HISTORIC PRESERVATION LAW

IN A NUTSHELL®

by

SARA C. BRONIN
Professor of Law
Faculty Director, Center for Energy and
Environmental Law
University of Connecticut School of Law

RYAN ROWBERRY
Assistant Professor of Law
Associate Director, Center for the Comparative
Study of Metropolitan Growth
Georgia State University College of Law

WEST ACADEMIC PUBLISHING

Mat #40591051

Nutshell Series, In a Nutshell and the Nutshell Logo are trademarks registered in the U.S. Patent and Trademark Office.

© 2014 LEG, Inc. d/b/a West Academic

      444 Cedar Street, Suite 700
      St. Paul, MN 55101
      1-877-888-1330

West, West Academic Publishing, and West Academic are trademarks of West Publishing Corporation, used under license.

Printed in the United States of America

ISBN: 978-0-314-18044-5

*To our friend, Professor J. Peter Byrne,
whose intellectual inquiries in historic
preservation law have helped to define the
field, and without whom this book would
not have been published.*

PREFACE

The purpose of this book is to provide a concise, coherent reference for the emerging field of historic preservation law for lawyers, policymakers, planners, architects, and students alike.

We consider preservation law to be "emerging" because it began to fully develop in the United States only in the last fifty years. Two key transition points happened at the federal level: the 1966 passage of the National Historic Preservation Act and the 1978 *Penn Central* Supreme Court decision, which upheld a landmarks law against a constitutional challenge and consequently encouraged other localities to adopt similar ordinances. (Of course, this book covers laws and judicial decisions prior to and subsequent to those two key transition points.)

Historic preservation law continues to evolve. Our book is intended to give a broad overview of the key issues as they stand today, supported by statutory references and caselaw. Some of the issues, particularly in the conservation/preservation restriction and the tax credit context, are very much "live," and we strive to highlight areas of current controversy. We will address the way these legal controversies come to be settled, if at all, in future editions of this book.

Most of the Chapters in this book focus on federal laws and jurisprudence implicating preservation, and we devote one Chapter to international preservation law. It is important to note, however, that the venue in which most people interact with historic preservation law is the local level. Hundreds of localities have stand-alone historic preservation ordinances, while others incorporate historic preservation considerations into their planning and zoning rules. While we could not survey every locality with a preservation ordinance, we present common legal strategies and areas of concern.

We hope that this resource is valuable and encourage you to contact us with any comments on how to improve the book in future editions.

Finally, special thanks to J. Peter Byrne, Lindsay Booth, Clinton Tankersley, Brooke Marie Thompson, and Joan Wood, whose contributions greatly improved this book.

SARA C. BRONIN
RYAN ROWBERRY

February 2014

OUTLINE

Chapter 16. International Preservation Law 497

TABLE OF CASES

References are to Pages

TABLE OF STATUTES

References are to Pages

HISTORIC PRESERVATION LAW

IN A NUTSHELL

CHAPTER 1
INTRODUCTION

The primary goal of historic preservation law is to protect significant historic resources from destruction, inappropriate alteration, and neglect. The most enduring historic preservation laws manage to achieve this protective aim while balancing a range of other values, including (among others): individual property rights, architectural design innovations, free speech, cultural identity, access for persons with disabilities, and economic development. These values need not be in tension with the goal of protecting historic resources. When tensions do arise, however, the law should create a fair and efficient process for parties to resolve their disputes.

Historic preservation law has developed to balance and respond to competing values—in some ways quite gracefully. This Chapter contextualizes our later discussion of the legal issues. Part A discusses the origins of historic preservation movement, and Part B describes the general legal framework which developed to support it. Part B also previews the more substantive, in-depth treatment of specific laws, cases, and legal ideas found in later Chapters. Finally, in Part C, we offer a brief description of two issues related to federal judicial decision-making—standards of review and standing—which would otherwise be unduly repetitive if included in each relevant Chapter.

A. WHAT IS HISTORIC PRESERVATION?

Historic preservation is the process of identifying resources of historic, cultural, or architectural significance and then protecting, interpreting, maintaining, and/or rehabilitating such resources. It is important to distinguish historic preservation, as a political movement and professional endeavor, from historic preservation *law*, which is the supporting legal regime. Humans have engaged in historic preservation in some form or another for millenia; it is human nature to preserve objects and sites we find meaningful. But only fairly recently have countries around the world begun to develop robust legal regimes for the preservation of historic resources.

This Part describes the history of three distinct but overlapping movements, and how those movements came to influence the development of preservation law. In the next Part, we discuss how the law in turn evolved to support the objectives of these movements.

1. THREE MOVEMENTS IMPACTING HISTORIC PRESERVATION LAW

The origins of the modern historic preservation movement in the United States may be traced through three distinct movements:

- First, the movement to collect archaeological and tribal resources;

- Second, the movement to protect natural landscapes; and

- Third the movement to preserve buildings, structures, and human-altered (that is, not entirely natural) sites.

Each movement influenced the development of historic preservation law in different ways. Below, we focus on national trends and federal government activity, but much of this activity occurred at the state and local levels as well.

a. Collecting Archaeological and Tribal Resources

In tracing the American approach to archaeology and tribal resources, it is important to remember that humans have always had an interest in their past and have always collected, catalogued, and honored objects and sites they find significant. Early Americans were no different, taking a keen interest in archaeological artifacts, "antiquities," and Native American anthropology. Several digs in the late eighteenth century, including one by Thomas Jefferson of an ancient burial mound in Virginia, reflected this interest. In 1812, the American Antiquarian Society was established to provide a forum for like-minded antiquities-seekers. By the mid-nineteenth century, the Smithsonian Institution had been created to manage the burgeoning federal museum collection. As the frontier expanded, various groups searched for tribal and archaeological artifacts. Guidance as to excavation techniques or the moral judgment regarding the appropriateness of collecting or selling artifacts was elusive and certainly did not affect many of those working on the frontier or those motivated purely by profit. All activity happened in the absence of any regulatory framework for dealing with even the most extraordinary sites.

This changed as the nineteenth century drew to a close and the public became increasingly aware of vandalism of national treasures such as the Mesa Verde Cliff Dwellings in Arizona. In 1906, Congress passed the Antiquities Act, and committed conservationist President Theodore Roosevelt signed it into law. The Antiquities Act is the first federal statute dealing with historic preservation which addressed more than one specific site. Among other things, it authorized the President to designate "landmarks, historic and prehistoric structures, and other objects of historic or scientific interest" on federal land. 16 U.S.C. § 431. The Historic Sites Act of 1935 followed, expanding federal protection of sites to allow the Secretary of the Interior to, among other things, create a "survey of historic and archaeologic sites, buildings, and objects . . . which possess exceptional value." *Id.* § 462(b). The Historic Sites Act was passed during a decade of federal engagement with archaeology, including field explorations, site surveys, and research assignments funded through various New Deal programs.

In the postwar period, large-scale federal projects, including the construction of dams and the interstate highway system, created concerns that important resources might be harmed by such projects. Congress passed several federal laws to address these concerns, including the National Historic Preservation Act of 1966, the National Environmental Policy Act of 1969, the Archaeological Resources Protection Act of 1979, and the Native American Graves Protection and Repatriation Act of 1990. These statutes, and others creating more specific regulatory regimes governing activities relating to archaeological and tribal resources on federal and tribal land, are covered in great depth in later Chapters.

The federal government was not the only level of government which has responded to the need to formalize protection of archaeological and tribal resources. State counterparts to the federal statutes mentioned above were also passed throughout the second half of the twentieth century. The United States has operated on the international stage as well, with delegates playing a key role in drafting the 1970 UNESCO Convention on the Means of Prohibiting the Illicit Import, Export, and Transfer of Ownership of Cultural Property, which addressed illegal trafficking in cultural patrimony.

b. Protecting Natural Landscapes

The second movement involved the desire to protect natural landscapes, also known as the conservation movement. While early Americans may have respected the opportunities nature provided or appreciated its beauty, there was no cohesive conservation movement until the second half of the nineteenth century. At this time, thinkers such as Henry David Thoreau, with his 1854 book *Walden* and other writings, introduced as a philosophical matter the human need for a strong relationship with nature.

By the early twentieth century, ideas on how this relationship might manifest itself diverged. On the one hand were the conservationists, such as Theodore Roosevelt, who profoundly appreciated nature but also wanted to manage resources for economic benefit. This perspective guided his actions as President (1901–1909). Roosevelt created national parks, monuments, and forests, and helped form the U.S. Forest Service. Yet he also anticipated that federal land would be used by loggers, miners, and other companies aiming to extract goods. On the other hand were the environmentalists, such as John Muir (founder of the Sierra Club in 1892), who believed that humans should not exploit natural resources, but instead preserve nature for its intrinsic value and as a haven from modern, industrial society.

As the debate between conservationists and environmentalists played out on the national stage, the federal government took action to set aside certain public lands for continued public ownership and use. In addition to Presidential designation of monuments and forests, Congress acted to allocate funding to specific parks and conservation initiatives. It created Yellowstone National Park in 1872 and Yosemite National Park in 1890. Then, in 1916, Congress formed the Department of the

Interior to manage the ever-expanding portfolio of federal land. Eventually, Congress established the National Park Service as a bureau within the Department of the Interior to administer many of the scenic areas open to the public.

After three decades of ever-increasing reservation of federal and state lands, the New Deal era swept in and left an indelible mark. The infrastructure in and around important natural resources was greatly improved by Public Works Administration and Civilian Conservation Corps teams who paved roads, built rest stops, and developed trails which facilitated public enjoyment of such resources. Some of the larger New Deal projects—dams, canals, tunnels, and bridges—had little-understood and potentially harmful impacts on natural, archaeological, and tribal resources.

The conservation and environmental movements largely smoldered until another book, Rachel Carson's 1962 *Silent Spring*, helped to reignite them. Activists in the 1960s focused on the protection of landscapes and natural resources—the protection and purification of air, water, and land—of which historic resources are a part. A broad coalition pushed for the passage of the National Environmental Policy Act of 1970, covered in Chapter IV. This important federal statute requires federal agencies to prepare environmental impact statements that address adverse effects of major federal actions on certain historic and natural resources. 42 U.S.C. § 4332(C). Various states also passed counterparts to this federal law, some of which are also covered in Chapter IV.

Nonprofit organizations have had other impacts. Groups like the Nature Conservancy became more active in assisting donors to place and enforce conservation restrictions (a topic covered in Chapter XIII) and working with federal and state officials to co-manage scenic land. The Trust for Public Land (founded in 1972) and the Land Trust Alliance (founded in 1982) also engage in the conservation of a range of property types. Other groups, such as the Sierra Club, frequently challenge government decisions affecting land.

c. Preserving Buildings, Structures, and Other Sites

The third movement—the movement to preserve buildings, structures, and human-altered (as opposed to purely natural) sites—is probably what most people consider to be the primary aspect of historic preservation. (We hope the descriptions in the two preceding subsections have emphasized that other areas, too, play a significant role.)

The story of the building preservation movement begins in the nineteenth century, when a variety of citizens' associations purchased, or encouraged public bodies to purchase, historically significant sites. Among these was Independence Hall, the site of the signing of the Declaration of Independence. The City of Philadelphia bought Independence Hall in 1816 after local groups raised alarms about its potential demolition to make way for a subdivision.

Other single-purpose efforts focused on the preservation of frontier settlements or battlefield sites from the Revolutionary War or the War of 1812. Perhaps the most famous nineteenth century preservation project involved Mount Vernon, George Washington's estate in Virginia. One of his descendants, John Washington, agreed in 1858 to sell the estate to the Mount Vernon Ladies' Association after efforts to convince the federal or state government to acquire the estate had failed. The Ladies' Association was an active group of patriotic individuals, mostly women, who painstakingly restored the site to its former glory even as the Civil War approached. Their widely publicized efforts set the stage for similar groups to focus on individual landmarks. Toward the end of the century, the Civil War battlefield at Gettysburg was the subject of another high-profile preservation effort, including an 1896 Supreme Court opinion regarding Congress's efforts to condemn and purchase the land, efforts we review in Chapter VIII. *See* United States v. Gettysburg Electric Railway Co., 160 U.S. 668 (1896). At the same time, local and regional private groups, such as the Society for the Preservation of New England Antiquities (today known as Historic New England), purchased and restored impressive examples of significant architecture.

It was not until the 1930s, however, that efforts were made to regulate the demolition or alteration of historic buildings and the development of incompatible structures within historic districts. Localities, not federal or state governments, were the prime movers in this respect. Historic district legislation was enacted by three large cities: Charleston, South Carolina, in 1931; New Orleans, Louisiana, in 1936; and San Antonio, Texas, in 1939. A handful of other cities, mostly in the mid-Atlantic region, followed suit in the 1940s. These local ordinances were motivated by public sentiment that sites worth saving required rules preventing property owners from destroying structures or making incompatible alterations. Many of these ordinances established aesthetic principles for new construction or changes to existing structures. At times, these ordinances were challenged for violating the state or federal constitution. The most prominent decision rejecting such a constitutional challenge was the 1978 Supreme Court case, *Penn Central*, covered in Chapter VIII. *See* Penn Central Transp. Co. v. City of New York, 438 U.S. 104 (1978). Local ordinances continue to form the backbone of preservation law and are the subject of Chapter VI.

So what was happening at the federal level during this time? A few pieces of federal legislation supported the largely local building preservation movement. In 1933, President Roosevelt authorized the Historic American Building Survey, as a New Deal program that set out to employ thousands of Americans in the act of documenting the historic built environment. The Historic Sites Act of 1935, mentioned above, authorized the Department of the Interior to create a list of places of national significance. For the first twenty or so years of its existence, however, this list primarily included sites slated to become national parks, not historically significant buildings. In 1949, Congress chartered the National Trust for Historic Preservation, a nonprofit whose aim was the preservation of the built environment. And in 1960, the National Park Service named the first National Historic Landmarks.

Although each of these federal actions was significant, the National Historic Preservation Act of 1966 (the subject of Chapter III) has been the most far-reaching piece of federal activity in historic preservation law. One of the central features of the statute is that it required federal agencies to review certain federal undertakings that impacted certain historic properties. It also expanded the list of historic places compiled under the Historic Sites Act, renaming it the National Register of Historic Places. The Register, covered in Chapter II, must list "districts, sites, buildings, structures, and objects significant in American history, architecture, archaeology, engineering, and culture." 16 U.S.C. § 470a(a)(1)(A). With this language, Congress recognized that historic preservation included all three distinct movements (the protection of archaeological and tribal resources and the conservation of landscapes) that we discussed previously. In addition, the National Historic Preservation Act created a legal framework that strongly encouraged states to name state historic preservation officers: public officials who lead state preservation efforts and liaise with federal officials. In 1992, tribal historic preservation officers were granted similar responsibilities and serve as representatives of federally-recognized tribes. Finally, the statute created the Advisory Council on Historic Preservation, an independent federal administrative agency that advises the President and other federal agencies on federal roles and responsibilities with respect to preservation. The Advisory Council also issues regulations related to the National Historic Preservation Act, which agencies must follow.

Also worth mentioning are later laws, including revisions to the Internal Revenue Code, that promoted private adoption of preservation and conservation restrictions, as well as private investment in qualifying rehabilitation projects. These incentives will be discussed in Chapters XIII and XIV. Today, the preservation of the built environment involves local governments, states, and federal officials, often working in concert and under established regulatory regimes to achieve the goals of preservation.

2.   RATIONALES FOR PRESERVATION

Different rationales have supported and energized historic preservation, among them: patriotism, education, aesthetics, community-building, economic development, and sustainability.

a. Patriotism

Patriotic sentiment was among the first motivators of historic preservation in the United States. In the first half of the nineteenth century, a few high-profile groups emerged to preserve homes and sites linked with the Founding Fathers, such as Independence Hall and Mount Vernon. Patriotism also motivated the preservation of battlefields of the Revolutionary and Civil Wars. In the case of Gettysburg Battlefield in Pennsylvania, for example, local entrepreneurs first capitalized on Gettysburg's significance. As their development in and around the battlefield grew out of control, political leaders, and by the end of the nineteenth century Congress, stepped in to preserve the site in a more dignified and public-minded way. Around the same time, Congress was also motivated in part by patriotism when voting to preserve the majestic Yellowstone and Yosemite Parks as symbols of America's vast bounty. No doubt this rationale still motivates decisions about what we preserve today.

b. Education

The educational rationale developed later in the historic preservation movement. We can learn many things from resources that embody unique techniques, styles, materials, or configurations. The early twentieth century efforts to protect Mesa Verde and similar archaeological sites recognized that significant information about prehistory and history could be lost forever without protective rules. A good example of a building worth preserving for its educational value is the West House in Yorktown, Virginia: an eighteenth century timber frame structure whose timbers have markings of artillery fire the house endured in 1781. Not only is the West House a rare example of a surviving colonial-era construction technique, but

its very structure tells a story about battlefield
events of national significance.

c. Aesthetics

An obvious rationale for historic preservation—
ultimately a strategy for protecting and enhancing
the way some things look—is the aesthetic
rationale. Many historic resources are physically
beautiful, and their rehabilitation can transform the
look and feel of neighborhoods. Moreover, beautiful
buildings preserved as an ensemble can create
visual harmony with each other and as part of a
broader environment.

There are, however, several critiques of the
aesthetic rationale for preservation. Requiring all
preservation activities to be judged on the basis of
aesthetics would mean that we would not preserve
resources that are unattractive, which is a
supremely subjective criterion. Conversely,
resources that we deem beautiful may be preserved
merely as a caricature, perhaps without any other
concerns in mind. Finally, the aesthetic rationale
might be seen as elitist when so many are deprived
of basic needs; preservation requirements imposed
on low-income housing developers renovating
historic buildings are often criticized on these
grounds.

d. Community-Building

Some commentators, including law professor
Carol Rose, have noted that between the mid-1960s
and 1980, "the chief function of preservation

[became] to strengthen local community ties and community organization." Carol M. Rose, *Preservation and Community: New Directions in the Law of Historic Preservation*, 33 Stan. L. Rev. 473, 479 (1981). Preservation can build community both by protecting the distinctive built heritage of a neighborhood and by giving residents a voice about changes. Local historic district ordinances that gained popularity during this time period reflect this sentiment. Several publications—including Jane Jacobs' 1961 book, *The Death and Life of Great American Cities*, and the U.S. Conference of Mayors' 1966 report, *With Heritage So Rich*—spurred this feeling on.

e. Economic Development

There is also increasing awareness about the economic benefits of preservation. Donovan Rypkema and David Listokin are among the top researchers finding economic benefits to preservation. Their work has revealed that preservation activity has significantly and positively impacted the building industry, housing production, heritage tourism, and downtown revitalization, with multiplier effects affecting a broad range of other activities. One of their findings is that preservation-related construction activity is much more likely than non-preservation-related construction activity to result in local jobs for laborers and apprentices. We encourage you to consult their work for the latest statistics. Preservation as a means for economic development has taken hold in the law through programs such as the state and federal tax credits offered to qualifying rehabilitation projects.

f. Sustainability

More recently, the slogan "the greenest building is one already built" has found traction with environmentalists. Intuitively, this saying makes sense: rehabilitating an existing building must take less energy than building the same building from scratch. Indeed, researchers have reached this conclusion by studying a concept called "embodied energy," which is the sum of all energy used to make a building. Beyond embodied energy comparisons, which focus on construction, historic buildings have operational benefits as compared to modern structures. The U.S. Energy Information Administration has analyzed data showing that buildings built before 1920 are more energy efficient than buildings built between 1920 and 2000. They also tend to be built in ways that respond to the natural environment—capturing breezes, sunlight, and vistas—much better than modern structures. Accordingly, some older buildings may be less costly to operate and more pleasant to occupy.

g. Federal Codification of Rationales

The National Historic Preservation Act of 1966 codifies some of these rationales, explaining why preservation should be a national priority. *See* 16 U.S.C. § 470(b). Congress declared that preservation "give[s] a sense of orientation to the American people" and protects a "vital legacy of cultural, educational, aesthetic, inspirational, economic, and energy benefits." *Id.* State and local laws often recite similar motivations.

B. NATURE AND SCOPE OF HISTORIC PRESERVATION LAW

Historic preservation law has evolved at the local, state, and federal levels to protect a wide range of physical resources. Early on, private citizens and public bodies focused on individual archaeological, natural, or built sites. By the 1930s, the scope of preservation had begun to expand: the federal government passed legislation recognizing nationally significant archaeological resources; public works projects made hundreds of natural wonders more accessible; and a few localities adopted citywide preservation ordinances. After a postwar lull in activity, the 1960s marked the transformative decade for historic preservation law. Most significantly, Congress enacted statutes that required the federal government to consider or prioritize historic preservation in all of its major development decisions. These statutes had a profound impact on state and even local rules. At the same time, the number of local historic districts regulating private property multiplied.

Judicial interpretations have also by and large strengthened the preservation movement. The constitutionality of the most common historic preservation regulations is no longer in question; they are well within the police power as state and federal courts have defined that term. Preservation laws have for the most part survived other constitutional challenges, including those relating to substantive due process, vagueness, free speech or religious liberty rights, and takings. These challenges, variations of which still arise today, are discussed in the relevant Chapters.

This Part explains where this dynamic history finds us today. It catalogues the types of resources that are protected, the four primary categories of preservation law, and the various groups that play some role in regulation.

1.   WHAT IS PROTECTED?

The applicability of historic preservation law almost always depends on whether the resource is judged to be either historically significant and thus "designated" historic (or eligible for preservation) or not historically significant. Designation is a formal, technical process (covered further in Chapter II) during which a nominated resource is evaluated to determine whether it meets legal requirements regarding its significance and its integrity. Some laws require federal agencies to consider protecting any property eligible for designation, not just those that have actually been designated.

Significance and integrity are terms of art that are defined by the jurisdiction doing the designation. Significance usually refers to the association that a resource has with significant persons or historical events; the architectural or technical merit of the resource; or the ability of the resource to provide information about history or prehistory. Integrity refers to the ability of a resource to communicate its significant elements. A stone fence that was once a technical masterpiece of local craftsmanship, but that was disassembled and strewn about a field would lack the integrity required to be designated historic. On the other hand, structures that have significantly deteriorated may still be deemed to have integrity, especially if designation will lead to rehabilitation.

With criteria as broad as "significance" and "integrity," the designation process combines both subjective and objective evaluations of nominated resources. Usually, nominations may come from any source; sometimes, the property owner must consent before the resource is designated under the applicable law. Nominators rely on oral histories, local archives, newspaper clippings, drawings, surveys, and other primary sources to document the significance of a resource. Up until the 1980s or so, nomination forms were often submitted by interested amateurs. These days, private firms, mostly regional in scope, provide consulting services to survey, document, and prepare nominations for historic resources.

Unless a property is evaluated to be historically significant, legal protections or incentives may not apply. There are some exceptions to this general rule. For example, the federal rehabilitation tax credit, covered in Chapter XIV, offers a 10 percent tax credit to owners doing qualifying rehabilitation work on a building built prior to 1936, whether or not the building is designated. (A higher tax credit of 20 percent is offered only to owners of designated historic structures.) *See* 26 U.S.C. § 47.

Typically, the term "historic preservation" conjures up images of old, famous buildings and structures—Grand Central Terminal, say, or the Brooklyn Bridge. But historic resources need not be famous to be legally protected. Many resources now protected, particularly under local historic ordinances, are vernacular structures used by ordinary people. Nor is old age a necessity when the resource has exceptional significance. For example, some especially significant buildings may be designated by federal officials as historic even before they are fifty years old; in New York City, the local historic preservation ordinance uses thirty years as the benchmark age. Resources other than buildings or structures also trigger legal protection. In this book, we include commentary on the preservation of landscapes, cultural objects, tribal artifacts, sites, artworks, and natural resources.

Different resources require different legal treatments. Archaeological resources, for example, may require regulations about how resources may be transported—something that is irrelevant to most buildings and structures. Projects that may disturb tribal resources may require consultation between government officials, private parties, and tribes before the potentially harmful action is taken. Buildings and structures may be subject to more specific guidelines depending on their architectural style. Historic roads and bridges may raise special issues relating to their functionality—how to preserve their historic features while still allowing vehicular movement. The preservation of landscapes may require consideration of animal habitat, public access, vegetation, and historically appropriate fencing. We cover these differences throughout the book.

2.   FOUR CATEGORIES OF PRESERVATION LAW

Historic preservation law uses four primary methods to advance the goals of the preservation movement:

- First, regulating;

- Second, providing incentives;

- Third, allowing conservation and preservation restrictions;

- Fourth, gathering and disseminating information.

Each of these categories of law is generally considered well within the constitutional and/or statutory authority of the relevant level of government. However, some specific laws may run afoul of constitutional or statutory provisions. We consider constitutional challenges to local historic district regulation in Chapters VII, VIII, IX, and X and other legal challenges, where relevant, in other Chapters.

a. Regulation

Regulation, the most important category of preservation law, refers simply to the imposition of rules on activities related to historic preservation. (We use the term "regulation" here more broadly than one might in administrative law, where it refers just to those rules and codes issued by government agencies.)

Federal, state, and local authorities may all impose rules on both public and private preservation activity. Often, the rules are applied to resources that have been designated as historic by the jurisdiction imposing the rules. But this is not always the case. For example, state environmental policy acts, discussed in Chapter IV, often protect properties designated as historic on the National Register of Historic Places, not just historic properties on the State Register. Local ordinances, too, may cover properties designated as historic under federal, state, and/or local registers of historic places.

At the federal level, there are rules relating to an agency's need to consider or curb its harmful effects on historic resources. Several important statutes, including the National Historic Preservation Act and the National Environmental Policy Act, considered in Chapters III and IV respectively, establish procedures that agencies must follow before they can undertake a large-scale activity. Other statutory provisions, such as Section 4(f) of the Transportation Act, considered in Chapter V, impose substantive requirements on agencies to minimize all harm to protected properties. There are also federal rules for private actors, including extensive guidance on how archaeological and tribal resources should be treated. State legislatures often pass counterparts to the federal preservation statutes, a fact we emphasize throughout the book.

Localities, meanwhile, have adopted individual ordinances related to historic preservation. These include both stand-alone historic preservation ordinances and special provisions of planning and zoning codes, including regulating the activities of private owners. These are administered by commissions of local residents, who make decisions about whether plans or proposals are compatible with the historic resource and/or its surroundings. Local ordinances often exempt public institutions from compliance. These ordinances are examined in Chapter VI.

b. Incentives

Preservation law has institutionalized incentives for private parties to engage or invest in historic preservation projects. These incentives come in three forms: direct subsidies, tax relief, and procedural relief.

Direct subsidies include grants or loan programs. The federal government provides grants to state historic preservation offices for specific projects, such as the preservation of historic cemeteries. Several states give grants to municipalities and nonprofit institutions to study the feasibility of preserving designated historic structures or to create affordable housing in historic structures. Some states also have revolving loan funds that offer low interest rate loans for qualifying private projects.

Tax relief comes in a variety of forms. Tax credits for some percentage of a project's qualified rehabilitation expenditures are offered by the federal rehabilitation credit discussed in Chapter XIV and state counterparts. Tax credits are desirable because they reduce a taxpayer's tax liability dollar for dollar. Tax deductions are also popular. They reduce a taxpayer's income subject to tax, which means that their value is relative to the rate the taxpayer pays. Taxpayers who donate a preservation or conservation restriction to a qualifying nonprofit are eligible for a federal tax deduction, as discussed in Chapter XIII. Taxpayers who rehabilitate single-purpose agricultural structures may also be eligible for a federal tax deduction. At the state or local level, property taxes may be frozen for, or phased in over, a period following the rehabilitation of the property. This benefits owners of historic properties because they do not have to immediately absorb the presumably higher post-rehabilitation appraised value of their properties. Property tax rates may also be reduced for rehabilitating certain types of projects into a new use.

Incentives might also include procedural relief, such as exemptions from zoning ordinances, relaxation of building codes, or waivers of building permit or occupancy permit fees.

c. Authorization of Restrictions

The first two categories of preservation law, regulating and providing incentives, are time-tested legal strategies that have been used in many different fields. The third category of historic preservation law—conservation and preservation restrictions—actually represents a legal innovation that pushes the boundaries of traditional property law. These restrictions allow private property owners to protect their historic properties for any length of time, including forever, by placing restrictions on development or other activities that might negatively affect the historic features of their properties. These property owners grant the restriction to a nonprofit organization or locality (depending on state law), which holds the restriction and enforces its terms. Conservation restrictions usually protect landscapes, while preservation restrictions usually protect buildings. For reasons we explain in Chapter XIII, we view these restrictions as innovations in property law, and call them restrictions rather than easements or covenants, two traditional areas of property law which restrictions merely resemble.

d. Information

The collection and dissemination of information has also been an important function of the law. Registers of historic places are an obvious example of public institutions serving an information-gathering role. These registers tell people about historic resources in their communities and provide a catalogue (albeit never comprehensive) of places worthy of attention. Building surveys, such as the Historic American Buildings Survey and the Historic American Engineering Record, serve as extremely valuable repositories of information. Beyond registers and surveys are public notice statutes for federal and state agencies. These require agencies to create a record, analyze, and notify the public about threats to historic resources—a critical source of information to those who know where to look. Finally, localities' historic preservation personnel (usually housed in the planning and zoning office) can be a valuable resource for property owners seeking information on local history and pending projects.

3. KEY PLAYERS

Key players in historic preservation law fall into one of four categories: property owners, public entities and officials, nonprofit organizations, and preservation professionals.

Owners of historic properties have great power, because they often have significant freedom to enhance, neglect, or even destroy their properties. This is because the vast majority of historic resources are protected only in limited ways—if legal protection exists at all. Most regulatory-type preservation laws apply only to private property owners, not public ones. But governments acting as property owners also have some obligations to consider the consequences of their actions and may serve as role models in their stewardship of land.

Public entities and officials—associated with federal, state, local, or tribal governments—also play a major role in historic preservation. Congress and state legislatures pass laws binding public or private actors to behave in certain ways. Presidents and governors can direct agencies to act or issue executive orders relating to preservation. Legislatively created advisory groups, such as the Advisory Council on Historic Preservation or state historic preservation councils, provide critical guidance. The Secretary of the Interior and head of the National Park Service, and their state and tribal historic preservation officer counterparts, make decisions and consult with multiple bodies in accordance with the framework created by the National Historic Preservation Act. State and tribal historic preservation officers also have national organizations that help coordinate and convey their concerns. At the local level, historic preservation commissions and planning and zoning staff can often make or influence decisions significantly impacting their communities.

Nonprofit organizations have also been instrumental in communicating a pro-preservation message and facilitating change. The key national nonprofit organization is the National Trust for Historic Preservation, chartered by Congress in 1949. It has an expansive mission that includes legal assistance, regional initiatives, historic site ownership, investment in specific towns and projects, and publicizing preservation-related news. Preservation Action, another national nonprofit, advocates that Congress pass laws promoting preservation. State historic trusts for preservation and state advocacy groups fulfill similar roles. We also have a proud tradition of local historical societies and other groups who advocate and engage on the local level.

Finally, there are those professionals who work "in the trenches" to turn preservation projects into reality. Over the last fifty years, historic preservation has become increasingly professionalized. Training programs in anthropology, archaeology, architecture, and history boast educational tracks devoted to historic preservation. Graduates of these programs (and others with preservation experience) survey historic resources, prepare nominations for registers of historic places, fill out grant, tax, and other incentive applications, engage in historic architectural design, conserve fragile archaeological resources, figure out complex financing schemes for preservation projects, and/or assist public or private entities with long-term resource management.

C. HISTORIC PRESERVATION IN FEDERAL COURT

Historic preservation laws, regulations, and decisions have been the subjects of a large number of cases litigated in federal court. Before proceeding with a case, litigants should be aware of two issues related to federal judicial decision-making. First is the standard of review a court will apply in reviewing a federal agency action or a lower court decision. Second are the standing requirements a plaintiff must meet before her case may proceed in federal court. These issues are covered here, rather than in individual Chapters, to avoid duplicative treatment.

1. STANDARDS OF REVIEW

Voluminous caselaw has outlined the parameters of federal standards of review. We give only the barest introduction here because many practitioners have considered these issues before.

a. Federal Agency Actions

Courts reviewing challenges to federal agency actions, which are governed by federal statutes, will abide by the Supreme Court's findings of *Chevron* and its progeny. *See* Chevron U.S.A. v. NRDC, 467 U.S. 837 (1984). The *Chevron* standard of review has two possible outcomes. If Congress has "directly spoken to the precise question at issue" and its intent is clear, then the court and agency "must give effect to the unambiguously expressed intent of Congress." *Id.* at 842–43. That is the end of the matter. If, however, Congress has not addressed the question and the statute is silent or ambiguous, the court must defer to agencies' reasonable interpretations of the statute. *Id.* at 843.

Chevron deference is not absolute, however. An agency's factual findings may be reviewed on the substantial evidence standard—that is, whether the whole record reasonably supports the factual conclusions of the agency. Agency actions may also be reviewed as to whether they were arbitrary and capricious or an abuse of discretion. Arbitrariness and capriciousness might be found if the agency: made a decision based on erroneous facts, erred in its judgment, acted irrationally (including offering highly inconsistent interpretations of a statute), had no authority to act, or failed to weigh all relevant factors. Thus courts are also able to review whether the agency has acted consistently with the law and exercised its discretion reasonably and in accord with fair procedures.

b. Lower Court Decisions

Judicial decisions may be reviewed on appeal, and the standard of review depends on the issue being appealed. Questions of law are reviewable de novo— that is, an independent, full review in which the appellate court views the case from the same fresh perspective as the court below. Questions of law include issues related to the constitutionality of a statute, statutory interpretation, and certain issues related to procedure, such as standing. Generally, questions that mix law and fact are reviewed by appellate courts using the de novo approach.

Questions of fact are considered by appellate courts under the clearly erroneous standard—that is, a review of the record to determine whether the lower court's finding of fact is implausible or resulted in a mistake. Appellate courts review questions of fact with some deference to the court below. Thus if stipulations, the written record, or other evidence may have two or more interpretations and the lower court adopted one interpretation, its interpretation will be upheld by the appellate court.

Questions of judicial discretion—including errors of law or errors in applying the law, or decisions based on clearly erroneous findings of material facts—are reviewable as to whether the lower court abused its discretion. An appellate court may only find an abuse of discretion if the lower court committed a clear error or acted irrationally.

2.   STANDING

Standing rules tell a litigant if they have the right to be heard in court. If a litigant has standing, she may have her day in court; otherwise, her case is dismissed without the court considering the merits of the controversy. Rules for determining whether a party has standing in a particular case derive both from the Constitution and from federal statutes.

a. Standing from the Constitution

Article III of the Constitution limits federal courts' jurisdiction to actual "cases or controversies." *See* U.S. CONST. art. III, § 2. This provision impacts standing because only litigants with a sufficient stake in the challenged activity can bring a case or controversy, meaning that the court will consider the merits of the dispute. *See* Warth v. Seldin, 422 U.S. 490, 518 (1975) (rejecting plaintiffs' standing claims).

The Supreme Court has set forth three elements that a plaintiff must show to qualify for Article III standing: (1) an injury in fact; (2) an injury fairly traceable to the action of the defendant; and (3) the ability for the injury to be redressed by a favorable court decision. *See* Lujan v. Defenders of Wildlife, 504 U.S. 555, 560–61 (1992) (finding that the plaintiffs failed to show that they suffered an injury in fact because they did not show how an agency's damage to certain animal species overseas would produce "imminent" injury to them).

Regarding (1) an injury in fact: a plaintiff must show an imminent injury that is "distinct and palpable, and not abstract or conjectural or hypothetical." Allen v. Wright, 468 U.S. 737, 751 (1984) (citations and quotation marks omitted) (finding that African American plaintiffs challenging government grants of tax exemptions to racially discriminatory schools had only an abstract, stigmatic injury that did not satisfy standing requirements). It is important to note that purely aesthetic and environmental concerns may give rise to an injury in fact. *See, e.g.*, Sierra Club v. Morton, 405 U.S. 727, 734 (1972) ("Aesthetic and environmental well-being, like economic well-being, are important ingredients of the quality of life in our society, and the fact that particular environmental interests are shared by the many rather than the few does not make them less deserving of legal protection through the judicial process.").

Regarding (2) an injury fairly traceable to the action of the defendant: the plaintiff must show that the defendant's actions actually caused a specific injury to the plaintiff. *See, e.g.*, Friends of the Earth,

Inc. v. Laidlaw Envtl. Servs., Inc., 528 U.S. 167, 181–84 (2000) (finding that plaintiffs who once fished, hiked, drove, and camped in and around a specific polluted river but now avoided such activities because of defendant's activities had shown an injury fairly traceable to the defendant); Warth v. Seldin, 422 U.S. 490, 505–06 (1975) (finding that plaintiffs associated with minority racial or ethnic groups lacked standing to challenge zoning ordinances because they failed to establish a causal relationship between the ordinance and their stated injury, namely, the inability to live in the community subject to the ordinance).

Regarding (3) the ability for the injury to be redressed by a favorable court decision: the plaintiff must show that the court has the ability to remedy the injury. *See*, *e.g.*, Lujan v. Defenders of Wildlife, 504 U.S. 555, 569–70 (1992) (finding that the plaintiffs had failed to show redressability because the agency officials who could remedy any injuries would not be bound by the Court's rulings).

b. Standing from Federal Statutes

The Administrative Procedures Act (APA) establishes rules for plaintiff standing which are applicable to requests for judicial review of decisions made by federal agencies pursuant to federal statutes that do not contain specific judicial review provisions. In essence, if a federal statute does not have its own procedures for judicial review of agency actions, courts will apply the APA standing rules. The three primary federal statutes that we consider in this book—the National Historic Preservation Act, the National Environmental Policy Act, and the Department of Transportation Act—are all covered by the APA standing rules.

The key language of the APA states that: "A person suffering legal wrong because of agency action, or adversely affected or aggrieved by agency action within the meaning of a relevant statute, is entitled to judicial review thereof." 5 U.S.C. § 702. The APA thus has two main requirements that must be met before someone can sue: (1) there must be a final agency action; and (2) the party must have suffered a "legal wrong" or be "adversely affected or aggrieved" pursuant to a "relevant statute."

The meaning of "agency action" is "the whole or a part of an agency rule, order, license, sanction, relief, or the equivalent or denial thereof, or failure to act." *Id.* § 551. The primary constraint on agency action is that the action must be final, not merely preliminary, procedural, or intermediate. *Id.* § 704.

The question of whether someone has suffered a "legal wrong" or been adversely affected or aggrieved within the meaning of a relevant statute requires more explanation. In addition to the three elements required to satisfy Article III, described above, the Supreme Court has said that the APA requires that a plaintiff show that the injury she complains of falls within the "zone of interests" sought to be protected by the statutory provision at issue *See* Clarke v. Securities Industries Ass'n, 479 U.S. 388, 396–97 (1987). The federal statutes we include in this book all have as their primary purpose the protection and preservation of historic and natural resources. Accordingly, courts have found that aesthetic, conservation, preservation, and recreational interests are all within the zone of interests being protected by these three statutes. *See, e.g.*, Pa. Envtl. Council, Inc. v. Bartlett, 315 F. Supp. 238, 245 (M.D. Pa. 1970). Moreover, the Supreme Court has required (with narrow exceptions) a plaintiff to direct attacks "against some *particular* 'agency action' that causes it harm . . . [in other words,] some concrete action applying the regulation to the claimant's situation in a fashion that harms or threatens to harm him." Lujan v. Nat'l Wildlife Fed'n, 497 U.S. 871, 891 (1990). The plaintiff, therefore, cannot simply allege that a broad regulatory framework or agency-wide approach has caused her harm under the relevant statute. She must connect a particular agency action to a specific harm that falls within the zone of interest of the statute.

Who can survive these constraints on standing? A broad assortment of individuals and entities have met standing requirements, which has in turn enabled aggrieved parties to bring lawsuits that have defined historic preservation law. Indeed, the amount of caselaw involving the federal statutes discussed in this book is immense, particularly so for the National Historic Preservation Act, the National Environmental Policy Act, and the Department of Transportation Act. State and tribal historic preservation officers, state and tribal governments, organizations of property owners, and citizens who use affected historic resources all have the ability to challenge agency actions under the National Historic Preservation Act. *See*, *e.g.*, Vieux Carré Prop. Owners, Residents & Assocs. v. Brown, 875 F.2d 453, 458 (5th Cir. 1989); Neighborhood Development Corp. v. Advisory Council on Historic Pres., 632 F.2d 21 (6th Cir. 1980); Weintraub v. Rural Electrification Admin., 457 F. Supp. 78, 88 (M.D. Pa. 1978). National Environmental Policy Act challenges implicating historic resources have also been successfully brought by a similar range of plaintiffs including municipal and county governments, nonprofit organizations, Indian tribes, and even individual private citizens. *See*, *e.g.*, Mid States Coal. for Progress v. Surface Transportation Bd., 345 F.3d 520 (8th Cir. 2003); Te-Moak Tribe of Western Shoshone of Nevada v. U.S. Dep't of Interior, 608 F.3d 592 (9th Cir. 2010); Recent Past Pres, Network v. Latschar, 701 F. Supp. 2d 49 (D.D.C. 2010). Towns, local civic organizations, nonprofit organizations (even unincorporated ones) with a conservation or preservation purpose, organizations that had been active in administrative proceedings, residents living near a proposed project, individuals who used threatened resources, and others have been held to be aggrieved parties under Section 4(f). *See*, *e.g.*, Brooks v. Volpe, 329 F. Supp. 118, 119 (W.D. Wash. 1971); Pa. Envtl. Council, Inc. v. Bartlett, 315 F. Supp. 238, 244–45 (M.D. Pa. 1970); Citizens to Preserve Overton Park, Inc. v Volpe (W.D. Tenn. 1970), 309 F. Supp 1189, *aff'd* 432 F.2d 1307 (6th Cir. 1970), *rev'd on other grounds* 401 U.S. 402 (1971).

CHAPTER 2
DESIGNATION

Historic preservation law only protects resources that are "designated" historic and resources that are eligible for such designation. Through the designation process, decision-makers evaluate the integrity of the resource and the physical characteristics or relationships to history which make the resource significant. The process is largely conducted by non-lawyers who use their backgrounds (often in architecture, archaeology, or history) to evaluate resources within a legal framework. When a federal, state, or local official decides a resource meets the applicable designation criteria, it will be listed on the requisite public register of historic places and/or given another special name (such as a "landmark" or "scenic byway").

This Chapter focuses on the designation process at the federal level, and adds brief commentary about the designation process at the state and local levels. The content of this Chapter is foundational to an understanding of historic preservation law, because the laws in this book largely deal with resources that have been designated through the processes we describe here.

A. FEDERAL DESIGNATION

At the federal level, the process for designating resources as historic is laid out in the National Historic Preservation Act of 1966 (NHPA). The

NHPA provides that the National Register of Historic Places (commonly called the National Register) will catalogue the resources that have gone through the federal process of being designated as historic. Currently, the National Register lists over eighty thousand historic resources, of which twenty-five hundred have special designation as National Historic Landmarks. To be listed on the National Register, a resource must meet certain criteria and must undergo a formal nomination and evaluation process. This Part describes the federal criteria and designation process.

1.   NATIONAL REGISTER CRITERIA

To be listed on the National Register of Historic Places, a resource must satisfy all of the following basic criteria:

• It must be one of the five *types* of resources eligible for the National Register: district, site, building, structure, or object.

• It must be relevant to a prehistoric or historic *context*: American history, architecture, archaeology, engineering, or culture.

• It must be *significant*: important events must have happened there; important people must have lived there; it must have architectural or artistic merit; or it must provide information important to history or prehistory.

• It must have *integrity*: in other words, the resource must be able to communicate its significance.

These four criteria are broad enough to allow for many different types of tangible resources to be considered for listing. After discussing the four criteria in greater detail, we discuss special criteria applicable to National Historic Landmarks and describe exceptions and special cases.

a. Type

A resource must be one of the five types of resources eligible for inclusion on the National Register: building, structure, object, site, or district. 16 U.S.C. § 470a(a)(1)(A). All of these categories require that the resource be tangible; intangible resources, such as ideas, are not eligible. Federal regulations define each of these five terms, and the National Register Bulletin No. 15, *How to Apply the National Register Criteria for Evaluation*, provides further insights, which are incorporated into the discussion below.

A building is "a structure created to shelter any form of human activity, such as a house, barn, church, hotel, or similar structure." 36 C.F.R. § 60.3(a). Historically related complexes, such as courthouses and jails, or houses with carriage houses, are also included in this term. *Id.* Parts of buildings, such as interiors or façades, cannot be listed on the National Register independent of the whole building; only whole buildings are considered for the National Register.

A structure is "a work made up of interdependent and interrelated parts in a definite pattern of organization. Constructed by man, it is often an engineering project large in scale." *Id.* § 60.3(p). Structures include bridges, canals, lighthouses, water towers, and similar uses that may be used by man but (in contrast to buildings) are not primarily intended to be places of human habitation. As is the case with buildings, parts of structures are not eligible standing alone; the whole structure must be considered.

An object is "a material thing of functional, aesthetic, cultural, historical or scientific value that may be, by nature or design, movable yet related to a specific setting or environment." *Id.* § 60.3(j). Examples of objects include steamboats, monuments, fountains, and sculptures. To qualify for the National Register, an object must be in an appropriate setting; relocation of an object to a museum may render it ineligible for listing.

A site is "the location of a significant event, a prehistoric or historic occupation or activity, or a building or structure, whether standing, ruined, or vanished, where the location itself maintains historical or archeological value regardless of the value of any existing structure." *Id.* § 60.3(l). Sites include battlefields, natural features with cultural significance, trails, landscapes, and ruins of buildings and structures that have lost basic structural elements and are no longer suitable for their original purpose. Documentation of the exact location of certain sites may be difficult, but locational accuracy is an important piece of a National Register eligibility determination. *See*

Hoonah Indian Ass'n v. Morrison, 170 F.3d 1223 (9th Cir. 1999).

Finally, a district is "a geographically definable area, urban or rural, possessing a significant concentration, linkage, or continuity of sites, buildings, structures, or objects united by past events or aesthetically by plan or physical development." *Id.* § 60.3(d). A district may be composed of different types of resources, but all of the resources must interrelate to each other. Examples of districts include groups of archaeological sites, neighborhoods of homes not eligible for individual listing on the National Register, historic mill complexes, and college campuses. Districts may be noncontiguous if they are "linked by association or history," *id.*, and if space between the elements is not related to the significance of the district, among other factors.

Categorizing certain resources may be confusing. For example, an aircraft is typically considered a structure, even though a good argument could be made that it is an object. Similarly, a stable is considered a building, even though stables are not usually meant for human habitation. Finally, while steamboats are listed in federal regulations as an example of an object, the National Park Service says that shipwrecks will be considered as sites. For the most part, the categories do not matter and may overlap. But an important question is "what is considered to be a building?," since rehabilitations of buildings are eligible for tax credits (discussed in

Chapter XIV) or may be subject to special regulations (discussed in Chapter XV).

b. Context

In addition to being identified as one of the five types of resources eligible for the National Register, a resource must be a good representative of a qualifying historic or prehistoric context: American history, architecture, archaeology, engineering, or culture. 16 U.S.C. § 470a(a)(1)(A).

The geographic scale of the historic context may be local, state, or national. The National Register does not require that listed resources be of national significance, although some nationally significant properties will be named National Historic Landmarks, discussed below.

All of these contexts have one thing in common: they involve human activity. A natural formation or scenic vista is not eligible for listing just because it is beautiful; it must also be linked to some human activity.

Some resources may relate to more than one historic context. For the National Register nomination, nominators need only document the resource's significance in one historic context.

c. Significance

To qualify for the National Register, a resource must also be considered significant when evaluated within its historic context. Significance may be found in resources:

(a) that are associated with events that have made a significant contribution to the broad patterns of our history; or

(b) that are associated with the lives of persons significant in our past; or

(c) that embody the distinctive characteristics of a type, period, or method of construction, or that represent the work of a master, or that possess high artistic values, or that represent a significant and distinguishable entity whose components may lack individual distinction; or

(d) that have yielded, or may be likely to yield, information important in prehistory or history.

36 C.F.R. § 60.4. Some resources may be significant in more than one of these areas. A National Register nomination must include careful documentation of at least one of these areas but need not include documentation of more.

Each of the four criteria for significance will be evaluated differently. Criterion A may involve the resource's relationship either to a specific event, such as a battle or discovery, or to a pattern of events or trends, such as a migration trail or downtown commercial development. Criterion B must involve a person who gained importance within her profession or group, not just someone about whom little specific information can be obtained, or who represented a profession or group in a general capacity but did not obtain special status. Criterion C applies to properties with special architectural or artistic merit, which can be expressed through design, planning, engineering, or decorative elements. Criterion D applies primarily to archaeological resources, but any resource with important informational value, supported by adequate data and research, may be deemed eligible for the National Register under this criterion.

d. Integrity

To be listed on the National Register, the resource must have "*integrity* of location, design, setting, materials, workmanship, feeling, and association." 36 C.F.R. § 60.4. The concept of integrity is based on an establishment of significance: the resource must be able to convey its significance through most (if not all) of seven aspects of integrity. A resource need not retain each and every historical element to convey its significance.

Each of the seven aspects of integrity captures a different dimension, and further explanation may be helpful:

• To have integrity of location, the historic resource must remain in the place from which it derives its significance; most resources that have been moved or separated from their original location are ineligible for the National Register.

• Integrity of design relates to the coherence of the form, plan, space, structure, and style of a resource.

• Integrity of setting refers to the character of the environment and its relationship to the resource.

• To have integrity of materials, a resource has to retain key physical elements from the period of its historic significance; a property reconstructed from new materials will not normally be eligible for the National Register.

• Workmanship, which is the physical evidence of craft of a particular culture or people during a given historical or prehistorical period, shows integrity if it remains obvious in all or parts of a resource.

• Integrity of feeling is perhaps the most subjective aspect of integrity, referring to the way the resource expresses a sense of the historic or prehistoric context during which it became significant.

• Finally, integrity of association occurs when the resource retains its link to the event or activity that conveyed its significance.

The particular aspects of integrity a resource must retain will depend on the reason it is significant in the first place. For example, Criterion A and Criterion B resources, which are significant for their association with specific events or important persons, need only retain those key physical characteristics that would convey important associations with events or persons. Criterion C resources, which have special architectural or artistic merit, must retain key features that relate to the applicable type, period, method of construction, workmanship, or artistic characteristics. Criterion D resources are significant because they provide information important to history and prehistory; they need not be in perfect condition, but they must retain enough historic fabric that information can actually be provided.

e. National Historic Landmark Criteria

"[P]roperties of exceptional value to the nation as a whole rather than to a particular State or locality" are eligible to become designated as National Historic Landmarks, which are listed on the National Register. 36 C.F.R. § 65.2(a). A Landmark must meet all of the basic criteria for the National Register and more: a Landmark must be "judged by the Secretary to possess national significance." *Id.* § 65.3. More specifically, the Secretary may only designate as Landmarks those resources:

(1) That are associated with events that have made a significant contribution to, and are identified with, or that outstandingly represent, the broad national patterns of United States history and from which an understanding and appreciation of those patterns may be gained; or

(2) That are associated importantly with the lives of persons nationally significant in the history of the United States; or

(3) That represent some great idea or ideal of the American people; or

(4) That embody the distinguishing characteristics of an architectural type specimen exceptionally valuable for a study of a period, style or method of construction, or that represent a significant, distinctive and exceptional entity whose components may lack individual distinction; or

(5) That are composed of integral parts of the environment not sufficiently significant by reason of historical association or artistic merit to warrant individual recognition but collectively compose an entity of exceptional historical or artistic significance, or outstandingly commemorate or illustrate a way of life or culture; or

(6) That have yielded or may be likely to yield information of major scientific importance by revealing new cultures, or by shedding light upon periods of occupation over large areas of the United States.

Id. § 65.4(a). Words like "outstandingly," "exceptionally," and "major"—not found in the language for Criterion A, B, C, and D described above—highlight the elevated nature of Landmarks as compared to the other resources on the National Register. Landmarks enjoy more protection than other properties listed on the National Register. For example, the National Historic Preservation Act requires agencies to "minimize harm" to Landmarks, as opposed to just "taking into account the effect" of agency actions on National Register properties that are not Landmarks. *Compare* 16 U.S.C. § 470h–2(f) *with id.* § 470f.

f. Exclusions and Exceptions

Some types of resources, such as intangible resources and resources lacking in significance or integrity, will always be excluded from the National Register. Other types of resources will usually be excluded, with some exceptions. The National Register normally excludes "cemeteries, birthplaces, or graves of historical figures, properties owned by religious institutions or used for religious purposes, structures that have been moved from their original locations, reconstructed historic buildings, properties primarily commemorative in nature, and properties that have achieved significance within the past 50 years." 36 C.F.R. § 60.4.

For each of these exclusions, however, there are exceptional circumstances under which a resource will be listed. Cemeteries will be eligible, despite the usual exclusion, if they are distinctively designed or if they are associated with historic events. Birthplaces or graves will be eligible if they relate to a "historical figure of outstanding importance" and if there is no site or building associated with that person's life. *Id.* Moved structures will be eligible if their significance relates primarily to their architectural value. Reconstructed buildings can be eligible if the quality of the reconstruction is high and if there are no other buildings with the same association. Commemorative properties are eligible if "design, age, tradition, or symbolic value has invested it with its own exceptional significance." *Id.* Likewise, properties achieving significance within the last fifty years will be eligible if they are "of exceptional importance." *Id.*

The treatment of religious properties deserves more discussion. They will be eligible for listing only if they derive their "primary significance from architectural or artistic distinction or historical importance." *Id.* Many religious properties are listed on the National Register because they were architecturally significant or because they became historically important as centers of community activity beyond religious activity. It is important to note that religious resources will not be judged on their religious significance or religious merit. As Chapter IX points out, evaluations on the basis of religious principles may be subject to constitutional challenge on the basis of the federal establishment clause. Note, however, that the National Historic Preservation Act allows for "[p]roperties of traditional religious and cultural importance to an Indian tribe or Native Hawaiian organization" to be eligible for the National Register. 16 U.S.C. § 470a(d)(6)(A). The reason for the differing treatment is discussed further in Chapter IX.

2.   FEDERAL DESIGNATION PROCEDURES

The process for designating significant properties to the National Register is handled by the National Park Service, a bureau of the U.S. Department of the Interior. First, a property must be nominated for the National Register. Then, the nomination will be evaluated by the National Park Service, with the final decision being made by a National Park Service official called the Keeper of the National Register of Historic Places (the Keeper). Once a property is designated, it may be removed from the National Register through the de-listing process. Each of these stages is discussed in greater detail below.

a. Nominations

National Register nominations come to the Keeper from three primary sources: (1) state historic preservation officers, (2) tribal historic preservation officers, and (3) federal preservation officers from the federal agencies. Private parties may not submit a nomination directly to the Keeper. Here we cover the procedures each of these three primary sources follow to submit nominations to the National Register. (The National Historic Landmark designation process requires special procedures not discussed here. *See* 36 C.F.R. § 65.5.)

Most National Register nominations come through state historic preservation officers (SHPOs): individuals who have been designated by their states as being responsible for their respective statewide preservation programs. The SHPO must "identify and nominate eligible properties to the National Register and otherwise administer applications for listing historic properties on the National Register." 16 U.S.C. § 470a(b)(3)(B). In practice, members of the public typically identify properties and draft nominations for the SHPO's consideration, rather than the SHPO surveying properties and drafting nominations herself. The SHPO makes decisions about which properties to nominate in light of the state's historic preservation plan and need not submit every suggested property to the Keeper.

Before submitting a nomination to the Keeper, the SHPO must notify and attempt to collect comments from three specific groups. First, the SHPO must provide notice of intent to nominate to the chief elected official (usually the mayor) of the local jurisdiction in which the resource is located. 36 C.F.R. § 60.6(c). Second, the SHPO must provide notice to any private owners of the property being considered for nomination. (More on the role of these owners is discussed in the next subsection.) Third, the SHPO must submit the draft nomination to the State Review Board. *Id.* § 60.6(j). This board is comprised of representatives from the fields of architecture, architectural history, history, and other professional disciplines. *Id.* § 60.3(o). If the State Review Board and SHPO disagree on the outcome, then the opinions of both parties may be forwarded on to the Keeper, along with the nomination. *Id.* § 60.6(l). If they agree a nomination should proceed, then the SHPO may submit the nomination after correcting any technical errors. *Id.* § 60.6(l).

Tribal historic preservation officers (THPOs) "may assume all or any part of the functions of a State Historic Preservation Officer." 16 U.S.C. § 470a(d)(2). This assumption of duties will be completed pursuant to a plan for a comprehensive tribal preservation program, approved by the Secretary of the Department of the Interior in consultation with affected SHPO(s). *Id.* §§ 470a(d)(2)–470a(d)(3). The exact manifestation of the THPO nomination process within particular tribal areas may vary somewhat from the SHPO nomination process, but many THPOs take on the basic SHPO role of shepherding nominations through the evaluation process at the federal level.

Federal preservation officers (FPOs) are the third primary source of National Register nominations. Each federal agency must name a FPO within the agency who identifies, evaluates, and nominates properties eligible for the National Register. 16 U.S.C. § 470h–2(a)(2). Agencies are also required to survey all properties they own or control to determine whether any are eligible for listing. Exec. Order No. 11,593, 3 C.F.R. 154 (1971–1975), *reprinted in* 16 U.S.C. § 470 note. Moreover, agencies must consider whether properties that may be affected by certain agency actions—such as those actions triggering Section 106 (discussed in Chapter III) or Section 4(f) (discussed in Chapter V) processes—are eligible for the National Register. *See, e.g.* 36 C.F.R. § 800.4(b); 23 C.F.R. § 774.11(e). During agency determinations of eligibility, if the SHPO agrees with the agency that the criteria are not met, the property will be considered ineligible. 36 C.F.R. § 800.4(c)(2). If the agency decides to proceed with a nomination, the agency must submit a draft to the SHPO or THPO with jurisdiction and notify and collect comments from local elected officials. *Id.* § 60.9(c). The FPO may submit the nomination after taking any comments received into account, and must append the comments of the SHPO and chief local official to the nomination. *Id.* § 60.9(f).

If any nominating authority refuses to nominate a property, any person or local government can appeal to the Keeper. *Id.* § 60.12(a). The Keeper will respond to the appellant and the relevant nominating authority with a written explanation either denying or sustaining the appeal. *Id.* § 60.12(c).

b. **Evaluation of Nominations**

Once a nomination is submitted, there is a period of forty-five days during which several different activities will occur. The National Park Service will publish a notice in the Federal Register that a nominated property is being considered for listing in the National Register, providing a fifteen-day commenting period. 36 C.F.R. § 60.13. At the same time, National Park Service staff will review the nomination to ensure that the four primary criteria for listing—type, context, significance, and integrity—have been satisfactorily documented, and that the case for any applicable exceptions to ordinarily excluded resources has been made. At the conclusion of this process, the reviewing staff will advise the Keeper on whether she should approve or disapprove of a nomination.

Appeals and objections may come in any time before the property is actually listed. As noted above, objections from certain key consulting parties that arrive before the nomination is submitted must be appended to the nomination. In addition, any individual or organization may petition the Keeper to accept or reject a nomination. *Id.* §§ 60.6(t) & 60.9(i).

Prior to listing, private owners of property being considered in the nomination process may also object. They may object to designation by sending a notarized statement to the federal historic preservation officer or state historic preservation officer, as applicable. *Id.* §§ 60.6(g) & 60.10(d). A property will not be listed on the National Register if: the sole owner of a property objects; the majority of partial owners of a single property object; or the majority of property owners in a proposed district object. 16 U.S.C. § 470a(a)(6). Note that owner objection will not prevent a property from being considered "eligible" for the National Register. As will be seen in later Chapters (including Chapters III, IV, and V), eligibility triggers certain protections from third party actions.

If, after reviewing all of the documentation, the Keeper does not affirmatively act, the default rule is that nominated properties will be listed on the National Register after the forty-five day period. 36 C.F.R. §§ 60.6(r) & 60.9(h). The Keeper's decisions will be reviewed pursuant to the reasonableness standard of the Administrative Procedures Act. *See* Moody Hill Farms Ltd. P'ship v. U.S. Dep't of the Interior, 205 F.3d 554, 558 (2d Cir. 1999).

c. De-Listing Properties

How can a resource be removed from the National Register? The resource must go through a process known as a de-listing. Any person may request in writing for the removal of a National Register property, and such a request must be routed to the Keeper through the state or tribal historic preservation officer, or an agency's federal preservation officer. 36 C.F.R. § 60.15(c). The Keeper may remove a property on her own motion after notifying the nominating authority of the basis for removal. *Id.* § 60.15(k). Removal may only be justified on one the following four grounds:

(1) The property has ceased to meet the criteria for listing in the National Register because the qualities which caused it to be originally listed have been lost or destroyed, or such qualities were lost subsequent to nomination and prior to listing;

(2) Additional information shows that the property does not meet the National Register criteria for evaluation;

(3) Error in professional judgment as to whether the property meets the criteria for evaluation; or

(4) Prejudicial procedural error in the nomination or listing process.

Id. § 60.15(a). A resource that is removed for merely procedural errors (the fourth ground listed above) remains eligible for re-nomination. *Id.* § 60.15(a)(4).

Courts will not recognize de-listing based on equitable principles beyond those specifically listed in the regulations. *See* Amoco Production Co. v. U.S. Dep't of the Interior, 763 F. Supp. 514, 522–23 (N.D. Okla. 1990) (rejecting the property owner's request for the application of equitable principles to force a de-listing after determining that the property owner's changes to a National Register building did not destroy qualities that caused it to be originally listed).

The notification and review procedures for de-listings are similar to those for listings. If a state historic preservation officer (SHPO) receives a petition for de-listing, she must forward it to the State Review Board, the chief elected official, and affected property owners. *Id.* §§ 60.15(d) & (h). If a federal preservation officer receives a petition for de-listing, she must forward it to the SHPO and include any comments from the SHPO with a recommendation to the Keeper. *Id.* § 60.15(d).

As is the case for listing properties, the Keeper has the final say over de-listings. The Keeper must respond within a forty-five day period (with some exceptions). *Id.* § 60.15(j). A party wishing to remove a resource from the National Register must exhaust all administrative remedies with the Keeper before attempting to get a court to order removal of the resource. *See* White v. Shull, 520 F. Supp. 11 (S.D.N.Y. 1981).

B. STATE AND LOCAL DESIGNATION

Historically and/or culturally significant resources may be eligible for historic designation at the state and/or local levels. Most states have a state register of historic places, state historical resources survey, or state historic site file, which includes information about listed resources. In addition, there are more than 2,300 local historic districts across the country, which include properties of local significance. Designation at the state and local level may affect property owners more than National Register designation, because state and local designation may impose substantive responsibilities on property owners—such as requiring them to refrain from renovating, moving, or destroying their resources without the approval of a public board or official—which the National Register designation does not.

As is the case with the National Register, state and local jurisdictions require that resources meet specific criteria and go through a formal process before they can be designated historic. This Part discusses a few issues specific to state and local registers, including designation criteria and the process for designation.

1. STATE AND LOCAL REGISTER CRITERIA

To be designated on a state or local register of historic places, a resource must meet the applicable criteria. In many jurisdictions, these criteria are developed by program officers or related advisory boards and are not enshrined in state statutes or local ordinances. This makes criteria difficult to survey comprehensively. But some common features emerge from the criteria that are readily available.

a. Type

State and local registers of historic places most often track the National Register in setting forth a range of resources that are eligible for inclusion. These may include buildings, structure, objects, sites, or districts. *Compare* 16 U.S.C. § 470a(a)(1)(A) *with* GA. CODE. ANN. § 12–3–50.2(a)(1)(B). At times, these categories may be folded into one another; Pittsburgh, for example, includes buildings in the definition of "historic structure" and leaves the other categories intact. PITTSBURGH, PA. CODE § 1101.02. Intangible resources are not eligible for state and local registers.

b. Context

State and local registers of historic places also set forth the historic context within which significance must be established. The historic contexts that are contemplated by state and local registers may go beyond the contexts—"American history, architecture, archaeology, engineering, and culture"—allowed for National Register properties. 16 U.S.C. § 470a(a)(1)(A). New Hampshire, for example, recognizes properties that are "meaningful in. . . the traditions of the state," in addition to properties meeting the National Register criteria. *See* N.H. REV. STAT. ANN. § 227–C:33. Maryland includes "prehistory" and "upland and underwater

archaeology" in its list of available contexts. MD.
CODE. ANN. STATE FIN. & PROC. § 5A–323.

c. Significance

All jurisdictions require that a resource be
considered "significant," but jurisdictions vary as to
criteria they will use for a finding of significance.
Some jurisdictions provide that the National
Register significance criteria should be used for
resources on their registers. One benefit to adopting
the National Register criteria is that they have not
been subject to any meaningful or successful legal
challenge on the basis of vagueness or arbitrariness.
A potential disadvantage is that the designation
criteria do not reflect the more expansive findings of
significance more appropriate to smaller levels of
government.

Other jurisdictions use the National Register
criteria but modify or augment them to suit their
own needs. A popular addition by states and
localities to the National Register criteria is one
that relates to the geographic importance of a
resource whose unique location or physical
characteristics offers an easily identifiable visual
feature. *See*, *e.g.*, SEATTLE, WASH. CODE
§ 25.12.350(F); OMAHA, NEB. CODE § 24–52(c); COLO.
REV. STAT. § 24–80.1–107(d). Wisconsin has added a
fifth criterion to the four National Register criteria
for significance: "[r]epresentation of a significant
and distinguishable entity whose components may
lack individual distinction." WIS. STAT. ANN.

§ 44.36(2)(a)(4). Hawaii, meanwhile, adds two additional criteria:

(2) Environmental impact, i.e., whether the preservation of the building, site, structure, district, or object significantly enhances the environmental quality of the State;

(3) The social, cultural, educational, and recreational value of the building, site, structure, district, or object, when preserved, presented, or interpreted, contributes significantly to the understanding and enjoyment of the history and culture of Hawaii, the pacific area or the nation.

HAW. ADMIN. CODE § 13–198–8. The environmental and cultural values reflected in the Hawaii legislation expand designation to properties beyond those that would be considered through simple adoption of the National Register criteria.

Still other jurisdictions formulate criteria for designation that have no basis in the National Register criteria. Minneapolis has seven designation criteria that include landscape design and properties "associated with distinctive elements of city or neighborhood identity." MINNEAPOLIS, MINN. CODE § 599.210. Chicago also has seven criteria, with specific references to Chicago development and history. Like other states and localities, Chicago deems eligible properties whose "unique location or distinctive physical appearance or presence representing an established and familiar visual feature of a neighborhood, community, or the City of

Chicago." CHICAGO, ILL. MUN. CODE § 2–120–620(7). One concern about deviating too far from the National Register criteria is that due process challenges may be made against vague language. In a case challenging Chicago's ordinance, a much-criticized state appellate court decision held that the plaintiff had stated a cause of action on due process grounds and sent the matter back to the trial court on the merits. Hanna v. City of Chicago, 907 N.E.2d 390 (Ill. App. 2009). On remand, the trial court found that the words used "provide a description of the observable historic character of the districts" and were not void for vagueness. Hanna v. City of Chicago, No. 06 CH 19422 (Cook County, Ill. Chancery Div. May 2, 2012).

d. Integrity

Interestingly, many jurisdictions altogether skip the concept of integrity found in the National Register criteria. *Cf.* 36 C.F.R. § 60.4 (requiring "integrity of location, design, setting, materials, workmanship, feeling, and association"). Even if the concept cannot be located in statutes, ordinances, and regulations, in practice it may nonetheless be evaluated since decision-makers may be reluctant to designate a resource as historic if it has lost the ability to convey its significance. This may especially be the case in places like Georgia, where there are requirements on localities to investigate and report on resources being considered for designation. *See* GA. CODE. ANN. § 44–10–26(b)(1).

e. Exclusions and Exceptions

Some states and localities have statutes that track the exclusions and exceptions of the National Register. Miami–Dade County replicates the language exactly. MIAMI–DADE COUNTY, FLA. CODE § 16A–10(II). Other jurisdictions have minor exceptions. For example, Wisconsin's state register, unlike the National Register, does not exclude properties that have been moved. WIS. STAT. ANN. § 44.36(b).

Most jurisdictions completely ignore the National Register exclusions and exceptions. Several states, including Indiana and Texas, have registers that include cemeteries and burial grounds—which are expressly excluded from being listed on the National Register. *See, e.g.*, IND. CODE § 14–21–1–13.5 (authorizing a state register of cemeteries and burial grounds); 13 TEX. ADMIN. CODE § 22.6 (establishing the "Historic Texas Cemetery" program); *see also* 36 C.F.R. § 60.4. Along the same lines, not all jurisdictions require that resources meet a minimum fifty-year requirement, which is the default minimum age of properties under the National Register, absent "exceptional importance." 36 C.F.R. § 60.4. New York City's local ordinance only requires that properties be significant for thirty years before they will ordinarily be considered historic, while Seattle requires a mere twenty-five years. N.Y.C. ADMIN. CODE § 25–302(n); SEATTLE, WASH. CODE § 25.12.350.

f. Designation by Reference

Sometimes, state and local decision-makers may not apply designation criteria at all. Instead, they may include properties "by reference." Many states, for example, call for all resources listed on the National Register to be included on the state register of historic places. *See, e.g.*, ARK. CODE ANN. § 13–7–109(b)(2); COLO. REV. STAT. § 24–80.1–105(c); OKLA. STAT. tit. 53, § 355; N.Y. PARKS REC. & HIST. PRESERV. § 14.07.1.(a). Local historic districts and landmarks may also be included on state registers. *See, e.g.*, MASS. GEN. LAWS. Ch. 9, § 26C. Similarly, National Register-designated properties may be included on local registers by reference. *See, e.g.*, MIAMI–DADE COUNTY, FLA. CODE § 16A–10(I)(e).

2. STATE AND LOCAL DESIGNATION PROCEDURES

States and localities have a wide range of designation procedures. Some states fully delineate procedures in their statutes. Others make bare mention of a state register in their statutes and delegate authority for the development of relevant criteria and procedures to the state historic preservation officer or state historical commission. *See, e.g.*, MASS. GEN. LAWS ch. 9, § 26D(2); NEV. REV. STAT. 381.002.4(c); N.C. GEN. STAT. § 121–4.1(b); OR. REV. STAT. § 358.622(5). In rare cases, a state will delegate a key role in the designation process to a nonprofit organization. OHIO REV. CODE ANN. § 149.30(M) (delegating the inventory process for a state register to a statewide nonprofit group). Cities often have more information about designation procedures in their ordinances, although there are many exceptions. The city with perhaps the most highly-developed rules is New York City, which requires 128 pages to catalogue them. *See* N.Y.C., LANDMARKS PRES. COMM'N, RULES OF THE NEW YORK CITY LANDMARKS PRESERVATION COMMISSION (2013). Information about nominations, evaluations of nominations, and de-listing of properties follows.

a. Nominations

Nominations to state and local registers of historic places can often be submitted by any person. *But see, e.g.*, MASS. GEN. LAWS ch. 9, § 26D (authorizing nominations to the state register only from local governments or state agencies); MINNEAPOLIS, MINN. CODE § 599.220 (allowing nominations to the local register to come from a member of the local historic commission, city councilmember, mayor, planning director, or "any person with a legal or equitable interest in the subject property"). In this way, the state and local nomination process is more open to direct engagement and citizen participation than the National Register process, which requires nominations to be submitted only by state and tribal historic preservation officers, federal preservation officers, or the Keeper of the National Register. The process at the state and local level is also much simpler, since nomination need not be preceded by a series of reviews by other parties.

A typical nomination form will require a statement of significance, a map of the property boundaries, and photographs that visually represent the property and its setting. *See, e.g.*, HAW. ADMIN. CODE § 13–198–3. Nominations to state and local registers are usually conducted separately from nominations to the National Register. Some jurisdictions, however, will accept a nomination that is completed on National Register forms.

b. Evaluation of Nominations

In general, nominations to state and local registers of historic places will go through an evaluation process in which a decision-maker or a decision-making body will assess whether the nomination adequately documents that the resource meets the requisite criteria.

At the state level, the state historic preservation officer or the State Review Board (a public, appointed body created pursuant to the National Historic Preservation Act) makes the decision about nominations. *See, e.g.*, VT. STAT. ANN. tit. 22, § 742(a) (granting the state review board the ability to approve nominations to and removals from the state register); GA. CODE ANN. § 12–3–50.2(a)–(b) (granting a state agency such powers); *see also* 36 C.F.R. § 60.6(j).

At the local level, the decision may be handled by the local legislative body, the local historic commission, or even the mayor. *See, e.g.*, D.C. CODE § 6–1103 (granting designating responsibilities to the local historic district commission but not the city council); NEW ORLEANS, LA., CODE § 84–50(1) (limiting the local commission's designation powers to buildings and vacant sites of less than five acres); OMAHA, NEB., CODE § 24–60(1) (empowering the council to make a landmark designation in consultation with the local historic commission and planning board). Alternately, one body may have veto power over the other. *See, e.g.*, N.Y.C. CHARTER § 3020(9) (allowing the city council to modify or disapprove of any designation by the local commission, and allowing the mayor to disapprove of the disapproval, which could be overridden by a two-thirds vote of the city council). In either case, the makeup of any local historic commission— including qualifications such as professional background or residency requirements—is specified in the local ordinance.

In all designation procedures, due process is required. Adequate meeting rules, notices, note-taking, and other rules of procedure should be created and followed consistently. Reasons for decisions should be explicitly stated whenever a nomination is approved or rejected. Designation decision-makers who apply consistent criteria and articulate reasonable bases for their actions stand a good chance of overcoming challenges that their decisions are arbitrary or capricious or violate due process. *See, e.g.*, Citizens Emergency Comm. to Preserve Pres. v. Tierney, 896 N.Y.S.2d 41 (App. Div. 2010).

One area where due process is essential is the notification of private owners of properties being considered for designation. Such notice is almost always explicitly required in the law creating the register, but if it is not, the practice should be followed nonetheless. *See, e.g.,* UTAH CODE ANN. § 9–8–403. There is also the issue of whether and how private property owners may object during the process. In some places, private property owners may object to a listing, and their objection, standing alone, will be enough to keep a property from being listed on the applicable register. *See, e.g.,* CAL. PUB. RES. CODE § 5024.1(f)(4); N.C. GEN. STAT. § 121–4.1(c). In other places, objection may not prevent a property from being listed, but it will be considered by the party making a decision. *See, e.g.,* IND. CODE § 14–21–1–7(c); N.Y. PARKS REC. & HIST. PRESERV. § 14.07.1.(c) (allowing either property owners or municipalities to register an objection to listing during the state designation process). For state registers, local governments are sometimes given the opportunity to object, although local government objections do not typically stop the process altogether and instead are just taken into account as part of the general decision-making process. *See, e.g.,* CAL. PUB. RES. CODE § 5024.1(f)(3). A handful of jurisdictions require property owners to affirmatively approve the listing of a property before it will be included in the applicable register. *See, e.g.,* COLO. REV. STAT. § 24–80.1–107(2).

c. De-Listing Properties

Removal of properties from state and local registers may follow procedures similar to those used in removing properties from the National

Register. At the state level, removal will occur if the state historic preservation officer or other official, in consultation with a State Review Board, finds that the qualities that gave a resource significance no longer exist. *See, e.g.,* N.Y. PARKS REC. & HIST. PRESERV. § 14.07.1.(e); GA. CODE ANN. § 12–3–50.2(b). At the local level, there may not be a formal procedure for removing a property from a local register; such decisions may be made on an ad hoc basis.

CHAPTER 3

NATIONAL HISTORIC PRESERVATION ACT

The National Historic Preservation Act of 1966 (NHPA) is a sweeping statute that established a detailed federal program for historic preservation. Among other things, it:

• Created the National Register of Historic Places and established the criteria by which properties are evaluated for listing on the National Register, as discussed in Chapter II.

• Created the Advisory Council on Historic Preservation, a federal agency that advises the President, sets federal historic preservation policy, and plays an integral role in the process through which agencies fulfill their obligations under the NHPA.

• Created the roles of state and tribal historic preservation officers and encouraged states and tribes to appoint individuals to such positions— each charged with carrying out certain aspects of the NHPA and setting forth historic preservation policy within their jurisdictions.

• Required federal agencies to establish historic preservation planning and programs to identify, evaluate, and protect their historic properties.

• Established a process under Section 106 of the NHPA, which requires federal agencies to review the impacts of their undertakings on certain historic properties.

Thus the NHPA created a multi-level framework for designation and protection which has had significant ramifications in areas discussed here and in other Chapters.

This Chapter focuses on Section 106, noted in the last bullet point. It provides an overview and explanation of its key terms, describes its application, and outlines the relationship between the Section 106 process and other federal statutes. Despite its limitations (which will become clear in the course of this Chapter), Section 106 is the most important federal provision on historic preservation.

A.   OVERVIEW

Section 106 of the National Historic Preservation Act (NHPA) protects properties that are listed on or eligible for the National Register of Historic Places by requiring federal agencies to take into account the impacts of certain undertakings on those properties before they proceed with the undertaking. The relevant language is as follows:

> The head of any Federal agency having direct or indirect jurisdiction over a proposed Federal or federally assisted undertaking in any State and the head of any Federal department or independent agency having authority to license any undertaking shall, prior to the approval of the expenditure of any Federal funds on the undertaking or prior to the issuance of any

license, as the case may be, take into account the effect of the undertaking on any district, site, building, structure, or object that is included in or eligible for inclusion in the National Register. The head of any such Federal agency shall afford the Advisory Council on Historic Preservation established under part B of this subchapter a reasonable opportunity to comment with regard to such undertaking.

16 U.S.C. § 470f. In Section 106, Congress created a "stop, look, and listen" process through which agencies consider the effects of their actions on historic places.

Congress did not, however, mandate that agencies reach a particular conclusion at the end of this review process. That is, Section 106 does not require agencies to actually preserve the properties covered by Section 106. Some have criticized the "procedural" nature of Section 106, especially when comparing it to the "substantive" protection of Section 4(f) of the Department of Transportation Act, discussed in Chapter V. Despite its lack of substantive "teeth," however, Section 106 has had important effects. It has ensured that agencies at a minimum consider historic properties and has provided incentives for federal officials to avoid or mitigate harm to historic resources. It has also allowed various parties (including the Advisory Council on Historic Preservation, state and tribal historic preservation officers, and other consulting parties) to play a role in the review process. And it offers a way for members of the public to enforce agencies' duties through lawsuits.

The regulations for Section 106, located in 36 C.F.R. Part 800, lay out the review process in further detail. When one reads through these regulations, one might get the sense that the process is mechanical, simply requiring that agencies check a few boxes to ensure compliance. But in practice, the requirements at each stage have proven to be quite nuanced and demanding. The next two Parts, describing the key terms and the application of Section 106, underscore that the duties Section 106 imposes on federal agencies are significant.

B.   KEY TERMS

Section 106 of the National Historic Preservation Act is only two sentences long, but it contains six key terms requiring our attention. The first five terms help us understand when Section 106 applies and the scope of its application. Section 106 constrains only an action of a federal "agency" which is considered an "undertaking." The important but unwieldy statutory definition for undertaking delineates four different categories of undertakings, all of which we consider here. Only the "effect" of the undertaking must be taken into account by agencies. The fourth term, "National Register," limits the types of properties subject to Section 106 review. And the fifth term, "eligible for inclusion," refers to those protected properties that are not actually listed on the National Register but still protected by Section 106.

The sixth term, "Advisory Council on Historic Preservation," refers to the only entity legally entitled to comment during every agency review conducted pursuant to Section 106.

1.   AGENCY

The National Historic Preservation Act refers to the Administrative Procedure Act for its definition of "agency." *See* 16 U.S.C. § 470w(1). The Administrative Procedure Act defines an agency as "each authority of the Government of the United States, whether or not it is within or subject to review by another agency," excluding Congress, federal courts and courts martial, federal territories and possessions, the District of Columbia, military commissions, and a few other entities. 5 U.S.C. § 551(1). This term includes not only Cabinet-level departments but also subagencies and independent agencies.

Most of the time, determining whether a federal entity is an agency for the purposes of Section 106 is a simple task. However, there are a few entities— such as the U.S. Postal Service, the branches of the Federal Reserve Bank, and the Federal Deposit Insurance Corporation—that have both public and private functions and characteristics. To determine whether these entities are in fact agencies for the purposes of Section 106, a court will review a range of factors, including: the entity's functions, the way the entity was created, the relationship between the entity and the federal government, the nature of the private functions or characteristics of the entity, and the rights and roles of the entity in federal judicial proceedings. *See, e.g.,* Comm. to Save the Fox Bldg. v. Birmingham Branch of the Fed. Reserve Bank, 497 F. Supp. 504, 509–10 (N.D. Ala. 1980) (finding that a Federal Reserve branch is a federal agency because, among other reasons, it was created to satisfy the needs of the federal government); Nat'l Trust for Historic Pres. v. FDIC, 995 F.2d 238, 240–41 (D.C. Cir. 1993), *rehearing granted and judgment vacated,* 5 F.3d 567 (D.C. Cir. 1993), *opinion reinstated in part on rehearing by* 21 F.3d 469 (D.C. Cir. 1994), *cert. denied,* 513 U.S. 1065 (1994) (finding the Federal Deposit Insurance Corporation is not a federal agency because of its immunity from judicial restraint when exercising the function at issue).

The term agency may also encompass units of state, tribal, or local government, if the unit of government has been delegated the responsibilities of a federal agency. 36 C.F.R. § 800.2(a). This occurs when another federal statute has authorized a nonfederal unit of government to act as a federal agency. *See, e.g.,* 42 U.S.C. § 5304(g)(1) (allowing local governments to "assume all of the responsibilities for environmental review, decisionmaking, and action" relating to the receipt of community development block grants from the federal government). (There is also the question of whether the action, including a delegated action, taken by an agency is covered by Section 106. This question is discussed in the next subsection, which deals with the definition of an "undertaking.")

Courts have emphasized that even when nonfederal parties are involved, Section 106 compliance and independent assessments of undertakings rests with the federal agency (either the head of the agency or agency official, depending on the stage of the process). *See, e.g.*, Hall County Historical Soc'y, Inc. v. Ga. Dep't of Transp., 477 F. Supp. 741, 751 (N.D. Ga. 1978) (finding that a federal agency had failed to comply with Section 106 because of its "blind reliance . . . upon the state's determination and findings" and failure to make independent assessments). When multiple agencies are engaged in an undertaking, a "lead federal agency" is chosen to have primary responsibility for compliance with the Section 106 process. 36 C.F.R. § 800.2(a)(2).

When an agency is identified, who may represent it? Both the "head of the agency" and the "agency official" play a role at different stages of the Section 106 review process. The head of an agency is the chief official of the agency or the head of the unit of state, local, or tribal government if such government has assumed or been delegated responsibility for Section 106 compliance. *Id.* § 800.16(k). This term includes the Secretary of an agency, governor of a state, chief of a tribe, or mayor of a town. An agency official is usually a lower-ranking individual within the agency or unit or government who is tasked with approving and implementing the undertaking subject to Section 106. *Id.* § 800.2(a). For example, for National Park Service undertakings, the Secretary of the Interior is the head of the agency, and park superintendents are usually the agency officials. In achieving her tasks, an agency official may (and often does) consult with "applicants, consultants, or designees," but she remains "legally responsible for all required findings and determinations." *Id.* § 800.2(a)(3). She also maintains financial responsibility, *id.* § 800.2(a), meaning that the agency cannot impose the financial burden of the Section 106 process on other parties.

2. UNDERTAKING

Section 106 only requires federal agencies to review the impacts of their actions on historic properties when those actions are deemed "undertakings." An undertaking is defined in the Advisory Council on Historic Preservation regulations as:

> a project, activity, or program funded in whole or in part under the direct or indirect jurisdiction of a Federal agency, including [a] those carried out by or on behalf of a Federal agency; [b] those carried out with Federal financial assistance; and [c] those requiring a Federal permit, license or approval.

36 C.F.R. § 800.16(y). Note that there is no requirement that the undertaking be a certain size or cost a certain dollar amount.

The statutory definition of undertaking, however, refers to a fourth type of undertaking, which we call a type-(D) undertaking: "those subject to State or local regulation administered pursuant to a delegation or approval by a Federal agency." 16 U.S.C. § 470w(7). As we explain below, the D.C. Circuit has determined that this type of undertaking is not covered by Section 106. *See* Nat'l Mining Ass'n v. Fowler, 324 F.3d 752 (D.C. Cir. 2003). All four types of undertakings—the three in the regulations and the type-(D) undertaking only mentioned in the statute—are discussed below.

a. Carried Out by or for the Agency

The most straightforward undertakings are those carried out by or for a federal agency. Such undertakings encompass a range of agency actions, the most common being construction activities: paving roads, erecting large-scale infrastructure (such as bridges and dams), demolishing existing structures, excavating for utilities, and changing the use of agency properties. Other undertakings have ranged from fencing livestock watering facilities and managing land to solarizing lighthouses.

Section 106 undertakings necessarily involve agency action. At a minimum, agencies must be substantially involved in the undertaking and/or must have an opportunity for the agency to exercise discretion to consider environmental values. An agency's failure to act, without more, is not considered an undertaking. *See* Nat'l Trust for

Historic Pres. v. Blanck, 938 F. Supp. 908, 919 (D.D.C. 1996).

Often times, undertakings can unfold in phases or over a long period of time. For Section 106 review to apply, the agency's role in the undertaking must involve continuous and/or periodic monitoring, approval, and/or funding. *See*, *e.g.*, Morris County Trust for Historic Pres. v. Pierce, 714 F.2d 271, 275 (3rd Cir. 1983). By contrast, actions taken without federal involvement or funding and occurring years after an undertaking once subject to Section 106 will not revive Section 106 obligations. *See*, *e.g.*, Waterford Citizens' Ass'n v. Reilly, 970 F.2d 1287, 1292 (4th Cir. 1992) (declining to find an undertaking where a private developer not assisted by federal funding wanted to add sewer lines to a system reviewed under Section 106 and completed twelve years before). Similarly, if the Advisory Council on Historic Preservation finds that a federal action complies with Section 106 and a second federal agency engages in the same action with "no new, unreviewed elements," Section 106 will not apply. *See* McMillan Park Comm. v. Nat'l Capital Planning Comm'n, 968 F.2d 1283, 1289 (D.C. Cir. 1992) (declining to find the National Capital Planning Commission's review of an amendment to a comprehensive plan an undertaking where such amendment had been previously considered by the Advisory Council on Historic Preservation).

The acquisition of property is not typically considered an undertaking, although later decisions regarding the use of such land may be considered undertakings. Courts in at least three circuits have found that acquisition of property through eminent domain is not an undertaking. *See*, *e.g.*, Paulina Lake Historic Cabin Owners Ass'n v. U.S.D.A. Forest Serv. 577 F. Supp. 1188, 1192 (D. Or. 1983). Similarly, the federal reassumption of control of federal land is not considered an undertaking. The Ninth Circuit has said that an agency's refusal to renew a permit to a private resort operator located on federal land is not an undertaking "because the mere exercise of ownership rights does not affect the historic character of the site, even when the assumption of control is clearly preparatory to action that will affect the site's historical aspects." Yerger v. Robertson, 981 F.2d 460, 465 (9th Cir. 1992).

In contrast to the acquisition of property, the disposition of property is often considered an undertaking. A decision not to excess federal property, for example, is an undertaking because such a decision could have long-term effects on historic resources located on the property. *See* Nat'l Trust for Historic Pres. v. Blanck, 938 F. Supp. 908, 920 (D.D.C. 1996). Similarly, sales of leases on federal property containing historic resources are considered undertakings. *See* Mont. Wilderness Ass'n v. Fry, 310 F. Supp. 2d 1127, 1151 (D. Mont. 1992).

b. Financial Assistance

Undertakings include projects "carried out with Federal financial assistance." 16 U.S.C.

§ 470w(7)(B). Such projects involve state or local governments or private entities which receive either direct or indirect assistance from the federal government. Direct assistance is often used to fund transportation projects or housing and urban development projects; indirect assistance includes block grants and federal loan guarantees.

Mere expenditure of funding is not sufficient to trigger Section 106. Rather, the meaning of financial assistance hinges on whether an agency has control over an "approval of the expenditure of funds." The regulations define this term to mean "any final agency decision authorizing or permitting the expenditure of Federal funds or financial assistance on an undertaking." 36 C.F.R. § 800.16(c).

The regulations require that the final decision must be made by an "agency," as that term is defined above. An authorization of the expenditure of federal financial assistance that is not made by an agency is not considered an undertaking. *See*, *e.g.*, Lee v. Thornburgh, 877 F.2d 1053 (D.C. Cir. 1989) (finding no undertaking because Congress, and not a federal agency, authorized and disbursed the funding).

Furthermore, the final decision must involve some element of agency discretion and control with respect to approving or disapproving the expenditure of funds. For example, an agency's expenditure of funds which is required by federal statute, without any agency discretion, is not an undertaking. *See* Sac & Fox Nation of Missouri v.

Norton, 240 F.3d 1250 (10th Cir. 2001). As another example, if an agency disburses block grants to a state but has no ability to influence the state's subsequent disbursement of such grants, the agency's initial disbursement will not be considered an undertaking. This is the case even if the later disbursement by the state may impact the historic resources Section 106 aims to protect.

One court has read a federal funding requirement into Section 106—meaning that only those projects receiving federal funding should trigger Section 106 review. *See* W. Mohegan Tribe & Nation v. New York, 100 F. Supp. 2d 122, 127 (N.D.N.Y. 2000), *aff'd in part, vacated in part*, 246 F.3d 230 (2d Cir. 2001). This narrow reading was rejected by the D.C. Circuit, *see* Sheridan Kalorama Historical Ass'n v. Christopher, 49 F.3d 750, 755 (D.C. Cir. 1995), and in our opinion the *Western Mohegan Tribe* court was incorrect in its reasoning.

c. Permit, License, or Approval

A broad range of federal permits, licenses, and approvals may also be considered undertakings. This category of undertaking involves both federal and nonfederal parties, because federal permits, licenses, and approvals are often sought by nonfederal actors. Perhaps the most common federal authorizations in this category is the authorization of private activity on federal land. Key considerations to finding an undertaking include: the nature of the nonfederal party's activities (including whether such activities require agency approval); the level of discretion and control of the agency; and/or whether the agency actually acted, or merely failed to act.

In general, activities that require a federal agency's prior approval are undertakings. *See*, *e.g.*, Fein v. Peltier, 949 F. Supp. 374 (D.V.I. 1996). For Section 106 to be triggered, the request or application for approval must actually be submitted to the federal agency. *See* Pres. Pittsburgh v. Conturo, No. 2:11cv889, 2011 WL 4025731, at *9 (W.D. Pa. Sept. 9, 2011). Without such a request or application, the agency will have no ability to take actions pursuant to Section 106.

Similarly, undertakings do not arise when the agency has no discretion over its ability to grant permits and/or retains no control over the permitting process. Certifications and approvals over which an agency has no discretion are not undertakings. *See*, *e.g.*, Sugarloaf Citizens Ass'n v. FERC, 959 F.2d 508, 513 & 515 (4th Cir. 1992) (finding federal certification of a waste-to-energy facility not an undertaking because the agency had no discretion regarding the issuance of the certification). Activities over which an agency has no regulatory authority are also not undertakings— even if the agency is entitled to comment. *See*, *e.g.*, Techworld Dev. Corp. v. D.C. Pres. League, 648 F. Supp. 106 (D.D.C. 1986). And in the case of phased or ongoing projects, an undertaking will not be found unless the federal agency has the continuing ability to require changes to a license. *See*, *e.g.*, Vieux Carré Prop. Owners, Residents & Assocs., Inc.

v. Brown, 948 F.2d 1436, 1444–45 (5th Cir. 1991) (involving a waterfront park project under federal license).

We stated above the general rule that mere inaction, without more, is not a Section 106 undertaking. The same rule holds true for licenses: a license within the meaning of Section 106 does not include an agency's failure to disapprove a project when the agency had discretion on whether or not to act. *See* Sheridan Kalorama Historical Ass'n v. Christopher, 49 F.3d 750, 756–57 (D.C. Cir. 1995) (finding the Secretary of State's failure to disapprove the Republic of Turkey's plans to demolish its historic chancery building to not be an undertaking).

Finally, there is an issue related to interpretation which deserves mention. Section 106 itself mentions only "license" and makes no mention of either "permit" or "approval." 16 U.S.C. § 470f. The National Historic Preservation Act does not define "license," but the definition of undertaking in both the statute and the regulations includes "permit[,] license, or approval." *See* 16 U.S.C. § 470w(7)(C) & 36 C.F.R. § 800.16(y). Courts should defer to the Advisory Council on Historic Preservation regulatory definition of an undertaking as a reasonable interpretation of ambiguous statutory language. A broad, inclusive interpretation is also supported by the definition of "license" in the Administrative Procedure Act (APA), which "includes the whole or a part of an agency permit, certificate, approval, registration, charter, membership, statutory exemption or other form of permission." 5 U.S.C. § 551(8). We suggest consulting the APA—despite the fact that the APA and National Historic Preservation Act are two separate statutes—because the APA applies to all federal agency actions, including Section 106 reviews, and because in other instances (including the APA's definition of "agency") the National Historic Preservation Act explicitly references the APA. Courts have generally reconciled the discrepancy between Section 106 and the statutory and regulatory definitions by including agency authorizations and permits that might not technically be considered to be licenses. *See, e.g.,* Nat'l Indian Youth Council v. Andrus, 501 F. Supp. 649, 676 (D.N.M. 1980), *aff'd* 664 F.2d 220 (10th Cir. 1981) (finding a "mining project entered into pursuant to a federally-approved lease" to be an undertaking and agency authorization of same to be a "license"); Walsh v. U.S. Army Corps of Eng'rs, 757 F. Supp. 781, 789 (W.D. Tex. 1990) (applying Section 106 to a permit related to the construction of a dam and reservoir).

d. Subject to State/Local Regulation

The statute defines undertaking to include federal activities "subject to State or local regulation administered pursuant to a delegation or approval by a Federal agency." 16 U.S.C. § 470w(7)(D). However, Section 106 makes no mention of this type of undertaking. Rather, Section 106 only addresses the first three types of undertakings: federal undertakings, federally assisted undertakings, and licenses. *See id.* § 470f. Clumsy drafting by Congress is to blame for this contradiction.

One important case has held that Section 106's omission of any reference to the type of undertaking contemplated by 16 U.S.C. § 470w(7)(D) means that such undertakings are not subject to Section 106 review. *See* Nat'l Mining Ass'n v. Fowler, 324 F.3d 752, 759–60 (D.C. Cir. 2003). As a result of this case, the regulations for Section 106 were revised to omit type-(D) undertakings from the definition. *See* 36 C.F.R. § 800.16(y). Counter-arguments to this case's interpretation are threefold: (1) a type-(D) undertaking is "federally assisted" because it operates under the auspices of federal law; (2) Section 106 refers to "any license," rather than to federal licenses, suggesting that some licenses issued by state and local bodies may be covered by Section 106; and (3) the Advisory Council on Historic Preservation, which adopted the definition including the type-(D) undertaking, should have received deference from the court, given that the issue is ambiguous. A court has yet to adopt any of these counter-arguments.

3. EFFECT

Section 106 applies only to the "effects" of undertakings on historic resources. The regulations define an effect as an "alteration to the characteristics of a historic property qualifying it for inclusion in or eligibility for the National Register." 36 C.F.R. § 800.16(i). Thus to understand whether an undertaking has produced an effect, one must first understand the reason a historic resource is seen as significant and the physical characteristics that express this significance. Part A of Chapter II thoroughly discusses the federal designation process and the finding of significance. Here, we must only remember that Section 106 only protects those characteristics of a historic resource that qualify a historic resource for the National Register; insignificant aspects of a historic resource receive no protection. The discussion of the application of Section 106 in Part C below will clarify the role this term plays in limiting the scope of Section 106.

4.   NATIONAL REGISTER

The National Register is the National Register of Historic Places established by the National Historic Preservation Act and maintained by the Secretary of the Interior. *See* 16 U.S.C. § 470w(6); 36 C.F.R. § 800.16(q). It is a list "of districts, sites, buildings, structures, and objects significant in American history, architecture, archeology, engineering, and culture." 16 U.S.C. § 470a(1)(A). The process for listing a property on the National Register involves at least two levels of review (usually state and federal). More information about the National Register criteria and eligibility for listing is contained in Chapter II.

Section 106 protects only those historic resources listed on or eligible for the National Register. It does not protect properties listed on state, tribal, or local registers of historic places, unless those properties meet the criteria for listing on the National Register.

5.   ELIGIBLE FOR INCLUSION ON THE NATIONAL REGISTER

Section 106 protects both properties listed on, and properties eligible for, the National Register. The regulations define properties that are "eligible for inclusion in the National Register" as "properties formally determined as such in accordance with regulations of the Secretary of the Interior and all other properties that meet the National Register criteria." 36 C.F.R. § 800.16(l)(2).

One might ask why Section 106 covers properties eligible for inclusion, when it might be simpler to cover only those properties that are already listed on the National Register. The reason is that protection of eligible properties achieves the goal of the National Historic Preservation Act by accounting for circumstantial or technical reasons for the property's omission from the National Register. One reason a historic property might not be listed is that the property is owned by a private party who has objected to listing. *See* 16 U.S.C. § 470a(a)(6); 36 C.F.R. §§ 60.6(g) & 60.10(d). Another reason might be timing: a resource may be discovered during the part of the Section 106 process (discussed below) in which federal agencies are required to search for and identify historic resources. Section 106 requires agencies to evaluate the significance of any historic properties discovered during this phase and treat non-listed properties that meet the National Register criteria in the same way as those properties already listed on the National Register.

6. ADVISORY COUNCIL ON HISTORIC PRESERVATION

The Advisory Council on Historic Preservation (ACHP) is an independent federal agency created by the National Historic Preservation Act and composed of members of the Cabinet, a governor, a mayor, a Native American representative, members of the public, and others. *See* 16 U.S.C. § 470i(a). The ACHP has several key functions including: advising the President and Congress on historic preservation issues; encouraging public interest in preservation; assisting state and local governments in drafting preservation legislation; and reviewing agency policies and programs. *Id.* § 470j(a). Importantly for this Chapter, the ACHP also promulgates the regulations for Section 106 and plays a crucial role in commenting on reviews conducted pursuant to Section 106. Its role in that process is discussed in Part C.

C. APPLICATION

Section 106 of the National Historic Preservation Act requires federal agencies to take into account the impact of certain undertakings on properties on or eligible for listing on the National Register of Historic Places, and to afford the Advisory Council on Historic Preservation the opportunity to comment. 16 U.S.C. § 470f.

Agencies satisfy their Section 106 responsibilities by completing a series of four steps set forth in regulations promulgated by the Advisory Council on Historic Preservation. *See* 36 C.F.R. §§ 800.3–800.6. These include: (1) the initiation of the process, (2) the identification of historic properties affected, (3) the evaluation of adverse effects, and (4) the resolution of adverse effects. After describing these four steps in detail, this Part discusses alternative procedures that agencies may use to satisfy Section 106 requirements.

Note that there are two types of resources subject to Section 106 which deserve more comprehensive treatment than we can provide in this Chapter: archaeological resources and Native American resources. Chapter XI includes a discussion of the issues raised by archaeological resources, while Chapter XII covers Native American resource issues.

1. INITIATION OF PROCESS

According to the regulations, agencies must take several steps to initiate the Section 106 review process. First, they must evaluate their projects, programs, and activities to determine if they are undertakings subject to Section 106. Second, they must set up the Section 106 process so that it is coordinated with agency reviews required by other federal statutes. Third, they must identify consulting parties—perhaps the most important step in the initiation phase, since consultation is at the heart of the Section 106 process. And fourth, they must develop a plan for public involvement. *See* 36 C.F.R. § 800.3.

Ideally, all of these activities will occur "prior to" the commencement of the undertaking, as required by Section 106—that is, as soon as the scope of the proposed undertaking is identified. *See* 16 U.S.C. § 470f. Agencies are expected to factor Section 106 reviews into their plans and engage in the review process early enough that any comments received can be fully considered. Agencies may, however, conduct or authorize "nondestructive project planning activities before completing compliance with Section 106, provided that such actions do not restrict the subsequent consideration of alternatives to avoid, minimize or mitigate the undertaking's adverse effects on historic properties." 36 C.F.R. § 800.1(c). This provision makes sense because agencies often need to conduct planning activities for their undertakings and should not be constrained by Section 106 if the activities' impacts are minimal. Once Section 106 review is completed, there are some situations in which unanticipated discoveries will re-open the Section 106 process, in which case the agency will repeat certain steps, as the regulations prescribe. *See id.* § 800.13.

a. Evaluate Undertaking Status

To initiate the Section 106 process, an agency must first determine if its project, activity, or program is an undertaking—a term discussed in Part B above. Some federal actions are very obviously undertakings; others require more careful evaluation. Unless there is an undertaking, Section 106 does not apply.

There are two other determinations that must be made by the agency at this stage. One is determining whether the undertaking has the potential to cause effects on historic properties. If the undertaking does not have this potential, then the agency can end its Section 106 inquiry. 36 C.F.R. § 800.3(a)(1). Another is whether the undertaking is governed by one of the program alternatives described in 36 C.F.R. § 800.14. *Id.* § 800.3(a)(2). (Three program alternatives are discussed below.) In that case, the review of the undertaking will be analyzed according to the rules of the applicable program alternative.

If the undertaking has the potential to cause effects and is not subject to the program alternatives, the agency will continue initiating the Section 106 process. If not, the process will conclude here.

b. Coordinate with Other Reviews

Another step in the initiation of the Section 106 process is the agency's coordination of the Section 106 review with reviews required by other federal statutes, such as the National Environmental Policy Act (discussed in Chapter IV of this book), Section 4(f) of the Department of Transportation Act (Chapter V), the Archaeological Resources Protection Act (Chapter XI), and the Native American Graves Protection and Repatriation Act (Chapter XII). 36 C.F.R. § 800.3(b). By coordinating review efforts under the applicable statutes, the agency may save time and money, while ensuring consistency across reviews. The nature of this coordination is discussed further in Part D below.

c. Identify Consulting Parties

Perhaps the most significant step in the initiation phase of the Section 106 process is the identification of consulting parties. Consultation forms the core of the Section 106 process. The regulations define consultation as "the process of seeking, discussing, and considering the views of other participants, and, where feasible, seeking agreement with them regarding matters arising in the section 106 process." 36 C.F.R. § 800.16(f). The consultation required by Section 106 is thus meant to be inclusive, with participants working toward the goal of common resolution. This goal is facilitated by the access to information and to agency officials provided to consulting parties. A common resolution is not always achieved, however, as the agency is not required to act on input received during the consulting process; it must merely take this input into account when proceeding through the Section 106 process.

Given the importance of consultation to the Section 106 review process, who must be consulted by the agency? The Advisory Council on Historic Preservation (ACHP) is entitled to participate as a consulting party in any Section 106 action and is the only entity allowed a "reasonable opportunity to comment." 16 U.S.C. § 470f. The right to comment is greater than the right to consult. The regulations define a comment as "the findings and recommendations of the [ACHP] formally provided in writing to the head of a Federal agency under section 106." 36 C.F.R. § 800.16(e).

Additional mandatory consulting parties include the state historic preservation officer (SHPO) and/or tribal historic preservation officer (THPO) with jurisdiction over the property on which the undertaking will occur or on which the historic resource is located. *Id.* § 800.3(c). A SHPO is the individual, designated by her state, with responsibility for the state's preservation programs. Among other responsibilities, a SHPO identifies, evaluates, and nominates eligible properties to the National Register of Historic Places, as further described in Chapter II. *See* 16 U.S.C. § 470a(b)(3)(B). A THPO is the chosen representative of a Native American group who "may assume all or any part of the functions of a State Historic Preservation Officer." *Id.* § 470a(d)(2). Normally, if a THPO has jurisdiction, only the THPO will be named a consulting party, not the SHPO. However, the owners of properties on tribal lands "which are neither owned by a member of the tribe nor held in trust by the Secretary for the benefit of the tribe" may request that the SHPO also participate in the Section 106 process. 36 C.F.R. § 800.3(c)(1).

After identifying the SHPO and/or THPO, the agency must consult with the SHPO/THPO to identify any other parties entitled to be consulting parties and invite them to be a part of the process. *Id.* § 800.3(f). Parties entitled to participate include: representatives of local governments with jurisdiction over the area of potential effects of the undertaking; applicants for federal assistance, permits, licenses, and approvals; and representatives of Indian tribes not represented by a THPO and Native Hawaiian organizations that "attach religious and cultural significance to historic properties off tribal lands." *Id.* § 800.2.

After identifying all parties entitled to consult, the agency has discretion to invite other parties to participate. In addition, the regulations provide that individuals and organizations may request in writing to be consulting parties. *Id.* § 800.3(f)(2). Those "with a demonstrated interest in the undertaking may participate as consulting parties due to the nature of their legal or economic relation to the undertaking or affected properties, or their concern with the undertaking's effects on historic properties." *Id.* § 800.2(c)(5). When fielding requests by interested individuals and organizations, the agency will consult with the SHPO or THPO to determine whether to grant the request. Parties with special interests should try to be consulting parties to ensure they have a seat at the table.

The need or desire to involve additional consulting parties may arise throughout the course of the undertaking, especially during a phased undertaking. An agency may add consulting parties throughout the process but should try to involve them as early as possible to ensure they have adequate opportunity to provide input.

d. Develop Public Involvement Plan

An agency must consult with the SHPO and/or THPO to develop a plan for involving the public in the Section 106 process. 36 C.F.R. § 800.3(e). The regulations require agency officials to "seek and consider the views of the public in a manner that reflects the nature and complexity of the undertaking and its effects on historic properties, the likely interest of the public in the effects on historic properties, confidentiality concerns of private individuals and businesses, and the relationship of the Federal involvement to the undertaking." *Id.* § 800.2(d)(1). The agency is also required to provide certain findings to the public and to provide a mechanism for the public to provide comment. *Id.* § 800.2(d)(2). The regulations articulate standards for documenting agency findings, including both format and content. *Id.* § 800.11. Aside from the documentation standards, the precise method of disseminating information and obtaining public input is left up to the agency officials.

2. IDENTIFICATION OF HISTORIC PROPERTIES AFFECTED

After an agency has successfully initiated the Section 106 process, it must identify the historic properties affected by the undertaking. This second stage of the process, like the first, involves several steps.

First, the agency official must consult with the state historic preservation officer (SHPO) and/or the tribal historic preservation officer (THPO) to determine the scope of its identification efforts. 36 C.F.R. § 800.4(a). The agency first determines the "area of potential effects," defined as "the geographic area or areas within which an undertaking may directly or indirectly cause alterations in the character or use of historic properties." *Id.* § 800.16(d). The area of potential effects may be public or private property. Proper documentation through photographs, maps, and/or drawings is critical because it establishes the geographic boundaries of the agency's efforts. The agency official must review information on known historic properties within the area of potential effects and must seek information from consulting parties and others "likely to have knowledge of, or concerns with, historic properties in the area." *Id.* §§ 800.4(2)–(3).

Once the area of potential effects has been delineated, the agency official must make a "reasonable and good faith effort" to identify historic properties, in consultation with the consulting parties. *Id.* § 800.4(b)(1). If a property is listed on the National Register of Historic Places, the agency official has an easy task. But when an agency official discovers a property within the area of potential effects which is not listed but may be eligible for the National Register, compliance with the reasonable and good faith standard is harder. The agency official must then seek information from consulting parties, apply the National Register criteria, and formally determine whether the property is eligible for the National Register. *Id.* § 800.4(c). To meet the reasonable and good faith effort standard, the agency must do more than just send out form letters, and agency officials must follow up with targeted parties to ensure engagement. A court will find unreasonable efforts to identify historic properties that violate the agency's own rules. *See, e.g.,* Mont. Wilderness Ass'n v. Connell, 725 F.3d 988, 1008–09 (9th Cir. 2013) (noting that the Bureau of Land Management failed to follow its internal protocols regarding the survey techniques used and thus failed to make a reasonable and good faith effort to identify historic resources). Courts will also scrutinize agency efforts to identify tribal resources, as agencies should be sensitive to confidentiality concerns of Native Americans. *See, e.g.,* Pueblo of Sandia v. United States, 50 F.3d 856, 860–62 (10th Cir. 1995) (finding no reasonable and good faith effort where the agency used form letters to request tribal input about historic and cultural resources, did not adequately consider confidentiality concerns, failed to act on information obtained, and did not timely distribute comments of a tribal elder and an anthropologist to the SHPO).

If the agency and SHPO/THPO agree on whether the property is eligible or not, then the agreed-upon view will prevail. If the parties do not agree, then the agency official will submit the matter to the

Keeper of the National Register of Historic Places, who makes a final decision.

Should the agency official determine that there are no historic properties in the area of potential effects or that the undertaking will have no effect on them, then the agency documents this conclusion and provides notice to the SHPO and all consulting parties. The SHPO/THPO may object to such a finding, and if she does, the agency must consult with her to resolve the disagreement or send relevant documentation to the Advisory Council on Historic Preservation (ACHP). After reviewing this documentation, the ACHP may provide a written opinion to the head of the agency. Even in the absence of a SHPO/THPO objection, the ACHP may object to an agency finding that no historic properties are affected and may provide written comments to the agency. All written documentation should be made available to the public. *See* 36 C.F.R. § 800.4(d). If at the end of this consultation the agency still determines that there are no historic properties affected by the undertaking, then the agency must document this determination and the Section 106 process may conclude.

If, however, the agency official finds that there are historic properties affected by the undertaking, then she must notify consulting parties and proceed to the next stage in the process: the evaluation of adverse effects. The agency official should take care to note which characteristics qualify a historic property for the National Register. As we will see in the next stage, it is these characteristics that Section 106 aims to protect.

3. EVALUATION OF ADVERSE EFFECTS

In the third stage of the Section 106 process, the agency official, in consultation with others, evaluates whether any effects on historic properties are adverse effects. A finding of an adverse effect occurs "when an undertaking may alter, directly or indirectly, any of the characteristics of a historic property that qualify the property for inclusion in the National Register in a manner that would diminish the integrity of the property's location, design, setting, materials, workmanship, feeling, or association." 36 C.F.R. § 800.5(a)(1). This language underscores why it is important for agency officials to determine which characteristics qualify a historic property for inclusion on the National Register. Without identifying these characteristics, the agency will not be able to determine whether there are adverse effects.

The regulations also clarify that a finding of adverse effect should be made when the undertaking "may" affect historic properties. The agency official need not be certain that an undertaking will affect historic properties to make a finding of adverse effect. These effects may also unfold over long periods of time and need not be immediate.

Several broad categories of adverse effects, which are described in further detail in the regulations, include: physical destruction, neglect, removal of the property from its historic location, changes in use, and alteration inconsistent with the Secretary of the Interior's Standards for the Treatment of Historic Properties (found in 36 C.F.R. Part 68). *See id.* § 800.5(a)(2) (explaining these examples further). The agency official need not find an adverse effect unless the effect impacts the significance or integrity of the historic property. Accordingly, the removal of an object from its historic location may not produce an adverse effect if the setting does not contribute to its historic designation. Similarly, a change in use will only be deemed an adverse effect where continuation of the historic use is essential to a property's historic designation. Another issue the agency official must keep in mind is that while neglect may be considered an adverse effect, mere inaction by an agency will not be an undertaking; there must first be an undertaking—perhaps some affirmative act by the agency—which leads to the neglect in order for Section 106 to apply.

If the agency official finds that the undertaking produces no adverse effects on historic properties, she should follow a process similar to the process of notifying consulting parties, addressing disagreements, and distributing documentation described for the second stage of Section 106 review (for findings that there are no affected historic properties). *Id.* §§ 800.5(c)–(d). If at the conclusion of this process the agency official determines again that there are no adverse effects, the agency may document this finding and proceed with the undertaking. *Id.* § 800.5(d)(1). Especially when all the parties agree that there are no adverse effects, a party attempting to challenge this finding in court will have a heavy burden. *See, e.g.*, Neighborhood Ass'n of the Back Bay v. Federal Transit Admin., 463 F.3d 50 (1st Cir. 2006) (rejecting a plaintiff's challenge to an agency's finding of no adverse effect because the agency's finding was not arbitrary and capricious).

If, however, the agency official finds that there are adverse effects on historic properties, the agency proceeds to the fourth stage of the Section 106 process: the resolution of adverse effects.

4.   RESOLUTION OF ADVERSE EFFECTS

The fourth and final stage of a typical Section 106 review process is for the agency to resolve adverse effects. The goal of this stage is to consult with the Advisory Council on Historic Preservation (ACHP), other consulting parties, and members of the public "to develop and evaluate alternatives or modifications to the undertaking that could avoid, minimize, or mitigate adverse effects on historic properties." 36 C.F.R. § 800.6.

Although the ACHP may provide comments at any time in the Section 106 process, its participation at this fourth stage is particularly important. The regulations require the agency official to invite the ACHP to participate when the undertaking will have an adverse effect on a National Historic Landmark (a category of historic properties listed on the National Register with truly national significance) or when a programmatic agreement will be prepared. *Id.* § 800.6(1)(i). Failure to notify the ACHP of an adverse effect is considered a serious procedural flaw in the Section 106 process, because it fails to provide the ACHP with a "reasonable opportunity to comment," as required by Section 106. 16 U.S.C. § 470f. The ACHP may (and often does) decline to participate, in which case the agency official proceeds with consultation with the other parties.

Whether the ACHP participates at this stage or not, the end goal is that the key parties in the Section 106 process—the agency official, the SHPO/THPO, and the ACHP (if participating)— execute a memorandum of agreement. This document "records the terms and conditions agreed upon to resolve the adverse effects of an undertaking upon historic properties." 36 C.F.R. § 800.16(o). The regulations prescribe the form of the memorandum of agreement, including the required signatories and required duration, and provide a process for amendment and termination. *Id.* § 800.6(c). However, no federal law mandates that the memorandum of agreement include specific substantive conclusions, choose any of the alternatives considered, or adopt any of the consulting parties' views. A properly executed memorandum of agreement will allow the undertaking to proceed and will be enforced by courts.

In the rare circumstance that the parties cannot agree on a memorandum of agreement, the agency official, SHPO/THPO, or ACHP may terminate the consultation process, with notification to other parties. *Id.* § 800.7(a). At this point, the agency official must request comments from the ACHP and must consider these comments on reaching a final decision about the undertaking. The agency official need not adopt the ACHP's views; she has discretion regarding the extent to which the ACHP's views are taken into account in her final decision.

There is one exception to the general rule that a Section 106 review does not mandate a particular substantive outcome: situations in which an undertaking affects a National Historic Landmark. When a historic property is designated a Landmark, agency officials must "undertake such planning and actions as may be necessary to minimize harm to such landmark." 16 U.S.C. § 470h–2(f). The harm-minimization requirement goes beyond the consultation requirements for properties on or eligible for the National Register that are not Landmarks. However, even the harm-minimization requirement for Landmarks does not require that all harm be eliminated. *See* Presidio Historical Ass'n v. Presidio Trust, No. C12–00522, 2013 WL 2435089, at *22 (N.D. Cal. June 3, 2013) (declining to require an agency to eliminate harm to a National Historic Landmark by halting the undertaking because the agency's redesign of the undertaking did minimize harm).

5. PROGRAM ALTERNATIVES

The four-stage process described above applies to standard Section 106 reviews. There are several program alternatives that an agency may follow to achieve the purposes of Section 106 without strict adherence to the four-stage process, including: (1) a programmatic agreement, which is used for specific projects, including complex or long-term undertakings; (2) alternate procedures applicable to all agency undertakings and approved by the Advisory Council on Historic Preservation as adequately implementing Section 106; and (3) categories of undertakings exempt from review under Section 106. *See* 36 C.F.R. § 800.14 (describing these and other program alternatives). Each program alternative is intended to save time, cost, and effort for all parties typically involved in the Section 106 process by removing repetitive or inapplicable steps.

a. Programmatic Agreements

A programmatic agreement is a streamlined alternative to the standard Section 106 review for certain complex, phased, or repetitive undertakings. It is "a document that records the terms and conditions agreed upon to resolve the potential adverse effects of a Federal agency program, complex undertaking or other situations." 36 C.F.R. § 800.16(t). Among other circumstances, it may be used: when effects on historic properties are similar and repetitive; when effects cannot be fully determined prior to approval of an undertaking; when nonfederal parties are delegated major decision-making responsibilities; and when the federal action at issue is a routine land management activity. *Id.* § 800.14(1). The Advisory Council on Historic Preservation (ACHP) maintains a list of programmatic agreements on its website: www.achp.gov/palist.html. These include a Department of Homeland Security programmatic agreement covering maintenance, automation, and leasing of lighthouses; a Department of Defense agreement covering the demolition of World War II-era temporary buildings; and a Department of Agriculture agreement covering rangeland management activities within National Forests.

In disputes as to whether a programmatic agreement applies to an agency action, courts will give deference to the ACHP, because it promulgated the regulations in the first place. *See, e.g.*, Lesser v. City of Cape May, 110 F. Supp. 2d 303, 318–21 (D. N.J. 2000) (finding that the agency did not act arbitrarily and capriciously in executing and acting upon a programmatic agreement approved by the ACHP where the undertaking involved a multi-phased renovation of a historic building).

Some aspects of the programmatic agreement process are the same as, or similar to, the standard Section 106 review process. For example, the agency official must arrange for public participation appropriate to the subject matter and scope of the program. In addition, she must consult with the ACHP and any relevant SHPO/THPO, representatives of tribes, and Native Hawaiian organizations. The key difference is that while in the standard Section 106 process consulting parties need not ratify the agency's actions, in a programmatic agreement, all consulting parties must execute the programmatic agreement to make it effective. *Id.* § 800.14(b)(2)(iii).

b. Alternate Procedures

In lieu of strict adherence with Section 106, an agency may develop alternate procedures that meet the goals of Section 106. *See* 36 C.F.R. § 800.14(a). Unlike programmatic agreements, which follow a process set forth in the regulations to deal with specific undertakings or types of undertakings, alternate procedures allow individual federal agencies to develop new processes that apply to certain actions they wish to cover. These procedures must be developed in consultation with the Advisory Council on Historic Preservation, the National Conference of State Historic Preservation Officers, and any relevant state or tribal historic preservation officers, Indian tribes, and Native Hawaiian organizations. Once the procedures are developed, the Advisory Council on Historic Preservation must formally approve them.

Few agencies have opted for alternate procedures. The United States Army is an exception, having adopted alternate procedures that include proposals of five-year plans for historic properties on Army bases.

c. Exempted Categories

It may be surprising to learn that entire categories of undertakings may be exempted from Section 106 review through a program alternative for "exempted categories" of undertakings. 36 C.F.R.

§ 800.14. An agency or the Advisory Council on Historic Preservation (ACHP) may propose such exemptions, as long as the potential effects of the undertakings on historic properties are "foreseeable and likely to be minimal or not adverse" and if exemption is consistent with the purposes of the National Historic Preservation Act. *Id.* § 800.14(c)(1)(iii).

As is the case with the other program alternatives, the proponent of the exemption (whether the agency official or ACHP) must consult with state and/or tribal historic preservation officers and relevant Indian tribes and Native Hawaiian organizations, with input from members of the public. Ultimately, the ACHP decides whether to approve or reject the exemption request. *Id.* § 800.14(c)(5). The ACHP can also terminate the exemption if it falls out of compliance with the statutory requirements or if the agency official requests termination.

Only a handful of exemptions have been granted by the ACHP over the years. The most important current exemption applies to federal interstate highways. According to this exemption, federal agencies do not need to take into account the effects of their undertakings on the interstate highway system, except for a limited number of individual elements—such as historic bridges, tunnels, and rest areas—that possess national significance and meet other National Register eligibility criteria.

D.   RELATIONSHIP WITH OTHER FEDERAL STATUTES

The National Historic Preservation Act is the most important federal statute dealing with historic preservation policy and programs. Accordingly, several of its key provisions have been interwoven into the text and administration of a variety of federal statutes.

Several statutes require federal agencies to conduct reviews of the impact of their actions on historic resources. These include the National Environmental Policy Act, Section 4(f) of the Department of Transportation Act, the Archaeological Resources Protection Act, and the Native American Graves Protection and Repatriation Act, discussed in Chapters IV, V, XI, and XII of this book, respectively. When an agency is conducting a Section 106 review and is also subject to one of these other statutes, the agency must coordinate all required reviews. *See* 36 C.F.R. § 800.3(b). We discuss coordination between Section 106 of the National Historic Preservation Act and the National Environmental Policy Act in Part D of Chapter IV, coordination with Section 4(f) of the Department of Transportation Act in Part D of Chapter V, and coordination with the Archaeological Resources Protection Act in Part C of Chapter XI.

An agency conducting a Section 106 review may also benefit from the public input gathered from other statutory review processes and from documentation prepared to comply with other statutes (and vice versa). *See id.* §§ 800.2(d)(3) &

800.11(b). However, the outcomes of these various statutory review processes may differ because the standards of review within the various federal statutes and the historic resources they protect are different.

Other federal statutes reinforce or expand the same kind of review required by Section 106. A federal statute related to surface mining control and reclamation, for example, prohibits new surface coal mining operations "which will adversely affect any publicly owned park or places included in the National Register of Historic Sites unless approved jointly by the regulatory authority and the Federal, State, or local agency with jurisdiction over the park or the historic site." 30 U.S.C. § 1272(e)(3). The concepts of "adverse effects" and protection of National Register properties are, of course, central to Section 106.

We should not forget that the National Historic Preservation Act contains many key provisions other than Section 106. The National Register and its designation criteria, both established in the National Historic Preservation Act, play a role in the enforcement and administration of other legal regimes. These include the Abandoned Shipwrecks Act discussed in Chapter XI and the federal rehabilitation tax credit discussed in Chapter XIV. *See* 43 U.S.C. §§ 2102(b) & 2105(a)(3); 26 U.S.C. § 47(c)(3).

CHAPTER 4

NATIONAL ENVIRONMENTAL POLICY ACT

Federal and state environmental protection statutes focus on the conservation of natural resources, but they often protect historic resources as well. This Chapter conveys how environmental protection statutes have become an important tool for preservationists seeking to ensure that historic resources receive due consideration before public or private parties take certain actions that might affect them.

The most significant of these statutes is the National Environmental Policy Act of 1969 (NEPA), which formally established environmental protection as a federal policy. NEPA requires federal agencies to consider certain environmental resources, including historic resources, before they undertake any major federal actions. This Chapter explains NEPA's contributions to historic preservation, providing an overview of NEPA, analyzing key terms, and describing its application to major federal actions involving historic resources. It also reviews NEPA's close relationship with provisions of the National Historic Preservation Act. Finally, this Chapter discusses a few state environmental protection acts that have been modeled on NEPA.

A. OVERVIEW

The National Environmental Policy Act of 1969 (NEPA) is the centerpiece of federal environmental law. It ensures that our environment—defined to include natural and historic resources—is given consideration in federal project planning by requiring federal agencies to analyze the environmental impact of their major actions prior to beginning such actions. Like the National Historic Preservation Act discussed in Chapter III, NEPA is a procedural, rather than an outcome-based statute: NEPA does not mandate any particular result, but it requires an agency to follow certain procedures in its decision-making process. Accordingly, NEPA has been characterized (and sometimes criticized) as a "stop, look, and listen" statute. This characterization, while technically correct, probably understates NEPA's profound impact on federal decisions affecting the environment, including the preservation of historic resources.

NEPA was signed into law on January 1, 1970 by President Nixon. It formalized the federal government's commitment to environmental protection, including historic resources, by stating that:

[I]t is the continuing responsibility of the Federal Government to use all practicable means, consistent with other essential considerations of national policy, to improve and coordinate Federal plans, functions, programs, and resources to the end that the Nation may * * * (4) preserve important historic, cultural, and natural aspects of our national heritage.

42 U.S.C. § 4331(b).

To fulfill its statutory purpose, NEPA requires that federal agencies prepare a "detailed statement" for "major federal actions significantly affecting the quality of the human environment" prior to initiating any such action. *Id.* § 4332(C). This detailed statement, called an environmental impact statement (EIS), must include a thorough discussion of the environmental impact of the proposed action, alternatives to the proposed action, and the resources that will be committed to the proposed action. *Id.* An EIS must be prepared in consultation with other federal agencies that have jurisdiction in the project area, other federal agencies that wield expertise with respect to any environmental impact involved, and the public.

In addition to requiring federal agencies to consider the impact of their actions before they begin, NEPA also created an agency in the executive office of the President to implement environmental policies that shape federal project planning: the Council on Environmental Quality (CEQ). The CEQ has promulgated detailed regulations for NEPA that set forth federal environmental review procedures. *See* 40 C.F.R. Part 1500. These regulations bind all federal agencies and are afforded substantial deference by courts. *See* Andrus v. Sierra Club, 442 U.S. 347 (1979) (holding that the CEQ's interpretation of NEPA is entitled to substantial deference). Note that in many respects, the CEQ is the environmental counterpart to the Advisory Council on Historic Preservation (ACHP), the federal agency created by the National Historic Preservation Act of 1966 and discussed in Chapter III. Similar to the CEQ's role under NEPA, the ACHP promulgates regulations for the National Historic Preservation Act which bind all federal agencies and are afforded substantial deference by courts. We will further discuss the relationship between these two agencies and the statutes that created them below.

B.   KEY TERMS

As the National Environmental Policy Act (NEPA) is a procedural statute, it is highly technical and filled with terms and phrases of art. Nearly all of these are defined in regulations promulgated by the Council on Environmental Quality. NEPA contains six key terms and phrases that are important to understanding its application. The first is "federal agency," because NEPA only applies to actions taken by federal agencies.

The next four key terms discussed in this section are all found in one critical clause in NEPA which determines whether or not a proposed federal action is subject to NEPA review procedures: "major federal actions significantly affecting the quality of the human environment." 42 U.S.C. § 4332(C). Proposed federal actions that are not major federal actions, or do not have a significant effect on the human environment, are exempt from NEPA review requirements.

The sixth term, "historic resources" is never defined in NEPA or in its accompanying regulations. Below, we discuss the most likely meaning of this term given the context of the statute, the regulations, and guidance from the Council on Environmental Quality.

1. FEDERAL AGENCY

In determining whether NEPA applies to a particular project, a key threshold question is whether the agency whose actions are at issue is a "federal agency." NEPA regulations define federal agency as:

> all agencies of the Federal Government. It does not mean the Congress, the Judiciary, or the President, including the performance of staff functions for the President in his Executive Office. It also includes . . . States and units of general local government and Indian tribes assuming NEPA responsibilities under section 104(h) of the Housing and Community Development Act of 1974.

40 C.F.R. § 1508.12. Excluded from NEPA's reach, therefore, are the entire federal legislative and judicial branches. Only agencies in the federal executive branch are covered, along with state, local, and tribal governments that have assumed NEPA responsibilities.

In determining whether an entity is a federal agency for purposes of NEPA, courts have typically examined the issues of authority and control. For instance, in *D'Agnillo v. Hill*, a federal district court held that a local housing agency is a federal agency under NEPA where it has received community development block grants—and thus a delegated responsibility to comply with NEPA—from a federal agency. *See* No. 89 CIV. 5609 (CSH), 1995 WL 110597, at *10 (S.D.N.Y. 1995). Another district court held, however, that the Port Authority of New York and New Jersey, which was created with the approval of Congress, did not qualify as a federal agency under NEPA because the federal government exercised no authority over the operations of the Port Authority, nor did the federal government give any financial support to the Port Authority. Brooklyn Bridge Park Coal. v. Port Auth. of N.Y. & N.J., 951 F. Supp. 383 (E.D.N.Y. 1997). And the Ninth Circuit has determined that a federal agency that takes actions under a plan created pursuant to a consent decree may not claim NEPA's "Judiciary" exemption because the federal agency actions occurred subsequent to the creation of the plan. Ramsey v. Kantor, 96 F.3d 434 (9th Cir. 1996).

To encourage and emphasize cooperation within the NEPA environmental review process, the regulations also delineate the concepts of lead agencies and cooperating agencies. A lead agency is the "agency or agencies preparing or having taken primary responsibility for preparing the environmental impact statement." 40 C.F.R. § 1508.16. A cooperating agency is a federal agency "other than a lead agency which has jurisdiction by law or special expertise with respect to any environmental impact involved in a proposal (or a reasonable alternative) for legislation or other major Federal action significantly affecting the quality of the human environment." *Id.* § 1508.5. State agencies, local agencies, and Indian tribes may also be designated as cooperating agencies under NEPA if a federal agency action impacts a state, locality, or Indian reservation. *See id.* This extension of cooperating agency status is important in the historic preservation context, as state and/or tribal historic preservation officers are usually cooperating agencies under NEPA when a federal agency action impacts historic resources within a state, locality, or reservation. The selection and responsibilities of cooperating agencies are described in 40 C.F.R. § 1501.6.

2.   MAJOR FEDERAL ACTION

Only "major federal actions" are subject to the requirements of the National Environmental Policy Act (NEPA). The regulations for NEPA define such actions as "actions with effects that may be major and which are potentially subject to federal control and responsibility." 40 C.F.R. § 1508.18. The key phrase here is "federal control and responsibility": NEPA does not apply to an action over which a federal agency has no ongoing control or responsibility. The adjective "major" is synonymous with "significantly" (see below) and has no independent meaning. *Id.*

Major federal actions include new and continuing projects or programs conducted by a federal agency and any "new or revised agency rules, regulations, plans, policies, or procedures; and legislative proposals." *Id.* § 1508.18(a). They also include activities, projects, and programs "entirely or partly financed, assisted, conducted, regulated, or approved by federal agencies." *Id.* Remember, however, the "federal control and responsibility" limitation of 40 C.F.R. § 1508.18, which covers all of the types of actions just mentioned. How does this limitation work in practice? As one example, the distributions of Department of Housing and Urban Development community development block grants to state and local governments to redevelop blighted neighborhoods or demolish derelict structures constitute major federal actions. However, federal funding assistance from general revenue sharing funds to states and localities with no federal agency control over the subsequent use of such funds is not considered a major federal action.

A federal agency's inaction or failure to act may also be considered a major federal action under NEPA. As the regulations state, "[a]ctions include the circumstance where the responsible officials fail to act and that failure to act is reviewable by courts." *Id.* § 1508.18. In other words, if a federal agency fails to act when it is required to act then such failure to act is considered a major federal action. If, however, a federal agency has discretion on whether or not to act and chooses not to act, such failure to act is not a major federal action. A case from the D.C. Circuit illustrates this point. The National Trust for Historic Preservation and other preservation groups brought suit against the U.S. State Department to prevent the demolition and expansion of the Republic of Turkey's chancery building in Washington, D.C., which was located in two overlapping historic districts. The National Trust argued that the State Department's Director of the Office of Foreign Mission's (OFM) decision not to exercise her veto power regarding the proposed chancery project constituted a major federal action triggering the NEPA review process. The court concluded, however, that OFM's decision not to veto the project was not a major federal action under NEPA because the statute authorizing the OFM to supervise the Turkish chancery project gave discretion to the Director to veto or not. Nat'l Trust for Historic Pres. v. Dep't of State, 834 F. Supp. 443 (D.D.C.), *aff'd in part, rev'd in part sub nom.*, Sheridan Kalorama Historical Ass'n v. Christopher, 49 F.3d 750 (D.C. Cir. 1995).

Although courts disagree as to the amount of federal involvement that is necessary for an action to be a major federal action, courts have held that the following federal actions involving historic preservation concerns do not qualify as major federal actions under NEPA:

• Approving a contract between an Indian tribe and a municipality, where federal approval was unnecessary (*see* Ringsred v. City of Duluth, 828 F.2d 1305 (8th Cir. 1987))

• Reviewing plans to realign sewers (*see* People for Responsible Omaha Urban Dev. v. Interstate Com. Comm'n, CV88–0–247 (D. Neb. Feb. 14, 1989), *aff'd*, No. 89–1342 NE (8th Cir. Sept. 14, 1989))

• Approving and providing financial assistance for a local environmental study (*see* Vill. of Los Ranchos de Albuquerque v. Barnhart, 906 F.2d 1477 (10th Cir. 1990))

• Certifying a power facility where the facility could have relied on self-certification (*see* Sugarloaf Citizens Ass'n v. FERC, 959 F.2d 508 (4th Cir. 1992))

• Approving a land exchange between private parties (*see* Gettysburg Battlefield Pres. Ass'n v. Gettysburg C. 799 F. Supp. 1571 (M.D. Pa. 1992), *aff'd*, 989 F.2d 487 (3rd Cir. 1993))

3.   SIGNIFICANTLY

The National Environmental Policy Act (NEPA) only applies to actions that "significantly" affect the human environment. The NEPA regulations analyze significance through "considerations of both context and intensity." 40 C.F.R. § 1508.27.

Regarding context, "the significance of an action must be analyzed in several contexts such as society as a whole (human, national), the affected region, the affected interests, and the locality." *Id.* § 1508.27(a). Several contexts must be considered; a significance analysis of an action in only one context in insufficient. The regulations explain that since "significance varies with the setting of the proposed action," it is not necessary to always include such broad considerations as society as a whole. *Id.* For example, "in the case of a site-specific action, significance would usually depend upon the effects in the locale rather than in the world as a whole. Both short- and long-term effects are relevant." *Id.*

Intensity considerations analyze severity of impact. The regulations state that ten factors should be considered in evaluating intensity, two of which explicitly refer to potential impacts on historic resources:

(1) Impacts that may be both beneficial and adverse. A significant effect may exist even if the Federal agency believes that on balance the effect will be beneficial.

(2) The degree to which the proposed action affects public health or safety.

(3) Unique characteristics of the geographic area such as proximity to historic or cultural resources, park lands, prime farmlands, wetlands, wild and scenic rivers, or ecologically critical areas.

(4) The degree to which the effects on the quality of the human environment are likely to be highly controversial.

(5) The degree to which the possible effects on the human environment are highly uncertain or involve unique or unknown risks.

(6) The degree to which the action may establish a precedent for future actions with significant effects or represents a decision in principle about a future consideration.

(7) Whether the action is related to other actions with individually insignificant but cumulatively significant impacts. Significance exists if it is reasonable to anticipate a cumulatively significant impact on the environment. Significance cannot be avoided by terming an action temporary or by breaking it down into small component parts.

(8) The degree to which the action may adversely affect districts, sites, highways, structures, or objects listed in or eligible for listing in the National Register of Historic Places or may cause loss or destruction of significant scientific, cultural, or historical resources.

(9) The degree to which the action may adversely affect an endangered or threatened species or its habitat that has been determined to be critical under the Endangered Species Act of 1973.

(10) Whether the action threatens a violation of Federal, State, or local law or requirements imposed for the protection of the environment.

Id. § 1508.27(b). As this excerpt shows, proximity to historic resources and adverse effects on historic properties are required considerations in the determination of significance.

In deciding whether a federal action will have a significant impact, courts have held that mitigation measures may be considered. This means that agencies that reduce the negative impacts of their actions may not have to engage in NEPA review at all. *See, e.g.*, Abenaki Nation of Mississquoi v. Hughes, 805 F. Supp. 234 (D. Vt. 1992), *aff'd*, 990 F.2d 729 (2d Cir. 1993) (finding that conditions for obtaining a permit reduced the impact of a hydroelectric project so substantially that an environmental impact statement was unnecessary).

4.   AFFECTING

Federal regulations define "affecting" as it is used in the NEPA simply as "will or may have an effect on." 40 C.F.R. § 1508.3. Note that the use of the phrase "will or may" in this definition connotes that the likelihood of an effect need not be certain—a mere possibility of an effect is enough.

The regulations further clarify the term "effect." An effect and an impact under NEPA are synonymous and may be: (1) direct (caused by the action and occurring at the same time and place); (2) indirect (caused by the action but occurring later in time or farther removed in distance but still reasonably foreseeable); or (3) cumulative (incremental impact of the action when added to other past, present, and reasonably foreseeable future actions). *See id.* §§ 1508.7–1508.8. Importantly for historic preservation, the term effect encompasses aesthetic, historic, and cultural values, whether direct, indirect, or cumulative. *See id.* § 1508.8. Effects may also include impacts resulting from "actions which may have both beneficial and detrimental effects, even if on balance the agency believes that the effect will be beneficial." *Id.*

5.   HUMAN ENVIRONMENT

When conducting a review under NEPA, a federal agency must identify the "human environment" that will potentially be affected by the major federal action at issue. This term is broadly defined as "the natural and physical environment and the relationship of people with that environment." 40 C.F.R. § 1508.14. As discussed in the next subsection, historic resources are included within the concept of the human environment.

In explaining the meaning of human environment, the NEPA regulations refer readers to the definition of "effect" in 40 C.F.R. § 1508.8 (discussed in the preceding section). For historic preservation law, this reference is important, as it confirms that "aesthetic, historic, [and] cultural," *id.*, effects will be reviewed, and that the corresponding resources impacted by such effects— historic resources—are covered by NEPA.

Other effects include "ecological . . . economic, social, or health" effects. *Id.* Note that since economic or social effects involve human to human relationships (rather than human to natural or physical environment relationships), "economic or social effects are not intended by themselves to require preparation of an environmental impact statement." *Id.* § 1508.14. However, if "economic or social and natural or physical environmental effects are interrelated" in a proposed major federal action, then the environmental impact statement should discuss all of these effects on the human environment. *Id.*

6. HISTORIC RESOURCES

The term "historic resources" is never explicitly defined in NEPA or its implementing regulations. But we can discern its most likely meaning by reviewing the context of the statute, the regulations, and guidance from the Council on Environmental Quality (CEQ).

By clear language in the statute, NEPA establishes as one of its goals the preservation of "historic [and] cultural . . . aspects of our natural heritage." 42 U.S.C. § 4331(b). The statute also protects "the human environment," *id.* § 4332(C), and the regulations explain that this term must "be interpreted comprehensively," 40 C.F.R. § 1508.14. The term "human environment" in NEPA, as noted above, also refers to the definition of "effect," which includes "aesthetic, historic, [and] cultural" effects. *Id.* § 1508.8. Piecing all of these parts together, it is obvious that NEPA intends to protect historic resources and to address effects on those resources.

But what, exactly, are the historic resources that NEPA protects? On this question, we get no specific guidance from the statute or regulations. Rather, guidance from CEQ suggests that in practice, agencies have been tasked with identifying a range of historic resources. A 2013 report from the CEQ and the Advisory Council on Historic Preservation (the federal agency overseeing historic preservation programs and policies) says that NEPA protects all historic resources listed on or eligible for the National Register of Historic Places, as well as a few other resources not eligible for the National Register. *See* COUNCIL ON ENVIRONMENTAL QUALITY, EXEC. OFFICE OF THE PRESIDENT, & ADVISORY COUNCIL ON HISTORIC PRES., NEPA AND NHPA: A HANDBOOK FOR INTEGRATING NEPA AND SECTION 106 (2013) at 4, 12–13. In theory, therefore, NEPA casts a wider net than does the National Historic Preservation Act, which requires federal agencies to review the impact of undertakings affecting only those resources listed on or eligible for the National Register of Historic Places. In practice, however, such an expansive interpretation is rare, because the requirements NEPA imposes on federal agencies with regard to identifying historic resources are often equated with the identification requirements imposed by the National Historic Preservation Act. This means that a federal agency required to review effects under both statutes usually needs only to identify resources on or eligible for inclusion on the National Register to satisfy both statutes.

C. APPLICATION

The National Environmental Policy Act (NEPA) requires federal agencies to assess proposed federal actions, including their impacts on historic and cultural resources, prior to beginning the action. Federal agencies satisfy their NEPA review responsibilities by completing the NEPA processes set forth in their NEPA implementing regulations or protocols along with the Council on Environmental Quality regulations at 40 C.F.R. §§ 1500–1508.

Compliance procedures for NEPA vary depending on the potential of the proposed action to cause environmental effects. There are three forms of NEPA review: (1) categorical exclusions, (2) environmental assessments (EAs), and (3) environmental impact statements (EISs). Federal agencies determine the type of NEPA review for a proposed action based on the context and intensity of its impacts. Each form of NEPA review will be discussed in turn below, followed by a discussion of how agencies may supplement finalized environmental reviews and tier completed reviews to avoid duplication. Finally, this section analyzes how courts have construed the adequacy of EAs and EISs.

1. CATEGORICAL EXCLUSION

When a federal agency proposes an action that may affect the environment, it first reviews whether that action falls within a categorical exclusion to NEPA. A categorical exclusion describes a category of actions that a federal agency expects will not "individually or cumulatively have a significant effect on the human environment." 40 C.F.R. § 1508.4. Most federal agencies have procedures for implementing NEPA which describe their categorical exclusions, which are established through the administrative rulemaking process. Each agency's list of categorical exclusions is agency-specific and is based on that agency's determination that the activities described typically have no potential for significant effects. A proposed action that falls within an agency's categorical exclusions does not require further review through an EA or EIS unless there are "extraordinary circumstances in which a normally excluded action may have a significant environmental effect." *Id.*

The majority of federal actions reviewed under NEPA are routine agency actions that qualify for a categorical exclusion. For example, the National Aeronautics and Space Administration (NASA) divides its categorical exclusions into five categories covering a wide range of activities:

• Administrative Activities (e.g., personnel actions; program budget proposals; software development; inventories; audits)

• Operations and Management Activities (e.g., routine maintenance at NASA facilities; NASA ceremonies or commemorative events; contributions of software, equipment, and technical advice to other agencies and public or private entities)

• Research and Development Activities (e.g., the use of lasers for research and development; the use of small quantities of radioactive materials in a laboratory or in the field; development and testing in compliance with all applicable laws)

• Real and Personal Property Activities (e.g., the acquisition of any personal property; granting or acceptance of easements; transfer of real property administrative control to another federal agency)

• Aircraft and Airfield Activities (e.g., routine periodic flight training activities; routine period flight research and development activities; relocation of similar aircraft)

See 14 C.F.R. § 1216.304(d). Courts typically sustain reasonable agency decisions to treat certain actions as categorical exclusions under NEPA. *See, e.g.*, City of Grapevine, Tex. v. U.S. Dep't of Transp., 17 F.3d 1502 (D.C. Cir. 1994) (upholding an agency's categorical exclusion for actions that caused noise under a certain level in the vicinity of historic resources).

2. ENVIRONMENTAL ASSESSMENT (EA)

When a categorical exclusion is inapplicable or inappropriate but a federal agency has not determined that a proposed action has the potential to cause significant environmental effects, the agency prepares an environmental assessment (EA). *See* 40 C.F.R. § 1501.3. The purpose of an EA is to determine whether a major federal action will have a significant impact on the human environment, including historic resources. *See id.* §§ 1508.8 & 1508.9(a).

The EA is a typically a concise public document that provides enough evidence and analysis to determine whether the agency should prepare a more thorough environmental impact statement or a finding of no significant impact (FONSI). The EA includes brief discussions of the need for the proposed action, the environmental impacts of the proposed action and alternatives, and a listing of agencies and persons consulted. *See id.* § 1508.9(b). It also includes the study, development, and description of "appropriate alternatives to recommended courses of action in any proposal which involves unresolved conflicts concerning alternative uses of available resources." 42 U.S.C. § 4332(E).

If a federal agency's EA concludes that there are no significant impacts on the human environment, then the agency issues a FONSI, a document that briefly explains why a proposed action will not significantly affect the human environment, and no further NEPA action is required. *See* 40 C.F.R. § 1508.13. If, however, significant impacts are found then a federal agency must move to the next phase of the NEPA process: the preparation of an environmental impact statement.

3.   ENVIRONMENTAL IMPACT STATEMENT (EIS)

When a federal agency determines at the outset of its review process, or through preparation of an environmental assessment, that a proposed action is a major federal action that may have a significant impact on the human environment, the agency prepares an environmental impact statement (EIS). *See* 42 U.S.C. § 4332(C); 40 C.F.R. § 1501.4. As discussed above, historic resources are included in NEPA's definition of the human environment.

Consequently, impacts on historic resources must be considered in the EIS.

Whereas an EA is designed to provide brief evidence and analysis about the potential significant impacts of a proposed action, an EIS must be detailed. *See* 40 C.F.R. §§ 1508.9(b) & 1508.11. Specifically, NEPA requires EISs to include detailed discussion of the following:

(i) the environmental impact of the proposed action,

(ii) any adverse environmental effects which cannot be avoided should the proposal be implemented,

(iii) alternatives to the proposed action,

(iv) the relationship between local short-term uses of man's environment and the maintenance and enhancement of long-term productivity, and

(v) any irreversible and irretrievable commitments of resources which would be involved in the proposed action should it be implemented.

42 U.S.C. § 4332(C). NEPA regulations stress that the discussion of alternatives is "the heart" of the EIS and requires that the agency "[r]igorously explore and objectively evaluate all reasonable alternatives." 40 C.F.R. § 1502.14. For proposed actions involving potential significant impacts to historic or cultural resources, specialized studies— including historic and cultural resource surveys—

are typically required. Exhaustive requirements regarding the content, format, and language of an EIS can be found at 40 C.F.R. § 1502.

The NEPA EIS review process proceeds in several stages. First, the lead federal agency for the proposed action should consult with other affected agencies, state and/or local governments, and the general public as to the appropriate scope of the EIS. *See id.* § 1501.7. (We expand on the consultation requirements of NEPA in Part D of this Chapter.) The scope of the EIS depends upon the level of probable effects and the complexity of the issues and alternatives. Once the scope of an EIS is determined, the agency prepares a draft EIS and presents it for public comment. *See id.* § 1503.1(a). After responding to all comments, the agency issues a Final EIS followed by a record of decision (ROD). The ROD is the agency's final decision on the proposed major federal action. It includes a statement identifying what the decision was, a discussion of why the agency selected one alternative over others, and provides information on how it will avoid or mitigate harmful environmental impacts in the selected alternative. *See id.* § 1505.2.

Agencies that act before completing the entire NEPA review process are in violation of NEPA and must begin the process anew. *See, e.g.,* Pit River Tribe v. U.S. Forest Serv., 469 F.3d 768 (9th Cir. 2006) (holding that agencies violated NEPA by failing to complete a EIS before extending leases that granted rights to develop a geothermal plant on federal land that had religious and cultural significance to tribes).

4. SUPPLEMENTAL ENVIRONMENTAL IMPACT STATEMENT (SEIS)

A supplemental draft or final environmental impact statement (SEIS) may be prepared by the agency if it makes "substantial changes in the proposed action that are relevant to environmental concerns" or there are "significant new circumstances or information relevant to environmental concerns and bearing on the proposed action or its impacts." *See* 40 C.F.R. § 1502.9(c).

Courts are in disagreement as to whether an SEIS must be prepared when new information regarding historic resources is discovered after completion of the initial environmental impact statement. *See, e.g.*, Aluli v. Brown, 437 F. Supp. 602 (D. Haw. 1977), *aff'd in part, rev'd in part on other grounds*, 602 F.2d 876 (9th Cir. 1979) (finding that the discovery of new historic resources after a final environmental impact statement triggered an SEIS); Natural Ress. Defense Council v. City of New York, 528 F. Supp. 1245 (S.D.N.Y. 1981), *aff'd*, 672 F.2d 292 (2d Cir. 1982) (holding that historic resources discovered after an EIS was completed were not so significant a change as to warrant a SEIS). When a SEIS is necessary, it need not include an initial scoping process, but it must proceed through the same public notice and comment procedures as draft or final environmental impact statements. *See* 40 C.F.R. § 1502.9(c).

5.   TIERING EAs AND EISs

To eliminate repetitive discussions of the same issues in EAs or EISs, federal regulations encourage agencies to tier them. *See* 40 C.F.R. §§ 1502.4(c), 1502.20, 1508.28. This means that whenever a broad EA or EIS has been prepared (such as a program or policy statement), and a subsequent EA or EIS is prepared on an action included within that program or policy (such as a site-specific action), the subsequent EA or EIS need only "summarize the issues discussed" in the broader EA or EIS "and incorporate discussions" from the broader EA or EIS "by reference." *Id.* § 1502.20. Materials incorporated by reference must be accurately cited and available for review by interested parties. Tiering allows the subsequent EA or EIS to "concentrate on the issues specific to the subsequent action" without wasting time, energy, or resources on duplicative analysis. *Id.*

6.   ADEQUACY OF AN EA OR EIS

When environmental assessments (EAs) and/or environmental impact statements (EISs) are prepared, those challenging the agency's NEPA review typically argue that it was inadequate in some aspect of content and/or scope. NEPA is a heavily litigated statute and the outcome is largely fact dependent, so we cannot cover all NEPA cases involving historic resources. Rather, what follows is a discussion of the types of arguments that have been used to challenge the adequacy of the NEPA review process in cases involving historic resources.

Challenges to EAs or EISs have been based on a variety of rationales. One of the most common is that an agency failed to consider the cumulative impacts of its proposed actions. *See, e.g.*, Te-Moak Tribe of Western Shoshone of Nevada v. U.S. Dep't of Interior, 608 F.3d 592 (9th Cir. 2010) (finding that an agency's EA for an amendment to a plan of operation for an existing mineral exploration project that would impact sacred tribal areas failed to account for the project's cumulative impacts); Lesser v. City of Cape May, 110 F. Supp. 2d 303 (D. N.J. 2000) (finding that the city's bifurcation of a historic hotel renovation project into rehabilitation and construction phases did not violate NEPA's aggregation requirement).

Courts have also ruled on whether the agency properly considered the alternatives to the proposed action. *See, e.g.*, City of Grapevine, Tex. v. U.S. Dep't of Transp., 17 F.3d 1502, 1506–07 (D.C. Cir. 1994) (holding that the agency took a hard look at the environmental alternatives to the expansion of a runway that would impact historic properties).

Claiming that agencies performed an inadequate analysis of mitigation measures for a proposed major federal action is another well-tread NEPA argument. *See, e.g.*, Communities, Inc. v. Busey, 956 F.2d 619 (6th Cir. 1992) (upholding an agency EIS that identified and discussed potential mitigation measures to an airport improvement plan that would affect historic properties, even though the EIS did not specify which mitigation measures would be adopted).

Moreover, courts have held that an agency's general management plan (which included a broad EIS) could not properly evaluate the site-specific impacts of the demolition of a historic building and required a site-specific environmental analysis. *See* Recent Past Pres. Network v. Latschar, 701 F. Supp. 2d 49 (D.D.C. 2010).

Courts have offered conflicting opinions on how thoroughly historic resources, and effects upon them, must be analyzed. Some courts hold that an EIS must include a penetrating discussion of the historic and archaeological resources involved in the project, the impact of the project on those resources, and alternatives that would allow for their preservation and rehabilitation. *See, e.g.,* Nat'l Indian Youth Council v. Andrus, 501 F. Supp. 649 (D.N.M. 1980), *aff'd*, 664 F.2d 220 (10th Cir. 1981) (finding that an EIS for a mining lease on the Navajo Reservation thoroughly discussed the significance of and potential impact upon historic and archaeological resources); Wis. Heritages, Inc. v. Harris, 490 F. Supp. 1334 (E.D. Wis. 1980) (holding that an EIS had carefully considered the impact of the contemplated demolition of a historic mansion and alternatives for preserving it). Other courts, however, have held that EISs containing incomplete or no mention of historic and archaeological resources were also adequate. *See, e.g.,* Warm Springs Dam Task Force v. Gribble, 378

F. Supp. 240 (N.D. Cal. 1974) (finding an EIS for dam construction was adequate even though its discussion of historic resources was incomplete because the agency had planned additional archaeological surveys and could avoid harming the resources in the meantime); James v. Lynn, 374 F. Supp. 900 (D. Colo. 1974) (declining to require an EIS for an urban renewal area to discuss historic resources because the evidence on historic resources developed at trial was sufficient to inform agency of the historic impacts).

In sum, NEPA is concerned with the process of how federal agencies gather and share information. If an agency strictly and conscientiously follows the procedures outlined in NEPA and the regulations implementing NEPA, courts will find the agency's NEPA review adequate. However, if an agency does not follow the procedural requirements of NEPA, it may be required to start the process again.

D. RELATIONSHIP WITH SECTION 106 OF THE NATIONAL HISTORIC PRESERVATION ACT

The National Environmental Policy Act (NEPA) and Section 106 of the National Historic Preservation Act (NHPA), discussed in Chapter III, appear to have striking similarities. Both statutes: are primarily procedural in nature and impose no substantive outcomes; created agencies (the Council on Environmental Quality and the Advisory Council on Historic Preservation) to implement programs and promulgate regulations that profoundly influence federal project planning; require federal agencies to generate information about the impacts of their actions on historic resources; and mandate that federal agencies take a hard look at the collected information before proceeding.

Indeed, the statutes and regulations relating to both statutes anticipate the NEPA and Section 106 review processes occurring simultaneously. The Advisory Council on Historic Preservation (ACHP) regulations for NHPA provide the most comprehensive discussion of this coordination. In appropriate cases, the regulations even allow substituting NEPA reviews for the Section 106 process. *See* 36 C.F.R. §§ 800.8(a) & 800.8(c). The ACHP's authority to issue regulations harmonizing the NHPA and NEPA has been upheld by courts. *See, e.g.*, Pres. Coal. of Erie County v. Fed. Transit Admin., 356 F.3d 444 (2d Cir. 2004). The use of these coordinating regulations by agencies, however, has not always been smooth. *See, e.g.*, Mid States Coal. for Progress v. Surface Transp. Bd., 345 F.3d 520 (8th Cir. 2003) (finding an agency's approval of a proposal to construct and upgrade hundreds of miles of rail line improperly followed the procedures harmonizing NEPA and the NHPA). For practical guidance on how federal agencies synchronize the NEPA and Section 106 processes, see a joint report published in 2013 by the Council on Environmental Quality and the ACHP: *NEPA and NHPA: A Handbook for Integrating NEPA and Section 106.*

Despite their apparent closeness, however, there are significant differences between NEPA and the

NHPA which have critical implications on how historic resources are protected from potentially adverse federal agency actions. The two most important differences between NEPA and the NHPA involve: (1) the scope of protection offered by each statute, and (2) the consultation requirements of each statute. Each of these is discussed below.

1. DIFFERENCES IN SCOPE

NEPA and Section 106 of the NHPA have separate but overlapping requirements that require federal agencies to consider the effects their programs and projects might have on historic resources. The "human environment" reviewed under NEPA is very broad, with aesthetic, historic, and cultural resources (such as sacred sites) representing only a fraction of the covered resources. *See* 40 C.F.R. § 1508.8. But NEPA only requires a detailed environmental impact statement (EIS) for potentially affected historic resources when there are "major federal actions significantly affecting the quality of the human environment." 42 U.S.C. § 4332(C). In contrast, Section 106 of the NHPA requires review of all undertakings impacting historic properties that are "included in, or eligible for inclusion on the National Register" irrespective of the scale of its probable effects. 16 U.S.C. § 470(w)(5); McMillan Park Comm. v. Nat'l Capital Planning Comm'n, 968 F.2d 1283 (D.C. Cir. 1992) (finding that any project, activity, or program that may result in changes in the character or use of historic properties is an undertaking under the NHPA requiring compliance with Section 106 review procedures). Thus, while NEPA's reach is extremely broad in scope but limited to projects considered major federal actions, the scope of the NHPA's Section 106 review requirements applies to a narrower range of historic resources but protects them more comprehensively.

Unsurprisingly, some courts have mistakenly elided the subtle, but important, distinctions between NEPA and the NHPA. *See* Sugarloaf Citizens Ass'n v. FERC, 959 F.2d 508 (4th Cir. 1992) (stating that the criteria for finding an undertaking under the NHPA were the same as those for finding a major federal action triggering NEPA).

Some federal projects involving historic resources will trigger both NEPA and NHPA Section 106 reviews, while others require review under only one of the statutes. All federal projects involving historic resources that are significant enough to warrant NEPA review are also subject to Section 106 of the NHPA. And when historic properties are affected by proposed federal actions, courts have made it clear that the requirements of both statutes must be fulfilled. *See, e.g.*, Pres. Coal. Inc. v. Pierce, 667 F.2d 851 (9th Cir. 1982). Some undertakings requiring Section 106 compliance, however, will not be considered major federal actions requiring NEPA review. Similarly, even if an agency decides that a project qualifies for a categorical exclusion under NEPA (the most common agency decision under the NEPA review process), this does not exempt the agency from performing a NHPA Section 106 review of the project. *See* 36 C.F.R. §§ 800.8(a)(1) & (b). On the other hand, historic resources that are not covered by NHPA because they are not eligible for or listed in the National Register might still warrant consideration under NEPA.

For these reasons, the NHPA review process is far more protective of historic resources than the NEPA review process—a fact borne out by the hundreds of thousands of Section 106 reviews completed annually to the mere hundreds of environmental impact statement reviews completed annually under NEPA.

2. DIFFERENCES IN CONSULTATION REQUIREMENTS

Another significant difference between NEPA and the NHPA is the consultation process. NEPA consultation procedures are subject to broad agency discretion. Agencies must "make diligent efforts to involve the public in preparing and implementing their NEPA procedures" and "to provide public notice of NEPA-related hearings, public meetings, and the availability of environmental documents so as to inform those persons and agencies who may be interested or affected." 40 C.F.R. §§ 1506.6(a)–(b). Moreover, an agency may request that other agencies or tribes cooperate in a NEPA review, particularly if these groups have jurisdiction over the project area or special expertise. *See id.* § 1501.6. In reality, this means that NEPA consultation with other agencies, Indian tribes, and the general public takes many forms and depends upon the level of NEPA review. Categorical exclusions typically provide very limited opportunities for public and tribal involvement; whereas for an environmental assessment, the extent of public involvement is at the discretion of the agency. Preparation of an environmental impact statement requires the strongest form of consultation under NEPA. The scoping process for an environmental impact statement involves notification and opportunities for comments on a proposed action by other affected agencies, organizations, tribes, local governments, and the public. *See id.* § 1501.7. Agencies are also required to make draft environmental impact statements available for public review, invite comments, and respond to any comments submitted. *See id.* § 1503.1–4.

Compared to the loose NEPA consultation process, the NHPA consultation requirements are much stronger. Like NEPA, Section 106 obligates a federal agency to assess, disclose, and solicit comments from the general public about the effects of its actions on historic resources. In addition, Section 106 also mandates consultation with certain parties to discuss ways to avoid or reduce the adverse impact of the undertaking. These parties include: (1) the relevant SHPO and/or THPO, or the representative officially designated by the tribe for tribal lands; (2) Indian tribes and Native Hawaiian organizations which attach religious and cultural significance to historic properties that may be affected by the undertaking; (3) applicants for federal assistance, permits, licenses, or other approvals; and (4) representatives of local governments with jurisdiction over the area in which the effects of an undertaking may occur. *See* 36 C.F.R. §§ 800.2(c)(1)–(4). Parties with legal or economic interests in the undertaking may also participate in consultation. *See id.* § 800.2(c)(5). While the decision on whether to proceed with the undertaking ultimately resides with the agency, the NHPA's robust consultation provisions typically result in negotiated solutions that offer more powerful protections to historic resources than consultations under NEPA.

E. STATE LAWS MODELED AFTER THE NATIONAL ENVIRONMENTAL POLICY ACT

Many states have adopted state environmental policy acts (SEPAs) that are modeled to some extent on the National Environmental Policy Act (NEPA). As the preceding Part explained, NEPA requires federal agencies to create environmental impact statements (EISs) for "major federal actions significantly affecting the quality of the human environment." 42 U.S.C. § 4332(C). An EIS must consider historic and cultural resources, among other things, when it analyzes "the environmental impact of the proposed action," "alternatives to the proposed action," and "any adverse environmental effect which cannot be avoided." *Id.* § 4332(C); 40 C.F.R. § 1508.8. NEPA merely creates a process that agencies must follow to adequately consider the impact of their actions; it does not require specific substantive outcomes. This Part considers the scope of SEPAs and the types of historic resources they protect.

1.   SCOPE OF STATE ENVIRONMENTAL
POLICY ACTS

State environmental policy acts (SEPAs) vary widely in scope. The threshold for determining whether a SEPA applies to a particular state agency action differs from state to state. Some SEPAs apply to a narrower range of actions than NEPA. For example, Virginia's SEPA only requires state agencies to prepare an environmental impact report for "major state projects" when the costs exceed a financial threshold. VA. CODE ANN. § 10.1–1188. And Hawaii's SEPA limits environmental review to an enumerated list of proposed state actions usually involving state or county lands, sensitive ecological areas, and, importantly, historic sites. *See* HAW. REV. STAT. ANN. § 343–5.

The scope of most SEPA threshold requirements, however, closely tracks NEPA by requiring an environmental review when a proposed agency action significantly impacts, or is likely to significantly impact, the environment. Indiana's Environmental Policy Act, for example, applies to "state actions significantly affecting the quality of the human environment." *See* IND. CODE ANN. § 13–12–4–5(C). Likewise, state agencies in Maryland must prepare an environmental effects report "in conjunction with each proposed State action significantly affecting the quality of the environment." MD. NAT. RES. CODE ANN. § 1–304. Minnesota's SEPA requires an environmental impact statement when "there is potential for significant environmental effects resulting from any

major governmental action." MINN. STAT. ANN.
§ 116D.04. Similarly, Massachusetts' SEPA requires
an environmental impact report when there is
actual or probable "damage to the environment," but
also includes a unique mandate to consider
"reasonably foreseeable climate change impacts,
including additional greenhouse gas emissions, and
effects, such as predicted sea level rise." MASS. GEN.
LAWS ANN. 30 § 61. The SEPAs of California,
Connecticut, Georgia, and South Dakota require an
environmental impact statement whenever a state
project "may" significantly affect the environment.
CAL. PUB. RES. CODE § 21100(a); CONN. GEN. STAT.
§ 22a–1c; GA. CODE ANN. § 12–16–3(4); S.D.
CODIFIED LAWS § 34A–9–4. And the Supreme Court
of Washington has interpreted Washington's SEPA
to apply to state actions "whenever more than
moderate effect on the quality of the environment is
a reasonable probability." Leschi v. Improvement
Council v. Wash. State Highway Comm'n, 525 P.2d
774 (Wash. 1974); *see also* WASH. REV. CODE ANN.
§ 43.21C.031. SEPAs that have a similar scope to
NEPA sometimes sweep local government actions
and private projects requiring permits within their
ambit as well. *See, e.g.,* CONN. GEN. STAT. § 22a–1c;
WASH. REV. CODE ANN. §§ 43.21C.030; 43.21C.060;
CAL. PUB. RES. CODE § 21002.1(b); S.D. CODIFIED
LAWS § 34A–9–2.

California's SEPA, the California Environmental
Quality Act (CEQA), deserves particular mention as
it has generated an immense amount of litigation
compared to other SEPAs. *See* CAL PUB. RES. CODE
§§ 21000–21177. This is likely due to a confluence of

several factors. First, CEQ establishes a low threshold for when an environmental impact report is required (noted above). *See id.* § 21100(a). Second, the Supreme Court of California has broadly interpreted environmental review under CEQA to include "private activities for which a government permit or other entitlement for use is necessary." Friends of Mammoth v. Bd. of Supervisors, 502 P.2d 1049, 1056 (Cal. 1972). Third, CEQA specifies the level of judicial review authorized for any disputes under the Act and allows for public enforcement. CAL. PUB. RES. CODE §§ 21168; 21168.5. Fourth, CEQA requires state agencies to "mitigate or avoid the significant effects on the environment of projects that it carries out or approves whenever it is feasible to do so" rather than simply study the issue. CAL. PUB. RES. CODE § 21002.1(b). Consequently, numerous lawsuits in California, some of them involving historic resources, allege that an agency failed to select the least harmful option or to sufficiently adopt necessary, reasonable mitigation measures for its projects. *See, e.g.*, Architectural Heritage Ass'n v. County of Monterey, 19 Cal.Rptr.3d 469 (Ct. App. 2004) (holding that a county's proposed mitigation measures for the demolition of a historic jail did not sufficiently reduce the adverse environmental impacts of the project to a level that would obviate the need for an environmental impact report).

2.   TREATMENT OF HISTORIC RESOURCES

SEPAs also vary as to whether they protect historic resources, and if they do, the types of historic resources that must be thoroughly considered during the environmental review. Some states omit explicit reference to historic resources in their SEPAs. Other SEPAs—like those of Indiana, Minnesota, Montana, Washington—mandate that the state "preserve important historic, cultural, and natural aspects," but offer no further clarification into what types of resources qualify as historic or cultural resources. IND. CODE § 13–12–4–4(4); MINN. STAT. ANN. § 116D.02, Subd. 2(4); MONT. CODE ANN. § 75–1–103(e); WASH. REV. CODE ANN. § 43.21C.020(2)(d). Similarly, the SEPAs of California and South Dakota are vague as to the exact types of historic resources that fall under its protection, covering "objects of historic or aesthetic significance." CAL. PUB. RES. CODE § 21060.5; S.D. CODIFIED LAWS § 34A–9–1(4). Virginia's SEPA protects "historic resources," and adds a unique provision for local government actions "costing more than $500,000 and less than $2 million" which requires that local government to "consult with the Department of Historic Resources to consider and make reasonable efforts to avoid or minimize impacts to historic resources" if the project has the potential to adversely affect historic resources. VA. CODE ANN. § 10.1–1188.

Other states, like Georgia and Massachusetts, offer slightly more guidance as to what types of historic resources are covered when a state action requires environmental review under its SEPA. Georgia's SEPA expects state agencies to be stewards of "historical and cultural resources" and any environmental effects report must include an assessment of the proposed project's adverse impacts on "historical sites or buildings, or cultural resources." GA. CODE ANN. §§ 12–16–2(2) & 12–16–3(1). Massachusetts' SEPA explicitly protects "underwater archaeological resources" along with "historic districts or sites." MASS. GEN. LAWS ANN. ch. 30 § 61.

Still other states tether the historic resources covered under their respective SEPAs to the State Register of Historic Places and/or the National Register of Historic Places, discussed in Chapter III. For instance, Maryland specifically defines the historic resources covered under its SEPA to be "those resources included in the Maryland inventory of historic sites." MD. NAT. RES. CODE ANN. §§ 1–301(c); 1–302(c). Hawaii's SEPA covers a somewhat broader array of historic resources as it protects any "historic site as designated in the National Register or Hawaii Register" and sites "under consideration for placement on the National Register or the Hawaii Register of Historic Places" that may be impacted by the expansion or modification of existing helicopter facilities in the state pending completion of the state historic resources inventory. HAW. REV. STAT. ANN. §§ 343–5(4) & (8)(c). Connecticut's SEPA is broader still, explicitly protecting all properties listed or under consideration for listing on the National Register from "unreasonable destruction." CONN. GEN. STAT. § 22a–19a. Connecticut courts have construed the phrase "unreasonable destruction" to include the demolition of a historic building identified as a contributing structure to a listed National Register

Historic District. *See also* Conn. Historical Comm'n v. Town of Wallingford, No. CV020468446S, 2011 WL 1087088 (Conn. Super. Ct. Feb. 22, 2011).

While the SEPAs discussed above are not a comprehensive list of all SEPAs, they offer a good overview of the many types of state laws inspired by NEPA and how these laws aim to protect historic resources. Unfortunately, studies analyzing the effects of these state statutes on historic resources are lacking.

CHAPTER 5

SECTION 4(f)

Section 4(f) of the Department of Transportation Act of 1966 provides the most substantive protection for historic resources threatened by federal action. It applies only to federal transportation programs or projects and holds that such programs or projects may adversely affect a significant historic site only if two criteria are met. First, there must be no prudent and feasible alternative to using the site. Second, the program or project must include all possible planning to minimize harm to the protected site. One can see why preservationists cheered when Congress passed this law in 1966: the statute prevents federal transportation officials from harming historic resources without considering every reasonable alternative, and choosing the one that does the least harm.

This Chapter provides an overview of Section 4(f), as well as an analysis of both its key terms and its application to federal agency projects. A review of the relationships between Section 4(f) and two other federal statutes follows. This Chapter concludes by discussing state transportation acts modeled after Section 4(f).

A. OVERVIEW

Section 4(f)—the most substantive protection for historic resources threatened by federal action—was created in 1966. It was a small part of the Department of Transportation Act, a sweeping piece of legislation that created the U.S. Department of Transportation by consolidating several different transportation-related functions from other departments and several independent agencies. The key language for our purposes is as follows:

[T]he Secretary [of the Department of Transportation] may approve a transportation program or project. . . requiring the use of publicly owned land of a public park, recreation area, or wildlife and waterfowl refuge of national, State, or local significance, or land of an historic site of national, State, or local significance (as determined by the Federal, State, or local officials having jurisdiction over the park, area, refuge, or site) only if—

(1) there is no prudent and feasible alternative to using that land; and

(2) the program or project includes all possible planning to minimize harm to the park, recreation area, wildlife and waterfowl refuge, or historic site resulting from the use.

49 U.S.C. § 303(c). Congress was motivated to adopt this language after hearing from constituents outraged by transportation-related urban renewal projects that destroyed, or threatened to destroy, parks and historic neighborhoods such as San Antonio's Breckenridge Park or New Orleans' French Quarter. Legislators clearly intended Section 4(f) to eliminate, or at least limit, potential damage done to such important community

resources by the activities of the newly created Department of Transportation.

So what, exactly, does Section 4(f) require? It requires the Secretary of the Department of Transportation to make a series of determinations before approving a project. First, the Secretary must determine that Section 4(f) actually applies— including determining whether there are protectable resources that would be "used" by a program or project. If this answer is yes, the Secretary must evaluate the impact of the proposed action on the protectable resources. If the impact is more than de minimis, the Secretary must review alternatives to the proposed action. If a feasible and prudent alternative to using the land exists, then the Secretary must select it. If not, then the Secretary must select the alternative that does the least harm to the protected resource.

Application of Section 4(f) to federal transportation programs and projects, described in Part C below, is highly technical. Its disposition depends almost entirely on the meanings of the key terms in Part B.

B. KEY TERMS

Section 4(f) has seven key terms and phrases which are critical to understanding the application of the statute. The first three terms considered in this Part help answer the question: does Section 4(f) apply to this project? Without a "transportation program or project" or a "use," the statute does not apply at all. In the case of "historic sites," the site must meet certain criteria to be protected by the statute. The fourth term, "official with jurisdiction," has a simple definition, but the identification of the official with jurisdiction has significant legal consequences because it determines who can consult at several key stages in the Section 4(f) process.

The final three terms all determine whether the Secretary may use the resource protected by Section 4(f). If no studied alternative to the proposed federal action is "prudent and feasible," and if the Secretary has engaged in "all possible planning to minimize harm" to the protected resource, then the resource may be used. Those challenging the Secretary's actions often argue that a particular alternative to use is prudent and feasible, or that the Secretary did not do everything she could to minimize harm. The exact meaning of the seventh phrase, "de minimis," is significant because a finding of de minimis impact offers the Secretary a way to proceed with a program or project without having to undergo a full evaluation of alternatives and harm-minimizing strategies under Section 4(f).

Other important terms in Section 4(f) that apply primarily to parks, recreation areas, and wildlife and waterfowl refuges, are not considered here.

1. TRANSPORTATION PROGRAM OR PROJECT

The scope of federal activities potentially subject to Section 4(f)—transportation programs or projects—is vast. The Department of Transportation houses several different entities that regularly engage in such activities, including: the Federal Highway Administration (which funds the construction of highways); the Federal Aviation Administration (which oversees civil aviation and operates airport towers, air traffic control centers, and other infrastructure); the Federal Transit Administration (which funds mass transportation programs); and the Maritime Administration (which funds various projects located in maritime transportation hubs). "Project" is defined through a cross reference to the Federal-Aid Highways Act from the Section 4(f) regulations to include "any undertaking eligible for assistance" from the Department of Transportation. 23 U.S.C. § 101(18). The more ambiguous "program" is not separately defined in the Section 4(f) statute or in the related regulations. Whether a program or project, the initiative must be in its final stages, not merely an idea or concept, to trigger Section 4(f) review.

The activities of the Department of Transportation are subject to Section 4(f) whether the Department has taken a lead role in planning and executing the program or project, or is simply funding a project being done by a state highway authority, airport authority, mass transit authority, port facility, or other nonfederal entity. There is no objective statutory threshold, in terms of cost per project or otherwise, that distinguishes between what is considered to be a transportation program or project and what is not. Often, minor programs or projects fall under the definition of transportation programs or projects, but fail to trigger the full Section 4(f) harm-minimization evaluation because they are considered to have de minimis impacts or are not considered to be a use—a term we turn to next.

2. USE

According to Section 4(f), the only types of federal programs and projects subject to Section 4(f) are those that "use" a protected resource. In general, a use occurs in any of three circumstances: (1) when land is permanently incorporated into a transportation facility; (2) when there is a temporary occupancy of land that is adverse to the resource; or (3) when there is a constructive use of the resource. 23 C.F.R. § 774.17. Each of these three circumstances merit further description, with an emphasis on how they affect historic sites.

Permanent incorporations occur when a historic site is purchased, acquired, demolished, or dismantled, or when a permanent right of access (an easement) is granted over the historic site. It also occurs when the historic site is converted to a highway or transit right of way. Certain types of minor permanent incorporations, such as the construction of a trail or boat ramp, are not generally considered to be uses under Section 4(f).

Temporary occupancies occur when project-related construction activities use the historic site in a way adverse to the preservation purpose of Section 4(f). For example, when a historic site operates seasonally, such as a historic beachside amusement park, then a temporary occupancy may be found to occur only during the season of operation. The contours of a temporary occupancy become clearer when one understands what it is not. A temporary occupancy is not a use when five criteria are met: (1) it is temporary (for a time that is less than the duration of project construction); (2) involves a minor scope of work; (3) has no permanent adverse impacts and does not interfere with the protected features of the property (even temporarily); (4) is followed by a full restoration of any affected aspect of the resource; and (5) is subject to a written agreement from the official having jurisdiction over the resource that the preceding four conditions have been met. *Id.* § 774.13(d). With respect to the restoration criteria, the resource has to be restored to a condition at least as good as its condition before the project commenced. These rules encourage agencies to design federal construction activities to meet these five criteria and fall under the exception to the temporary occupancy rules. Similarly, temporary easements that do not involve a long-term or indefinite interest, and involve only a minor amount of land, are not likely to be considered to be a use.

Constructive uses are very complex and the most difficult to identify. In such cases, the historic site is neither permanently incorporated nor temporarily and adversely occupied. Rather, some federal transportation activity happening on nearby land substantially impairs the activities, features, or attributes of the historic site which rendered the site protectable under Section 4(f) in the first place. *Id.* § 774.15(a). Substantial impairment can only be found when the protected activities, features, or attributes of the historic site will be "substantially diminished," that is, meaningfully reduced or lost. *Id.* It is easy to imagine the kinds of activities that might create a so-called "proximity impact" on protected resources: vibrations, visual impacts, noise, air pollution, access restrictions, and similar externalities. It may be harder to think of how such activities can substantially impair the key features of a historic site. Federal regulations, *id.* § 774.15(e), offer several examples of when a constructive use is a use:

  • A noise level increase attributable to a federal transportation project, when it interferes with the "[e]njoyment of a historic site where a quiet setting is a generally recognized feature or attribute of the site's significance."

  • The location of a proposed transportation facility in a way that obstructs or eliminates views of an architecturally significant historical building.

  • A restriction of access that substantially diminishes the utility of a historic site.

  • Vibration from construction that physically damages a historic building.

Thus, federal activities that are not minor and cause an indirect but substantial impairment to a historic site will be considered to be constructive uses, and Section 4(f) will apply. *See, e.g.*, Citizen Advocates for Responsible Expansion, Inc., v. Dole, 770 F.2d 423, 441–42 (5th Cir. 1985) (finding a constructive use where an overhead highway project would have been nearly touching a "magnificent" historic building, destroying views of it); Stop H–3 Ass'n v. Coleman, 533 F.2d 434, 445 (9th Cir. 1976), *cert. denied*, 429 U.S. 999 (1976) (finding that an interstate highway designed to pass near a petroglyph rock on the National Register would use that resource). *But see* Nashvillians Against I–440 v. Lewis, 524 F. Supp. 962, 976–77 (M.D. Tenn. 1981) (finding no constructive use where plaintiffs challenging transportation project provided no "proof that the claimed harm [of air pollution] will affect the historic value or quality of the properties").

The Department of Transportation may also avoid having its activities qualify as constructive uses by mitigating their proximity impacts through restoring the resource to a condition equivalent to, or better than, the condition if the project were not built, in accordance with Department consultation with the official(s) with jurisdiction over the historic site. 23 C.F.R. § 774.15(f)(6). Certain activities, such as changes in airport schedules or plane types, are not considered to be uses subject to Section 4(f) review because of the likelihood that the impacts will be minor and the administrative burdens of evaluating each instance of the activity. *See* Sierra Club v. Department of Transp., 753 F.2d 120, 130 (D.C. Cir. 1985) (noting that the land alleged to be affected had been operated as an airport for more than four decades and that "[it] can hardly be expected, once an airport has been in operation, that every change in flight scheduling or operations must be accompanied by" a Section 4(f) use analysis).

3.   HISTORIC SITE

Section 4(f) does not apply to a historic resource unless the resource is deemed to be a "historic site." This term includes any public or private "prehistoric or historic district, site, building, structure, or object included in, or eligible for inclusion in, the National Register." 23 C.F.R. § 774.17. This definition has several important dimensions, all covered below.

a. Listed Properties

A listing on the National Register of Historic Places provides the surest degree of protection. Listing includes both properties individually listed on the National Register and properties that are not individually listed but lie within the boundaries of a listed historic district and are considered to contribute to the historic character of that district. Properties within the boundaries of a listed historic district but not considered to contribute to the district may still trigger Section 4(f) protection if the use of such property would adversely affect the integrity or attributes of the district itself. In such cases, the constructive use would be said to affect either individually eligible or contributing properties within a historic district, or the district as a whole. Noncontributing properties in a historic district are not deemed historic sites, so if the proposed transportation program or project affects only the noncontributing properties within a historic district, there will be no use under Section 4(f).

The National Register also includes all National Historic Landmarks, which are designated separately but automatically listed on the National Register (and afforded protection greater than the protection given to the National Register properties under various statutory schemes).

b. Eligible and Unlisted Properties

Federal transportation officials must determine during the planning stage whether resources that they may use may have historic significance, even if that resource is not yet listed on the National Register. 23 C.F.R. § 774.11(e). In such a situation, they complete a process to determine whether the resource is "eligible" for the National Register.

Such a determination is usually made through consultation with the state or tribal historic preservation officer. The determination may be referred to the Keeper of the National Register if there is disagreement between the federal and state/tribal authorities, or if a third party requests the involvement of the Keeper through the Advisory Council on Historic Preservation. In such instances, the Keeper's finding that the property is eligible for the National Register will supersede any contrary determinations made by state authorities. *See generally* Stop H–3 Ass'n v. Coleman, 533 F.2d 434 (1976) (ruling for the protection of a historic site that the Secretary of the Interior declared eligible for the National Register, even though state officials said it had merely marginal significance). If the property is reviewed and the parties agree that the property is not historic, then documentation of this consensus should be collected as part of the Section 4(f) record. If the property is located within a historic district, the parties must also document that the property does not contribute to the historic significance of the district, and that the property could be used without adversely affecting the district.

Even if a site is not listed on or even eligible for the National Register, federal transportation officials may decide to apply Section 4(f) when asked to do so by a state or local official that provides information about the significance of a site.

c. Historic Sites with a Transportation Function

Bridges, highways, and transit stations (such as railroad depots) which are listed on or eligible for the National Register present special issues because they are both historic sites and parts of the transportation system. The Federal Highway Administration has determined that repair, maintenance, and improvement of these resources are not typically subject to Section 4(f) review. Only when these resources are being demolished, or if their historically significant characteristics are adversely affected, will Section 4(f) review apply. 23 C.F.R. § 774.13(a). A determination as to whether a historic bridge or highway is adversely affected is made by the Federal Highway Administration in consultation with the state or tribal historic preservation officer. What about the replacement of a historic bridge, where the historic bridge is left in place and the new bridge is built nearby? Section 4(f) does not apply if the historic characteristics of the old bridge will be maintained and the proximity impacts of the new bridge will not substantially impair the historic bridge.

There is another dimension to sites with a transportation function. In 2005, Congress exempted the 46,700–mile interstate highway system from Section 4(f) review by stating that the system "shall not be considered to be a historic site." 23 U.S.C. § 103(c)(5)(A). (A similar provision was passed to exempt the interstate highway system from review under Section 106 of the National Historic Preservation Act.) Why would Congress do this? Consider the timing: properties may be considered for National Register listing as soon as they reach fifty years of age (unless they are exceptionally significant), which for the interstate highway system was June 29, 2006. The fear in 2005 was that some would imminently attempt to designate the entire interstate highway system as historic, thereby inhibiting the Department of Transportation's ability to maintain, upgrade, or replace it.

The 2005 amendment allowed the Secretary to determine if individual elements of the interstate system possess "national or exceptional historic significance (such as a historic bridge or a highly significant engineering feature)," and these individual elements will be deemed to be historic sites. *Id.* § 103(c)(5)(B). In 2006, the Federal Highway Administration released its "Final List of Nationally and Exceptionally Significant Features of the Federal Interstate Highway System." This list includes 132 properties—the vast majority of which are bridges and tunnels—that are excluded from the interstate highway exemption. We comment on the way historic bridges are treated by Section 4(f) in Part C.

d. Archaeological Sites

Archaeological sites may be considered to be historic sites under Section 4(f). However, Section 4(f) regulations have evolved to protect only those archaeological sites worth preserving in place, and courts have approved this interpretation as reasonable. *See, e.g.*, Town of Belmont v. Dole, 766 F.2d 28 (1st Cir. 1985). Officials engaging in the federal program or project may merely document or relocate any archaeological sites not worth preserving in place.

e. Timing

Some resources that would otherwise be deemed to be historic sites will not be protected by Section 4(f) if they were discovered, listed on the National Register, or deemed to be eligible for the National Register too late in the Section 4(f) process. If the discovery or determination that a site is historic occurs after the site is acquired, but an adequate effort was made to identify protectable properties before the site was acquired, Section 4(f) review will not be triggered. The one exception to this general rule is archaeological resources, because it can be difficult to know exactly where these resources are until they are disturbed by underground construction activity.

When a late discovery requiring additional Section 4(f) review occurs, then the project sponsor and the federal transportation officials must determine whether an individual, programmatic, or amended Section 4(f) evaluation is required. These different types of evaluations are discussed in Part C.

f. Nature of Historic Significance

There are several points in the Section 4(f) process where the nature of the historic significance of a resource—that is, the reason why it is considered to be historic—is critical. For example, a constructive use only occurs if the "proximity impact" affects the feature or attribute that conveys the site's historic significance. Moreover, the legal determination as to whether there is an adverse effect on the protected property also depends on a clear link to those features and attributes that contribute to the property's historic significance. *See also* 36 C.F.R. § 800.5 (mandating review under Section 106 of the National Historic Preservation Act where there is an effect on historic significance). Thus understanding the reason why non-lawyers call a property significant is critical for attorneys dealing with Section 4(f) cases.

4.   OFFICIAL(S) WITH JURISDICTION

Section 4(f) gives "official(s) with jurisdiction" a role at several key points in the process. The definition, found at 23 C.F.R. § 774.17, identifies different individuals as official(s) with jurisdiction depending on the location of the site and the characteristics of the resource.

For historic sites, the official with jurisdiction is the state or tribal historic preservation officer where the historic site is located. When a historic site is located on tribal land but there is no tribal historic preservation officer, then the tribe may designate a representative of the tribe to serve as an official with jurisdiction, alongside the state historic preservation officer. The Advisory Council on Historic Preservation may also be named an official with jurisdiction when it has been involved in a consultation for the same property in a Section 106 review under the National Historic Preservation Act.

For National Historic Landmarks, which are the properties with the highest level of historic significance and consequently the highest level of legal protection, the National Park Service is also an official with jurisdiction.

5.   PRUDENT AND FEASIBLE

One of the responsibilities of the Secretary during the Section 4(f) process is to consider whether there are alternatives to using the historic site. An avoidance alternative—that is, an alternative that avoids the use of the historic site—must be selected if it is prudent and feasible. If an alternative is found to be imprudent or infeasible, it may be rejected.

Prudence refers to how reasonable the alternative is. An alternative is not prudent if it involves one or more of the following factors:

(i) It compromises the project to a degree that it is unreasonable to proceed with the project in light of its stated purpose and need;

(ii) It results in unacceptable safety or operational problems;

(iii) After reasonable mitigation, it still causes:

(A) Severe social, economic, or environmental impacts;

(B) Severe disruption to established communities;

(C) Severe disproportionate impacts to minority or low income populations; or

(D) Severe impacts to environmental resources protected under other Federal statutes;

(iv) It results in additional construction, maintenance, or operational costs of an extraordinary magnitude; [or]

(v) It causes other unique problems or unusual factors.

23 C.F.R. § 774.17. So if the alternative is extremely expensive, or excessively disrupts the community around it, it has a good chance of being not prudent.

Courts' interpretation of the prudence factor has diverged. The First Circuit, for example, said that the Secretary's decision that three alternatives to the construction of an airport facility were imprudent was not arbitrary or capricious because: (1) the no-build alternative did not meet the transportation needs of the project; (2) an alternative project location was rejected based on "the combined effect of a number of considerations which weighed heavily against" the alternative; and (3) adaptation of an existing facility would require code compliance and cost $500,000, while still not necessarily being efficient or structurally feasible. Safeguarding The Historic Hanscom Area's Irreplaceable Resources, Inc. v. FAA, 651 F.3d 202, 209–12 (1st Cir. 2011). The Ninth Circuit rejected the Secretary's decision to call imprudent (1) an alternative that cost an extra $42 million, because that amount was not extraordinary; and (2) a no-build alternative that would require the purchase of extra buses and would result in increased congestion and delays. Stop H–3 Ass'n v. Dole, 740 F.2d 1442, 1452 & 1456 (9th Cir. 1984). And a Florida district court upheld the Department of Transportation's decision to deem a comparatively very costly alternative imprudent where the alternative presented "problems of disposal of excavated soil and other environmental impacts. . . that would not mitigate all environmental concerns, despite the very high cost." Citizens for Smart

Growth v. Peters, 716 F. Supp. 2d 1215, 1234–35 (S.D. Fla. 2010).

Feasibility is a simpler term, and is less likely to be the subject of a legal battle than is the term prudent. It refers to whether the alternative is technically possible, meaning whether it can be achieved through current construction methods, technologies, and practices. An alternative is not feasible if it cannot be built as a matter of sound engineering judgment. *Id.* This formulation allows for little administrative discretion in the determination of feasibility.

6. ALL POSSIBLE PLANNING TO MINIMIZE HARM

Once federal transportation officials have rejected all alternatives to using a historic site as imprudent and infeasible, they may only use a historic site if they have engaged in "all possible planning to minimize harm." Like "prudence," "reasonableness" is an important definitional concept: federal officials have responsibility to engage only in those harm-minimizing activities that are reasonable. Activities are reasonable if they preserve the historic activities, features, or attributes of the site. In evaluating the reasonableness of harm-minimizing activities, the Secretary must consider: the preservation purpose of Section 4(f); the views of the officials with jurisdiction over the resource; a cost-benefit analysis with regard to the impact and benefit to the resource; and any impacts on communities or environmental resources outside of the Section 4(f) property. *See* 23 C.F.R. § 774.17.

The meaning of "all possible planning to minimize harm" was clarified in *Merritt Parkway Conservancy v. Mineta*, 424 F. Supp. 2d 396 (D. Conn. 2006). There, the court found inadequate Federal Highway Administration (FHWA) planning to reconstruct parts of a historically significant highway. The court stated that the agency need not choose the alternative inflicting the least harm on the resource regardless of cost or technical feasibility. It found that the administrative record failed to show that the FHWA had (1) evaluated "the feasibility and prudence of alternative construction designs with less impact on the Merritt Parkway" and (2) complied with "mitigation measures compensating for residual impacts . . . to the extent feasible." *Id.* at 418. The court stressed the narrowness of its judgment: it intimated no judgment as to whether the proposed plan "in fact minimizes harm to the Merritt Parkway or complies to the extent feasible with the Merritt Parkway Guidelines. The Court holds only that the administrative record before it does not show that FHWA made such a determination or on what basis the FHWA did so." *Id.* at 424.

7. DE MINIMIS

For historic sites, the Secretary may find that a program or project has a de minimis net impact on the protected property after harm-minimizing measures are taken. A de minimis impact can be found either if no historic site is affected by the federal program or project, or if the program or project will have no adverse effect on the historic site. 49 U.S.C. § 303(d)(2)(A); 23 C.F.R. § 774.17(5). Thus, de minimis does not mean minor or negligible impact: it actually means no impact.

Before the Secretary can make a finding of de minimis impact on historic sites, she must consult with the official(s) with jurisdiction and consulting parties who are part of the Section 106 review process (pursuant to the National Historic Preservation Act), and obtain a written concurrence from them. Compliance with the National Historic Preservation Act suffices to satisfy all requirements for public input. *Id.* § 774.5(b)(1)(iii). Note that the requirements for public notice and comment differ for historic sites than for other resources protected by Section 4(f). The Secretary's determination of de minimis impact on parks, recreation areas, and wildlife or waterfowl refuges is the only part of the Section 4(f) process that explicitly requires public input. The statute requires "public notice and opportunity for public review and comment," 49 U.S.C. § 303(d)(3), which may take the form of a public meeting, public hearings, project websites, newsletters, advertisements, or other means, prior to the final determination of de minimis impact.

The legal impact of a de minimis finding is that the Secretary need not proceed with an individual or programmatic evaluation of the proposed federal action.

C. APPLICATION

Section 4(f) establishes the process that federal transportation officials must follow to ensure compliance with the statute. At first glance, the steps are simple. The Secretary (in reality, various designees of the Secretary) must first determine whether Section 4(f) applies. If it does apply, the Secretary must evaluate the impact of the proposed program or project on the protected resource using either a full evaluation or a programmatic evaluation. As part of the evaluation stage, the Secretary must identify alternatives to the proposed program or project, including avoidance alternatives (alternatives that avoid using the resource altogether). Finally, the Secretary must select the most suitable alternative. If no alternative is prudent and feasible, the Secretary may use the protected resource only if the program or project includes all possible planning to minimize harm to the site. At various points in the process, there is a consulting role for officials with jurisdiction. Challenging and unique circumstances may arise at any point.

1.   APPLICABILITY OF SECTION 4(f)

Prior to commencing a program or project, federal transportation officials must determine whether Section 4(f) applies at all. Of course, there has to be a transportation program or project. In the case of historic sites, there has to be a historic site that is designated or determined to be eligible for the National Register *prior* to the commencement of the program or project; late discoveries (other than archaeological discoveries) may not trigger reconsideration by the Secretary. Most importantly (and most often litigated among these applicability issues), there must be a "use" of the protected resource. Part B of this Chapter describes how each of these concepts has been defined and thus outlines the scope of the applicability of Section 4(f).

2.   EVALUATIONS

Once federal transportation officials determine that Section 4(f) applies, they must begin the process of evaluating the impact of the proposed program or project. If they determine the impact to be de minimis, a term defined in Part B, then the evaluation ends there, provided that there is documentation of the impact and official(s) with jurisdiction agree in writing. In such a circumstance, there is no requirement to evaluate alternatives, nor is there a requirement to engage in all possible planning to minimize harm because harm-minimization strategies have been contemplated in the de minimis finding.

If, however, the impact is not de minimis, the relevant officials must engage in either an individual evaluation or a programmatic evaluation, as applicable.

a. Individual Evaluation

An individual Section 4(f) evaluation is complex, requiring extensive analysis, consultation, and documentation, all specific to the project. An individual evaluation is chosen when the protected resource will be used, when the impact of the proposed program or project is greater than de minimis, and when a programmatic evaluation cannot be applied (see below). It involves two parts: a draft and a final evaluation.

The draft evaluation introduces the proposed federal action, describes the protected resource(s), identifies and evaluates alternatives to using the historic site (including avoidance alternatives), describes harm-minimizing or harm-mitigating features of the proposed action, and recounts how federal transportation officials have coordinated with official(s) with jurisdiction and other relevant parties.

The review of alternatives to using the historic site(s) and the potential impacts of these alternatives is a central part of the draft evaluation. Federal officials must select a reasonable number of alternatives to review or must justify why studying additional alternatives would not be worthwhile. One of the options reviewed should be a "no-build" alternative, which means that the program or project would not be built, avoiding negative impacts entirely. *See*, *e.g.*, D.C. Fed'n of Civic Ass'ns v. Volpe, 459 F.2d 1231, 1238 (D.C. Cir. 1971), *cert. denied* 405 U.S. 1030 (1972) (finding that the Secretary was required to review a no-build alternative to a new bridge in a historic neighborhood). Alternatives that avoid the use of the resource should also be considered where possible. Such "avoidance alternatives" may involve re-routing or relocating the project to avoid the use of a historic site, proposing an entirely different mode of transportation (such as transit, rather than vehicular travel), or redesigning or resizing the project to eliminate adverse impacts to the historic site. When there is more than one historic site (or other type of Section 4(f) protected property) being considered during an evaluation, an alternative is not an avoidance alternative if it requires the use of any of the protected properties. *See* Druid Hills Civic Ass'n v. FHWA, 772 F.2d 700 (11th Cir. 1985).

Once the various alternatives have been identified, the prudence and feasibility of each should be evaluated. If there is a prudent and feasible alternative that avoids the use of the historic site, that alternative must be selected. If there are no feasible and prudent avoidance alternatives—that is, if all alternatives result in a "use"—then the alternative that does the least harm to the historic site must be selected.

The selection of the non-avoidance alternative that does the least harm to the historic site can be tricky. When it comes to historic resources, harm-minimization measures may be judged relative to their ability to preserve the historic activities, features, or attributes of the site. Several factors may be balanced to help rank the harm caused by each alternative: the ability to mitigate adverse impacts; the severity of the harm after mitigation to the significant features of the historic site, or to other resources; the relative significance of the historic site(s); the views of the relevant officials with jurisdiction; the degree to which each alternative meets the "purpose and need" for the program or project; and the differences in costs of alternatives. 23 C.F.R. § 774.3(c)(1). Even though the statute does not explicitly state that the agency may reject an alternative that does the least harm to protected areas because it is infeasible or imprudent, courts have recognized that the agency may do so. *See, e.g.,* Druid Hills Civic Ass'n v. FHWA, 772 F.2d 700, 716 (11th Cir. 1985); La. Envtl. Soc'y, Inc. v. Coleman, 537 F.2d 79, 86 (5th Cir. 1976). In Section 4(f) cases, which often involve a complicated administrative record, a court will look carefully at the manner in which the agency carries out or prepares to carry out the harm-minimizing steps it has offered. *See, e.g.,* Merritt Parkway Conservancy v. Mineta, 424 F. Supp. 2d 396, 399 (D. Conn. 2006) (engaging in a "thorough, probing" review of the administrative record to find that the Federal Highway Administration failed to minimize harm to a historic parkway).

The draft evaluation also involves consultation and coordination with and among those considered "official(s) with jurisdiction" and others. (The role of these officials is discussed in greater detail in the next section.) The statute does not explicitly require public input during the draft evaluation, but public input may be obtained and considered through the public input process of a state agency partner, or through simultaneous federal reviews such as reviews under the National Environmental Policy Act. *See* 23 U.S.C. § 771.111 (describing the requirement for a coordination of public involvement and public hearings during federal environmental reviews). Once a draft is completed, these parties will have the opportunity to comment on the draft for forty-five days, and the relevant Department of Transportation personnel are required to consider these comments in good faith. If no comments are received or the Department addresses any comments received, the final evaluation may be issued.

The final evaluation includes the information contained in the draft and more detail about the reasons why the preferred alternative was selected. A copy of a final Section 4(f) evaluation is usually included in a National Environmental Policy Act environmental impact statement, if required.

b. Programmatic Evaluation

The alternative to the individual evaluation is the programmatic evaluation, which prescribes predetermined rules for certain minor, common, and/or special uses (all with greater than de minimis impact) of historic sites. The Department of Transportation developed the programmatic evaluation route through federal regulations; it does not appear in the language of the statute. It is intended to save time and cost as compared to individual evaluations. Before a programmatic evaluation may be applied, the official(s) with jurisdiction must agree that a programmatic evaluation is appropriate.

Programmatic evaluations may be used in several circumstances: where there is a net benefit to a protected resource; where there is only a "minor involvement" with historic sites; historic bridge projects; and independent bikeway or walkway construction projects. 23 C.F.R. § 774.3(d). Each of these circumstances comes with its own set of rules. At first glance, programmatic evaluations look somewhat similar to individual evaluations. The Department of Transportation must evaluate the applicability of Section 4(f), identify alternatives, describe anticipated measures to minimize harm, and consult with the official(s) with jurisdiction. However, programmatic evaluations need not make the two critical findings that are required by an individual evaluation: namely, that there is no feasible and prudent alternative that completely avoids the use of the historic site, and that the project includes all possible planning to minimize harm.

It is easy to see why federal officials would want to fast-track projects with a net benefit to a historic resource, or why they might consider bikeway or walkway projects, or other projects with "minor involvement" in historic sites, to be low-impact activities not requiring a full individual evaluation. However, the inclusion of historic bridges on the list of project types subject to programmatic evaluations may be puzzling. Programmatic evaluations of historic bridges apply when the bridge is to be replaced or rehabilitated with federal funds. Such evaluation must consider at least three alternatives: (1) a no-build alternative; (2) an alternative in which a new bridge is built in a different location; and (3) an alternative that rehabilitates the bridge without threatening its historic integrity. A no-build alternative may be rejected if the reason (e.g., making necessary repairs or accommodating increased traffic flows) for planning the project in the first place demonstrates that some construction is needed. The second and third alternatives may be rejected because of extraordinary cost, engineering challenges, or other external impacts. As for a showing of harm-minimization of the proposed program or project, federal officials have in the past been able to say that documentation through surveys and photographs was enough to mitigate the harm done to a bridge being demolished. All of these facts suggest that historic bridges are not well-protected by programmatic evaluations.

3.   ROLE OF OFFICIALS WITH JURISDICTION

Throughout the Section 4(f) process, official(s) with jurisdiction may or must provide input at certain stages. Officials with jurisdiction have the right to consult, coordinate, and provide an objection to, or concurrence with, certain actions. Their cooperation with federal transportation officials is critical to a timely resolution of the Section 4(f) evaluation.

In terms of consultation, officials with jurisdiction must be consulted during the substantive portion of any of the three routes that a program or project may take—finding of de minimis impact, individual evaluation, or programmatic evaluation. Coordination must occur with officials with jurisdiction at every stage, including the points at which the parties:

• Determine whether a property is significant and whether Section 4(f) applies to historic sites

• Apply Section 4(f) to archaeological sites discovered during construction

• Apply certain programmatic evaluations

• Make approvals for uses of historic sites

• Determine whether a constructive use has occurred

• Determine if proximity impacts will be mitigated to equivalent or better condition

• Evaluate proposed harm-minimization measures

• Evaluate which alternative imposes the least harm

In addition, the official(s) with jurisdiction may provide objections or concurrences at certain stages during the Section 4(f) process. For example, a statement regarding the relevant official(s)' lack of objection must be collected before federal transportation officials may proceed with two exceptions to full review. (These are the exception for restoration, rehabilitation, or maintenance of historic transportation facilities, and the exception for archaeological sites of minimal value for preservation in place. 23 C.F.R. §§ 774.13(a)–(b).) In addition, written concurrence of official(s) with jurisdiction is required before the Secretary can find that there are no adverse effects (prior to making de minimis impact filings) or before applying the exception for temporary occupancies or the exception for transportation enhancement activities and mitigation activities. *See id.* §§ 774.5(b), 774.13(d) & (g).

D.   RELATIONSHIP WITH SECTION 106 OF THE NATIONAL HISTORIC PRESERVATION ACT

Both Section 4(f) of the Department of Transportation Act and Section 106 of the National Preservation Act (considered in Chapter III) impose duties on federal agencies to address the effects of their actions on historic resources. They provide different types of protection for historic resources, but do interact in a few ways.

Although agencies will often engage in Section 4(f) and Section 106 reviews simultaneously, the statutory and regulatory schemes are quite different. Section 4(f) requires one federal agency, the Department of Transportation, to review alternatives and minimize harm if it is going to proceed with a transportation program or project that will "use" a property on or eligible for the National Register. 49 U.S.C. § 303. Section 106, on the other hand, requires *all* federal agencies to "take into account the effect" of their federal undertakings on properties on or eligible for the National Register. 16 U.S.C. § 470f. While Section 4(f) applies only to the Department of Transportation, Section

106 applies to all federal agencies. Furthermore, Section 4(f) actually dictates certain substantive results, while Section 106 review just requires agencies to "take into account" the effect of their actions—a "stop, look, and listen" provision. And finding a "use" under Section 4(f) requires a very different analysis than finding an "effect" under Section 106, so the same federal project may use a historic property without imposing any adverse effect, or vice versa.

So how do these two statutes interact? Most significantly, the Section 4(f) review can "piggyback" on certain findings made through the Section 106 review. First, federal law has established as an integral part of the Section 106 process the identification of properties that are potentially historically significant, and the evaluation of whether these properties are eligible for the National Register. A Section 106 eligibility determination may be used in the Section 4(f) process when a federal transportation program or project is being reviewed under both schemes. Second, the Section 106 process requires identification of the "National Register boundary" of a property, which does not necessarily coincide with property lines. For a Section 4(f) review, where the outcome can hinge on whether there are proximity impacts on a historic resource, understanding the National Register boundary (and thus the limits of protection) can be very important. Third, the Section 106 review process can name both contributing and noncontributing resources within historic districts. Section 4(f) reviewers can benefit from knowing these distinctions because noncontributing resources are not protected. Fourth, the Section 106 process can determine whether archaeological resources should be protected in place—an important question when an archaeological resource is discovered late in the process of constructing a transportation program or project. Fifth, a Section 106 review that concludes with a finding of no adverse effect on a historic property can be used by federal transportation officials to cut short a Section 4(f) review, because such a finding during the Section 106 process can justify either a finding of de minimis impact and/or a finding of no constructive use.

Another area of interaction between the statutes is the consultation requirements: who must or may be consulting parties to the Department of Transportation officials reviewing a federal transportation program or project. Both statutes require that the Department consult with the state or tribal historic preservation officers, or a tribal representative alongside the state historic preservation officer if there is no tribal historic preservation officer and the tribe names a representative. Section 4(f) also provides that any consulting parties in a Section 106 review, including the Advisory Council on Historic Preservation or local parties, be consulting parties in a Section 4(f) review.

Finally, the Department of Transportation often makes an effort to coordinate Section 4(f) and Section 106 reviews (and simultaneous reviews under the National Environmental Policy Act). So even though the substance and outcomes of the reviews will be different, a certain amount of internal streamlining may occur to reduce redundancies.

E. RELATIONSHIP WITH THE FEDERAL-AID HIGHWAY BILL

Someone combing through federal transportation legal canon might notice some language in 23 U.S.C. § 138—part of the Federal-Aid Highway Act—which is very similar to Section 4(f). The difference in the substantive portion of the two provisions is very minor. While Section 4(f) says that the Secretary "may approve" a program or project "only if" it meets the relevant criteria (no feasible/prudent alternatives and all possible planning to minimize harm), 23 U.S.C. § 138 says that the Secretary "shall not approve" a program or project "unless" it meets the criteria.

The explanation for the similarity may be found in the legislative histories of the Federal-Aid Highway Act and the Department of Transportation Act. In short, the two statutes were being considered concurrently, and the protections shielding certain resources from damaging consequences of federal transportation programs and projects ended up being slightly strengthened in the later statute, the Department of Transportation Act. *See* 23 U.S.C. § 138; 49 U.S.C. § 1653(f), nicknamed Section 4(f). In 1983, Section 4(f) was moved to its current location at 49 U.S.C. § 303.

The important point to remember, however, is that both the Federal-Aid Highway Act and Transportation Act language remain in effect and, while slightly different, they serve to reinforce each other. Other statutes refer to both provisions simultaneously. For example, 23 U.S.C. § 103(c)(5) contains the provision that the interstate highway system cannot be considered to be a historic resource either under section 138 of that title, or under Section 4(f).

Several law review articles say more about the legislative history of Section 4(f). *See*, *e.g.*, Oscar S. Gray, *Section 4(f) of the Department of Transportation Act*, 32 MD. L. REV. 327 (1973).

F.   STATE LAWS MODELED AFTER SECTION 4(f)

The success of Section 4(f) at the federal level as a tool to ensure substantive protection of historic resources has inspired states to pass similar laws. Many 4(f)-inspired state statutes apply to all state agency actions, and even some county and locality actions, rather than being limited to just state transportation agency actions. There are also a variety of 4(f)-inspired statutes that apply to specific types of state actions or specific resources.

Only a few states have adopted both aspects of Section 4(f)'s central enforcement mechanism: the review of the feasibility and prudence of the alternatives and the requirement to minimize harm. Kansas, for example, prevents the state from proceeding with any project that will damage or destroy properties on the National Register or state register of historic places unless the governor or other relevant official has determined that "there is no feasible and prudent alternative to the proposal and that the program includes all possible planning to minimize harm to such historic property resulting from such use." KAN. STAT. ANN. § 75–2724(a). (Until the 2013 legislative session, this language also protected the "environs" surrounding the landmarked property.) South Dakota has adopted identical language, except that the South Dakota statute adds that "encroach[ing] upon" historic properties is a prohibited activity unless the review of alternatives and planning to minimize harm occurs. S.D. CODIFIED LAWS § 1–19A–11.1.

Similarly, New Mexico prevents state agencies from spending money on any program or project "that requires the use of any portion of or any land from a significant prehistoric or historic site unless there is no feasible and prudent alternative to such use, and unless the program or project includes all planning to preserve and protect and to minimize harm." N.M. STAT. ANN. § 18–8–7. In California, no state agency can alter historic fabric or "transfer, relocate, or demolish historic resources" in a way that has adverse effects on a listed historic resource without adopting "prudent and feasible measures that will eliminate or mitigate the adverse effects." CAL. PUB. RES. CODE §§ 5024.5(a)–(b). Florida has a very similar provision, adding that the agency may also "undertake an appropriate archaeological salvage excavation or other recovery action to document the property as it existed prior to

demolition or alteration." FLA. STAT. ANN. § 267.061.
In Texas, parks, recreation areas, scientific areas,
wildlife refuges, and historic sites are protected
from public bodies' use and taking unless the
appropriate official determines that: "(1) there is no
feasible and prudent alternative to the use or taking
of such land; and (2) the program or project includes
all reasonable planning to minimize harm to the
land, as a park, recreation area, scientific area,
wildlife refuge, or historic site, resulting from the
use or taking." TEX. CODE ANN. § 26.001. And in
South Carolina, agencies proposing easements,
rights-of-way, or other encroachments on state
parks or historic areas must demonstrate that:
"[t]here is an important public necessity for the
encroachment;" alternative routes are neither
prudent nor feasible; and the applicable agency
must "make reasonable mitigation of the impacts of
the proposed encroachment." S.C. CODE ANN. § 10–
1–135 (Law. Co-op. 1976).

Illinois has a hybrid approach, adopting both
Section 4(f) key concepts but failing to provide any
real legal protection. An Illinois state agency must
explore "all feasible and prudent plans which
eliminate, minimize, or mitigate adverse effects on
historic resources," 20 ILL. STAT. ANN. 3420/4–4(c),
and the state historic preservation officer must
agree whether there is or is not an alternative that
eliminates, minimizes, or mitigates the adverse
effect of the undertaking. However, there does not
appear to be a requirement that the agency select
the alternative with no adverse effect, or halt the

project even if there are feasible and prudent alternatives.

In a different vein, several state statutes require agencies to refrain from impairing natural and/or historic resources as long as there is a prudent and feasible alternative, but make no mention of a harm-minimization requirement. Connecticut, Minnesota, and South Dakota have nearly identical laws stating as much. *See* CONN. GEN. STAT. § 22a–19(b); MINN. STAT. ANN. § 116B.09; S.D. CODIFIED LAWS § 34A–10–8. These three states' laws affect all state agencies' administrative, licensing, and similar proceedings, not just those of the state transportation agency. In Maryland, for capital projects affecting historic properties, units of state government must be sure "that the activities will not "have an adverse effect on the historic and cultural resources of the certified heritage area, unless there is no prudent and feasible alternative." MD. CODE ANN., FIN. INST. § 13–1112. An Oregon statute is more limited in scope, requiring the state transportation agency, "whenever prudent and feasible," to provide for the rehabilitation, restoration, maintenance, and preservation of certain features of a "historic and scenic highway;" it also provides that the agency may not dismantle, destroy, abandon, or significantly transform such a highway "when it is prudent and feasible not to take such action." OR. REV. STAT. §§ 377.105(1) & (5).

An assortment of other laws protect certain types of resources using a Section 4(f)-like prudent and feasible standard. In North Carolina, property encumbered by a conservation restriction may not be condemned unless the condemning party "sufficiently consider[s] alternatives to the action" or if "a prudent and feasible alternative exists." N.C. GEN. STAT. § 40A–82. In Massachusetts, American Indian remains must remain in place unless "prudent and feasible alternatives exist to avoid, minimize, or mitigate harm to the Indian burial site." MASS. GEN. LAWS ch. 7C, § 43. If not, the state archaeologist must excavate and recover the remains. Similar provisions exist in Connecticut. *See* CONN. GEN. STAT. § 10–388(c). In New Jersey, the New Jersey Water Supply Authority may not use public lands, reservations, highways or parkways unless there is no prudent and feasible alternative to doing so. N.J. STAT. ANN. § 58:1B–7.m.

Finally, two states have adopted judicial remedy provisions that evoke concepts at the heart of Section 4(f). In California, a person sued by the Attorney General for polluting, impairing, or destroying the state's "natural resources" pursuant to CAL. GOV. CODE § 12607 may use as a defense that "there is no more feasible and prudent alternative to the defendant's conduct." *Id.* § 12608. (California's definition of "natural resources" includes "historic or aesthetic sites." *Id.* § 12605.) Rhode Island, meanwhile, allows courts to provide a judicial remedy to "protect the air, water, land, or other natural resources located within the state from pollution, impairment, or destruction, considering the health, safety, and welfare of the public, and the availability of feasible, prudent, and economically viable alternatives." R.I. GEN. LAWS § 10–20–6 (1956). (Rhode Island's definition of "natural resources" includes both "land" and "recreational resources," but not historic sites specifically. *Id.* § 10–20–2.)

While the above list is not exhaustive, it provides a good overview of the many types of state laws inspired by Section 4(f). Academic study to determine the effects of these state statutes is sadly lacking.

CHAPTER 6
LOCAL REGULATION

Hundreds of localities around the country have passed historic preservation ordinances: rules governing development and rehabilitation of privately owned historic properties. These rules might encompass a range of restrictions, from preventing demolition of historic structures, to imposing aesthetic standards on exterior alterations, to dictating how new construction in historic districts should be built. Historic preservation ordinances focus on historic buildings and districts of historic buildings—rarely do they impact structures, objects or sites.

Whatever its content, a historic preservation ordinance is almost always administered by a small group of people, usually residents of the jurisdiction, called the historic preservation commission. (This group may also be called the historic properties commission, historic district commission, or landmarks commission.) Commissioners may be required to have expertise in architecture, planning, history, and/or real estate development. In addition to its powers to make decisions pursuant to the historic preservation ordinance, the commission may also have advisory responsibilities in other matters affecting historic properties, including the process of designating properties as historic, planning and zoning applications, and local legislative body actions.

Localities derive their authority to draft historic preservation ordinances and empower local commissions from state enabling statutes. This means that practices vary from state to state, though some legal issues are common. In this Chapter, we focus on historic preservation ordinance provisions restricting demolition, alteration, and new construction. We conclude by discussing how zoning ordinances—general land use regulations not specific to historic properties—can also affect historic properties.

A. RESTRICTIONS ON DEMOLITION

Local ordinances may limit or delay the ability of private property owners to demolish all or part of their historic (or older) properties. There are three different types of ordinances that limit demolition: (1) ordinances restricting demolition by affirmative act, (2) ordinances requiring delays before demolition by affirmative act occurs, and (3) ordinances restricting demolition by neglect. We cover each of these types of ordinances and how they affect historic properties in turn.

1. ORDINANCES RESTRICTING DEMOLITION BY AFFIRMATIVE ACT

Demolition by affirmative act occurs when a property owner intentionally tears down part or all of a building. Most localities require property owners to obtain a permit before demolition occurs, whether the building slated to be demolished is historic or not. Some localities provide heightened review of proposed demolitions of historic and/or older properties. This section illustrates the heightened restrictions localities may impose, and then describes an exception offered by some jurisdictions: the public interest exception.

a. Types of Restrictions

There are two main types of restrictions on demolition: requirements that a building permit be simultaneously filed and requirements that the demolition be "appropriate."

Some localities require a building permit for new construction to be filed before the demolition of a historic property will be approved. Such provisions reduce the chance that the demolition of a significant building will result in a vacant lot. Beverly Hills, California, for example, will not issue a permit for demolition or removal of a building unless: (1) a building permit for a replacement building or for a restoration of a partially demolished building is also issued, (2) a local architectural commission has approved an alternative use not requiring a building permit, or (3) a landscape, fencing, and maintenance plan is approved. *See* BEVERLY HILLS, CA., CODE § 10–3–4201.

Other localities require that an application for partial or total demolition be reviewed by the local historic commission for "appropriateness"—that is, compatibility with existing historic features of the subject property and its surroundings. The process for determining appropriateness is described further in the Part B of this Chapter. If the commission finds that the demolition is not appropriate, the commission may prohibit the demolition. If it finds that the demolition is appropriate, the demolition will be allowed to proceed. Typically, decision-makers seek to avoid the destruction of historic fabric with a high degree of physical integrity and historic fabric in a prominent location.

In Dallas, for instance, the local historic commission reviews for appropriateness all applications for demolition or removal of structures in historic overlay zones. *See* DALLAS, TEX., CODE § 51A–4.501(h). The commission will only approve the demolition on only four grounds:

(i) To replace the structure with a new structure that is more appropriate and compatible with the historic overlay district.

(ii) No economically viable use of the property exists.

(iii) The structure poses an imminent threat to public health or safety.

(iv) The structure is noncontributing to the historic overlay district because it is newer than the period of historic significance.

Id. § 51A–4.501(h)(2)(B). Property owners seeking demolition must provide documentation supporting one or more of these grounds for approval, and the commission must deny applications unless the owner meets her burden of proof. *See id.* § 51A–4.501(h)(4). The economic viability exception (also called an "economic hardship" exception) also arises in the context of restrictions on alterations, as described in the next Part.

b. Public Interest Exception

A small number of jurisdictions recognize a public interest exception, allowing property owners who show that the demolition is in the public interest to proceed with demolition, even if historic fabric will be destroyed.

The three most prominent cities that offer this exception are Philadelphia, Washington, D.C., and San Antonio. Philadelphia issues a demolition permit if the local historic commission finds that "issuance of the permit is necessary in the public interest." PHILADELPHIA, PA., HISTORIC PRES. ORDINANCE § 14–1005(6)(d). D.C. allows a demolition permit to issue for the same reason, D.C. CODE § 6–1104(e), and adds that "necessary in the public interest" means "consistent with the purposes of [the historic preservation ordinance]. . . or necessary to allow the construction of a project of special merit." *Id.* § 6–1102(10). San Antonio's ordinance is based on Washington D.C.'s. *See* SAN ANTONIO, TEX., CODE §§ 35–7002, 35–7051.

Property owners seeking to prove that their proposed project possesses special merit or otherwise show that their demolition is within the public interest should review cases within the relevant jurisdiction. If no cases are available, we recommend turning to precedents from Washington, D.C. At least four D.C. circuit court cases and two dozen opinions of the Mayor's Agent (the one-person appeal board from decisions of the local historic commission) have considered the public interest exception.

2. ORDINANCES REQUIRING DELAYS BEFORE DEMOLITION BY AFFIRMATIVE ACT

Localities may limit demolition of historic and/or older properties by requiring that a certain period of time pass before demolition can occur. A delay period may be required by a stand-alone "demolition delay ordinance," or through a provision in the building code, zoning code, or historic preservation ordinance adopted by the locality. This delay is intended to allow for the property owner and/or preservation proponents to consider alternatives to demolition, such as moving the building, finding a new owner, or identifying a new purpose for the building. Delay periods are often applied to buildings over a certain age (say, fifty or sixty years), whether they are historic or not. Accordingly, another use of the delay period may be to determine whether the subject property is eligible for listing on relevant registers of historic places.

Some localities have very robust demolition delay ordinances. In Cambridge, Massachusetts, the local historic commission will review subject properties over fifty years old to confirm whether they either are designated historic or are "preferably preserved significant buildings" that have not been designated historic but whose preservation is in the public interest. *See* CAMBRIDGE, MASS., CODE § 2.78.090.E.

Owners of such buildings must wait six months before demolition. *Id.* The six-month period may be shortened only if the commission finds either that no party "would be willing to preserve, rehabilitate or restore such building," or that the property owner has already made "continuing, bona fide, reasonable and unsuccessful efforts to locate such a purchaser" over a six-month period. *Id.* If the property owner demolishes any building more than fifty years old without going through the process, the city will not issue any building permit for two years after the demolition. *Id.* § 2.78.120.B. Similarly, Alexandria, Virginia, requires that most historic properties be marketed for sale for one year before a demolition permit will be issued. ALEXANDRIA, VA., ZONING ORDINANCE art. X, § 108(A)(2).

Other localities have demolition delay ordinances that require shorter waiting periods or allow for more liberal waivers. For example, Greenwich, Connecticut, imposes a ninety-day waiting period, but if the building official receives no objection to the demolition within twenty days, the balance of the ninety-day waiting period is waived. GREENWICH, CONN., CODE §§ 6–313 & 6–318.

3.   ORDINANCES PROHIBITING DEMOLITION BY NEGLECT

Localities may also prohibit "demolition by neglect," which occurs when property owners allow a property to fall into such a state of disrepair that it becomes necessary to demolish it. Many localities have housing codes, which require that property owners maintain interiors to certain standards of habitability. Housing codes alone, however, are insufficient to prevent demolition by neglect because they focus on occupant comfort and not on the maintenance of aesthetic characteristics of historic features (including decorative elements whose retention may be important for the building's integrity). Only a few localities go beyond housing codes to adopt targeted demolition by neglect ordinances, which require that historic or older buildings be kept in a good state of repair inside and out, with special attention to the maintenance of exterior historic features.

The biggest issue in demolition by neglect situations is ensuring that the local ordinance is strong enough to compel property owners to comply with maintenance and repair requirements. The demolition by neglect ordinances in Washington, D.C., and Dallas illustrate two approaches to enforcement. D.C. defines demolition by neglect as "neglect in maintaining, repairing, or securing an historic landmark or a building or structure in an historic district that results in substantial deterioration of an exterior feature of the building or structure or the loss of the structural integrity of the building or structure." D.C. CODE ANN. § 6–1102(3A). Upon determining that the treatment of a building has met this definition, the mayor of D.C. may, after obtaining an order from the D.C. Superior Court, require the owner to repair the offending conditions or may direct city personnel to make repairs necessary, at the owner's expense. *Id.* § 6–1109.03. Dallas allows the local historic commission to certify a property as a demolition by neglect case and to refer the case to the city attorney for enforcement. *See* DALLAS, TEX. CODE § 51A–4.501(k).

It is important to note that many localities with demolition by neglect ordinances also constrain demolition by affirmative act. *See*, *e.g.*, BEVERLY HILLS, CA., CODE §§ 10–3–3206 & 10–3–4201. In this way, localities interested in preservation may combat both types of demolition that concern preservationists.

B.   RESTRICTIONS ON ALTERATION

Many localities restrict the way property owners can alter the visible features of their historic buildings. These restrictions typically take the form of a review by the local historic commission, which is triggered when the owner of a historic property (or a nonhistoric property located within a historic district) applies for a building permit to change some aspect of her building. The property owner must convince the commission that the alterations are appropriately compatible with the historic aspects of the property and its setting. If the commission agrees with the property owner, it will issue a "certificate of appropriateness," which allows the building permit to be issued and the alterations to proceed.

This Part focuses first on the process by which property owners obtain certificates of appropriateness for proposed alterations. It then turns to economic hardship—the primary ground upon which owners may be excused from obtaining certificates of appropriateness. (Another less common ground for excusal is the public interest exception, discussed in Part A of this Chapter.)

1.   CERTIFICATES OF APPROPRIATENESS

A certificate of appropriateness (COA) is a document issued by a local historic commission to indicate that a property owner's proposal for altering her building is compatible with the historic fabric of the property and/or its setting. The following aspects of COAs vary by jurisdiction: covered properties and activities; evaluation process; and content. Each of these aspects is discussed below.

a. Covered Properties and Activities

A locality will require COA review if the property and the alteration activity being undertaken by the property owner are covered by local law. Covered properties may include properties in one or more of the following categories: (1) individually listed on a register of historic places; (2) contributing properties within listed historic districts; (3) noncontributing properties within listed historic districts; and (4) vacant lots within listed historic districts. Some jurisdictions cover all of property types and hold them all to the same requirements; others apply different criteria to the different categories. Houston, for example, only requires COAs for categories (1) and (2). (Category (4), which involves new construction, is the focus of the next section.) Properties that are not within historic districts and not otherwise listed on any register of historic places are not typically subject to the COA process.

Only some alterations activities will trigger COA review. The local historic commission in Washington, D.C., for example, has authority to regulate only alterations involving "a change in the exterior appearance of a building or structure or its site." D.C. CODE § 6–11102(1). In D.C., as in most other jurisdictions, interior alterations of ordinary historic properties do not require a COA to proceed. (Interior alterations to exceptional properties or properties with interiors that are designated historic may still require a COA.)

In addition, many jurisdictions distinguish between major work, minor work, and routine maintenance. Major work to covered properties will always require a COA. For alterations that are considered to be minor, a COA may or may not be required. If a COA is required for minor work, staff approval may be deemed to be an acceptable substitute for approval by the full commission. Routine maintenance and repairs do not typically require COAs and thus are not usually reviewed by either commissions or staff. Jurisdictions differ on whether changing an exterior paint color requires a COA.

b. Evaluation Process

The COA process typically begins when the owner of a covered property files for a building permit for covered alteration activities. The owner usually sends her building permit application to the building department (sometimes called the office of licenses and inspections), which redirects applications to the planning or economic development department, or other department housing the historic preservation staff. The staff will review the building permit and any supplemental information provided by the applicant to confirm that the alteration activities fall within the COA process. Staff may be authorized to approve minor work, but any major work (and minor work whose disposition may set a new precedent in the locality) will go before the local historic commission.

If the commission needs to evaluate the application, the commission will typically hold a public meeting to discuss the application within a time frame prescribed by the local ordinance. At this meeting, the application will be presented by the property owner or by members of the locality's professional staff (or consultants acting on behalf of the city). Then the staff may provide an opinion to the commission as to the merit of the application. The commission may then ask questions of the applicant and may invite testimony from neighbors or others.

The next step is commission deliberation, which is usually public. The criteria used by commissions to evaluate appropriateness vary. Often localities tether their standards to the Secretary of the Interior's Standards for the Treatment of Historic Properties. *See* 36 C.F.R. § 68.3. Localities may also catalogue architectural styles common in the community and provide design guidelines (usually based on the Secretary's Standards) for each architectural style. To see how one city approaches COA criteria, find Miami's *Historic Preservation Guidelines*, a document that illustrates how the Secretary's Standards apply to certain properties, catalogues common architectural styles (such as Art Deco and Mission styles), and explains the city's requirements for certain common alterations, such as hurricane shutters and awnings. *See* CITY OF MIAMI, HISTORIC PRESERVATION GUIDELINES (2011).

Applying the relevant criteria, the local historic commission will vote on the application. If the commission decides to issue the COA, the commission may also add conditions to the approval. If the commission declines to issue the COA, the reasons for its decision are usually included in the COA. Such reasons may include that the proposal was not appropriate within the standards of the jurisdiction or that the applicant failed to provide enough information or assurances regarding her plans.

An applicant disappointed by the commission's decision may appeal, depending on the locality, to an administrative official or board, the local legislative body, the chief local elected official, or to a court.

c. Content

In terms of content, the COA is usually fairly straightforward. It lists the property address and property owner, describes the proposed alterations, identifies relevant documents (such as the plans and elevations being approved), and states the decision of the local historic commission. In some cases, the COA may include conditions for approval. For example, a bond may be required to ensure the improvements will be made in accordance with the plans. Approval may also be conditioned on certain changes to the proposed design. Once the COA is completed, the commission sends it back to the building department, which then issues the building permit.

Some COAs may be issued with a statement that the alteration produces "no effect" on historic elements. These are sometimes also called "certificates of no effect."

2. ECONOMIC HARDSHIP EXCEPTION

Many jurisdictions offer an economic hardship exception for property owners who would otherwise have to obtain a certificate of appropriateness (COA) for their alteration proposals. This exception relieves property owners of the need to obtain a COA if they can show that their proposed alteration is the only way that they can make some minimum economic return on the property. A property owner usually must present evidence of an economic hardship to the local historic commission, although some localities have a separate staff member or body that makes decisions on economic hardship claims.

The standards for economic hardship vary widely. In Hartford, Connecticut, an applicant may show economic hardship if she provides two "realistic comparable professional estimates" showing that the level of compliance needed to obtain a COA is 20 percent greater than the applicant's preferred alteration technique. HARTFORD, CONN., CODE § 28–219(c). Bloomfield, Indiana, requires the commission to weigh many pieces of evidence supplied by the applicant to determine whether the property "may yield a reasonable return to the owners," including: construction costs, engineering reports, market analysis showing price in current condition and condition after proposed alterations, purchase price, two years' of statements of income from the property, real estate taxes, and the like. BLOOMINGTON, IND., CODE § 44.11–6.A. Berkeley, California, has more nebulous language, requiring applicants to show that the disapproval of the building permit "will work immediate and substantial hardship because of conditions peculiar to the particular structure or feature involved, and that failure to disapprove the application will be consistent with the purposes of this chapter." BERKELEY, CA., CODE § 3.24.270. Finally, Washington, D.C., ties the concept of economic hardship to the takings clause in the U.S. Constitution, defining unreasonable economic hardship as "a taking of the owner's property without just compensation, or, in the case of a low-income owner(s) as determined by the Mayor . . . an onerous and excessive financial burden." D.C. CODE § 6–1102(14).

These four examples illustrate the wide variety of economic hardship exception provisions. Hartford's provides the simplest guidance for applicants, but its low threshold may allow too many applicants to avoid compliance. Bloomington's long list of factors does not provide the commission with clear direction, but it may allow flexibility. Berkeley's language provides perhaps the maximum flexibility to determine that an economic hardship claim has been substantiated. D.C.'s link to the takings clause means that proof of economic hardship may be more difficult for applicants to provide, since they would likely have to consult with lawyers familiar with constitutional law before seeking a hardship exception.

Given the numerous cases litigating economic hardship, the fact-dependent nature of these cases, and the constraints of this book, we do not highlight any cases here. We add that economic hardship exceptions may be applied to allow property owners to proceed with demolition by affirmative act, discussed in the prior Part.

C.   RESTRICTIONS ON NEW CONSTRUCTION

New construction on vacant lots within historic districts presents special problems. On the one hand, it seems odd, or even anti-creative, to constrain construction that does not demolish or alter extant historic fabric. On the other hand, one can see how incompatible new construction within a historic district could negatively affect the ensemble effect of a district.

Jurisdictions vary as to how they treat new construction within historic districts. Some jurisdictions will hold new construction to the same standards as alterations, described in the preceding Part. Aggrieved property owners may question whether the vacant lot should have been included in the designation of the district at all. *See, e.g.*, A–S–P Assocs. v. City of Raleigh, 258 S.E.2d 444 (N.C. 1979) (rejecting challenges to the inclusion of a vacant lot within a historic district because inclusion was reasonable given the regulatory aims of the locality). Washington, D.C. reverses the burden of proof, providing that the permit must be granted unless the mayor finds that the proposal is incompatible with the character of the historic district. D.C. CODE § 6–1107(f).

Other jurisdictions will not evaluate the appropriateness of new construction. Because rules on this topic vary so widely, consultation with local officials and careful review of the relevant documents is advised.

D. HISTORIC PRESERVATION AND ZONING

Localities use many strategies to regulate land use. One common strategy involves implementing zoning ordinances that govern the use, bulk, height, and location of buildings in particular areas. Zoning ordinances do not typically address building appearance or aesthetic concerns. Historic preservation ordinances, meanwhile, focus almost entirely on building appearance and aesthetics and do not usually regulate building uses. This Part details the intersection between zoning and preservation, and discusses two recent zoning innovations with some bearing on historic preservation: conservation districts and form-based codes.

1. INTERSECTIONS BETWEEN PRESERVATION AND ZONING

Understanding how zoning and historic preservation intersect (and do not intersect) can explain how localities regulate historic properties. As a structural matter, the regulation of zones and of preservation often occurs under two different regulatory schemes: the zoning ordinance and the historic preservation ordinance. Sometimes, a zoning ordinance will incorporate aspects of historic preservation, as we discuss below.

Zoning and historic preservation have different aims. Traditional zoning ordinances focus primarily on building uses. They place land into different zones and impose specific rules for development in each zone. Zoning has as its primary objective the separation of incompatible uses; for example, an industrial zone may be located far from a residential zone. As a secondary objective, zoning aims to create a sense of visual order by controlling the general look of certain zones. To do this, zoning may require that buildings be set back a certain distance from the street, may limit the height of buildings, and may limit the square footage (or the bulk) of buildings. While these restrictions can affect the general look of a building or neighborhood, zoning regulations do not usually address decorative elements, façade features, or fenestration of a building.

Historic preservation ordinances, by contrast, focus on these aesthetic details. Their primary objective is the preservation of the physical characteristics of historic buildings and districts that are important to their historic character. As a secondary objective, they regulate new construction to ensure that it is compatible with protected historic fabric. To accomplish these goals, preservation ordinances usually create a process for reviewing proposed changes to ensure compatibility with historic character and restrict other kinds of activities, such as demolition.

How do these two complimentary but distinct types of land use regulatory schemes interact? First, a zoning ordinance may establish a historic overlay district and set forth special rules for that district. This is most likely to happen where there is not a stand-alone historic preservation ordinance. Second, a zoning ordinance may require that the local historic commission be consulted in certain zoning decisions, such as requests for variances in historic districts or the development of a comprehensive plan for a jurisdiction. Third, zoning officials may relax use restrictions in historic areas in need of redevelopment, as was done in the SoHo neighborhood of New York City—thus spurring rehabilitation. Fourth, innovative schemes such as conservation districts and form-based coding may incorporate design goals of historic preservation into zoning ordinances, which has traditionally ignored such goals. Conservation districts and form-based codes are discussed in greater detail below.

There are also areas of possible conflict, usually in the case of new construction in historic districts. Zoning ordinance provisions governing setbacks, height, and bulk may provide property owners with more design flexibility than historic ordinance provisions, which govern the aesthetic details with the aim of compatibility. For example, a zoning ordinance may allow for a 20-story building to be built within a historic district containing only 2-to-5-story buildings. The 20-story building may, however, be incompatible with the smaller-scale historic structures as a result of its height. Property owners attempting to avoid the more restrictive historic preservation rules may try to challenge these rules on a variety of grounds. They may allege that state enabling acts or other statutory authorities require the zoning ordinance to take precedence. Some of these constitutional arguments are described in Chapters VII to X.

2.   CONSERVATION DISTRICTS

Conservation districts have developed in a few dozen localities around the country—including Phoenix, Nashville, Portland (Oregon), Atlanta, and San Antonio—as an alternative to historic districts. They are used to delineate districts which have a distinctive local identity, but where the application of strict preservation principles would be inappropriate, either because there is little political support for the ordinance or because the buildings do not have sufficient integrity to merit the more comprehensive protection provided by typical historic district regulations.

Conservation districts are often created pursuant to zoning ordinances as a type of floating zone, although they may also be included in historic preservation ordinances. Creating such districts varies in practice, from a simple presentation to the city council (Nashville) to the onerous process of garnering consensus among 100 percent of property owners (Portland, Oregon). The authority to create conservation districts is usually thought to exist in state planning and zoning enabling acts. Some states do, however, provide more specific guidance regarding the creation of, and evaluation process for, conservation districts.

Sometimes called "historic preservation light," a conservation district scheme will generally have fewer regulations than a historic district scheme. Localities generally allow demolition in conservation districts. Alterations and new construction will be reviewed pursuant to guidelines less onerous than those used to evaluate historic districts. If review guidelines reference the Secretary of the Interior's Standards for Rehabilitation, these will be relaxed when applied to conservation districts. Reviews may be conducted by the zoning department staff, zoning commission, historic preservation staff, or historic preservation commission. In Cambridge, Massachusetts, conservation districts are administered by a neighborhood group. The conclusions of these reviews may be binding or advisory. Official permits may or may not be issued.

A property owner may receive some advantages if her building is located within a conservation district. Many communities provide access to grant, tax credit, and low-interest loan programs. Other communities, such as Boise, Idaho, offer property owners more flexibility in meeting parking requirements, while the planning department of Riverside, California, waives permit fees.

3.   FORM-BASED CODES

Form-based codes are another innovative zoning technique that can be used to advance some of the aesthetic goals of historic preservation. They emerged as a concept in the 1980s, but jurisdictions have only recently begun to adopt them in greater numbers. Unlike traditional zoning, form-based codes do not primarily address uses, but instead focus on the massing, fenestration, shape, and other physical elements (such as porches and roofs) of a building and its site. Form-based codes seek to provide design guidelines at a human scale, while relaxing use restrictions that characterize traditional zoning.

Many people have criticized form-based zoning for being too complicated. Others have said that this type of zoning strives too hard to replicate traditional, walkable neighborhoods of the past. This criticism also reveals, however, why form-based codes are compatible with historic preservation concepts. When form-based codes are implemented in jurisdictions without historic districts or historic preservation ordinances, the codes may serve as a kind of design review, ensuring that alterations and new construction are performed in a way that is sensitive to the historic setting.

CHAPTER 7

POLICE POWER AND DUE PROCESS

This Chapter provides an overview of two of the most basic federal constitutional constraints on government activity: the requirement that governments conduct activities that are within their police power, and the requirement that governments not deprive individuals of property without due process. It aims to illuminate how these constitutional provisions affect historic preservation law at the federal, state, and local levels.

This Chapter is the first of four Chapters considering constitutional constraints on historic preservation laws. It is followed by Chapter VIII on takings; Chapter IX on religious liberty; and Chapter X on free speech.

A. POLICE POWER

Reasonable historic preservation laws that are not arbitrary and that are substantially related to public health, safety, morals, or general welfare (including aesthetic aims) are valid exercises of the police power. The police power, which constrains state governments and their political subdivisions (including localities), finds its conceptual origins in the Tenth Amendment of the U.S. Constitution. The Tenth Amendment states: "The powers not delegated to the United States by the Constitution, nor prohibited by it to the States, are reserved to the States respectively, or to the people." U.S. CONST. amend. X. Among the powers not specifically enumerated in the Constitution is the police power. This power allows states and their political subdivisions to make laws that promote health, safety, morals, and general welfare.

The acceptance of historic preservation as a valid exercise of the police power grew out of the acceptance of zoning ordinances as a valid exercise of the police power. State and local zoning ordinances have long been held to be within the police power of states and localities, as long as they are reasonable, not arbitrary, and substantially related to public health, safety, morals, or general welfare. In 1926, the Supreme Court confirmed this principle in the *Euclid* case, which upheld a common zoning ordinance against constitutional challenge. *See* Vill. of Euclid v. Ambler Realty Co., 272 U.S. 365, 395 (1926). In 1954, the Supreme Court clarified that the concept of public welfare included in the police power was:

> broad and inclusive. The values it represents are spiritual as well as physical, aesthetic as well as monetary. It is within the power of the legislature to determine that the community should be beautiful as well as healthy, spacious as well as clean, well-balanced as well as carefully patrolled.

Berman v. Parker, 348 U.S. 26, 33 (1954). Although *Berman* was not a police power case (it was an eminent domain case), it eventually became as important as *Euclid* in supporting the notion that aesthetic regulation is subsumed within the police power.

Between 1926 and 1978, several lower courts considering challenges to historic preservation regulations used *Euclid* or *Berman* (or both) to justify their findings that preservation regulation was a valid exercise of the police power. *See, e.g.,* Maher v. City of New Orleans, 516 F.2d 1051, 1061 (5th Cir. 1975) (opining that "considering the nationwide sentiment for preserving the country's heritage and with particular regard to the context of the unique and characteristic French Quarter, the [ordinance]. . . falls within the permissible scope of the police power"), *cert. denied,* 426 U.S. 905 (1976). In 1978, the Court finally took up this specific issue, confirming that historic preservation regulation does in fact fall within the police power. Penn Central Transp. Co. v. City of New York, 438 U.S. 104 (1978). The Court offered that it had "recognized, in a number of settings, that States and cities may enact land use restrictions or controls to enhance the quality of life by preserving the character and desirable aesthetic features of a city." *Id.* at 129.

Since 1978, the *Penn Central* decision has made it nearly impossible to successfully argue that the most common historic preservation laws enacted at the state and local levels—rules creating historic districts, providing for registers of historic places, or regulating the aesthetic features of private property—violate the police power. We know of no court decision upholding such an argument and do not believe that any of the laws mentioned in this book could reasonably be said to exceed the police power.

B. DUE PROCESS

The Fifth and Fourteenth Amendments state that in no case shall government deprive a person "of life, liberty, or property, without due process of law." U.S. CONST. amends. V & XIV. The due process clause does not protect government actors, and challenges are typically brought by private individuals as well as corporate persons. As a threshold matter, a plaintiff challenging a historic preservation law must demonstrate a deprivation of property by government. *See* Shanks v. Dressel, 540 F.3d 1082, 1087–88 (9th Cir. 2008) (rejecting neighbors' substantive due process challenge against a city that failed to enforce local historic preservation regulations because they failed to show such deprivation).

After this initial showing, the plaintiff must prove that either procedural or substantive due process rights (or both) have been violated. Procedural due process protects individuals' rights to adequate process when being deprived of a property interest, while substantive due process guarantees fundamentally fair government action. Historic preservation laws have been largely upheld by courts against procedural due process challenges, although there have been exceptions. Substantive due process challenges have also been mostly rejected, but the lack of clear, uniform thought as to what substantive due process requires adds volatility and unpredictability to legal decision-making. In both instances, the cases turn on the specific facts presented, not on abstract legal concepts. More on each area of law follows. Note that we do not cover state due process claims here, but interpretations of state constitutional due process provisions are very similar.

1. PROCEDURAL DUE PROCESS

Procedural due process requires that laws be implemented pursuant to fair, uniformly applied procedures. The Supreme Court has articulated what due process means on many occasions, recognizing that its applicability is flexible and fact dependent. *See, e.g.*, Morrissey v. Brewer, 408 U.S. 471, 481 (1972). In general, once a deprivation of property is found, a court must weigh three factors: (1) the nature of the private interest affected; (2) the likelihood of erroneous deprivations of property with the procedure used and the value of any alternative procedures; and (3) the burden on the state of alternative procedures. Matthews v. Eldridge, 424 U.S. 319 (1976).

Applying the Supreme Court's three-factor test to a historic preservation law is very fact-specific. For example, the nature of the private interest affected may range from mere inconvenience of having to choose from a limited palette of exterior paint colors to the inability of replacing a historic building with one better-suited to the plaintiff's needs and economic position. Courts apply these factors very differently (or fail to mention them at all), and outcomes are unpredictable. For historic preservation laws, procedural due process has generally meant that deprivations of property may not occur unless the affected party is given notice about the application of the law, the opportunity to be heard, an explanation of the decision, uniform standards, and qualified, neutral decision-makers.

Below, we discuss procedural due process challenges against local, state, and federal historic preservation laws.

a. Local Ordinances

Local historic preservation laws, discussed further in Chapter VI, have been the target of the majority of procedural due process challenges to historic preservation laws.

Most often, plaintiffs allege that a local ordinance regulating a property owner's construction activities fails to provide adequate guidance to the local commission regarding the exercise of its powers. Other times, plaintiffs charge that the local commission's designation of their property as historic ran afoul of due process. Nearly all of these challenges have failed. For example, a 1975 Fifth Circuit case dealt with a challenge to a local ordinance that set standards over alterations and demolitions in the French Quarter of New Orleans. *See* Maher v. City of New Orleans, 516 F.2d 1051 (5th Cir. 1975), *cert. denied*, 426 U.S. 905 (1976). The court found: "To satisfy due process, guidelines to aid a commission charged with implementing a public zoning purpose need not be so rigidly drawn as to prejudge the outcome in each case, precluding reasonable administrative discretion." *Id.* at 1062. The court added that the ordinance nonetheless provided specific guidance in several ways because it: delineated the boundaries of the regulated district; defined what alterations required approval; offered tailored rules for lighting, balconies, and signs; specified qualifications and the selection process for the commission; and generally relied on the observable character of the district. *Id.* at 1062–63.

Most local historic preservation laws offer the same features used in the *Maher* case to uphold the ordinance. Accordingly, they have almost universally been sustained against due process challenges. *See, e.g.,* Burke v. City of Charleston, 893 F. Supp. 589, 611–12 (D. S.C. 1995), *rev'd on other grounds,* 139 F.3d 401 (4th Cir. 1998); Rector, Wardens, & Members of the Vestry of St. Bartholomew's Church v. City of New York, 728 F. Supp. 958, 964–65 (S.D.N.Y. 1989) (rejecting plaintiff's argument that the standards for designating landmarks and granting certificates of appropriateness were "impermissibly vague"), *aff'd* 914 F.2d 348 (2d Cir. 1990), *cert. denied,* 499 U.S. 905 (1991); Mayes v. City of Dallas, 747 F.2d 323, 325–26 (5th Cir. 1984) (citing *Maher v. City of New Orleans*).

Over the years, there have been a handful of exceptions to courts sustaining local historic preservation ordinances against due process challenges. For example, in 1990 a North Carolina state court invalidated a historic preservation ordinance that a city enacted without complying with state statutory procedures regarding property owner's rights to object to the proposed ordinance. Unruh v. City of Asheville, 388 S.E.2d 235, 237 (N.C. Ct. App. 1990). Similarly, in 1979, a Texas state court found a city's ordinance unconstitutional on due process grounds because it failed to provide a reasonable time limit on final city council action after a parcel had been listed on the agenda of a landmark commission, where listing subjected the parcel to the same restrictions as if it were already designated as a landmark. Southern Nat'l Bank of Houston v. City of Austin, 582 S.W.2d 229, 238–39 (Tex. Civ. App. 1979). In both of these examples, local governments could have survived the due process challenges if they had paid better attention to the procedures being applied. A D.C. court hearing similar facts to the Texas state court just mentioned found for the local government in part because D.C. specified a time limit for the temporary designation. Weinberg v. Barry, 604 F. Supp. 390, 398 (D.D.C. 1985) (rejecting a due process challenge to a city's temporary designation of properties being reviewed for landmark status pending a hearing). The most recent case where a court allowed a plaintiff to proceed with a due process challenge alleging a local ordinance was too vague ended well for preservationists when the court found that the words used "provide a description of the observable historic character of the districts" and were not void for vagueness. *See* Hanna v. City of Chicago, No. 06 CH 19422 (Cook County, Ill. Chancery Div. May 2, 2012).

Revocations of building permits for historic properties after property owners have commenced construction have also been subjected to procedural due process challenges. These revocations have generally been upheld, especially where property owners were given sufficient notice of the pending revocation and an opportunity to be heard. *See, e.g.,* Elkins v. District of Columbia, 527 F. Supp. 2d 36, 47–49 (D.D.C. 2007). Similarly, where a building permit was revoked after a town determined that the historic commission was legally unable to issue a certificate of appropriateness due to a procedural error, the property owners were found not to have a protectable due process property right. Achtien v. City of Deadwood, 814 F. Supp. 808, 815 (D. S.D. 1993); *see also* Bozcar v. Kingen, 6 Fed. Appx. 471 (7th Cir. 2001) (dealing with property owner's misrepresentation of plans for construction). These examples, which seem to be the most obvious deprivations of property, indicate that courts are generally willing to view local historic preservation laws in a favorable light.

b. State Statutes

There are fewer procedural due process challenges involving state statutes dealing with historic preservation, mostly because such statutes do not generally deprive individuals of property. For example, state enabling acts allow localities to create historic districts and historic preservation commissions, but these enabling acts do not impose specific duties on property owners or implicate the designation process. That said, state statutes authorizing historic districts have been upheld against challenges that they are too vague to provide property owners with sufficient information about their regulatory scope. *See*, *e.g.*, Chabad Lubavitch of Litchfield County, Inc. v. Borough of Litchfield, 853 F. Supp. 2d 214, 234–35 (D. Conn. 2012) (upholding Connecticut's historic district enabling statute as "not so subjective that a reasonable person could not ascertain what factors" would be used to grant certificates of appropriateness and "not void for vagueness due to arbitrary enforcement").

c. Federal Statutes

Various federal historic preservation laws and activities have faced, and mostly survived, procedural due process challenges. As a threshold matter, plaintiffs must direct their due process complaints against the appropriate governmental party. The federal government cannot be held responsible for burdens that are actually imposed by the states or localities. A Second Circuit case illustrates this point. Plaintiff landowners could not challenge the National Park Service for a listing on the National Register where the burdens on the landowners were imposed by a state law that automatically listed National Register properties on the state register of historic places. *See* Moody Hill Farms Ltd. P'ship v. U.S. Dep't of the Interior, 205 F.3d 554 (2d Cir. 1999).

Plaintiffs that appropriately identify the federal government as the burden-imposing entity may proceed to challenge federal entities or statutes on the merits. The National Historic Preservation Act

and National Park Service have been targets for
miscellaneous procedural due process challenges.
Regulations regarding the definition of "adverse
effect," an important term in the National Historic
Preservation Act's Section 106 process, have been
upheld against constitutional challenge because the
National Park Service clarified the term in several
publications (e.g., Bulletins, websites) beyond the
regulation. *See* Nat'l Mining Ass'n v. Slater, 167 F.
Supp. 2d 265, 295 (D.D.C. 2001), *rev'd on other
grounds*, 324 F.3d 752 (D.C. Cir. 2003). There are
fewer regulations and publications regarding
National Historic Landmark designations. Perhaps
as a result, a Virginia district court rejected the
Secretary of the Interior's designation of a site as a
National Historic Landmark because "without
published rules of procedure and substantive
criteria for qualification as a landmark, they have
been denied any meaningful opportunity for
informal response to the proposed action and the
Court has been precluded from meaningful review of
the Secretary's decisions." Historic Green Springs,
Inc. v. Bergland, 497 F. Supp. 839, 854–55 (E.D. Va.
1980). That court added that the criteria were
"vague and open-ended" and did not limit the
Secretary's discretion, and that people affected by
landmark designation were informed of the criteria
too late in the process. *Id.* at 855.

Other historic preservation laws mentioned in
this book have also survived procedural due process
challenges. Some cases have involved federal agency
compliance with the National Environmental Policy
Act, discussed in Chapter IV, and its required

review of federal agency effects on historic properties. *See, e.g.*, City of Ridgeland v. Nat'l Park Serv., 253 F. Supp. 2d 888, 914–15 (S.D. Miss. 2002) (upholding the National Park Service's compliance procedures). As another example, the Tenth Circuit rejected a plaintiff's claim that the Native American Graves Protection and Repatriation Act (NAGPRA) was void for vagueness where an expert in Native American artifacts claimed that NAGPRA did not provide fair notice of the prohibited activities. United States v. Corrow, 119 F.3d 796, 803 (10th Cir. 1997). NAGPRA is discussed in much greater detail in Chapter XII.

2. SUBSTANTIVE DUE PROCESS

Substantive due process rights ensure that government does not deprive an individual of property by actions that shock the conscience, demonstrate bad faith, infringe on a fundamental liberty, or are arbitrary, egregious, or outrageous. Honest mistakes, negligence, and inadvertent errors do not typically give rise to successful due process challenges. *See, e.g.*, Elkins v. District of Columbia, 690 F.3d 554, 562 (D.C. Cir. 2012) (rejecting a property owner's substantive due process claim because the search of her home and revocation of a building permit "at most show[ed] agency confusion, not. . . grave unfairness"). These standards are very subjective, and have been criticized by jurists and scholars alike.

The subjectivity of substantive due process standards may lead one to believe that outcomes from substantive due process challenges to historic preservation laws have been all over the map. However, our review of the limited number of such cases suggests that plaintiffs tend to lose. Below, we briefly describe a few challenges to local preservation laws and mention a federal statute challenged for substantive due process violations.

A handful of cases—all resolved in favor of the locality—have involved substantive due process challenges to local preservation ordinances. A property owner's mere inability to develop her property as she sees fit will not substantiate a substantive due process allegation. *See* Van Horn v. Town of Castine, 167 F. Supp. 2d 103, 106–07 (D. Me. 2001). Nor will a locality's reversal of an issuance of a building permit when the reason for revocation was justified by a procedural error in the historic commission's issuance of a certificate of appropriateness. Achtien v. City of Deadwood, 814 F. Supp. 808, 816 (D. S.D. 1993). There have been other cases upholding localities' regulation of private property pursuant to historic preservation ordinances. *See, e.g.*, First Nat'l Bank of Highland Park v. Vill. of Schaumburg, No. 85 C2427, 1987 WL 17468, at *5 (N.D. Ill. 1987) (noting that the locality took several factors into account when making its decision, including compatibility with neighborhood uses and architectural styles).

We could not find a case where the designation of a property was struck down for violating substantive due process because governments almost always designate properties through the thorough analysis described in Chapter II and thus have legitimate and rational reasons for designating particular properties. Nonetheless, several property owners have advanced such arguments. *See, e.g.,* Nw. U. v. City of Evanston, No. 00 C7309, 2002 WL 31027981, at *9 (N.D. Ill. Sept. 11, 2002) (rejecting a university's allegation that a local historic designation was "invidious or irrational because it was designed to extort funds from the University"); Sameric Corp. of Del., Inc. v. City of Philadelphia, 142 F.3d 582, 594–96 (3rd Cir. 1998) (finding no improper motive, arbitrariness, or irrationality in the designation of a historic theater).

We could only locate one substantive due process challenge of a federal preservation statute mentioned in this book. The Abandoned Shipwreck Act, discussed in Chapter XI, was upheld against a substantive due process challenge based on the theory that its application to "embedded" shipwrecks is not rationally related to its purpose. Zych v. Unidentified, Wrecked, and Abandoned Vessel, Believed to be SB Seabird, 811 F. Supp. 1300, 1316–17 (N.D. Ill. 1992).

We conclude with some speculation about the reason there are so few cases involving substantive due process. It may be that plaintiffs recognize they are unlikely to win because the extreme governmental behavior that would make their challenge successful is so rare. It may also be that substantive due process jurisprudence is so subjective that attorneys are not advising their clients to litigate in that arena. Fundamentally, the broad social acceptance of reasonable preservation regulation of private property as a legitimate power of government precludes any judicial conclusion that preservation exceeds the police power or violates substantive due process.

CHAPTER 8

TAKINGS

This Chapter deals with the federal constitutional constraints on governmental appropriations of private property—more commonly known as "takings." The Fifth Amendment states that in no case "shall private property be taken for public use, without just compensation." U.S. CONST. amend. V. Takings clause caselaw has evolved, and courts now recognize that government may take private property in three ways: by physically appropriating it (either by eminent domain or otherwise); by regulating it in certain problematic ways; or by exacting concessions from the property owner before she is able to develop her property in her preferred manner. This Chapter considers how all three types of takings might arise for private owners of historic properties.

No matter the type of taking, just compensation must be provided to aggrieved property owners. Just compensation typically takes the form of fair market value, calculated through a comparable sales approach, income approach (particularly for commercial properties), or cost approach. Some jurisdictions require extra compensation for the taking of homes. We do not fully consider in this Chapter all of the possible ways to calculate just compensation.

It is widely accepted that the constraints of the takings clause apply not only to the federal government, but to the actions of the states, and by extension localities. This Chapter does not consider state constitutional equivalents to the federal takings clause, but many state constitutions provide similar protection from government takings, which are often analyzed using legal principles similar to the ones discussed below.

A. PHYSICAL TAKINGS

Government may physically appropriate historic properties in two ways. First, government may take over ownership of private property entirely through formal condemnation proceedings pursuant to government's power of "eminent domain." This term refers to the power of the sovereign to take private property for public use, even if the owner objects; it is limited by the requirement that government pay just compensation. Litigation arising over an exercise of eminent domain usually focuses on the question of whether the purpose of the government's condemnation falls within the meaning of "public use."

Second, government may occupy, or may allow a third party to occupy, some or all of a parcel of private property, without instituting formal condemnation proceedings. Property owners seeking compensation from the government for this type of intrusion would have to file an inverse condemnation action, claiming that a taking for which compensation is required had occurred. Usually, physical takings cases not involving an exercise of eminent domain focus on whether the occupation constituted a taking. Even though the public use requirement is generally not central to litigation, it still serves as an important limitation: if the physical occupation does not satisfy some public use, government may not engage in the taking at all.

We analyze relevant legal precedent for both types of physical appropriations and then highlight the applicability of this precedent to historic properties.

1.   EMINENT DOMAIN

Eminent domain refers to the power of government to condemn private property for public use. The federal government—including Congress as well as duly authorized administrative agencies, officials, and commissions—may condemn land pursuant to its inherent powers of eminent domain. Through statutes and constitutions, state legislatures have also claimed the power of eminent domain. States' eminent domain powers may be delegated to their political subdivisions—counties, cities, regional bodies, and special-purpose governments—and to private entities, such as railroads and utilities. State statutes regulate the exercise of eminent domain, for example, by requiring the entity exercising the power to make certain findings.

We begin by discussing the bases for federal judicial review of federal and state exercises of eminent domain, in light of constraints of the U.S. Constitution. We then turn to the key issue in most federal eminent domain cases: the interpretation of the public use requirement. Finally, we highlight the ways in which eminent domain and historic preservation intersect.

a. Bases for Federal Judicial Review

The bases for federal judicial review of federal and state exercises of eminent domain come from two different strands of judicial thought.

With respect to the federal government, the power of eminent domain was originally understood to be an inseparable incident of sovereignty. Accordingly, the U.S. Constitution does not expressly grant the power of eminent domain to Congress or to the executive branch. It does, however, anticipate the federal exercise of such power in the takings clause of the Fifth Amendment. In 1875, in the case of *Kohl v. United States*, 91 U.S. 367 (1875), the Supreme Court confirmed that this power was within federal authority.

In 1888, Congress passed the Condemnation Act, which codified some aspects of the *Kohl* decision. It states:

An officer of the Federal Government authorized to acquire real estate for the erection of a public building or for other public uses may acquire the real estate for the Government by condemnation, under judicial process, when the officer believes that it is necessary or advantageous to the Government to do so.

40 U.S.C. § 3113. The "other public uses" language in the Condemnation Act has been broadly interpreted to cover a range of activities. The Supreme Court has upheld federal exercises of eminent domain pursuant to the Condemnation Act, even against the interests of states and localities. *See, e.g.*, Chappell v. United States, 160 U.S. 499 (1896) (holding that the federal government is not barred from condemning land important to the state); United States v. Carmack, 329 U.S. 230 (1946) (authorizing the federal government to condemn land held by the city for public purposes such as a park, courthouse, city hall, and public library).

After *Kohl*, plaintiffs aggrieved by an exercise of federal eminent domain could sue in federal court. But plaintiffs aggrieved by an exercise of eminent domain from a state government or its political subdivisions had to wait a few more years before the Supreme Court confirmed their right to sue. The Fifth Amendment does not say that the protections of the takings clause apply to the states, and in 1833, a unanimous Supreme Court declined the opportunity to read this into the takings clause. *See* Barron v. Mayor of Baltimore, 32 U.S. 243 (1833).

The ratification of the Fourteenth Amendment in 1866, however, marked a turning point. Section 1 of that Amendment provides in relevant part, "nor shall any State deprive any person of life, liberty, or property, without due process of law." U.S. CONST. amend. XIV. In 1897, the Supreme Court incorporated the takings clause into the due process requirement of the Fourteenth Amendment, making the takings clause applicable to state actions as well as federal actions. *See* Chicago, Burlington & Quincy R.R. Co. v. City of Chicago, 166 U.S. 226, 241 (1897).

b. The Interpretation of the Public Use Clause

The key legal issue in the eminent domain cases reviewed by federal courts is whether there is a "public use" justifying the condemnation. Early on, courts interpreted the public use requirement narrowly, requiring public ownership of, or public access to, the condemned property. Valid public uses under this narrow view included public buildings, roads, bridges, and parks. But what about other activities which are not so obviously public uses? Federal courts have evolved to adopt a broader view of the public use requirement, allowing exercises of eminent domain that achieve a public benefit, without necessarily granting public use or access. This evolution is illustrated by a few key cases.

Discussion of an 1896 Supreme Court case regarding Congress's exercise of eminent domain over a portion of Gettysburg Battlefield is essential: not only does it reveal a modest departure from the requirement of public use or access, but its central substantive issue is historic preservation. *See* United States v. Gettysburg Elec. Ry. Co., 160 U.S. 668 (1896). Because of *Kohl*, decided in 1875, Congress's authority to exercise eminent domain was not in question by the time the Supreme Court was hearing *Gettysburg Railway*. Instead, the issue in this case was whether historic preservation constituted a public purpose justifying the use of eminent domain pursuant to the Condemnation Act, codified at 40 U.S.C. § 3113, or the Fifth Amendment of the U.S. Constitution. Congress had authorized $75,000 to be spent "[f]or the purpose of preserving the lines of battle at Gettysburg, Pa." and for the installation of tablets, improvement of battlefield avenues, and study of the battlefield site. 160 U.S. at 668. The Secretary of War appointed a commission to carry out these tasks, and the commission condemned property, including property of the plaintiff, Gettysburg Electric Railway Company. Note that at the time of the condemnation in 1893, there were no legal assurances that the site would be open to the public. (Two years later, however, Congress passed legislation to designate the site as a national battlefield park. *See* Ch. 80, 53d Cong., Sess. III, 28 Stat. 651 (Feb. 11, 1895).)

The Supreme Court identified the "really important question" in this case to be whether the preservation of Gettysburg constituted a public use. *Id.* at 679. The Supreme Court held that historic preservation was indeed a public use under both the Condemnation Act and the U.S. Constitution. It further explained:

> The battle of Gettysburg was one of the great battles of the world. The numbers contained in the opposing armies were great; the sacrifice of life was dreadful; while the bravery, and, indeed, heroism, displayed by both the

contending forces, rank with the highest exhibition of those qualities ever made by man. The importance of the issue involved in the contest of which this great battle was a part cannot be overestimated. The existence of the government itself, and the perpetuity of our institutions, depended upon the result. Valuable lessons in the art of war can now be learned from an examination of this great battlefield, in connection with the history of the events which there took place. . . . Such a use seems necessarily not only a public use, but one so closely connected with the welfare of the republic itself as to be within the powers granted congress by the constitution for the purpose of protecting and preserving the whole country. . . . [T]he sacrifices are rendered more obvious and more easily appreciated when such a battlefield is preserved by the government at the public expense.

Id. at 681–83. In *Gettysburg Railway*, the preservation purpose was enough to sustain the finding of public use. Of course, the Court may have assumed some future physical use/occupation by the public: what significance are monuments, unless they can be viewed by the public? But the essence of the lofty language used by the Court—reflecting the patriotic rationale for preservation discussed in Chapter I—was that the preservation aim could itself sustain the exercise of eminent domain.

Gettysburg Railway modestly expanded the interpretation of public use. Nearly six decades later, *Berman v. Parker*, 348 U.S. 26 (1954) expanded it much further. In that case, the Supreme Court considered Congressional authorization granted to a District of Columbia redevelopment agency to condemn and assemble land "for the redevelopment of blighted territory. . . and the prevention, reduction, or elimination of blighting factors or causes of blight." *Id.* at 29–30 (internal quotation marks omitted). Congress allowed the agency to transfer acquired property either to public agencies for "such public purposes as streets, utilities, recreational facilities, and schools" and to lease or sell the remainder to a private redevelopment organization. *Id.* at 30. A property owner whose department store—not itself blight—was slated for condemnation challenged this grant of authority, and its applicability to the specific condemnation, as unconstitutional.

Upon review, the Supreme Court determined that the elimination of blight was a valid "public purpose"—a concept that went beyond what had previously been deemed a public use. It linked this concept to the notion of "public welfare," which could justify an exercise of the police power, and said that legislative declarations of public purpose deserve judicial deference. The Court further opined:

> The concept of the public welfare is broad and inclusive. The values it represents are spiritual as well as physical, aesthetic as well as monetary. It is within the power of the legislature to determine that the community should be beautiful as well as healthy, spacious

as well as clean, well-balanced as well as
carefully patrolled. . . . If those who govern the
District of Columbia decide that the Nation's
Capital should be beautiful as well as sanitary,
there is nothing in the Fifth Amendment that
stands in the way.

Id. at 33. With this language, *Berman* provided a
legal justification for state and local governments
engaging in large-scale urban renewal pursuant to
their police powers (and in turn, large-scale
exercises of eminent domain).

The Supreme Court expanded upon *Berman* with
the controversial *Kelo v. City of New London*
decision. 545 U.S. 469 (2005). Owners of property
condemned by a city economic development
corporation were challenging the exercise of
eminent domain by claiming that the purpose for
which their property was taken—economic
revitalization—was not a public use. Dozens of
homes had been condemned so that the economic
development corporation could realize its plans for
creating a mixed use neighborhood with shops,
parking, office, and recreational uses—primarily
privately owned. Like the department store in
Berman, the homes were not considered to be
blighted, even though the city in which they were
located was economically depressed. Again, here,
the Court favored a broad reading of the public use
requirement. The Court found the taking to be part
of a "carefully considered development plan" that
was not adopted to benefit one particular party. *Id.*
at 478 (internal quotation marks omitted). The

economic revitalization plan was enough of a public purpose to justify the economic development corporation's exercise of eminent domain. The *Kelo* decision reaffirmed the notion in *Berman* that an action with a "public purpose" qualified as a "public use," and that courts should defer to the legislature's determination of a public purpose.

Many lower federal court decisions have also addressed the public use requirement of the takings clause, but there is not enough space to consider them all here.

c. Application to Historic Preservation

So what does this eminent domain caselaw mean for historic preservation? The expansiveness of the interpretation of the public use clause should cause some concern among preservationists because it could be used to justify exercises of eminent domain that destroy historic buildings. With the *Kelo* decision, the Supreme Court confirmed that entire neighborhoods may be razed to make way for modern development, as long as the relevant legislature determines that such development has a public purpose. *See* Kelo v. City of New London, 545 U.S. 469 (2005). Moreover, *Kelo* confirmed that federal courts will defer to legislative determinations of what constitutes a public purpose. If historically significant resources are not valued by the majority in a community, then the legislature (presumably representing the majority) may be unwilling to protect such resources against exercises of eminent domain which might achieve some other purpose (such as economic development) valued by the community. Of course, historic preservation statutes or ordinances might well restrict or condition the use of eminent domain before historic properties are demolished.

On the other hand, eminent domain caselaw can also be used to promote historic preservation, both directly and indirectly. One case illustrating the way eminent domain may directly benefit historic preservation is *Gettysburg Railway*. *See* United States v. Gettysburg Elec. Ry. Co., 160 U.S. 668 (1896). In that case, land was taken from private property owners so that it could be adequately preserved for future generations to study and visit. The Supreme Court confirmed that preservation itself is a public use that can justify the exercise of eminent domain. Governments at all levels thus have the power to use eminent domain to assume ownership of historically significant properties that are neglected or compromised by private property owners. Of course, political pressures and limited public financial resources may inhibit the frequent exercise of eminent domain for preservation purposes.

Another eminent domain case that has had a surprising effect on preservation law is *Berman v. Parker*. 348 U.S. 26 (1954). The immediate effect of *Berman* was to allow the condemnation and razing of existing stores and homes to make way for an urban renewal project. In that sense, the case enabled the large-scale destruction of buildings (some of them likely historic)—the antithesis of historic preservation. *Berman*, however, has impacted the way courts view the exercise of the police power in a way that has bolstered historic preservation. One of the purposes of the urban renewal project in *Berman* was to beautify the neighborhood. The Supreme Court explicitly identified aesthetic goals as valid justification for a state's (in that case, the District of Columbia's) exercise of its police power. Historic preservation advocates have used this aspect of *Berman* as legal justification for local preservation ordinances and the expansion of historic district and individual property designations.

2. PHYSICAL TAKINGS NOT INVOLVING EMINENT DOMAIN

Property taken through eminent domain is taken physically; the property undergoes a formal process by which it passes into public ownership. There are other circumstances, however, where government may physically take property without invoking eminent domain. To receive compensation in such circumstances, the property owner must file an inverse condemnation action claiming that a taking occurred. The key issue in physical takings cases not involving eminent domain is usually whether the taking occurred. However, the other requirements of the takings clause (namely that the taking be for a public use, and that the property owner be justly compensated) still apply.

The controlling Supreme Court precedent for physical takings not involving eminent domain is

Loretto v. Teleprompter Manhattan CATV Corp, 458
U.S. 419 (1982). In *Loretto*, the physical invasion
was of a very minor character: a cable less than one
half inch in diameter, two silver boxes, two
directional taps, and necessary bolts and screws to
attach the equipment to the building of the
aggrieved property owner. *Id.* at 422. This
equipment was installed by a cable company that
had received authorization from the State of New
York pursuant to a statute preventing property
owners from interfering with such installations. *Id.*
at 423. The Supreme Court held that even this
minimal permanent physical occupation could
constitute a taking: "a permanent physical
occupation authorized by government is a taking
without regard to the public interests that it may
serve." *Id.* at 426. Thus, physical occupations that
give rise to takings may either be imposed by
government or by private parties with governmental
authorization to do so. An aggrieved property owner,
therefore, may bring a takings claim against a
private party acting as a government agent.

Loretto applies to historic properties in the same
way it applies to other properties. One example of a
federal court case invoking *Loretto* and applying it
to historic buildings took place in Manhattan. *See*
Board of Managers of Soho Int'l Arts Condo. v. City
of New York, 2004 WL 1982520, at *4 (S.D.N.Y.
2004). Here, the controversy revolved around a
sculpture that was attached to the façade of a
historic building. The sculpture was owned by one
party, but the historic building to which it was
attached was owned by other parties. The owners of

the historic building sought to remove the artwork, but the local historic commission denied the request for removal as being incompatible with the historic nature of the building, because the artwork had acquired special significance in the years since its installation. Citing *Loretto*, the court found that the commission's denial amounted to a permanent physical occupation—a taking from the property owner—because it allowed a third party (the owner of the sculpture) to permanently occupy part of the building. *Id.* at *12. This case illustrates one way in which, without using eminent domain, a government action regarding a historic property could amount to a physical taking.

B.   REGULATORY TAKINGS

In addition to recognizing physical takings (through eminent domain or otherwise), courts have recognized regulatory takings. Regulatory takings involve a public decision or rule which regulates a property in a way that deprives the owner of some of the hallmarks of ownership to such an extent that the regulation can be said to have effected a taking. Regulatory takings do not result in transfers of ownership (as is the case with eminent domain). Rather, they infringe on the property owner's rights to use, transfer, or exclude in the way the property owner would prefer.

The Supreme Court first recognized regulatory takings in 1922, with *Pennsylvania Coal Co. v. Mahon*, 260 U.S. 393 (1922). In that case, the Court said that "while property may be regulated to a certain extent, if regulation goes too far it will be recognized as a taking." *Id.* at 415. Lower courts often had difficulty determining when a regulation went "too far."

Despite subsequent Supreme Court decisions, discussed below, it remains difficult to determine when a regulatory taking has occurred. In one scenario, a taking may occur when the property's value has not been entirely diminished; that is, when there is still some value remaining. Federal courts, in such situations, will typically weigh what are known as the *Penn Central* factors to determine if a taking has occurred. The second scenario occurs when a property's value has been diminished entirely, in which case federal courts will (with few exceptions) find a "total taking."

1.   PARTIAL TAKINGS

The most important case in regulatory takings jurisprudence, *Penn Central Transportation Co. v. City of New York*, 438 U.S. 104 (1978), happens to focus on historic preservation. The owner of a landmarked building—Grand Central Terminal in Manhattan—hoped to construct a 55-story office tower atop the Terminal. The local historic preservation commission determined that the tower, as designed, was incompatible with the historic features of the Terminal and thus could not be built. The property owner challenged this determination as an unconstitutional regulatory taking.

The Supreme Court identified three relevant factors, weighing them to determine that no taking had occurred. The factors are: (1) the character of the government action; (2) the economic impact of the regulation on the claimant; and (3) "the extent to which the regulation has interfered with distinct investment-backed expectations," *id.* at 124. Importantly, the Court found that the local preservation ordinance did not unfairly burden the Terminal's owner. Moreover, because the owners could still use the property as a railroad terminal— its primary use for the preceding sixty-five years— the character of the government action was not so invasive, nor did it so severely diminish the reasonable investment backed expectations of the claimant, that a taking had occurred.

The facts, holding, and impact of *Penn Central* are more involved and far-reaching than this brief description suggests. No court has declared that a designation of a historic resource constitutes a taking, and only two decisions (one state, one federal—both in Maryland) have found that a preservation restriction is a taking. *See* Keeler v. Mayor of Cumberland, 940 F. Supp. 879 (D. Md. 1996); Broadview Apartments Co. v. Comm'n for Historical & Architectural Pres., 433 A.2d 1214 (Md. Ct. Spec. App. 1981). We focus below on the three-factor balancing test used in all regulatory takings cases where it is alleged that the regulation diminished some portion of the property's value.

a. Character of the Government Action

The first *Penn Central* factor is the nature and purpose of the government action being challenged as a regulatory taking. The more broadly a regulation applies, the less likely it is to be considered to be a taking. Broad applicability may be shown if the action is part of a generally applicable regulatory scheme, if decisions are made in a consistent manner, and/or if a "reciprocity of advantage" (that is, a mutual benefit) among burdened parties exists. Similarly, the less invasive the regulation, the less likely it is to be called a taking. If the burden on the individual is small compared to the benefit to the public, this *Penn Central* factor may be weighed in favor of the government. Conversely, an otherwise constitutional, generally applicable regulation could be found to be taking if it is "unduly oppressive" to the property owner. *See* Goldblatt v. Town of Hempstead, 369 U.S. 590 (1962) (upholding a town action to enjoin the operation of a sand and gravel pit while requiring the owners of the pit to obtain the appropriate permit).

In *Penn Central*, the Supreme Court analyzed the government action at issue: the decision by the New York City Landmarks Preservation Commission to deny a certificate of appropriateness to the owner of Grand Central Terminal for its proposed rehabilitation. Penn Central Transportation Co. v. City of New York, 438 U.S. 104 (1978). The Court found that the historic preservation scheme applied broadly and was not applied to the property owner in an inconsistent manner. *Id.* at 132. The Court thus wholly rejected the property owner's contention that the law was "inherently incapable of producing the fair and equitable distribution of benefits and burdens of governmental action which is characteristic of zoning laws and historic-district legislation." *Id.* at 133. Moreover, the Court found that the property owners gained a reciprocity of advantage by participating in the regulatory scheme:

> Unless we are to reject the judgment of the New York City Council that the preservation of landmarks benefits all New York citizens and all structures, both economically and by improving the quality of life in the city as a whole—which we are unwilling to do—we cannot conclude that the owners of the Terminal have in no sense been benefited by the Landmarks Law.

Id. at 134–35. Note that the Court also relied upon the declaration of legislative body (the city council) that preservation was in the public interest.

Many local historic preservation ordinances contain declarations that preservation is in the public interest, are applied like the New York City ordinance was applied, and impose similar burdens (and benefits) on property owners. As a result, the *Penn Central* Court's analysis of the character of the government action has helped to buttress local historic preservation ordinances against takings challenges by declaring that preservation ordinances with a legitimate, stated public purpose cannot easily be declared unconstitutional.

b. Economic Impact on the Claimant

The economic impact on the claimant is the next *Penn Central* factor. A court must determine whether the economic impact on the property is so negative and burdensome that a taking has occurred. The value of the property before and after the regulation is typically compared, and may be measured in a variety of ways, such as the fair market value of the property or a value related to commercial productivity (e.g., capitalization of income). The more dramatic the diminution of value, the more likely it is that a taking will be found. As discussed in the next section, if the property's value has been reduced to nothing, then a slightly different analysis will be used.

In analyzing this second factor, the *Penn Central* Court reviewed both the present use of the Terminal as built and the future use of the undeveloped air rights above the Terminal. Regarding the present use, the Court noted that the property owner, Penn Central Transportation Company, could continue to use the building as a railway terminal. Penn Central Transportation Co. v. City of New York, 438 U.S. 104, 136 (1978). Accordingly, the economic impact on the property owner's present use was negligible. Regarding the air rights, the Court said that the property owner "exaggerate[s] the effect of the law on their ability to make use of the air rights above the Terminal in two respects." *Id.* at 136. First, the property owner was not "prohibited from occupying *any* portion of the airspace above the Terminal," *id.* at 136; the commission had only disapproved of this particular proposal. Second, the property owner had the ability to transfer the development potential of the air rights to several other property owners near the Terminal under the city's transferable development rights scheme. This ability to transfer the development rights could help "mitigate whatever financial burdens the law has imposed on appellants and, for that reason, are to be taken into account in considering the impact of regulation." *Id.* at 137.

As was the case with its analysis of the first *Penn Central* factor, the Supreme Court dealt with the economic impact factor in a way that has benefitted governments defending historic preservation ordinances from takings challenges. According to its logic, a decision that prohibits a property owner from making alterations to a historic property does not necessarily impose an undue economic impact when the decision allows the owner to retain her current use of the property. The reason is that there is still some value remaining in the property which may include, according to *Penn Central*, more than just the value of the current use of the building, but perhaps the potential value of future development or future rights as well.

c. Reasonable Investment-Backed Expectations

Closely related to the second *Penn Central* factor is the third factor: whether the reasonable investment-backed expectations of the property owner were diminished so much that a taking could be said to have occurred. Investment-backed expectations are the expectations that the property owner had when she acquired the property, primarily with respect to the size of her possible return on investment. A court may consider whether a property owner bringing a takings claim had notice of the possibility that her property would be affected by the regulation when she acquired the property. One aspect of notice is whether the regulation was in effect when the acquisition occurred. A court may also consider whether the owner purchased the property instead of acquiring it through other means (such as inheritance), which may indicate that the owner had no particular investment-backed expectations.

In *Penn Central*, the Supreme Court reviewed how the property owner, Penn Central Transportation Company, viewed the Terminal upon its acquisition. The property had been used as a railroad terminal (with office space and concessions) for sixty-five years, and the Court said that the decision of the historic preservation commission to reject a dramatic change to its façade "does not interfere with what must be regarded as Penn Central's primary expectation concerning the use of the parcel." *Id.* at 136. Rather, the Court suggested, the commission's decision helped to ensure that the property could continue to be put to the use the property owners had come to expect. *Id.*

The question of reasonable investment-backed expectations has led a complicated life after *Penn Central*, primarily because many have questioned why the expectations of the property owner should matter. Some have also questioned the difficulties in accurately evaluating the dollar value of the expectations. Why, for example, should it matter that a regulation passed *after* a property owner acquired her property? Similarly, why should someone who came to acquire a parcel by inheritance be treated differently (viewed as having a minimal investment-backed expectation in the property) than someone who came to acquire a parcel by purchase? Finally, what about the fact that some of the most prized possessions people have are heirlooms, which they inherited—how should property law value that subjective connection?

Courts considering this third *Penn Central* factor in historic preservation cases have often weighed in favor of the government. For example, a D.C. Circuit case determined that no taking had occurred in a situation in which a property owner was aware of federal and local landmark laws that might have affected its ability to redevelop the property, concluding that the owner had no reasonable expectation to redevelop it in a way that would maximize profit. District Intown Props. Ltd. P'ship v. District of Columbia, 198 F.3d 874, 883–84 (D.C. Cir. 1999), *cert. denied*, 531 U.S. 812 (2000).

d. Weighing the Three Factors

The Supreme Court gave little guidance in *Penn Central* as to how to weigh these factors and did not indicate which factor should take priority. Lacking direction from the Court, lower courts have used their judgment in applying the factors. While a few academic commentators have criticized the vagueness of *Penn Central*, and some cases have tried to weaken its reach, it remains as the primary precedent for regulatory takings cases involving less than one hundred percent diminution of value.

2. TOTAL TAKINGS

When a government action denies all economically beneficial or productive use of property, it is considered to be a total taking requiring just compensation, unless background principles of nuisance and property law would prohibit the activities that are proscribed by the regulation. The key Supreme Court decision on point is *Lucas v. South Carolina Coastal Council*, 505 U.S. 1003 (1992). An owner of two oceanfront lots brought a takings challenge against a state beachfront management law that prohibited him from building on those lots. *Id.* at 1007. In that case, both parties stipulated that under the state law, the lots lacked any value. The Supreme Court noted that the state's beachfront management scheme was broadly applicable, and that it applied to Lucas's parcel in a manner consistent with other applications of the statute. Nonetheless, the Court found that because the property owner lost all economically beneficial use of the property, he had suffered a taking. *Id.* at 1019.

Importantly, the Court added that a taking would not be declared if the regulation simply prohibited activities that the property owner would not have been able to engage in under "background principles of nuisance and property law." *Id.* at 1030. To determine whether this exception to the *Lucas* rule prevented the declaration of a taking, a court must examine:

> the degree of harm to public lands and resources, or adjacent private property, posed by the claimant's proposed activities, the social value of the claimant's activities and their suitability to the locality in question, and the relative ease with which the alleged harm can be avoided through measures taken by the claimant and the government (or adjacent private landowners) alike.

Id. at 1030–31. If a property owner or nearby property owners has engaged in a particular activity for some time, this activity is less likely to be prohibited by the common law.

The focus on total takings in *Lucas* raised the stakes for plaintiffs to appropriately identify the scope of relevant parcel—the "denominator" from which something has been taken. A well-defined denominator can help the property owner claim that one hundred percent of the property was taken by a government action. A parcel that is functionally coherent, is treated as a single unit, and was acquired at the same time will be considered to be a single "denominator" for the purposes of takings analysis. More difficult are factual scenarios involving a parcel with multiple uses, multiple parcels treated somewhat differently, or parcels acquired at different times.

One lower court case involving historic preservation which grappled with the denominator question is *District Intown*. District Intown Props. Ltd. P'ship v. District of Columbia, 198 F.3d 874, 883–84 (D.C. Cir. 1999), *cert. denied*, 531 U.S. 812 (2000). Here, the owner had subdivided a large parcel eligible for historic designation into nine lots, asked for the right to develop townhouses on eight of the nine lots, and sued alleging a taking when it was denied the ability to do so by a local preservation commission. The appellate court determined that subdivision was not determinative, and upheld the district court's use of the following factors to identify the relevant parcel: "the degree of contiguity, the dates of acquisition, the extent to which the parcel has been treated as a single unit, and the extent to which the restricted lots benefit the unregulated lot." *Id.* at 880. In applying these factors, the appellate court found that all nine lots should be treated as one parcel for the purpose of takings analysis because the property owners had treated it as a single, indivisible property for over twenty-five years and because the lawn lots were not managed separately. *Id.*

Delving further into the *District Intown* decision reveals why *Lucas* is not often applicable in takings cases involving historic preservation regulations. After the court determined that the relevant "parcel" was all nine recently subdivided parcels, it reviewed whether the property was rendered valueless. It determined that, even if the lots were viewed as separate parcels, the property owner had not presented evidence showing that the properties had been rendered valueless by the local historic commission's denial of the application to build townhomes on eight of the parcels. *Id.* Because the owner had not carried its burden of showing that the properties were rendered valueless, *Lucas* was inapplicable.

In reality, historic preservation regulations almost never rob a property of all of its economically beneficial use. *See* J. Peter Byrne, *Regulatory Takings Challenges to Historic Preservation Laws After Penn Central*, 15 Fordham Envt'l L. Rev. 313 (2004). A designation, for example, usually imposes no direct legal obligations, beyond triggering affirmative maintenance in a few jurisdictions, or, more commonly, requiring review by a local board if the property owner wishes to make changes. Furthermore, local historic ordinances might establish a board that reviews proposed changes to historic structures or consults with the local legislative body on matters of policy, but grant the board no power to condemn a property that simply maintains its existing use and physical features. State and federal laws may also require that property owners consider alternatives to proposed courses of action which would be less burdensome on historic resources without requiring that nothing be done; even "no-build" alternatives allow for the continued use of the historic resource as it had been used in the past.

C. EXACTIONS

When a developer seeks to change the use of, or build upon, a parcel of land, government may seek an "exaction" from her in exchange for public approvals of her proposal. These exactions may take several forms, including: dedications of off-site or on-site land for public uses such as walkways or parkland; incorporation of certain uses, such as affordable housing or day care centers; or payment of "impact fees" to offset the costs of the development on public services. The law treats monetary exactions the same way as physical exactions. *See* Koontz v. St. Johns River Mgmt. Dist., 133 S.Ct. 2586, 2601–03 (2013).

Public officials may see the redevelopment of historic sites, or vacant lots within historic districts, as attractive candidates for exactions because such redevelopments tend to require multiple public approvals. Many developers are willing to tender an exaction to smooth the development process and achieve their desired results. A regulator also could extract some commitment to preservation or restoration, perhaps an easement, as a condition for a permit on a property not designated.

Other developers, however, may challenge an exaction perceived as unfair by invoking the takings clause of the Fifth Amendment. They might argue that the exaction lacks a public use or that they were not justly compensated when government imposed the exaction. Federal caselaw offers developers facing exactions two additional arguments not generally available for regulatory takings: (1) there is no "essential nexus" between the exaction and a legitimate state interest; and (2) the exaction is not "roughly proportional" to the additional costs created by the development. We now turn to those arguments, which apply equally to historic and nonhistoric properties.

1.   ESSENTIAL NEXUS

An exaction may be declared to be an unconstitutional taking of property when the conditions imposed by the exaction do not have an "essential nexus" with a legitimate government purpose. The Supreme Court set forth this rule in *Nollan v. California Coastal Commission*, 483 U.S. 825 (1987). In that case, owners of beachfront property who wanted to build a home appealed to a state commission for approval of their plans. The commission approved the plans subject to a condition requiring a lateral easement that would allow the public to walk along the beachfront portion of their property. *Id.* at 828. The commission's primary concern with respect to the Nollan's property was the fact that the proposed house interfered with "visual access" to the beach and created a "psychological barrier" to public access. *Id.* at 838. The Nollans appealed this conditional approval all the way to the Supreme Court.

The Court sided with the property owners, asserting that the condition must "further the end advanced as the justification for the prohibition" and calling this relationship an "essential nexus." *Id.* at 837. In this case, the Court said:

It is quite impossible to understand how a requirement that people already on the public beaches be able to walk across the Nollans' property reduces any obstacles to viewing the beach created by the new house. It is also impossible to understand how it lowers any "psychological barrier" to using the public beaches, or how it helps to remedy any additional congestion on them caused by construction of the Nollans' new house.

Id. at 838–39. The Court added that if the state commission had simply required the property owners to tender the easement, rather than conditioning the easement on an approval, there would certainly have been a taking. *Id.* at 831. The Court declined to treat the same action differently just because it was couched as a condition instead of a taking.

Furthermore, whether a condition is combined with a permit approval or a permit denial, the law will treat the decision in the same way. The Supreme Court has clarified that *Nollan* applies equally to government's conditional approvals of permits and to permit denials when an applicant refuses to comply with a condition. *See* Koontz v. St. Johns River Mgmt. Dist., 133 S.Ct. 2586, 2597 (2013) (analyzing a water management district's denial of a permit to a property owner who refused to yield to a condition that he surrender an interest in the land to the district). This clarification is significant because it means that governments may not avoid constitutional scrutiny by denying a permit to a property owner just to hold out for a concession that they otherwise may have imposed as a condition for permit approval.

2.   ROUGHLY PROPORTIONAL

The second exaction-specific Supreme Court rule worth noting is the "rough proportionality" rule from *Dolan v. City of Tigard*, 512 U.S. 374 (1994): an exaction must be "related both in nature and extent to the impact of the proposed development." *Id.* at 391. In that case, a property owner wanted to expand her store and pave a parking lot. In exchange for a building permit, the local government requested dedication of a creekside greenway for flood control purposes and a public pathway for pedestrians and bicyclists. In making these requests, the locality was acting in accordance with city planning documents, which identified traffic congestion and flooding to be problematic urban conditions. *Id.* at 378. The Court first found there to be an "essential nexus" under *Nollan*, because the requested dedications furthered the legitimate public purposes of reducing traffic and preventing flooding established in the city's plans. *Id.* at 386–88; *see also* Nollan v. California Coastal Comm'n, 483 U.S. 825 (1987) (explaining the essential nexus requirement).

Expanding on *Nollan*, however, the *Dolan* Court added that exactions imposed on development should be roughly proportional to the additional costs created by the development (in other words, the impact of the development). *Dolan*, 512 U.S. at 391. Here, the local government's required dedications went too far. First, the Court acknowledged that the development imposed a cost with regard to flooding, which was remedied by providing a greenway. But the Court thought that the city was excessive in demanding that the property owner provide public access to this greenway—an unnecessary infringement on the property owner's right to exclude. *Id.* at 393. Second, the Court found that while in theory the pedestrian/bicycle pathway could potentially offset traffic demand, the city had not done enough to "quantify its findings in support of the dedication." *Id.* at 395–96.

In *Dolan*, the city imposed a condition on a permit approval. But the *Dolan* test also applies when government denies a permit after offering the applicant the chance to satisfy a condition. *See* Koontz v. St. Johns River Mgmt. Dist., 133 S.Ct. 2586, 2597 (2013).

The meaning of *Nollan* and *Dolan* for developers of historic sites is no different than it is for any other property owner. However, developers of historic sites, or vacant lots within historic districts, must often achieve various approvals before proceeding with a project. So they may need to understand caselaw on exactions—and limitations on government behavior—even more thoroughly than developers of non-historic sites.

CHAPTER 9

RELIGIOUS LIBERTY

Federal law provides individuals and institutions with certain religious rights, including the rights to free exercise (as defined in the U.S. Constitution), to religious exercise (as defined in a federal statute), and to be free of public establishment of religion. These rights have had implications for the development of historic preservation law in two key ways.

First and more significantly, the rights to free exercise and religious exercise may be invoked to constrain local governments' ability to enforce historic preservation ordinances on religious owners of historic properties. Property owners may claim that their ability to exercise their religion would be unconstitutionally or illegally inhibited if they had to abide by restrictions imposed upon them by historic preservation rules or decisions. Underlying their claim would be either the free exercise clause of the First Amendment of the Constitution or the provisions of the Religious Land Use and Institutionalized Persons Act (or both).

Second, the establishment clause of the First Amendment ensures that the law cannot advance or inhibit, or be excessively entangled with religion. A law that involves designation or regulation of historic properties might be challenged for violating the establishment clause if it treats religious properties (or religious owners) more or less preferentially than secular properties (or owners), or if it delves too deeply into issues related to religious belief.

More on each of these federal religious liberty protections follows. Although this Chapter does not consider state religious liberty laws, several closely track the federal Constitution's religion clauses and the federal statute mentioned below.

A. FREE EXERCISE CLAUSE

The religion clause of the First Amendment to the federal Constitution states: "Congress shall make no law respecting an establishment of religion, or prohibiting the free exercise thereof." U.S. CONST. amend. I. The free exercise clause has been interpreted separately from the establishment clause (considered below, in Part C), and focuses on the extent to which the religious beliefs or practices of an individual or institution may be burdened by a law that is grounded in some public interest.

The First Amendment refers to "Congress," which may at first glance suggest that only the federal government is constrained by the free exercise clause. However, the Supreme Court in 1940 clarified that the free exercise clause was applicable to the states and the actions of their political subdivisions (cities, counties, and the like) through incorporation into the due process clause of the Fourteenth Amendment. *See* Cantwell v. Connecticut, 310 U.S. 296, 303 (1940) ("hold[ing] that the statute, as construed and applied to the appellants, deprives them of their liberty without due process of law in contravention of the Fourteenth Amendment").

Free exercise jurisprudence has followed a complicated path, but a few key Supreme Court cases illuminate the current state of the law. We discuss these cases as well as their applicability to historic preservation, focusing on their constraints on government's ability to regulate religious properties or the nonreligious properties of religious owners.

1.   SUPREME COURT INTERPRETATIONS

At a minimum, the free exercise clause requires that government "neither compel affirmation of a repugnant belief; nor penalize or discriminate against individuals or groups because they hold religious views abhorrent to the authorities; nor employ the taxing power to inhibit the dissemination of particular religious views." Sherbert v. Verner, 374 U.S. 398, 402 (1963). Beyond this minimum, the Supreme Court has developed two different tests when considering whether laws that are not neutral laws of general applicability or neutral laws of general applicability violate the free exercise clause.

Before a court applies either test, a plaintiff must identify a relevant exercise of religion (such as assembly, participation in ceremonies, proselytizing, or avoiding certain activities). Then the court decides whether the law at issue is a neutral law of general applicability or not. Neutral laws of general applicability include laws that are facially neutral, do not target a religious group/person, and do not require individualized assessments. The Supreme Court has clarified that a law "that targets religious conduct for distinctive treatment cannot be shielded by . . . facial neutrality." Church of the Lukumi Babalu Aye, Inc. v. City of Hialeah, 508 U.S. 520, 534 (1993) (holding that a local ordinance banning ritual slaughter was not generally applicable because the evidence showed it targeted the Santería religion). In other words, a court may review the motivation behind a law, even if the law itself is facially neutral. Once this determination is made, a court will apply one of the two tests described below.

a. Laws That Are Not Neutral Laws of General Applicability

For laws that are not neutral laws of general applicability, the free exercise clause prevents government from substantially burdening the free exercise of religion absent a showing that the burden furthered a compelling government interest. This is known as the strict scrutiny standard.

The strict scrutiny test was laid out in *Sherbert v. Verner*, which rejected as an unconstitutional constraint on free exercise a state's denial of unemployment benefits to an individual who could not work on Saturdays because doing so violated her religious beliefs. *See* 374 U.S. 398, 403–10 (1963). The Court found that a burden had been imposed on the plaintiff's free exercise, and that to survive a constitutional challenge, "any incidental burden on the free exercise of appellant's religion [would have to] be justified by a compelling state interest in the regulation of a subject within the State's constitutional power to regulate." *See* 374 U.S. 398, 403 (1963) (quotation marks omitted). The Court found that the state did not demonstrate a compelling government interest justifying the burden, because granting the exemption to the plaintiff would not have compromised the state's goal in the statutory scheme. *Id.* at 408–09. (The Court did note that the state's interest in preventing exemptions that would "render[ ] the entire statutory scheme unworkable" could have risen to the level of a compelling government interest.)

Nearly ninety Supreme Court cases have cited *Sherbert*, the majority of them favorably. Several cases have dealt with the denial of unemployment benefits—the same government conduct at issue in *Sherbert*. *See, e.g.*, Hobbie v. Unemployment Appeals Comm'n of Fla., 480 U.S. 136 (1987); Thomas v. Review Bd. of the Ind. Emp't Sec. Div., 450 U.S. 707 (1981). Other cases have applied *Sherbert* to political activities, education, and other issues. *See, e.g.*, McDaniel v. Paty, 435 U.S. 618 (1978); Wisconsin v. Yoder, 406 U.S. 205 (1972).

Religious institutions and others concerned with religious liberty favor the strict scrutiny required by *Sherbert*. The primary reason is that the burden on the government to show a compelling government interest is difficult to overcome. *See, e.g., McDaniel*, 435 U.S. at 628–29 (rejecting as not compelling and not factually supported a state's interest in preventing religious ministers from serving at constitutional conventions to avoid unconstitutional establishments of religion); *Wisconsin*, 406 U.S. at 212–22 (rejecting as not compelling a state's interest in compulsory education in order to prepare students for effective participation in political life, in light of "separated agrarian community that is the keystone of the Amish faith").

b. Neutral Laws of General Applicability

For neutral laws of general applicability, a different test is used. The free exercise clause requires that neutral laws of general applicability only meet the rational basis test: the law must be rationally related to a legitimate government purpose.

The Supreme Court laid out this test in *Employment Division, Department of Human Resources of the State of Oregon v. Smith*, 494 U.S. 872 (1990), which upheld a state's denial of unemployment benefits to individuals who violated a state drug law prohibiting the possession of peyote. The individuals ingested peyote for sacramental purposes at a Native American religious ceremony. *Id.* at 874. They argued that the law's failure to provide a religious exemption constituted a free exercise violation, and that the law should not be applied to them; thus, they should be afforded unemployment benefits. *Id.* at 875. The Court rejected their argument, finding that the law they violated was a neutral law of generally applicability because it applied to those who used drugs for religious and nonreligious reasons alike. *Id.* at 878. Under the rational basis test, the law did not effect a free exercise violation, and thus was a valid bar to the individuals receiving any unemployment compensation. The Court expressed concern that: "To make an individual's obligation to obey such a law contingent upon the law's coincidence with his religious beliefs, except where the State's interest is 'compelling'—permitting him, by virtue of his beliefs, to become a law unto himself—contradicts both constitutional tradition and common sense." *Id.* at 885 (citation and quotation marks omitted).

With *Smith*, the Supreme Court clarified years of conflicting caselaw, including several previous Supreme Court cases that had used a rational basis test, and not the strict scrutiny test of *Sherbert v. Verner*, to decide free exercise claims. *See*, *e.g.*, Lyng v. Northwest Indian Ceremony Protective Ass'n, 485 U.S. 439 (1988) (holding that the free exercise clause did not prohibit government from building a road or allowing timber harvesting in an area traditionally used for religious purpose by Native American groups); Bowen v. Roy, 476 U.S. 693 (1986) (using a rational basis test to find that a federal statute requiring individuals to submit Social Security numbers did not violate the free exercise rights of Native American plaintiffs).

Although prior cases suggested that the Supreme Court might eventually declare the rational basis test as it did in *Smith*, religious liberty advocates seemed surprised by the case. They acted quickly to

mobilize support in favor of the Religious Freedom
Restoration Act, passed in 1993 by Congress, which
restored the strict scrutiny test of *Sherbert* for all
laws. The Supreme Court struck this statute down
as it applied to the states for exceeding Congress's
"remedial, preventive" enforcement power under
section five of the Fourteenth Amendment. *See* City
of Boerne v. Flores, 521 U.S. 507, 532–33 (1997)
(finding that the legislative record did not
adequately set forth the facts needed to substantiate
remedial action). RFRA still applies to actions by
the federal government. Congress tried again with
the Religious Land Use and Institutionalized Person
Act of 2000, discussed below in Part B. That statute
applied the strict scrutiny test only to the land use
and institutionalized persons contexts. So far, it has
survived challenges to its constitutionality.

2.   APPLICATION TO
HISTORIC PRESERVATION

The free exercise clause applies to a historic
preservation law when there is a conflict between
the law and exercise of religion. Once this conflict is
identified, a court will review the law's
characteristics and will apply either the rational
basis test or strict scrutiny test to determine
whether the application of the law constitutes a free
exercise violation.

a. Identifying the Free Exercise

The first step in using the free exercise clause to
evaluate a historic preservation law is to identify

the free exercise of religion at issue. Traditionally, these relate to expressions of religious views, the ability engage in religious practices, the rights to associate or assemble for religious reasons, and the right to be free of coercion with respect to religious beliefs or practices.

The kinds of free exercise at issue in historic preservation law cases typically relate to the use, configuration, construction, financing, or designation of a building or site. Issues that could give rise to a constitutional claim include: the availability of places for religious ceremonies, the ability to configure a building's plan or site's orientation to comport with religious doctrine, the desire to use certain techniques or materials in the construction of a religious structure, the ability to construct facilities that help a religious institution maximize revenues, or the desire to avoid listing religious sites on secular lists of historic places.

Whether these issues rise to the level of protectable free exercise is a question for the judicial decision-maker. Courts have not always agreed that preferences related to the built or natural environment necessarily implicate the right to express religious views or other broad rights traditionally associated with free exercise. For example, a Connecticut court found that a historic commission's decision to prevent a religious institution from installing vinyl siding did not implicate the institution's free exercise rights because the decision "has not interfered with the right of the plaintiff or its members to express their religious views, or associate or assemble for that purpose." *See, e.g.,* First Church of Christ, Scientist v. Ridgefield Historic Dist. Comm'n, 738 A.2d 244 (Conn. Super. Ct. 1998), *aff'd* 737 A.2d 989 (Conn. App. Ct. 1999). Similarly, in a zoning (but not historic preservation) case, the Sixth Circuit dismissed the claim by a religious group that construction of a place of worship constitutes free exercise. *See* Lakewood, Ohio Congregation of Jehovah's Witnesses v. City of Lakewood, 699 F.2d 303, 306–07 (6th Cir. 1982), *cert. denied*, 464 U.S. 815 (1993). That court also considered the religious beliefs of Jehovah's Witnesses to find that the construction or ownership of a physical structure was not a "fundamental tenet" of their religion. *Id.* at 307.

b. Identifying and Applying the Appropriate Test

After an incidence of free exercise is identified, the next step is to identify the type of law at issue, so that the appropriate test may be used to evaluate its constitutionality. Historic preservation laws— whether they involve regulation, incentives, land restrictions, or information-gathering functions— are typically considered to be neutral laws of general applicability. They tend to be facially neutral and are not written to target a religious group or religious person. Accordingly, they are generally analyzed using the rational basis test. Thus, to survive a constitutional challenge based on a free exercise claim, a historic preservation law must be rationally related to a legitimate government purpose.

This test is used even if the historic preservation law at issue requires individual assessments of the characteristics of the properties that fall under the laws' purview, as long as the assessments are made using common standards set forth in the law, regulations, or practice.

Using the rational basis standard, it is hard to imagine how a historic preservation law could be held unconstitutional. Indeed, courts applying the rational basis test have overwhelmingly rejected free exercise challenges to historic preservation laws. One excellent example is a Second Circuit case involving St. Bartholomew's Church in Manhattan. *See* Rector, Wardens, & Members of the Vestry of St. Bartholomew's Church v. City of New York, 914 F.2d 348 (2d Cir. 1990), *cert. denied*, 499 U.S. 905 (1991). The church wanted to replace a structure on its campus with an office tower, which would earn revenues that the church could use to support its religious mission. It contended that the local historic preservation commission's denial of a certificate of appropriateness for its building plans "unconstitutionally denies it the opportunity to exploit this means [fundraising through renting out the office tower] of carrying out its religious mission." *Id.* at 353–54. Finding that the local historic preservation ordinance used by the commission in its decision was a facially neutral regulation of general applicability, the court applied a rational basis test. It rejected the church's argument, because "no First Amendment violation has occurred absent a showing of discriminatory motive, coercion in religious practice or the Church's inability to carry out its religious mission in its existing facilities." *Id.* at 355.

Other courts have followed the logic of *St. Bartholomew's Church.* The New York supreme court held that a landmark designation did not infringe on a religious group's free exercise when "rather than argue its desire to modify the structure to accommodate these religious activities, the Society has suggested that it is improper to restrict its ability to develop the property to permit rental to nonreligious tenants," the latter not being an exercise of religion subject to First Amendment protection. Soc'y for Ethical Culture in City of New York v. Spatt, 415 N.E.2d 922, 926 (N.Y. 1980). *See also* First Church of Christ, Scientist v. Ridgefield Historic Dist. Comm'n, 738 A.2d 244 (Conn. Super. Ct. 1998), *aff'd* 737 A.2d 989 (Conn. App. Ct. 1999) (finding that "[t]he first amendment cannot be extended to such an extent that a claim of exemption from the laws based on religious freedom can be extended to avoid otherwise reasonable and neutral legal obligations imposed by government").

At least two cases have applied the strict scrutiny test to local laws allowing for the designation of historic landmarks—we think in contravention of the *Smith* holding and Supreme Court precedent. *See* First Covenant Church of Seattle v. City of Seattle, 840 P.2d 174, 183 (Wash. 1992); Mount St. Scholastica Inc. v. City of Atchison, 482 F. Supp. 2d 1281, 1295 (D. Kan. 2007). These cases are exceptions, and not the rule. Several commentators have noted that they overextend the free exercise clause without recognizing that secular activities such as construction do not require the application of the strict scrutiny test. Once *Sherbert*'s strict scrutiny test is applied to a historic preservation law, it may be difficult for the law to survive because the government interests underlying historic preservation laws may not be considered compelling.

B.   RELIGIOUS LAND USE AND INSTITUTIONALIZED PERSONS ACT

In 2000, Congress passed the Religious Land Use and Institutionalized Persons Act (RLUIPA) to require all levels of government to consider the impact of their land use regulations on religious institutions. (It also addresses the religious rights of institutionalized persons, including those in jails and mental institutions, but these are irrelevant for our purposes.) More specifically, RLUIPA prohibits government from imposing land use regulations that substantially burden religious people or institutions unless the burden furthers a compelling government interest and is the least restrictive means of achieving that interest.

Congress enacted RLUIPA after a 1990 Supreme Court case signaled that a rational basis test should be used to evaluate free exercise clause challenges of neutral laws of general applicability. *See* Employment Div., Dep't of Human Ress. of the State of Oregon v. Smith, 494 U.S. 872 (1990). Under rational basis review, a law must only be reasonably related to a legitimate government interest to survive free exercise clause challenges. The change in 1990 marked a departure from prior Supreme Court free exercise jurisprudence, which usually applied the more rigorous strict scrutiny test, requiring government to show a compelling government interest in the law before the law could be upheld. *See, e.g.*, Sherbert v. Verner, 374 U.S. 398 (1963). RLUIPA restores the pre-1990 strict scrutiny test for land use regulations, including historic preservation laws.

1. OVERVIEW

The Religious Land Use and Institutionalized Persons Act of 2000 (RLUIPA) is one of the few federal statutes that constrain state and local governments' abilities to regulate land use. It has two primary components: (1) a substantial burden provision and (2) a discrimination and exclusion provision. The discrimination and exclusion provision is fairly self-explanatory. It prohibits governments from treating religious and nonreligious institutions unequally, discriminating against any religious institution on the basis of religion, or excluding (or unreasonably limiting) religious institutions from the jurisdiction. *Id.* § 2000cc(b).

The substantial burden provision is more complex and will be the focus of this Part. It reads as follows:

> No government shall impose or implement a land use regulation in a manner that imposes a substantial burden on the religious exercise of a person, including a religious assembly or

institution, unless the government demonstrates that imposition of the burden on that person, assembly, or institution—

(A) is in furtherance of a compelling governmental interest; and

(B) is the least restrictive means of furthering that compelling governmental interest.

42 U.S.C. § 2000cc(a)(1). This language was drafted in response to the concerns of some constituents who believed that religious institutions suffered from discrimination in the way land use regulations were written and applied.

RLUIPA applies when the substantial burden: (1) is imposed by federally funded programs or activities; (2) affects foreign, interstate, or tribal commerce; and (3) is imposed in the implementation of land use regulations that permit government to make individualized assessments of proposals or properties. *Id.* § 2000cc(a)(2). The third scenario— individualized assessments—is most relevant for our purposes. A historic preservation law that might be deemed to be a neutral law of general applicability for the purposes of constitutional free exercise review, and thus require only rational basis scrutiny, may trigger strict scrutiny review under RLUIPA's individualized assessments provision.

RLUIPA's substantial burden provision is an important tool for religious persons and institutions, and in many ways more powerful than First Amendment constitutional constraints because of its clear adherence to the strict scrutiny approach and broad applicability to all land use regulations. Its power becomes clearer when one understands a few key terms, described in the next section.

2. KEY TERMS

The Religious Land Use and Institutionalized Persons Act's substantial burdens provision, excerpted above, has six terms worth discussing further. Three—"government," "land use regulation," and "religious exercise"—are defined in the statute and identify when RLUIPA applies. The first two have meanings that are obvious, perhaps, but the third offers a novel formulation for the types of activities the federal government will protect. The fourth, "substantial burden," fifth, "compelling government interest," and sixth, "least restrictive means," have been primarily defined in courts of law. To explain these last three concepts, courts have often borrowed from decisions involving the free exercise clause of the U.S. Constitution. This borrowing has helped religious institutions develop a sense of when and how RLUIPA may be applied to constrain government regulation of their desired land use activities.

a. Government

RLUIPA's definition of "government" is very broad. It includes branches, departments, agencies, instrumentalities, and officials of the federal government or "a State, county, municipality, or other governmental entity created under the authority of a State" 42 U.S.C. § 2000cc–5(4). It also includes any person acting under color of state or federal law.

Historic preservation laws are enacted and enforced at every level of government. Agencies and officials play a big role in the historic preservation scheme. Members of boards and commissions—from local preservation review boards all the way up to federal advisory commissions—act under color of law even if they are not public employees. Their actions, too, are subject to RLUIPA.

b. Land Use Regulation

Only a "land use regulation" is subject to the constraints of RLUIPA. This term includes the full range of regulatory activities:

> a zoning or landmarking law, or the application of such a law, that limits or restricts a claimant's use or development of land (including a structure affixed to land), if the claimant has an ownership, leasehold, easement, servitude, or other property interest in the regulated land or a contract or option to acquire such an interest.

42 U.S.C. § 2000cc–5(B)(5). The scope of application provision provides some limitation on this broad definition. It limits RLUIPA's applicability to those land use regulations "under which a government makes, or has in place formal or informal procedures or practices that permit the government to make, individualized assessments of the proposed

uses for the property involved." *Id.* § 2000cc(2)(C).
In general, neither government's exercise of eminent
domain nor its annexation of land will be considered
a land use regulation as RLUIPA defines that term.
See, e.g., St. John's United Church of Christ v.
Chicago, 502 F.3d 616 (7th Cir. 2007) (involving an
exercise of eminent domain); Vision Church v. Vill.
of Long Grove, 468 F.3d 975 (7th Cir. 2006)
(involving an annexation).

Historic preservation laws are specifically
mentioned, in the definition's reference to
"landmarking law[s]." They often require
individualized assessments of proposals for
properties and thus would fit within the limitation
provided by the scope of application provision.
Consider, for example: local historic preservation
ordinances that require property owners of historic
resources to submit plans for board scrutiny;
statutory schemes (at any level) requiring detailed
reviews before properties may be designated
historic; and public grant (or other incentive)
programs meant to benefit historic properties
meeting certain criteria. Indeed, other than
enabling legislation (such as legislation allowing
municipalities to create historic districts, or
legislation authorizing private creation of
preservation or conservation restrictions) or historic
preservation planning laws, it is hard to think of
many examples of historic preservation laws that
would not be subject to RLUIPA.

c. Religious Exercise

RLUIPA only protects "religious exercise," a term distinct from the "free exercise" protected by the federal Constitution. RLUIPA defines religious exercise to include "any exercise of religion, whether or not compelled by, or central to, a system of religious belief." 42 U.S.C. § 2000cc–5(7)(A). With the "centrality of belief" language, RLUIPA avoids delving into the connection between the protected activity and the content of an aggrieved party's religious beliefs. This approach differs from cases involving free exercise constitutional challenges, which may review whether a government burden implicates a belief or practice that is central to the aggrieved party's religion. *See*, *e.g.*, Hernandez v. Comm'r, 490 U.S. 680, 699 (1989) (stating that "[t]he free exercise inquiry asks whether government has placed a substantial burden on the observation of a central religious belief or practice").

In addition, RLUIPA states that "[t]he use, building, or conversion of real property for the purpose of religious exercise shall be considered to be religious exercise." *Id.* § 2000cc–5(7)(B). Here, too, RLUIPA broadens the definition of "religious exercise" to guarantee the protection of activities beyond those that would be protected by the U.S. Constitution's free exercise clause.

This definition clarifies that that activities normally subject to historic preservation laws (construction, land use, and the like) will be considered to be religious exercise—even if such activities are not central to the aggrieved party's religious beliefs. Indeed, courts have interpreted this provision broadly. For example, a federal district court in Michigan found that a student center that used a facility to sponsor social events, concerts, and other events engaged in religious exercise under the meaning of RLUIPA. Episcopal Student Found. v. City of Ann Arbor, 341 F. Supp. 2d 691, 700–01 (E.D. Mich. 2004).

d. Substantial Burden

The term "substantial burden" is not defined in RLUIPA. Though the Supreme Court has never opined on the land use provisions of RLUIPA, the "substantial burden" term has been interpreted by numerous lower federal courts in a manner that is generally in line with free exercise jurisprudence. Courts typically find that a historic preservation law creates a substantial burden when it coerces religious parties into abandoning or violating religious beliefs, requires them to choose between following their beliefs and following the law, or prevents them from pursuing their religious beliefs. Further articulation of the exact standard used has been the work of the federal circuit courts. Note that most of the federal circuit court cases that have expanded upon the substantial burden term under RLUIPA have involved zoning, not historic preservation.

In the only federal circuit court case dealing with RLUIPA's applicability to historic preservation, the First Circuit found no substantial burden where a church had to bear some costs of maintaining its building as a result of a historic designation. *See* Roman Catholic Bishop of Springfield v. City of Springfield, 724 F.3d 78, 100 (1st Cir. 2013). Similarly, a Michigan federal district court found no substantial burden where a religious student center claimed to be prevented from "seek[ing] growth or welcom[ing] new members, contrary to its religious mission" after a local board denied the center's application to demolish its historic building. Episcopal Student Found. v. City of Ann Arbor, 341 F. Supp. 2d 691, 695 & 704 (E.D. Mich. 2004). And a Connecticut federal district court found no substantial burden where the religious institution was required to submit plans for historic commission review, like secular applicants were required to do. Chabad Lubavitch of Litchfield County v. Borough of Litchfield, Conn., 853 F. Supp. 2d 214, 224–25 (D. Conn. 2012).

These cases track RLUIPA-based federal circuit court decisions dealing with zoning ordinances, which typically have a high threshold for a showing of substantial burden. The Second Circuit has perhaps the highest threshold, requiring the plaintiff to show "direct coerc[ion on] the religious institution to change its behavior" before a substantial burden may be found. Westchester Day Sch. v. Vill. of Mamaroneck, 504 F.3d 338, 349 (2d Cir. 2007). Several other circuits have set a lower bar for plaintiffs, equating a substantial burden with "substantial pressure" on a religious plaintiff to modify her behavior. This test has resulted in a range of outcomes, usually finding no substantial burden, except in unusual circumstances. *See, e.g.,*

Bethel World Outreach Ministries v. Montgomery Cnty. Council, 706 F.3d 548, 556 (4th Cir. 2013) (reversing summary judgment against a finding of substantial burden because church facilities were overcrowded, services were limited, and the pastor testified that "the lack of adequate facilities creates a sense of disunity"); Living Water Church of God v. Charter Twp. of Meridian, 258 F. App'x 729, 734 (6th Cir. 2007) (finding no substantial burden because the church could carry out its missions and ministries without its desired expansion of a religious school and gym on church grounds); Midrash Sephardi, Inc. v. Town of Surfside, 366 F.3d 1214, 1227 (11th Cir. 2004) (finding that the possibility that a religious institution may have to move a few blocks away to find a more appropriate site is not a substantial burden). The Seventh Circuit recently offered a relative approach to determining a substantial burden, which takes into account certain characteristics of the religious plaintiff, including its size, as well as its "needs and resources." World Outreach Conference Ctr. v. City of Chicago, 591 F.3d 531, 539 (7th Cir. 2009). Relevant factors may include whether the regulation targets a religion or religious practice or is imposed arbitrarily, capriciously, or unlawfully.

e. Compelling Government Interest

The meaning of "compelling government interest" has only been fleshed out in a few RLUIPA cases, in part because courts have focused so heavily on the substantial burden analysis. A court will only reach the compelling government interest requirement of

RLUIPA when a substantial burden has been found. Courts that do proceed to evaluate the nature of the public interest usually adopt, or offer variations on, the interpretation of that term in free exercise caselaw.

To be compelling, an interest must be "of the highest order." Church of the Lukumi Babalu Aye, Inc. v. City of Hialeah, 508 U.S. 520, 546 (1993). Interests in national security and public health are the kinds of interests that would normally be called compelling. Courts may also defer to government officials and legislative bodies that have publicly declared that certain interests are compelling. *See* *id.* at 547. Some courts have added that the government may have to show that its interest is specific to the application in question, and may not simply show that it has a compelling interest in general. *See*, *e.g.*, Westchester Day Sch. v. Vill. of Mamaroneck, 504 F.3d 338, 353 (2d Cir. 2007).

It may be difficult to show that a government has a compelling government interest in enforcing historic preservation laws, especially since historic preservation laws deal with primarily aesthetic concerns. Most courts considering free exercise challenges to historic preservation laws have characterized the laws as neutral laws of general applicability, a characterization that does not require a court to review whether there is a compelling government interest. Two decisions that have found historic preservation laws not to be neutral laws of general applicability (and thus proceeded to the compelling government interest question) have both said that historic preservation is not a compelling government interest. *See* First Covenant Church of Seattle v. City of Seattle, 840 P.2d 174 (Wash. 1992); Mount St. Scholastica Inc. v. City of Atchison, 482 F. Supp. 2d 1281, 1295 (D. Kan. 2007).

A compelling interest will not be found if the law at issue is inconsistent or arbitrary, or if the government is acting in bad faith. In addition, a locality that is disingenuous about its interests will not be found to have a compelling government interest. *See* Fortress Bible Church v. Feiner, 694 F.3d 208, 219 (2d Cir. 2012).

f. Least Restrictive Means

The "least restrictive means" requirement goes hand in hand with the compelling government interest requirement to ensure that government's imposition of a substantial burden on religious exercise is justified. In general, a government must show that there is no less-restrictive alternative to achieve the compelling government interest at issue other than the path that it has chosen.

This term is not defined in the statute, and it has not been well-considered by the courts either, because often RLUIPA cases are decided on whether there is a substantial burden or compelling government interest, and thus courts do not reach the least restrictive means question. The Eleventh Circuit has said that a complete prohibition on religious assemblies in residential zones is not a "narrowly tailored means of achieving the City's interest in preserving the residential character of neighborhoods." Covenant Christian Ministries, Inc. v. City of Marietta, Ga., 654 F.3d 1231, 1246 (11th Cir. 2011). Similarly, a Tennessee federal district court found that a locality had not used least restrictive means by denying or delaying a certificate of occupancy to a religious institution, as proven by the city's subsequent passage of an ordinance that used less restrictive means of achieving the same goal stated by the city. Layman Lessons, Inc. v. City of Millersville, Tenn., 636 F. Supp. 2d 620 (M.D. Tenn. 2008).

3.   APPLICATION

The Religious Land Use and Institutionalized Persons Act (RLUIPA) does not require governments to engage in a "religious impact review" prior to acting. (Such a review might be similar to environmental or adverse effects reviews required by the federal statutes discussed in Chapters III, IV, and V.) Rather, RLUIPA is applied primarily through lawsuits alleging that a government has violated the statute. These lawsuits happen in a fairly mechanical way.

First, a plaintiff asserts a violation of the statute pursuant to the cause of action contained in 42 U.S.C. § 2000cc–2. The plaintiff must provide enough prima facie evidence to support her claim and bears the burden of persuasion as to whether there is a substantial burden on the plaintiff's religious exercise. The government bears the remaining burdens of persuasion, including the burden of showing a compelling government interest. The statute offers a rule of construction that influences how these burdens are reviewed. It says that it "shall be construed in favor of a broad protection of religious exercise, to the maximum extent permitted by the terms of this chapter and the Constitution." *Id.* § 2000cc–3.

To bring a claim under the substantial burden provision (as opposed to the discrimination and exclusion provision) of RLUIPA, one of the three jurisdictional requirements laid out in section 2000cc(2) must be met. The substantial burden must: (1) be imposed in a program or activity receiving federal financial assistance; (2) affect foreign, tribal, or interstate commerce, or (3) be imposed in the implementation of a land use regulation in which government makes individualized assessments of the proposed uses for the affected property. Often, plaintiffs challenging historic preservation ordinances will say that religious institutions meet the third jurisdictional requirement because the laws they are challenging impose substantial burdens through a land use regulation system requiring individualized assessments. This is the case even though prior free exercise jurisprudence most often found that the laws were neutral laws of general applicability not requiring individualized assessments. Sometimes, however, religious institutions cite to the interstate commerce requirement of 42 U.S.C. § 2000cc(a)(2)(B) because religious institutions participate in the interstate markets for goods and services, use interstate communication and transportation, and move money across state lines. *See, e.g.,* Cottonwood Christian Ctr. v. Cypress Redevelopment Ag., 218 F. Supp. 2d 1203, 1221 (C.D. Ca. 2002).

4.   INTERSECTION WITH THE RELIGIOUS FREEDOM RESTORATION ACT

RLUIPA has some historical and substantive overlap with the Religious Freedom Restoration Act (RFRA), passed by Congress in 1993. 42 U.S.C. § 2000bb–bb–4. That statute was the first attempt by Congress to circumvent the Supreme Court's 1990 articulation of the rational basis test for free exercise challenges to neutral laws of general applicability. *See* Employment Div., Dep't of Human Ress. of the State of Oregon v. Smith, 494 U.S. 872 (1990). RFRA states:

Government may substantially burden a person's exercise of religion only if it demonstrates that application of the burden to the person—

(1) is in furtherance of a compelling governmental interest; and

(2) is the least restrictive means of furthering that compelling governmental interest.

Id. § 2000bb–1(b). In 1997, the Supreme Court struck down RFRA as it applied to the states, because in enacting RFRA Congress exceeded the enforcement powers granted to it by section 5 of the Fourteenth Amendment. *See* City of Boerne v.

Flores, 521 U.S. 507 (1997). RFRA remains applicable to actions of the federal government.

RLUIPA was passed three years later, after Congress established a more robust legislative record that justified the use of the strict scrutiny text in the two contexts (land use and institutionalized persons) to which RLUIPA applies. RLUIPA shares similar language with RFRA, and both statutes were passed for similar reasons. However, with few exceptions, these two laws are rarely cited in the same court case. *But see* Navajo Nation v. U.S. Forest Serv., 479 F.3d 1024 (9th Cir. 2007) (considering both RFRA and RLUIPA in a case involving federal actions on federal land eligible for inclusion on the National Register of Historic Places and important to Navajo spiritual practice). The primary reason is that most RLUIPA claims (in the land use, as opposed to institutionalized persons, context) are filed against local authorities, but RFRA no longer applies to local authorities. In addition, RLUIPA only applies to a limited range of federal government actions, while RFRA applies much more broadly. Despite the linkage of these two statutes by commentators and even courts, in practice there is not much reason for the land use practitioner to be overly concerned with RFRA.

C. ESTABLISHMENT CLAUSE

The establishment clause of the First Amendment states: "Congress shall make no law respecting an establishment of religion." U.S. CONST. amend. I.

The most obvious meaning of this clause is that Congress cannot establish a national religion or national religious institution. It also means that the federal government cannot prefer one religion over another, or religion to irreligion (or vice versa).

Going further, the Supreme Court has said that the religious liberty protections of the establishment clause also apply to actions of the states and their various political subdivisions. The Fourteenth Amendment, ratified in 1866, provided the legal grounds for this determination. It prevents the states from "depriv[ing] any person of life, liberty, or property, without due process of law." U.S. CONST. amend. XIV. The Supreme Court incorporated the establishment clause into the due process requirement of the Fourteenth Amendment in 1943. *See* Murdock v. Commonwealth of Pennsylvania, 319 U.S. 105, 108 (1943).

The Court has further defined the parameters of the establishment clause on several occasions. One can extrapolate from its cases that the establishment clause constrains government behavior in the historic preservation context in three key ways: the designation of significant resources as historic (the theme of Chapter II), the regulation of historic properties, and the provision of public historic preservation grants.

1.   SUPREME COURT INTERPRETATIONS

According to the Supreme Court, the establishment clause has two primary meanings. First, it prohibits governments from establishing a public religion or a public religious institution. This first meaning has essentially no bearing on historic preservation law. Second, and more pertinent to historic preservation, the establishment clause allows judicial review of laws that do not involve establishments of religion. We consider this second meaning more fully by exploring the Supreme Court's consideration of two primary tests: the minimum principle of neutrality and the more involved *Lemon* test. We conclude by noting inconsistencies in establishment clause jurisprudence, which make this area of law somewhat complicated and unpredictable.

a. The Principle of Neutrality

At a minimum, the establishment clause forbids governmental preference of one religion over another, or religion to irreligion. This neutrality principle may be violated if one religious sect is given preferential treatment. *See, e.g.*, Board of Educ. of Kiryas Joel Vill. Sch. Dist. v. Grumet, 512 U.S. 687 (1994) (finding unconstitutional a state law allowing a community comprised exclusively of members of one particular religious sect to have its own school district).

It may also be violated if religious groups are given opportunities not given to similarly situated secular groups. *See, e.g.*, Larkin v. Grendel's Den, Inc., 459 U.S. 116 (1982) (finding a state statute that granted religious bodies veto power over applications for liquor licenses to be an unconstitutional violation of the neutrality principle).

It is important to note that the establishment clause "does not depend upon any showing of direct governmental compulsion and is violated by the enactment of laws which establish an official religion whether those laws operate directly to coerce non-observing individuals or not." Engel v. Vitale 370 U.S. 421, 430 (1962) (finding that daily school prayer violated the establishment clause). In other words, proof of coercion of individuals is not required to declare a public law unconstitutional. This general rule contrasts with the rule in the free exercise context, discussed in Part A above.

b. The Lemon Test

Beyond this minimum, the Court has said that the establishment clause requires that laws meet three more specific criteria: "First, the statute must have a secular legislative purpose; second, its principal or primary effect must be one that neither advances nor inhibits religion, finally, the statute must not foster an excessive government entanglement with religion." Lemon v. Kurtzman, 403 U.S. 602, 612–13 (1971) (citations and quotation marks omitted) (finding unconstitutional states' financial aid to religious public schools).

The first criterion requires the law to have a secular legislative purpose. As two examples, the Court found that the following laws lacked a secular religious purpose: a state statute that required the posting of a copy of the Ten Commandments on the walls of each public school classroom, and a school district's policy allowing "student-led, student-initiated" prayer at public school sporting events. *See* Santa Fe Independent Sch. Dist. v. Doe, 530 U.S. 290, 314–15 (2000); Stone v. Graham, 449 U.S. 39, 41 (1980) (per curiam) (finding that "[t]he pre-eminent purpose for posting the Ten Commandments on schoolroom walls is plainly religious in nature").

The second criterion requires that the law neither advance nor inhibit religion. The legislature's stated justification for the law may be taken into account in making this determination. For example, a state law that allows parents to take state tax deductions for parochial school expenses does not impermissibly advance religion. Mueller v. Allen, 463 U.S. 388, 396–98 (1983) (noting that the "legislature's judgment that a deduction for educational expenses fairly equalizes the tax burden of its citizens and encourages desirable expenditures for educational purposes is entitled to substantial deference").

The third criterion recognizes that "[s]ome relationship between government and religious organizations is inevitable." *Lemon*, 403 U.S. at 614. This relationship, however, must pass constitutional muster. The Court has viewed a state statute allowing religious groups the right to object to liquor license applications as an unconstitutional entanglement between religion and government. Larkin v. Grendel's Den, Inc., 459 U.S. 116, 126–27 (1982) (finding that the statute "substitutes the unilateral and absolute power of a church for the reasoned decisionmaking of a public legislative body acting on evidence and guided by standards, on issues with significant economic and political implications").

c. Inconsistencies in Establishment Clause Caselaw

The principle of neutrality and the *Lemon* test are two strands of establishment clause jurisprudence. But even the Supreme Court has failed to use them consistently to decide cases.

In particular, the *Lemon* test has not been universally applied. For example, the Court has applied *Lemon* slightly differently in school aid cases than the three-pronged test described above. *See, e.g.*, Zelman v. Simmons-Harris, 536 U.S. 639, 668–69 (2002) (describing how different Court cases related to school aid have involved variations on the *Lemon* test). Other government aid programs have been reviewed based on whether they meet the principle of neutrality, and not the *Lemon* test. *See, e.g.*, Good News Club v. Milford Central Sch., 533 U.S. 98 (2001) (holding unconstitutional a public school's exclusion of a Christian club from meeting on its grounds, and failing to mention *Lemon* altogether). The Court has also recognized an "endorsement" test that seemingly folds together *Lemon*'s first two prongs. That test suggests that an action may be unconstitutional if a reasonable person would think that the government was endorsing the action. *See* Lynch v. Donnelly, 465

U.S. 668 (1984) (O'Connor, J., concurring) (setting forth the endorsement test for the first time).

In addition, the Court has sometimes not applied *Lemon*, including in *Van Orden v. Perry*, in which the Supreme Court considered the Ten Commandments display on the grounds of the Texas State Capitol. *See* 545 U.S. 677 (2005). In that case, the majority found that *Lemon* is "not useful in dealing with the sort of passive monument that Texas has erected on its Capitol grounds. Instead, our analysis is driven by both the monument's nature and by our Nation's history." *Id.* at 686. The Court upheld as constitutional the display of the Ten Commandments due to the Commandments' role in the state's political, legal, and even architectural history. *Id.* at 686–690. *See also* Marsh v. Chambers, 463 U.S. 783, 790–92 (1983) (using an alternative to *Lemon* to find unconstitutional the practice of a state legislature of beginning each of its sessions with a prayer, because the practice was in effect for over a century and because the Framers allowed a Congressional chaplain).

Several of the current justices have expressed dismay at the inconsistent direction of the Court's establishment clause jurisprudence. In 2011, Justice Thomas issued a dissent to a denial of certiorari, in part because he viewed the case at issue as "an opportunity to provide clarity to an Establishment Clause jurisprudence in shambles." *See* Utah Highway Patrol Ass'n v. American Atheists, Inc., *cert. denied*, 132 S.Ct. 12, 13 (U.S. Oct. 31, 2011) (Nos. 10–1276 & 10–1297) (Thomas, J., dissenting).

Given these views—and the even more inconsistent application of Supreme Court establishment clause jurisprudence by the lower courts—a practitioner should be wary of this area of the law.

2. APPLICATION TO DESIGNATION

The establishment clause of the U.S. Constitution applies to the public designation of historic properties, regardless of the level of government doing the designation. The typical designation ordinance will survive establishment clause challenges, as long as the process for evaluating resources does not involve analyzing religious beliefs or values.

As Chapter II describes in further detail, various forms of government designate resources— buildings, objects, structures, sites, and districts— as historic. The designation process identifies resources that are significant and that have the integrity required to convey their significance. These resources may receive special protection under the law: they may be protected from demolition or alteration; or their existence may trigger certain procedures to be taken before a project may proceed.

The designation process may run up against the establishment clause in the designation of religious properties—that is, properties with religious significance or religious affiliation. The National Register avoids establishment clause challenges by expressly stating that religious properties will not be eligible for listing unless they have independent architectural merit or historic significance. In other words, religious properties may not be listed for, or evaluated on the basis of, their religious significance. *See* 36 C.F.R. § 60.4. To evaluate establishment clause challenges to other designation processes, the three-pronged *Lemon* test is most likely to be used. *See* Lemon v. Kurtzman, 403 U.S. 602, 612–13 (1971). We believe that federal courts will continue to apply the *Lemon* test to cases involving land use regulations, as the Supreme Court did in *Larkin v. Grendel's Den, Inc.*, 459 U.S. 116 (1982).

To avoid violating *Lemon*, a government must ensure that the designation law has a secular legislative purpose, neither advances nor inhibits religion, and does not foster excessive government entanglement with religion. *Lemon*, 403 U.S. at 612–13. The typical designation law would easily survive scrutiny under *Lemon*'s first prong. Designation laws have a secular purpose: the identification of significant historic resources (an essentially educational endeavor) with the possible protection of such properties through companion legislation. As for the second prong—advancing or inhibiting religion—here, too, the typical designation law would survive scrutiny. Designation alone does not typically have a direct effect, physical or otherwise, on a designated resource.

The third prong of the *Lemon* test is relevant to the designation process because the process typically involves the evaluation of certain key attributes of a resource. Government involvement in evaluating the beliefs of the religious group affiliated with the property would likely violate *Lemon*'s third prong. Thus governments would be well-advised to avoid including any evaluation of religious beliefs during the designation process. The federal government's approach to designation follows this strategy. The National Register ordinarily excludes "properties owned by religious institutions or used for religious purposes," but it allows designation for religious properties "deriving primary significance from architectural or artistic distinction or historical importance." 36 C.F.R. § 60.4. This approach allows officials to avoid making decisions about religious values, and focuses the evaluation on purely secular concerns (architectural, artistic, and/or historic distinction). (Note that Native American religious properties are treated differently in that decision-makers may take their cultural and religious significance into account, as discussed in Chapter XII.)

One federal court recently rejected an establishment clause challenge to a local preservation ordinance that was used to designate a single-parcel historic district around a church. Roman Catholic Bishop of Springfield v. City of Springfield, 760 F. Supp. 2d 172 (D. Mass. 2011), *aff'd in part and rev'd in part*, 724 F.3d 78 (1st Cir. 2013). The plaintiff, a church, alleged that the ordinance, facially and as applied, violated all three prongs of the *Lemon* test. Easily dismissing the challenges based on the first two prongs of *Lemon*, the court focused on the church's argument that the ordinance's requirement that it submit plans for review before it altered its property was an "excessive entanglement" in violation of *Lemon*'s third prong. The court said that "this argument, if accepted, would exempt church property from all zoning limitations and simply is not sustainable. Indeed, even if Plaintiff had gone through the application process and had been denied, it is unlikely that Plaintiff could show that this entanglement was 'excessive.'" *Id.* at 194. This decision confirms that the typical designation process, if applied neutrally to religious and nonreligious properties alike, is likely to survive establishment clause scrutiny.

Another application of *Lemon* is a California Supreme Court decision that included a federal establishment clause challenge. East Bay Asian Local Dev. Corp. v. State of California, 13 P.3d 1122 (Cal. 2000). At issue was a state statute that granted nonprofit religious institutions the ability to circumvent the local historic designation of their property. Analyzing each prong of the *Lemon* test, the court reasoned that the statute had a secular purpose ("to relieve religious entities of a potential burden on free exercise"), did not inhibit or advance religion ("[t]he only impact of the exemption is that the owner may continue to use the property as it sees fit"), and that there was no excessive governmental entanglement with religion ("[t]here is no delegation of substantial governmental authorities to the religious entities that own exempt properties"). *Id.* at 1132–37. This reasoning has held sway over federal and state courts beyond California, which have by and large upheld local historic preservation ordinances against establishment clause challenges.

3. APPLICATION TO REGULATION

Courts may consider challenges based on the federal establishment clause to regulation of religious historic resources and nonreligious historic resources owned by religious institutions. The typical historic preservation regulation will survive an establishment clause challenge, as long as the regulation applies neutrally to religious and nonreligious properties and does not delve too far into the religious beliefs of affected religious parties.

As Chapter I describes, regulation may reach a wide range of activities, but primarily focuses on the use, alteration, and destruction of resources that have been designated as historic or are eligible for such designation. Regulation ranges from local ordinances designed to protect historic resources from historically incompatible alterations or demolition to federal statutes requiring agencies to study or minimize harm to protected resources.

As is the case with evaluations of historic preservation designations, the three-pronged *Lemon* test is the most likely to be used in evaluations of historic preservation regulation. *See* Lemon v. Kurtzman, 403 U.S. 602, 612–13 (1971). The average historic preservation regulation would comply with *Lemon*'s first prong, since it has a secular purpose: the protection of historic properties for educational, aesthetic, community-building, or other rationales. The average regulation has neither a direct effect on the advancement or inhibition of religion, nor is it excessively entagled with religion, as it provides a process for evaluating architectural and aesthetic matters, not religious beliefs or values.

One excellent example of the application of the *Lemon* test is *St. Bartholomew's Church v. City of New York*, in which a New York federal district court considered an establishment clause challenge. Rector, Wardens, & Members of the Vestry of St. Bartholomew's Church v. City of New York, 728 F. Supp. 958 (S.D.N.Y. 1989), *aff'd* 914 F.2d 348 (2d Cir. 1990), *cert. denied*, 499 U.S. 905 (1991). In that case, the local historic preservation commission denied a certificate of appropriateness to the owners of a church who sought to build an office tower on church grounds, even after reviewing extensive material regarding the financial affairs of the church to determine whether it had grounds for a finding of a certificate of appropriateness due to insufficient economic return. *Id.* at 962. The church claimed that the "tests for determining when a certificate of appropriateness may be granted on the grounds of hardship require an intrusive examination into the finances and internal workings of the Church," constituting "an excessive entanglement between government and religion in violation of the establishment clause" and of *Lemon*. *Id.* at 963. (The first two prongs of *Lemon* were not alleged to have been violated.) The district court found this establishment clause challenge meritless, because the examination of church finances was done for such a limited purpose. *Id.*

4.   APPLICATION TO GRANT PROGRAMS

The establishment clause constrains government's ability to provide historic preservation grants (or similar funding) to religious institutions that happen to own or manage historic properties. The federal governments and many states have designed grant programs for secular organizations and religious institutions to avoid establishment clause scrutiny. It is advisable for these grant programs to offer awards to both religious and nonreligious properties, avoid evaluating religious beliefs or values, and ensure that grant monies are expended only for designated, non-religious purposes.

In one of the few federal cases considering these issues, the Sixth Circuit held that a city program that gave grants to three churches did not violate the establishment clause. American Atheists, Inc. v. City of Detroit Downtown Dev. Auth., 567 F.3d 278 (6th Cir. 2009). Analyzing the program using the neutrality principle, the court reasoned that the city's program "makes grants available to a wide spectrum of religious, nonreligious and areligious groups alike and employs neutral, secular criteria to determine an applicant's eligibility, what projects may be reimbursed and how much each grantee receives," all of which ensures the program meets the neutrality requirement. *Id.* at 290. In addition, the program did not have a purpose of, or the effect of, advancing religion because it did not: (1) employ skewed selection criteria that favored religious groups, (2) lead to religious indoctrination, (3) have an inherently religious content, (4) allow for the diversion of grant money to further a religious mission, or (5) entangle the government in religious affairs. *Id.* at 290–94 (describing in detail relevant Supreme Court jurisprudence).

Federal historic preservation grant programs have so far also withstood establishment clause challenges. In 2003, the U.S. Department of Justice published a lengthy memorandum opinion on this topic. It had been asked by the Department of the Interior to opine on whether the federal government could offer grants for historic preservation purposes to religious institutions. The Department of Justice identified three reasons why the grant program designed by the Department of the Interior would pass establishment clause scrutiny:

> First, the federal government has an obvious and powerful interest in preserving all sites of historic significance to the nation, without regard to their religious or secular character. The context in which this issue arises distinguishes the Program from programs of aid targeted to education, which have been subjected to especially rigorous scrutiny by the Supreme Court. Second, eligibility for historic preservation grants extends to a broad class of beneficiaries, defined without reference to religion and including both public and private institutions. All sorts of historic structures—from private homes to government buildings—are eligible for preservation grants. Third, although the criteria for funding require a

measure of subjective judgment, those criteria are amenable to neutral application, and there is no basis to conclude that those who administer the Program will do so in a manner that favors religious institutions.

Memorandum Opinion for the Solicitor, Dep't of the Interior, Authority of the Department of the Interior to Provide Historic Preservation Grants to Historic Religious Properties such as the Old North Church (Apr. 30, 2003). Perhaps emboldened by this memorandum, Congress in 2004 passed the California Missions Preservation Act, which provided financial support to nineteen historic mission properties that still operated as active religious congregations but had independent historic significance. *See* California Missions Preservation Act, Pub. L. No. 108–420, 118 Stat. 2372 (2004). To address establishment clause concerns, section 3(b)(4) of that public law required that financial assistance provided: "(A) is secular; (B) does not promote religion; and (C) seeks to protect qualities that are historically significant."

CHAPTER 10
FREE SPEECH

When historic preservation regulations constrain behavior and avenues of expression, they may come into conflict with the free speech clause of the Constitution. This clause states: "Congress shall make no law . . . abridging the freedom of speech." U.S. CONST. amend. I. It has not been interpreted literally; it does not protect all speech. Rather, some types of speech and some avenues for expressing one's free speech may be regulated.

Importantly for historic preservation regulation (much of which happens at the local level) the free speech clause applies to localities. While the term "Congress" suggests that the free speech clause applies only to the federal government, the Supreme Court has made this clause applicable to the states and their various political subdivisions and instrumentalities. *See* Gitlow v. New York, 268 U.S. 652 (1925).

The analysis used in cases involving free speech challenges depends upon the nature of the law at issue (whether it is content-based or content-neutral) and the nature of the speech at issue (as some types of speech, such as political speech, merit more robust constitutional protection than other types). A look at Supreme Court interpretations can help one understand how lower courts have applied, or are likely to apply, these interpretations to historic preservation laws.

A. SUPREME COURT INTERPRETATIONS

The Supreme Court has said that government regulations cannot be a guise for restricting free speech on the basis of the personal tastes of local officials. Moreover, regulations may not be overbroad or vague: they must be specific enough to be fairly enforced.

Beyond these general rules, the Court has developed an array of specific rules that apply to certain regulations and/or types of speech. Most relevant to historic preservation are the Court's rules for land use ordinances and signage regulations. In these two areas, the Court will almost always review first whether the regulation at issue is content-based or content-neutral. A content-based regulation regulates content or viewpoint, and it will be evaluated using the strict scrutiny test. A content-neutral regulation regulates the avenue or form of expression, not the content or viewpoint, and it will be evaluated using the intermediate scrutiny test. The Court will review not only the text of the regulation but also its underlying purpose to ensure that a facially content-neutral regulation is not motivated by government disagreement with the content of the speech (and should thus be analyzed as a content-based regulation).

Below, we first offer simplified versions of the Supreme Court's application of strict scrutiny and intermediate scrutiny to free exercise challenges. We then explain why these simplified versions do not fully reflect the Court's inconsistent caselaw.

1. STRICT SCRUTINY

If a regulation is content-based, then the Supreme Court will apply strict scrutiny. A content-based regulation will be found constitutional if it is (1) justified by a compelling government interest, and (2) narrowly tailored to achieve (or the least restrictive means of achieving) that interest. The government has the burden of proving these two requirements. In general, the Court applies strict scrutiny less often than intermediate scrutiny, perhaps because communities are less likely to regulate based on content knowing the heightened standard they must meet if they do so.

One example of the Court's application of strict scrutiny was its decision involving a District of Columbia law prohibiting the display of any sign that brought a foreign government into "public odium" or "public disrepute," within five hundred feet of a foreign embassy. *See* Boos v. Barry, 485 U.S. 312 (1988). The Court decided to use strict scrutiny because the law prohibited the signs based on their content—whether they were supportive or critical of the foreign government—and because the speech being regulated was "political speech in a public forum" (restrictions on which are subject to "the most exacting scrutiny"). *Id.* at 321. The Court declined to determine whether the "dignity interest" of foreign governments was compelling, *id.* at 324, and instead focused on the second element of strict scrutiny review. It determined that the law was not narrowly tailored to serve the stated interest because a less restrictive alternative was available.

Id. at 329. And thus the law was held unconstitutional.

Strict scrutiny may also apply if there is a total ban on certain kinds of speech. For example, the Court applied strict scrutiny and struck down a local prohibition on real estate ("for sale") signs. In that case, the Court rejected a town's attempt to characterize the ban as a "time, place, or manner" restriction because the regulation targeted the message of the signs. Linmark Assocs., Inc. v. Township of Willingboro, 431 U.S. 85, 93–94 (1977). The Court found that the town failed to submit evidence proving that the ban would have the effect of achieving the town's stated goal of neighborhood stability and stemming white flight. *Id.* at 95–96. It also suggested that the alternatives available under the ban were not satisfactory because they were more expensive and less effective. *Id.* at 93.

2. INTERMEDIATE SCRUTINY

If a regulation is content-neutral, then the Supreme Court will apply a kind of intermediate scrutiny. The type of content-neutral regulation most often considered by courts is a "time, place, or manner" restriction, which restricts the duration, location, and/or format of an activity but does not affect the nature of the activity itself. These types of restrictions will be found constitutional if they: (1) do not refer to the content of the regulated speech; (2) are narrowly tailored to serve a significant (or substantial) government interest; and (3) leave open ample alternative channels for communication of the information. *See* Clark v. Community for Creative Non-Violence, 468 U.S. 288, 293 (1984). Note that the "narrowly tailored" language does not require that the government prove that its regulation is the least restrictive means of achieving this interest. *See* Ward v. Rock Against Racism, 491 U.S. 781, 798 (1989). Three decisions reveal how the Supreme Court has applied the intermediate scrutiny test to land use regulations.

In one case, the Court considered a zoning ordinance that had the effect of prohibiting all live entertainment (a form of expression). Schad v. Borough of Mount Ephraim, 452 U.S. 61 (1981). The plaintiffs' commercial establishment hosted nude dancing, and they alleged that the ordinance violated their rights of free expression. The Court held that the ordinance was unconstitutional because the borough did not show that it had a significant government interest in prohibiting nude dancing and because its exclusion of all live entertainment failed to leave open ample alternative channels of communication. *Id.* at 75–77. *Schad* suggests that the Court will apply intermediate scrutiny, rather than strict scrutiny, for total bans on certain kinds of commercial speech.

In a second case, the Court applied intermediate scrutiny to an ordinance that prohibited the posting of any sign (commercial or noncommercial) on public property. *See* Members of City Council v. Taxpayers for Vincent, 466 U.S. 789 (1984). Importantly for historic preservation law, the Court found that reduction of visual clutter "constitutes a significant substantial evil within the City's power to prohibit." *Id.* at 807 (referring to *Metromedia, Inc. v. City of San Diego*, 453 U.S. 490 (1981)); *see also* City of Ladue v. Gilleo, 512 U.S. 43, 54 (1994) (stating "the City's interest in minimizing the visual clutter associated with signs . . . is concededly valid"). Ultimately, the Court upheld the ordinance against the constitutional challenge since it (1) did not distinguish among different kinds of speech; (2) was narrowly tailored to directly eliminate the source of visual blight; (3) allowed for adequate alternate means of expression (such as leaflets). *Taxpayers for Vincent*, 466 U.S. at 812–815. The Court added that posting signs on public property was not a "uniquely valuable and important mode of communication." *Id.* at 812.

The Court also applied intermediate scrutiny to a zoning ordinance that prohibited adult movie theaters from locating within one thousand feet of any residential zone, church, park, or school, which it characterized as a time, place, or manner restriction. *See* City of Renton v. Playtime Theaters, 475 U.S. 41 (1986). Arguably, the regulation of adult movie theaters is a content-based regulation requiring strict scrutiny. However, the Court characterized the regulation as content-neutral after looking to the predominant intent of the ordinance, which was to curb "secondary effects" (such as crime and prostitution) directly related to the existence of these theaters. It found that the ordinance met the three-part test described above, since (1) the ordinance targeted secondary effects, not content; (2) the ordinance was narrowly tailored and the substantial interest was in the secondary effects; and (3) there were ample alternative channels for communication because 5 percent of the city's land could be used for adult theaters. *Id.* at 50–53.

3.　INCONSISTENCIES IN FREE SPEECH CLAUSE CASELAW

The Supreme Court has utilized the strict scrutiny and intermediate scrutiny tests described above in most of its free speech caselaw involving land use and signage regulations. However, the Supreme Court has not applied these two tests in a clear and consistent manner. Moreover, the Court has developed other tests that are similar to, but not exactly the same as, the two tests described above.

As one example of inconsistency in free speech clause caselaw, we note that the Court has not always clearly stated whether the regulation is content-based or content-neutral, and thus has not always clearly stated which level of scrutiny it should be applying. For example, in a 1994 case evaluating a locality's ban on all residential lawn signs, prior precedent suggested that the Court should have applied strict scrutiny because the ordinance worked as a total ban on an avenue for noncommercial speech. *See* City of Ladue v. Gilleo, 512 U.S. 43 (1994). The Court, however, avoided this issue—hinting it would apply strict scrutiny but really only taking to its logical conclusion the city's argument that the ordinance be reviewed on intermediate scrutiny (and finding that it failed). *Id.* at 56–57.

The Court has also applied different tests to different types of speech or restrictions on speech. For example, *United States v. O'Brien*, 391 U.S. 367 (1968), offers a four-part intermediate scrutiny test that applies to "incidental restrictions" on free speech. It allows incidental restrictions on speech if:

> [1] it is within the constitutional power of the Government; [2] if it furthers an important or substantial governmental interest; [3] if the governmental interest is unrelated to the suppression of free expression; and [4] if the incidental restriction on alleged First Amendment freedoms is no greater than is essential to the furtherance of that interest.

Id. at 377. This four-part test looks similar to the three-part intermediate scrutiny test discussed above, but it is more tailored to a particular type of speech.

Similarly, the *Central Hudson* test is a four-factor test that is used to evaluate regulations on commercial speech. *See* Central Hudson Gas & Electric Corp. v. Pub. Serv. Comm'n of N.Y., 447 U.S. 557 (1980). This analysis asks:

> At the outset, [1] we must determine whether the expression is protected by the First Amendment. For commercial speech to come within that provision, it at least must concern lawful activity and not be misleading. [2] Next, we ask whether the asserted governmental

interest is substantial. If both inquiries yield positive answers, we must determine whether the regulation [3] directly advances the governmental interest asserted, and [4] whether it is not more extensive than is necessary to serve that interest.

Id. at 566. Even the Court has difficulty applying the *Central Hudson* test, as can be seen in the 1981 Supreme Court case, *Metromedia, Inc. v. City of San Diego*, 453 U.S. 490 (1981) (dealing with a billboard ordinance allowing commercial on-site signs but banning both commercial off-site signs and most noncommercial advertising). In that case, the Court issued five opinions, none of which obtained a majority, and each of which interpreted prior tests slightly differently (or offered a few new arguments).

Other special rules for speech related to campaign finance, students' speech in schools, defamation/libel, the rights to assemble and associate, speech by anonymous persons, and the relationship between the free speech clause and other constitutional clauses (such as the religious liberty clauses) will not be discussed here. For a clearer view on this area of murky Supreme Court jurisprudence, see Professor Alan Weinstein's Chapter 6 in the 2001 *Context Sensitive Signage Design*, an American Planning Association research guide edited by Marya Morris and others.

B. APPLICATION TO HISTORIC PRESERVATION

The Supreme Court has never taken a case involving the conflict between free speech and historic preservation. However, its decisions in the land use and signage arenas (several of which are described above) suggest that the free speech clause constrains government behavior in the preservation context in a few key ways. As a general rule, a historic preservation law must not be a guise for restricting free speech on the basis of the personal tastes of local officials; nor may it be overbroad or vague. Beyond these broad guidelines, lower courts will likely apply two standards of review—strict scrutiny or intermediate scrutiny—in a manner similar to the Supreme Court.

1. STRICT SCRUTINY

A court will apply strict scrutiny to a historic preservation law that regulates speech on the basis of content. To survive, the law must be (1) justified by a compelling government interest, and (2) narrowly tailored to achieve (or be the least restrictive means of achieving) that interest.

Only very rarely will a historic preservation law be found to regulate on the basis of content, since such laws typically tend to focus on aesthetic or cosmetic issues and not speech. Consider, however, an ordinance that regulates signage in a local historic district and allows "flags or banners of the United States or other political subdivisions thereof" but prohibits other kinds of flags or banners. A

Georgia federal district court considered this exact scenario and determined the signage ordinance to be content-based. *See* Lamar Advertising Co. v. City of Douglasville, Ga., 254 F. Supp. 2d 1321, 1331 (N.D. Ga. 2003) (finding the regulation unconstitutional by applying Supreme Court rules relating to prior restraint).

If a court reviews a historic preservation law that restricts speech based on its content and applies strict scrutiny, then a government will have to show that its interest in enacting the law is compelling. Historic preservation laws are likely to fail this part of the strict scrutiny test. No federal court has found that historic preservation is a compelling government interest, even though many courts have found it to be a significant or substantial government interest. Similarly, aesthetic ends are not considered to be compelling government interests.

Illustrating this point is a federal district court decision analyzing a signage regulation that covered, among other areas, a National Historic Landmark and other historic properties. *See* Sandhills Ass'n of Realtors v. Vill. of Pinehurst, No. 1:98CV00303, 1999 WL 1129624 (M.D. N.C. Nov. 8, 1999). The court first determined that the signage regulation was content-based because it regulated the type of information that could be placed on realty sale and lease signs. *Id.* at *9. Consequently, the court applied strict scrutiny. It found that neither the village's "strong interest in maintaining its historical ambience and the charm of its lush green setting through land use," *id.* at *1, nor any other interests expressed by the village were compelling government interests. *Id.* at *10. In the *Sandhills Association* case, the regulation did not solely target historic properties. However, it is one example of a court applying strict scrutiny analysis and finding that historic preservation is not a compelling government interest.

We should mention two recent cases that applied the wrong Supreme Court test to historic preservation laws. The "prior restraint" test essentially mandates that content-based regulations will be found unconstitutional, as an alternative to the strict scrutiny analysis just described. It is typically used in cases involving government censorship (such as government approvals of art exhibitions or public injunctions on newspaper stories), not in cases involving land use regulations. In *Lusk v. Village of Cold Spring*, 475 F.3d 480 (2d Cir. 2007), a property owner contended that a historic district regulation requiring him to obtain a certificate of appropriateness before he could post a sign in a historic district violated his free speech rights. The court determined that the regulation effected a "prior restraint" on his expression because it required administrative approval of speech. *Id.* at 485. Under Supreme Court jurisprudence, there is a heavy presumption against the constitutionality of regulations characterized as be prior restraints on speech, and the regulation at issue in *Lusk* did not overcome this presumption. *Id.* at 487. Using similar reasoning, a Georgia federal district court also applied prior restraint rules to strike down as

unconstitutional a signage policy that allowed the
local historic commission some discretion in
reviewing applications for property owners to post
signs. *See Lamar Advertising Co.* at 1331. That
court found that a sign ordinance that allowed some
flags and banners but not others was content-based
and was therefore unconstitutional. *Id.* at 1331–32.
Both of these recent cases determined that fairly
common historic district regulations operated as
prior restraints on speech and handily dismissed
them as unconstitutional.

These cases are outliers whose reasoning should
not be incorporated into other courts' decisions.
Wooden application of the prior restraint
presumption would fatally undermine all
preservation regulation of private property if it
would apply strict scrutiny to, say, denying a permit
to build a modernist cube building in a Victorian
historic district. Historic preservation laws regulate
aesthetic expression but only in specified places and
thus should generally not be held to more than
intermediate scrutiny.

In sum, strict scrutiny will almost certainly be
fatal to a historic preservation law that is not
justified by some other interest a court would deem
compelling. Governments should therefore ensure
that their historic preservation laws do not regulate
on the basis of content.

2.   INTERMEDIATE SCRUTINY

If a historic preservation law is content-neutral,
then a court will apply intermediate scrutiny to

review how it holds up against a constitutional challenge that it infringes on the right to free speech. To survive, a content-neutral law must (1) not refer to the content of the regulated speech; (2) be narrowly tailored to serve a significant (or substantial) government interest; and (3) leave open ample alternative channels for communication of the information.

Historic preservation laws and decisions made pursuant to those laws are almost always considered content-neutral. The three federal circuit court decisions dealing with this question, for example, found that complete bans on newspaper racks, off-site signs, and street performances in historic districts were content-neutral time, place, or manner regulations because they did not refer to affected speech and did not discriminate on the basis of viewpoints of the speakers. *See* Horton v. City of St. Augustine, Fla., 272 F.3d 1318, 1333–34 (11th Cir. 2001); Globe Newspaper Co. v. Beacon Hill Architectural Comm'n, 100 F.3d 175, 183 (1st Cir. 1996); Messer v. City of Douglasville, Ga., 975 F.2d 1505, 1509 (11th Cir. 1992). Similarly, federal district courts have found regulations requiring property owners to obtain certificates of appropriateness prior to building within the historic district, as well as regulations governing the size and location of murals in historic districts, to be content-neutral. *See* Chabad Lubavitch of Litchfield County, Inc. v. Borough of Litchfield, 853 F. Supp. 2d 214, 233 (D. Conn. 2012); Burke v. City of Charleston, 893 F. Supp. 589, 609–10 (D. S.C. 1995), *rev'd on other grounds*, 139 F.3d 401 (4th Cir. 1998).

And a state court in Massachusetts characterized as content-neutral a local historic commission's decision preventing a property owner from erecting a sixty-eight foot radio antenna on a non-designated property within a historic district. *See* Sleeper v. Old King's Highway Regional Historic Dist. Comm'n, 417 N.E.2d 987 (Mass. App. Ct. 1981).

Once a court determines that a regulation is content-neutral, it will review whether the regulation is narrowly tailored to serve a significant or substantial government interest. A historic preservation regulation will almost always be deemed to further a significant or substantial government interest. The Supreme Court has repeatedly stated that aesthetics and reduction of visual clutter rise to the level of a significant or substantial government interest under the intermediate scrutiny standard. *See, e.g.,* City of Ladue v. Gilleo, 512 U.S. 43, 54 (1994); Members of City Council v. Taxpayers for Vincent, 466 U.S. 789, 807 (1984); Metromedia, Inc. v. City of San Diego, 453 U.S. 490, 510–12 (1981). Lower courts have consistently followed this approach. For example, the Ninth Circuit found a ban on handbills on a historic street within a state historic park to be justified by a significant government interest in "preserving the historic quality" of the historic street. Gerritsen v. City of Los Angeles, 994 F.2d 570, 577 (9th Cir. 1993).

The question of whether the law is narrowly tailored to meet the significant or substantial government interest, however, is more fact-specific.

This analysis involves deciding whether the regulation restricts more speech than is necessary to further the government interest. As noted above, regulations do not need to be the least restrictive means of achieving the government interest. Generally, historic district regulations have been considered to be narrowly tailored to further the government interest. *See, e.g.,* Hop Publications, Inc. v. City of Boston, 334 F. Supp. 2d 35, 43–44 (D. Mass. 2004) (determining that a ban on newsracks in a historic district did not burden more speech than necessary in part because the local commission had carefully considered alternatives to the ban).

Next, the court will review whether the law leaves open ample alternative channels of communication. On this issue, we turn to *Globe Newspaper Company v. Beacon Hill Architectural Commission*, 100 F.3d 175 (1st Cir. 1996), a First Circuit decision with excellent analysis of free speech issues related to historic preservation. The case involved a newspaper publishers' constitutional challenge of a local historic district commission's ban on newspaper racks in a historic district. The court determined this ban was content-neutral and applied intermediate scrutiny. *Id.* at 186. It first found aesthetics to be a significant government interest—even more so because the district was designated to be a historic district. *Id.* at 187. It also found that the ordinance was narrowly tailored for three reasons: (1) it promoted the commission's significant interest in preserving the district's aesthetics; (2) of the five alternatives considered by the commission, banning the newsracks would most completely address their inappropriateness; and (3) the ordinance did not burden or otherwise affect any other means of distribution. *Id.* at 188–89. Finally, the court reviewed whether the speakers (in this case, newspaper publishers) had ample alternative channels of communication. The court noted that the regulation "leaves unaffected the Newspapers' primary means of distribution within the District: home delivery, sales by stores, street vendors, and mail" and that no point in the historic district was more than one thousand feet from a source of publications. *Id.* at 192. In fact, the court noted, the newspaper publishers were able "to distribute publications through street vendors in the very public forum—the District's sidewalks—from which the newsracks are banned." *Id.* at 193. A group of newspaper publishers challenged another local commission's set of guidelines that banned all newsracks, with identical results. *See* Hop Publications, Inc. v. City of Boston, 334 F. Supp. 2d 35 (D. Mass. 2004).

Another interesting case involving free speech is *Board of Managers of Soho International Arts Condominium v. City of New York*, No. 01 Civ. 1226 (DAB), 2004 WL 1982520 (S.D.N.Y. Sept. 8, 2004). In that case, property owners of a building in the Soho-Cast Iron Historic District in Manhattan were denied a certificate of appropriateness from the local historic commission when they applied to remove a large piece of sculptural art appended to the historic building. They argued that they were "compelled" to speak by maintaining the artwork on their property, in violation of their free speech rights. The artwork was not included in the original designation for the historic district, but according to the local historic commission it had since come to "contribute[ ] to the special architectural and historic character of the historic district and. . . its permanent removal will adversely affect the district's special sense of place." *Id.* at *5. The court characterized the commission's decision as content-neutral because it was not targeting speech and, more specifically, did not intend to compel the property owners to speak by requiring them to display the artwork. *Id.* at *15. Moreover, the court found that "the Commission's denial of the [certificate of appropriateness] and its permit to repair and reinstall the Work further[ed] the substantial government objective of preserving aesthetics in an historic district" and did not burden more speech than necessary. Thus, the local historic district's decision withstood the constitutional challenge. *Id.* at *16.

In sum, historic preservation regulations analyzed under intermediate scrutiny will almost always pass constitutional muster. The cases above show courts upholding local ordinances regulating newsracks, signage, street performance, artwork, handbill distribution, and antenna locations within historic districts.

CHAPTER 11

ARCHAEOLOGICAL PROTECTIONS

Long before the United States existed, indigenous persons and early European settlers lived, worshiped, worked, and died here. These people left valuable tangible clues about their traditions, culture, and technologies—clues that modern researchers may piece together to solve questions about our past. In addition to the informational value of these resources, they may have cultural or religious significance, especially to modern-day Native American groups. Of course, countless archaeological resources remain undiscovered.

In modern times, destruction, alteration, and removal have become the biggest threats to archaeologically significant sites and artifacts because these resources may be in fragile condition, may lose their value if altered, and may be moved without detection. Beginning in the early twentieth century, Congress and state legislatures passed archaeological protection statutes to control access to these resources and prohibit their destruction or significant alteration. Whether at the state or federal level, such statutes usually address both known and unknown resources, and they usually limit their scope to those resources on public or tribal land.

The urge to protect archaeologically significant sites and artifacts has inspired several important pieces of federal legislation. This Chapter focuses on four federal statutes that specifically address

archaeological resources: Antiquities Act; Historic
Sites Act; Archaeological Resources Protection Act;
and Abandoned Shipwreck Act. The applicability of
Section 106 of the National Historic Preservation
Act (discussed in Chapter III) to archaeological
resources is also examined.

A. ANTIQUITIES ACT

At the turn of the twentieth century, there were
mounting concerns over the rising theft and
destruction of archaeological sites, particularly in
the southwestern United States. In response,
Congress passed the Antiquities Act of 1906, the
earliest piece of federal legislation designed to
preserve historic and prehistoric resources. It
authorizes the President to designate national
monuments on federal land; requires permits for
examining or excavating archaeological sites on
federal land; and imposes penalties on the unlawful
appropriation, excavation, injury, or destruction of
certain significant resources. This Part provides an
overview of these three primary functions, along
with an explanation of key terms.

1. OVERVIEW

The Antiquities Act has three primary functions.
See 16 U.S.C. §§ 431–33. First, it authorizes the
President to designate national monuments on
federal lands that contain historic or prehistoric
resources with scientific or educational value.
Second, it empowers three federal agencies to
manage the access to and protection of the historic

and scientific resources on federal lands through permits. Third, the Antiquities Act prescribes civil and/or criminal penalties for appropriating, excavating, injuring, or destroying certain resources on federal land without permission from the relevant federal official. Each of these functions is considered in greater detail below.

a. Designation of National Monuments

The Antiquities Act authorizes the President of the United States to proclaim national monuments on "lands owned or controlled by the Government of the United States" which contain "historic landmarks, historic and prehistoric structures, and other objects of historic or scientific interest." 16 U.S.C. § 431. President Theodore Roosevelt created the first national monument, Devil's Tower in Wyoming, shortly after the Antiquities Act was passed. Subsequent acts of Congress have limited Presidential authority under the Antiquities Act by requiring congressional authorization for monument extensions, for withdrawals exceeding 5,000 acres in Alaska, and for the establishment of any new monuments in Wyoming. *See id.* §§ 431a & 3213.

Courts have never reversed or otherwise limited a presidential designation. *See, e.g.,* Cameron v. United States, 252 U.S. 450, 455 (1920) (rejecting a claim that the President lacked authority to designate as a monument the Grand Canyon); Wyoming v. Franke, 58 F. Supp. 890 (D. Wyo. 1945) (holding that a state's loss of revenue from taxes and grazing fees through the designation of a national monument was not a legal basis to reject a monument designation). Rather, political pressures and limited federal resources are probably the biggest checks on the President's exercise of Antiquities Act authority. Since the promulgation of the Antiquities Act, sixteen presidents have created 137 monuments. Often, monuments are created to protect a resource from harm. For example, the Grand Canyon was declared a national monument to shield it from commercial developers, while the designation of the Petrified Forest protected it against the looting of mineralized remains of ancient forests.

Around half of the presidential monument proclamations have reserved areas of fewer than 5,000 acres. The smallest is the African Burial Ground National Monument in New York City at 0.345 acres, established by President George W. Bush. The Papahanaumokuakea Marine National Monument, also reserved by President Bush, is the largest monument at approximately 89 million acres in the Pacific Ocean. Nearly half of the current national parks (including the Grand Canyon National Park) were initially designated as national monuments under the Antiquities Act.

b. Issuance of Permits on Federal Land

The Antiquities Act also authorizes the Secretaries of three federal agencies to establish permitting systems for "the examination of ruins, the excavation of archaeological sites, and the gathering of objects of antiquity upon the lands under their respective jurisdictions." 16 U.S.C. § 432. The Secretary of Agriculture may develop permits for forest reserves, while the Secretary of the Army may do so for military reservations. 43 C.F.R. § 3.1. The Secretary of the Interior handles permitting for "all other lands owned or controlled by the Government of the United States." *Id.*

How do permit applications typically work? Only "museums, universities, colleges, or other recognized scientific or educational institutions" may apply for a permit to examine ruins, excavate archaeological sites, and gather objects of antiquity located on federal land. *Id.* § 3.3. Applicants must apply for a permit with the managing agency and include an "exact statement of the character of the work" that will be performed. *Id.* § 3.5. The managing agency then refers the application to the Smithsonian Institution for recommendation. *See id.* § 3.8.

Once a permit is granted, the permit holder must abide by all conditions, including time limits, seasonal reports, and the restoration of "the lands upon which they have worked to their customary condition." *Id.* § 3.11. Failure to adhere to permit conditions may result in permit termination and seizure of any objects of antiquity collected. *See id.* §§ 3.12 & 3.16.

c. Penalties

The Antiquities Act subjects anyone "who shall appropriate, excavate, injure, or destroy any historic or prehistoric ruin or monument, or any object of antiquity" on "lands owned or controlled by the Government of the United States" without permission to civil and/or criminal penalties. 16 U.S.C. § 433. Violations are punishable by fine of up to $500 and/or imprisonment of up to ninety days. Given the low stakes of these penalties, it may be easy to see why prosecutors prefer the penalty provisions of the Archaeological Resources Protection Act, discussed in Part C of this Chapter.

Two federal circuit courts have addressed the constitutionality of section 433 the Antiquities Act, with different results. In *United States v. Diaz*, the Ninth Circuit held it unconstitutional because the resources protected by section 433—ruins, monuments, objects of antiquity—were never defined and too vague, violating the due process clause of the U.S. Constitution. 499 F.2d 113 (9th Cir. 1974). However, in *United States v. Smyer*, the Tenth Circuit held that the terms of section 433 of the Antiquities Act offered a sufficiently definite warning to give a person of ordinary intelligence a reasonable opportunity to know that excavating prehistoric Indian burial grounds and taking antiquities is prohibited. 596 F.2d 939 (10th Cir. 1979). The different outcomes reflect the different factual scenarios in each case. Ultimately, courts interpreting the Antiquities Act will assess the vagueness of the statute in light of the particular conduct with which the defendant is charged.

2.   KEY TERMS

Neither the text of the Antiquities Act nor its implementing regulations define any individual term in the Act. Courts, therefore, have been tasked with interpreting the meaning of several important statutory phrases. The first is "public proclamation," the documentary vehicle through which national monuments under the Antiquities Act are created. The second phrase, "in his discretion," is concerned with the scope of the President's power under the Antiquities Act. The third phrase, "lands owned or controlled by the government," tells us what lands are protected under the Antiquities Act and where national monuments may be located, while the fourth phrase, "other objects of historic and scientific interest," identifies what may be designated as a national monument. The fifth phrase, "smallest area compatible," is concerned with presidential discretion as to the proper size for monuments.

a. Public Proclamation

To designate national monuments, the President must issue a public proclamation, also known as a presidential proclamation. It is a written document that delineates the monument's boundaries and describes the special qualities of the objects, landmarks, scenic vistas and/or structures receiving protection. The proclamation may also list threats to the resources being protected, as President Clinton did when he identified the threat of coal mining operations in his proclamation creating the Grand Staircase–Escalante National Monument.

Like executive orders, proclamations carry the force of law. The difference between the two is the target audience: executive orders are aimed at government agencies, while proclamations are aimed at those outside of the government. Note that proclamations designating national monuments are not subject to review under the National Environmental Policy Act (discussed in Chapter IV). *See, e.g.,* Alaska v. Carter, 462 F. Supp. 1155 (D. Alaska 1978).

b. In His Discretion

The Antiquities Act grants President authority to designate national monuments "in his discretion." With this broad language, no legal challenge to the President's authority has been successful. For instance, in *Tulare County v. Bush*, the D.C. Circuit held that the President's exercise of his discretion to establish national monuments under the Antiquities Act does not violate the property clause of the U.S. Constitution because the Act includes intelligible principles to guide the President's action. 306 F.3d 1138 (D.C. Cir. 2002). Similarly, courts have rejected challenges based on the nondelegation doctrine and the spending clause of the U.S. Constitution, because Congress clearly intended to delegate decision-making authority to the President. *See, e.g.,* Utah Ass'n of Counties v. Bush, 316 F. Supp. 2d 1172, 1185–86 (D. Utah 2004). Judicial review of the President's exercise of discretion in designating a national monument is limited to the narrow question of whether the President in fact invoked his powers under the Antiquity Act.

c. Lands Owned or Controlled by the Government

The Antiquities Act concerns itself primarily with "lands owned or controlled" by the federal government. *See* 16 U.S.C. §§ 431 & 433. Usually, federal ownership and control can be clearly demonstrated through chains of title or other documentation. Among the objects raising the most legally interesting questions are offshore shipwrecks. One federal court determined that an eighteenth century shipwreck located within a national park off the coast of Florida was protected by the Antiquities Act. *See* Lathrop v. Unidentified, Wrecked & Abandoned Vessel, 817 F. Supp. 953 (M.D. Fla. 1993). However, in *Treasure Salvors, Inc. v. Unidentified Wrecked and Abandoned Sailing Vessel*, the Fifth Circuit held that the Antiquities Act did not apply to a shipwreck resting on the continental shelf outside the territorial waters of the United States. 569 F.2d 330 (5th Cir. 1978).

In some cases, the boundaries of a national monument may surround "islands" of nonfederal lands located within such boundaries. These islands are not "lands owned or controlled" by the federal government. While a monument designation does not bring nonfederal lands into federal ownership or extinguish valid existing rights such as mineral leases, mining claims, or rights of way, it may severely restrict the development of these inholdings because development may be constrained by federal management of the surrounding monument lands. *See, e.g.*, Wilkenson v. U.S. Dep't of Interior, 634 F. Supp. 1265 (D. Col. 1986) (finding that the federal government could restrict, but not eliminate, travel on a pre-existing right of way through a national monument). State or private landowners within a monument may pursue land exchanges with the federal government, and some monument proclamations explicitly authorize land exchanges to further the protective purposes of the monument.

d. Other Objects of Historic or Scientific Interest

The Antiquities Act authorizes the President to protect "historic landmarks, historic and prehistoric structures, and other objects of historic or scientific interest." 16 U.S.C. § 431. Courts have construed "other objects of historic and scientific interest" broadly to include not just archaeologically significant resources but also entire ecosystems and scenic vistas. *See, e.g.*, Cameron v. United States, 252 U.S. 450 (1920) (finding that the term includes ecosystems and scenic vistas); Mountain States Legal Found. v. Bush, 306 F.3d 1132 (D.C. Cir. 2002) (holding that the term is not limited to rare and discrete man-made objects but may include natural wonders and wilderness values).

Among other resources appropriately covered by the Antiquities Act, President Obama recently designated the San Juan Islands National Monument in the State of Washington. This 970–

acre monument contains an archipelago of over 450 islands, rocks, and pinnacles in Puget Sound, including diverse habitats, numerous wildlife species, historic lighthouses, archaeological sites, and an "unmatched landscape." PRESIDENTIAL PROCLAMATION—ESTABLISHMENT OF THE SAN JUAN ISLANDS NATIONAL MONUMENT, Mar. 25, 2013.

e. Smallest Area Compatible

When the President designates a national monument under the Antiquities Act, the size of the national monument must be "the smallest area compatible with the proper care and management of the objects to be protected." 16 U.S.C. § 431. Unsurprisingly, the appropriate size for national monuments has been a contentious issue, and courts have consistently deferred to the President's judgment. *See, e.g.*, Tulare County v. Bush, 306 F.3d 1138, 1142 (D.C. Cir. 2002) (finding no factual basis for the claim that Grand Sequoia National Monument's size—327,769 acres—was not "the smallest area compatible with proper care and management").

B.   HISTORIC SITES ACT

Nearly three decades after the Antiquities Act authorized the President to designate national monuments, Congress passed the Historic Sites Act of 1935. This Act organized the myriad federally owned parks, monuments, and historic sites under the National Park Service of the Department of Interior and expanded the executive branch's ability to preserve, maintain, and acquire historic sites. In addition to providing an overview of the key provisions of the Historic Sites Act, this Part discusses a related statute, the Historic and Archaeological Data Protection Preservation Act.

1. OVERVIEW

The Historic Sites Act of 1935 (HSA) formed the foundation of the modern preservation movement. It articulated for the first time "a national policy to preserve for public use historic sites, buildings, and objects of national significance for the inspiration and benefit of the people of the United States." 16 U.S.C. § 461.

Beyond enshrining historic preservation as a government objective, the HSA also aimed to establish a framework for a system of national historic sites in three ways. First, it mandated that the Secretary of the Interior, through the National Park Service, collect extensive information about historically noteworthy places in the United States. Specifically, the HSA required the National Park Service to:

(a) Secure, collate, and preserve drawings, plans, photographs, and other data of historic and archaeologic sites, buildings, and objects.

(b) Make a survey of historic and archaeologic sites, buildings, and objects for the purpose of determining which possess exceptional value as commemorating or illustrating the history of the United States.

(c) Make necessary investigations and researches in the United States relating to particular sites, buildings, or objects to obtain true and accurate historical and archaeological facts and information concerning the same.

Id. §§ 462(a)–(c). The information collected through these efforts formed the basis for the Historic American Buildings Survey, the Historic American Engineering Record, the Historic American Landscapes Survey, and the National Historic Landmarks Program, which was later integrated into the National Register after the promulgation of the National Historic Preservation Act in 1966 (discussed in Chapter III). Information about the designation criteria for National Historic Landmarks is contained in Chapter II.

Secondly, the HSA authorized the Secretary of the Interior through the National Park Service to perform a broad range of historic preservation activities. Among other things, the HSA empowered the National Park Service to acquire, manage, operate, and restore nationally significant archaeological sites, buildings, and properties; enter into cooperative efforts with other agencies and with state and local governments to preserve historic resources; establish education programs and museums to promote historic resource literacy; and to erect and maintain tablets to commemorate historic or prehistoric places and events of national significance. *See id.* §§ 462(d)–(h) & (j). The power to acquire significant resources "by gift, purchase, or otherwise," *id.* § 462(d), deserves additional clarification. Courts have interpreted this phrase to include the use of eminent domain, which therefore allows the Secretary of the Interior to take private property without consent of the owner for the public purpose of preserving sites of national historic significance. *See*, *e.g.*, Barnidge v. United States, 101 F.2d 295, 299 (8th Cir. 1939) (holding that the HSA granted the government the authority to condemn private property for the public purpose of preserving sites of national historic importance to "commemorate and illustrate to nation's history").

Finally, to assist the National Park Service in its sundry activities, including historic preservation efforts, the HSA created the National Park System Advisory Board. It consists of up to twelve people from varied geographic regions of the United States. *See* 16 U.S.C. § 463.

2.   HISTORIC AND ARCHAEOLOGICAL DATA PROTECTION PRESERVATION ACT

The Historic and Archaeological Data Protection and Preservation Act of 1974 (HADPA) extends the powers of the Secretary of the Interior beyond those granted in the Historic Sites Act. 16 U.S.C. §§ 469–469c2. HADPA is designed to preserve:

historical and archeological data (including relics and specimens) which might otherwise be irreparably lost or destroyed as the result of (1) flooding, the building of access roads, the erection of workmen's communities, the relocation of railroads and highways, and other alterations of the terrain caused by the construction of a dam by any agency of the United States, or by any private person or corporation holding a license issued by any such agency or (2) any alteration of the terrain caused as a result of any Federal construction project or federally licensed activity or program.

Id. § 469. Under HADPA, federal agencies are required to inform the Secretary of the Interior if they discover, or are notified in writing by an appropriate historical or archaeological authority, that their activities "in connection with any Federal construction project of federally licensed project, activity or program may cause irreparable loss or destruction of significant scientific, prehistorical, historical, or archeological data." *Id.* § 469a–1(a). The Secretary may survey the affected site, and if any relics or specimens are found, she must consult with the appropriate federal and state agencies, or educational or cultural institutions to preserve the objects. *See id.* §§ 469a–2 & 469a–3. In short, HADPA's significance is that it protects historical and archaeological resources during the entirety of construction, not merely during the planning phase.

C. ARCHAEOLOGICAL RESOURCES PROTECTION ACT

Fears that archaeological resources on public and Indian lands were endangered prompted Congress to pass the Archaeological Resources Protection Act of 1979 (ARPA). *See* 16 U.S.C. §§ 470aa–470ll. ARPA expands upon the meager archaeological protections contained in the Antiquities Act by regulating and systematizing the excavation or removal of archaeological resources on public and Indian lands as well as providing stringent criminal and/or civil penalties for violations of the Act. ARPA has since become the primary tool for archaeological resources management and protection. Following a brief overview of ARPA, this Part covers key terms and the application of the statute. It concludes with notes on the issue of confidentiality and the relationship between ARPA and Section 106 of the National Historic Preservation Act.

1.   OVERVIEW

In the Archaeological Resources Protection Act of 1979 (ARPA), Congress declared that archaeological resources on public and Indian lands are "an irreplaceable part of the Nation's heritage." 16 U.S.C. § 470aa(a)(1). The purpose of ARPA is therefore "to secure, for the present and future benefit of the American people, the protection of archaeological resources and sites which are on public lands and Indian lands." *Id.* § 470aa(b).

ARPA accomplishes its stated purpose in several ways. First, it prohibits unauthorized excavation, removal, damage, alteration, and trafficking of protected resources. Second, ARPA establishes a management regime that prohibits the excavation and removal of archaeological resources from public and Indian lands without a permit. Finally, it imposes robust civil and/or criminal penalties for violations of the Act, with escalating penalties for repeat offenders. Each of these elements will be discussed further below.

2. KEY TERMS

The Archaeological Resources Protection Act (ARPA) has six key terms. The first, "archaeological resource," is vital to understanding the types of resources that ARPA protects. The second term, "person," and the third term, "Indian tribe," are important because they delineate the people to whom ARPA applies. The fourth term, "federal land manager," identifies the officials responsible for stewardship over public and Indian lands. And the final two terms, "public lands" and "Indian lands," define the jurisdictional boundaries of ARPA.

a. Archaeological Resource

The statute defines "archaeological resource" as "any material remains of past human life or activities which are of archaeological interest" and which are "at least 100 years of age." 16 U.S.C. § 470bb(1). The regulations implementing ARPA present a seemingly exhaustive list of broad classes of material remains: mounds, pits, tools, weapons, clothing, ornaments, debris, human remains, artwork, caves containing material remains, and shipwrecks. 43 C.F.R. § 7.3(3). However, some resources—including paleontological remains, coins, bullets, unworked materials, and rocks—are not considered archaeological resources under ARPA unless they possess a "direct physical relationship" with an archaeological resource. *Id.* § 7.3(4).

ARPA's broad definition for archaeological resources has been challenged in court as being unconstitutionally overbroad and vague, but to no avail. *See* United States v. Austin, 902 F.2d 743, 745 (9th Cir. 1990) (rejecting a vagueness challenge by finding that the statute provided fair notice to the defendant that scrapers and arrow points were "weapons" and "tools" under ARPA).

b. Person

A "person" as defined in ARPA's implementing regulations means "an individual, corporation, partnership, trust, institution, association, or any other private entity, or any officer, employee, agent, department, or instrumentality of the United States, or of any Indian tribe, or of any State or political subdivision thereof." 43 C.F.R. § 7.3(g). Thus ARPA applies to all private persons, any public official at the federal, state, or local level, and any tribal official.

c. Indian Tribe

The term "Indian tribe" as defined in ARPA means any "Indian tribe, band, nation, or other organized group or community, including any Alaska Native village or regional or village corporation as defined in, or established pursuant to, the Alaska Native Claims Settlement Act [43 U.S.C. 1601 et seq.]." 16 U.S.C. § 470bb(5). To add precision to this statutory definition, ARPA's implementing regulations clarify that an "Indian tribe" under ARPA is (1) any federally recognized tribal entity; (2) any "Alaska Native village or regional or village corporation as defined in or established pursuant to the Alaska Native Claims Settlement Act"; and (3) any "Alaska Native village or tribe which is recognized by the Secretary of the Interior as eligible for services provided by the Bureau of Indian Affairs." 43 C.F.R. § 7.3(f).

d. Federal Land Manager

ARPA designates different federal land managers for different types of lands. For public lands, the federal land manager is the Secretary of the department or the head of any other agency with "primary management authority" over such lands, unless the department or agency has delegated that responsibility to the Secretary of the Interior. 43 C.F.R. § 7.3(c)(1) & (3). For Indian lands, or public lands for which no department or agency is responsible, the federal land manager is the Secretary of the Interior. *See id.* § 7.3(c)(2).

e. Public Lands

ARPA protects archaeological resources on "public lands," which are defined by the statute as "lands which are owned and administered by the United States as part of the national park system, the national wildlife refuge system, or the national forest system; and all other lands the fee title to which is held by the United States." 16 U.S.C. § 470bb(3). The only caveat is that the statute explicitly states that "lands on the Outer Continental Shelf and lands which are under the jurisdiction of the Smithsonian Institution" are not subject to ARPA. *Id.*

Courts interpreting the term public lands under ARPA examine all of the interests in the parcel of land to determine whether the statute applies. *See* Fein v. Peltier, 949 F. Supp. 374, 379–380 (D.V.I. 1996) (holding that a one-acre parcel owned and operated as part of the ninety-four-acre Virgin Islands National Park is public land under ARPA, despite the fact that the one-acre parcel was subject to a holder's possessory interest for a term of years, because the United States holds fee title to the parcel).

f. Indian Lands

ARPA protects archaeological resources on "Indian lands," which means "lands of Indian tribes, or Indian individuals, which are either held in trust by the United States or subject to a restriction against alienation imposed by the United States, except for any subsurface interests in lands not owned or controlled by an Indian tribe or an Indian individual." 16 U.S.C. § 470bb(4).

Courts have interpreted the restriction against alienation clause of the definition broadly. *See* Starkey v. U.S. Dep't of Interior, 238 F. Supp. 2d 1188, 1193 (S.D. Cal. 2002) (holding that land owned in fee by the La Posta Band of Mission Indians was subject to ARPA because the Secretary of the Interior had to approve the conveyance of this property, which constituted a restriction against alienation imposed by the United States). But courts have refused to find that Indian land is subject to ARPA when the lands in question are ancestral rather than current. *See* Mashpee Tribe v. Watt, 542 F. Supp. 797 (D. Mass. 1982), *aff'd on other grounds*, 707 F.2d 23 (1st Cir. 1983) (finding that ARPA did not provide any cause of action for Native Americans who challenged the sale of ancestral lands owned by a town).

3. APPLICATION

The Archaeological Resources Protection Act (ARPA) protects archaeological resources located on public and Indian lands in several ways. ARPA specifically forbids unauthorized excavation, removal, damage, alteration, and trafficking of archaeological resources obtained from public and Indian lands. ARPA also establishes a permitting process to allow archaeological resources to be excavated or removed to support the public interest. Finally, ARPA imposes stiff civil and/or criminal penalties for violations of the statute. Each of these three mechanisms to protect archaeological resources will be discussed in turn below.

a. Prohibited Acts

ARPA places a strict prohibition on two kinds of actions involving archaeological resources. The first is that no one may "excavate, remove, damage, or otherwise alter or deface" any archaeological resources located on public lands or Indian lands, or attempt to do so, without a permit. 16 U.S.C. § 470ee(a). ARPA's second prohibition aims to stem illegal trafficking in looted items: no one may "sell, purchase, exchange, transport, receive, or offer to sell, purchase, or exchange any archeological resource" removed from public or Indian lands without permission. *Id.* §§ 470ee(b) & (c). This provision certainly includes those individuals who steal archaeological resources and try to sell them for profit. Perhaps less obviously, a museum would violate ARPA if it received or purchased historical items that were removed from public or Indian lands without a permit.

b. Permitting Process

Aside from prohibiting certain acts that would damage the archaeological record, ARPA provides a permitting process aimed at supporting and furthering the public's interest in archaeology. Any person may apply to the requisite federal land manager for a permit to "excavate or remove any archaeological resource located on public lands or Indian lands and to carry out activities associated with such excavation or removal." 16 U.S.C. § 470cc(a). The process for applying for a permit is outlined in 43 C.F.R. § 7.6, and includes, among other things, the nature and duration of the work, the qualifications of the applicant, and "the names of the university, museum, or other scientific or educational institution" where any archaeological resources collected will be stored. *Id.* § 7.6(b). If the issuance of an ARPA permit "may result in harm to, or destruction of, any Indian tribal religious or cultural site on public lands," the federal land manager must notify the tribes with historic ties to the land, and if requested, must meet with the tribes to determine ways to "avoid or mitigate potential harm or destruction." *Id.* § 7.7.

Not every activity on public or Indian lands requires an ARPA permit. An ARPA permit is only required for the excavation, collection, and/or removal of archaeological resources from public or Indian lands. The collection of items that are not archaeological resources (such as rocks, coins, or bullets) only requires a permit if it disturbs an archaeological resource. *See id.* § 7.5(b)(2). It is important to note that members of an Indian tribe may excavate and/or remove archaeological resources located on their respective Indian lands without a permit, provided that there is tribal law regulating such activities. If there is no tribal law on the subject, then a tribal member must apply for an ARPA permit. *See id.* § 7.5(b)(3).

There is also the issue of activities authorized by federal permits besides ARPA which are "exclusively for purposes other than the excavation and/or removal of archaeological resources." *Id.* § 7.5(b)(1). Such authorized activities only require an additional ARPA permit if they more than incidentally disturb archaeological resources. For example, neither the licensed drawdown of a reservoir for an irrigation project nor the authorized construction of fences and livestock watering facilities as part of a range restoration program requires an ARPA permit. San Carlos Apache Tribe v. United States, 272 F. Supp. 2d 860 (D. Ariz.

2003); Attakai v. United States, 746 F. Supp. 1395 (D. Ariz. 1990).

c. Penalties

ARPA authorizes powerful civil and/or criminal penalties for violations of the Act. For a first time offense, it provides that any person "who knowingly violates, or counsels, procures, solicits, or employs any other person to violate" the statute shall be fined up to $10,000, or imprisoned for up to one year, or both. 16 U.S.C. § 470ee(d). If the "commercial or archaeological value" of the resources involved "and the cost of restoration and repair of such resources exceeds the sum of $500," the fine may be up $20,000 and the prison term up to two years, or both. *Id.* For second or subsequent offenses a person may be fined up to $100,000, or imprisoned for up to five years, or both. *Id.*

Courts have interpreted various aspects of ARPA's penalty provisions. One particularly thorny issue is deciding when a person violates ARPA "knowingly." For example, the Ninth Circuit has reasoned that since "removing objects that are not 'archaeological resources' from public land is not a violation of ARPA, the knowingly requirement should apply to the term 'archaeological resources' as well as the prohibited act of removing." United States v. Lynch, 233 F.3d 1139, 1144 (9th Cir. 2000). But the Tenth Circuit rejected the argument that a person must "knowingly" be on federal land to violate ARPA because it would frustrate the purpose of the statute. United States v. Quarrell,

310 F.3d 664 (10th Cir. 2002). Prior acts of a defendant may also be considered in determining whether she acted knowingly. *See* United States v. Shumway, 112 F.3d 1413 (10th Cir. 1997). With respect to the reach of ARPA's penalty provisions, it is important to note that in *United States v. Gerber*, the Seventh Circuit concluded that ARPA penalties could be applied to archaeological resources unlawfully removed from private land that were subsequently placed in interstate commerce. 999 F.2d 1112 (7th Cir. 1993).

4. THE ISSUE OF CONFIDENTIALITY

Archaeological resources, especially human remains and items that are easily transportable, are prime targets for looters and traffickers. Recognizing this, ARPA strives to balance the public information disclosures typically required of government agencies with the need to keep archaeological sites secret to protect them from pillage. It does so by erring on the side of caution. The federal land manager issuing a permit for excavation or removal must keep information concerning "the nature and location of any archaeological resource" from the public unless she determines that the disclosure would further the purposes of ARPA and would "not create a risk of harm to such resources or to the site at which such resources are located." 16 U.S.C. § 470hh; 43 C.F.R. § 7.18. However, if the governor of any state makes a written request for specific information concerning the archaeological resources within her state and promises to adequately protect the confidentiality of the information, the federal land manager must make such information available. *See id.* § 7.18(a)(2).

5.   RELATIONSHIP WITH SECTION 106 OF THE NATIONAL HISTORIC PRESERVATION ACT

Section 106 of the National Historic Preservation Act (discussed in Chapter III) requires federal agencies to take into account the effect of their undertakings on any "district, site, building, structure, or object that is included in or eligible for inclusion in the National Register." 16 U.S.C. § 470f. This may require agencies to complete a lengthy process of evaluating the effects of their actions on sites or properties that include archaeological resources. The Archaeological Resources Protection Act (ARPA) states that the granting of an ARPA permit alone does not trigger Section 106 review requirements; but nor does permit issuance "excuse the federal land manager from compliance with Section 106 where otherwise required." 16 U.S.C. § 470cc(i); 43 C.F.R. § 7.12. If an agency, therefore, issues an ARPA permit as one piece of an undertaking requiring Section 106 review, the permit does not obviate the need for the agency to completely comply with Section 106.

D.   ABANDONED SHIPWRECK ACT

Congress passed the Abandoned Shipwreck Act in 1987 to resolve open questions as to the title of abandoned shipwrecks in state waters. It allows for the ownership of certain abandoned shipwrecks found embedded in, or on, a state's submerged lands to be transferred to the state. This Part describes the Abandoned Shipwrecks Act and its key terms, notes how it has been applied, and discusses the statute's relationship to the laws of salvage and finds.

1. OVERVIEW

Congress passed the Abandoned Shipwreck Act of 1987 (ASA) to clarify the ownership and the authority to manage and protect abandoned shipwrecks on states' submerged lands. Congress found that "States have the responsibility for management of a broad range of living and nonliving resources in State waters and submerged lands; and included in the range of resources are certain abandoned shipwrecks, which have been deserted and to which the owner has relinquished ownership rights with no retention." 43 U.S.C. § 2101. Accordingly, the United States asserts title and ownership over abandoned shipwrecks that are "embedded" in a state's submerged lands or, in the case of shipwrecks listed or eligible for the National Register, "on" a state's submerged lands. *Id.* § 2105(a). Title and ownership of such shipwrecks are then immediately transferred to the state wherein the shipwreck is located. *Id.* § 2105(c). The United States has retained its title to shipwrecks located in or on public lands, while Indian tribes hold title to shipwrecks located in or on Indian lands. *See id.* § 2105(d).

The ASA also authorized the National Park Service to prepare and publish guidelines "to encourage the development of underwater parks and the administrative cooperation necessary for the comprehensive management of underwater resources related to historic shipwrecks." *Id.* § 2104(a). The ASA Guidelines are only intended "to assist States and the appropriate Federal agencies in developing legislation and regulations to carry out their responsibilities under" the ASA and are not legally binding. *Id.* § 2104(c); *see also* Abandoned Shipwreck Act Guidelines, 55 Fed. Reg. 50116–01 (Dec. 4, 1990).

2.   KEY TERMS

There are eight key terms that are important in determining whether the ASA applies. The first two terms, "shipwreck" and "abandoned," are foundational, because the ASA only applies to resources that meet these two threshold criteria. Shipwrecks that are not abandoned are not affected by the ASA. The next two terms, "embedded" and "submerged lands," are found in a clause in the ASA that outlines the three categories of abandoned shipwrecks that trigger a title transfer under the statute: "(1) embedded in submerged lands of a State; (2) embedded in coralline formations protected by a State on submerged lands of a State; or (3) on submerged lands of a State and is included in or determined eligible for inclusion in the National Register." 43 U.S.C. § 2105(a). The fifth term, "historic shipwreck," is never defined in the ASA, but a definition is suggested in the ASA

Guidelines. Although non-binding, this definition is important because it offers one possible standard for determining the historical significance of resources affected by the ASA.

The three remaining ASA terms, "public lands," "Indian lands," and "Indian tribe," have meanings identical to those given in the Archaeological Resources Protection Act, discussed in Part C above, and are incorporated into the ASA by reference. *Id.* § 2102(c).

a. Shipwreck

The ASA defines "shipwreck" as "a vessel or wreck, its cargo, and other contents." 43 U.S.C. § 2102(d). The ASA Guidelines further expand this definition by suggesting the following clarification:

> The vessel or wreck may be intact or broken into pieces scattered on or embedded in the submerged lands or in coralline formations. A vessel or wreck includes, but is not limited to, its hull, apparel, armaments, cargo, and other contents. Isolated artifacts and materials not in association with a wrecked vessel, whether intact or broken and scattered or embedded, do not fit the definition of a shipwreck.

Abandoned Shipwreck Act Guidelines, 55 Fed. Reg. 50116–01 (Dec. 4, 1990). One court has interpreted the ASA Guidelines language about isolated artifacts to hold that an anchor was not a shipwreck subject to ASA. *See* Anchor Ventures LLC v. Marine

Prop. from Unidentified Sailing Vessel, C09–67 MJP, 2010 WL 4941441 (W.D. Wash. Nov. 30, 2010).

b. Abandoned

Although ASA does not expressly define the term "abandoned," it does describe abandoned shipwrecks as shipwrecks "which have been deserted and to which the owner has relinquished ownership rights with no retention." 43 U.S.C. § 2101(b). While the statutory language regarding abandonment requires a complete relinquishment of all ownership rights before a title transfer under ASA occurs, the statute offers no indication about the requisite method of relinquishment (i.e., what circumstances allow for an inference of abandonment).

Fortunately, the Supreme Court clarified the meaning of abandoned when it stated that "the meaning of 'abandoned' under the ASA conforms with its meaning under admiralty law." California v. Deep Sea Research, Inc., 523 U.S. 491, 508 (1998). In admiralty law, there is a presumption against abandonment. When there is no owner claiming an interest in the vessel, courts adjudicating abandonment under ASA have found that abandonment may be inferred from circumstantial evidence as long as the evidence is "clear and convincing." *See, e.g.*, Ne. Research, LLC v. One Shipwrecked Vessel, No. 11–1644–CV, 2013 WL 4753732 (2d Cir. Sept. 5, 2013) (finding that a shipwreck was abandoned due to lapse of time, the location and circumstances of the wreck, and lack of present claims of ownership).

c. Embedded

The statutory definition of "embedded" is "firmly affixed in the submerged lands or in coralline formations such that the use of tools of excavation is required in order to move the bottom sediments to gain access to the shipwreck, its cargo, and any part thereof." 43 U.S.C. § 2102(a). The ASA Guidelines suggest that tools of excavation should "include, but not be limited to, hydraulic, pneumatic, or mechanical dredges; explosives; propeller wash deflectors; air lifts; blowtorches; induction equipment; chemicals; and mechanical tools used to remove or displace bottom sediments or coralline formations to gain access to shipwrecks." Abandoned Shipwreck Act Guidelines, 55 Fed. Reg. 50116–01 (Dec. 4, 1990). However, diving equipment "normally worn by recreational divers while exploring or viewing shipwreck sites are not considered to be tools of excavation." *Id.* Thus, the analysis for determining whether a shipwreck is embedded turns on whether tools of excavation are required to gain access to the shipwreck.

Courts typically will assess whether or not a shipwreck is embedded using a "preponderance of the evidence" standard. *See, e.g.,* Deep Sea Research, Inc. v. Brother Jonathan, 883 F. Supp. 1343, 1356 (N.D. Cal. 1995). Courts have found that a shipwreck is not embedded when no technology is necessary to gain access to it. *See id.* at 1354–56 (finding a shipwreck covered with sediment was not embedded because the interior did not contain any significant amount of sand, mud, or dirt, and the external sediment covering was only one or two inches deep, fine, loose and powdery, and could easily be displaced by a human hand).

d. Submerged Lands

"Submerged lands" in the ASA is synonymous with the term "lands beneath navigable waters" as used in the Submerged Lands Act of 1953. 43 U.S.C. § 2102(f)(1). Thus, submerged lands include:

(1) all lands within the boundaries of each of the respective States which are covered by nontidal waters that were navigable under the laws of the United States at the time such State became a member of the Union, or acquired sovereignty over such lands and waters thereafter, up to the ordinary high water mark as heretofore or hereafter modified by accretion, erosion, and reliction;

(2) all lands permanently or periodically covered by tidal waters up to but not above the line of mean high tide and seaward to a line three geographical miles distant from the coast line of each such State and to the boundary line of each such State where in any case such boundary as it existed at the time such State became a member of the Union, or as heretofore approved by Congress, extends seaward (or into the Gulf of Mexico) beyond three geographical miles, and

(3) all filled in, made, or reclaimed lands which formerly were lands beneath navigable waters, as hereinabove defined.

Id. § 1301(a). Submerged lands, however, do not include streambeds that the United States conveyed to any state or person. *See id.* § 1301(f). Courts have yet to interpret the contours of submerged lands under the ASA.

e. Historic Shipwreck

The phrase "historic shipwreck" is not defined in the ASA, but the ASA Guidelines define it as "a shipwreck that is listed in or eligible for listing in the National Register of Historic Places." Abandoned Shipwreck Act Guidelines, 55 Fed. Reg. 50116–01 (Dec. 4, 1990). Federal courts have not yet weighed in on the matter.

3. APPLICATION

Congress passed the Abandoned Shipwreck Act of 1987 (ASA) to clarify the ownership and the authority to manage abandoned shipwrecks on state lands. There are three primary steps in the ASA process. First, one must determine if a shipwreck is covered by the ASA. Second, if a shipwreck is covered by the ASA, the United States asserts ownership, and then immediately transfers title to the shipwreck to the state in which the shipwreck is, provided that the state asserts ownership rights. Finally, once a court has adjudicated a state's title claim in its favor, the state has an obligation to provide protection for the shipwreck and allow public access to the wreckage. Each of these steps is discussed below.

a. Determining Which Shipwrecks Are Protected

Before a shipwreck may be governed by the ASA, it must meet two requirements. First, the shipwreck must be abandoned as defined above. *See* 43 U.S.C. § 2101(b). This abandonment requirement may be met by either express abandonment or implied abandonment. If an owner appears in court and asserts an ownership interest in a shipwreck, the shipwreck must be expressly abandoned before the ASA applies. *See, e.g.*, Sea Hunt, Inc. v. Unidentified Shipwrecked Vessel or Vessels, 221 F.3d 634, 640–41 (4th Cir. 2000) ("When an owner comes before the court to assert his rights, relinquishment would be hard, if not impossible, to show. Requiring express abandonment where an owner makes a claim thus accords with the statutory text."). This principle reflects the longstanding admiralty rule that when items are lost at sea, title remains in the owner. In contrast, implied abandonment occurs when the state asserts title over a shipwreck, and there is no owner "asserting any control over or otherwise indicating his claim of possession" over the shipwreck. *Id.* at 641. While express abandonment requires some words or overt actions that clearly communicate the shipwreck owner's relinquishment of all ownership interests, implied abandonment requires a consideration of several factors, including, but not limited to: lapse of time; location and circumstances of the wreck; whether parties claiming ownership have attempted to locate or salvage the vessel, and the technological feasibility of doing so. *See* Ne. Research, LLC v. One Shipwrecked Vessel, 11–1644–CV, 2013 WL 4753732 (2d Cir. Sept. 5, 2013).

The second requirement a shipwreck must meet to be covered by ASA is that it must be embedded (as the term is defined above) in, or on, the submerged lands of a state. Importantly, shipwrecks eligible for listing on the National Register of Historic Places do not need to be embedded in a state's submerged lands before a state may assert title to them. Such historic shipwrecks need only be "on" a state's submerged lands. 43 U.S.C. § 2105(a)(3).

b. Asserting State Title

When a shipwreck is subject to ASA, the United States may assert ownership over the shipwreck. At this point, the state in which the shipwreck is located may assert title to it and request immediate transfer from the federal government. To assert title, a state must present a colorable claim to the shipwreck. Courts, however, disagree as to the burden imposed by this colorable claim requirement. Some courts require that the state demonstrate by a preponderance of the evidence that the shipwreck has triggered the applicability criteria set forth in the ASA. *See*, *e.g.*, Deep Sea Research v. Brother Jonathan, 102 F.3d 379, 386 (9th Cir. 1996). Other courts have concluded that a state need only make a bare assertion to ownership of the shipwreck governed by the ASA. *See*, *e.g.*, Zych v. Wrecked

Vessel Believed to be the Lady Elgin, 960 F.2d 665, 670 (7th Cir. 1992).

c. Providing for Public Access and Protection

After a court confirms that a state has title to an abandoned shipwreck, the ASA imposes affirmative duties on the state to protect the shipwreck and provide public access to it. The statute recognizes that "shipwrecks offer recreational and educational opportunities to sport divers and other interested groups, as well as irreplaceable State resources for tourism, biological sanctuaries, and historical research." 43 U.S.C. § 2103(a)(1). As such, states that gain title to abandoned shipwrecks under the ASA have a responsibility to provide "reasonable access by the public to such abandoned shipwrecks." *Id.* § 2103(a)(2). Specifically, states are to "develop appropriate and consistent policies [to] guarantee recreational exploration of shipwreck sites; and allow for appropriate public and private sector recovery of shipwrecks consistent with the protection of historical values and environmental integrity of the shipwrecks and the sites" *Id.* States are also "encouraged to create underwater parks or areas to provide additional protection for such resources." *Id.* § 2103(b).

4.   RELATIONSHIP TO THE LAW OF SALVAGE AND THE LAW OF FINDS

The Abandoned Shipwrecks Act expressly states that the "law of salvage and the law of finds shall not apply to abandoned shipwrecks to which" title is asserted under the ASA. 43 U.S.C. § 2106(a). A few salvors have challenged this clause by arguing that it unconstitutionally divests federal courts of jurisdiction over traditional admiralty cases. Courts have rejected such challenges. *See, e.g.*, Zych v. Wrecked Vessel Believed to be the Lady Elgin, 960 F.2d 665 (7th Cir. 1992); Sunken Treasure, Inc. v. Unidentified, Wrecked & Abandoned Vessel, 857 F. Supp. 1129, 1136 (D.V.I. 1994).

E. ARCHAEOLOGICAL RESOURCES PROVISIONS OF SECTION 106 OF THE NATIONAL HISTORIC PRESERVATION ACT

The four statutes discussed previously in this Chapter focus exclusively on archaeologically significant sites and artifacts. We turn now to a fifth federal statute, the National Historic Preservation Act, which addresses archaeological resources but does not exclusively focus on them. Section 106 of the National Historic Preservation Act—the backbone of federal historic preservation law in the United States—protects, among other historic and prehistoric resources, archaeological resources listed or eligible for listing on the National Register of Historic Places. Specifically, it requires federal agencies to "take into account the effect of the undertaking on any district, site, building, structure, or object that is included in or eligible for inclusion in the National Register" prior to the issuance of any license or federal funds in support of the undertaking. 16 U.S.C. § 470f.

This Part describes how archaeological resources meet the National Register criteria and thus become eligible for protection under Section 106. It then describes federal agencies' duties under Section 106 to identify previously undiscovered archaeological resources and to protect archaeological resources. Finally, it discusses the various roles that archaeologists may take in the Section 106 consultation process.

1.   ARCHAEOLOGICAL RESOURCES AND THE NATIONAL REGISTER CRITERIA

Archaeological resources must meet certain criteria (discussed in Chapter II) to be listed in the National Register. In general, they must:

(1) be one of five types of resources: a district, site, building, structure, or object;

(2) represent a qualifying historic or prehistoric context: American history, architecture, archaeology, engineering, or culture;

(3) exhibit "integrity of location, design, setting, materials, workmanship, feelings, and association"; and

(4) be associated with significant historic events, persons, or architectural characteristics or "have yielded, or may be likely to yield, information important in prehistory or history."

See 36 C.F.R. §§ 60.3–60.4. Each of these criteria is discussed further in Chapter II, but the final criterion—that of significance—deserves special mention. Typically, archaeological resources satisfy the fourth type of significance, also known as "Criterion D," through their information-providing qualities. They must be associated with human activity and may not just be an unassociated natural feature; in addition, they must possess characteristics that would allow researchers to test hypotheses, corroborate available information, or reconstruct the sequence of archaeological cultures. *See* Patrick W. Andrus, *How to Apply the National Register Criteria for Evaluation* 21 (Nat'l Park Serv. Nat'l Reg. Bull. No. 15, 1990). Reconstructed properties, such as plowed sites that mix or superimpose artifact assemblages, or properties that cannot be identified with a particular time period or group are not eligible Criterion D resources. *See id.* at 21–24.

Completing a National Register nomination for archaeological resources can be daunting in terms of time and detail. To provide guidance on nominations, in 1997 the National Park Service published National Register Bulletin 16A, *How to Complete the National Register Registration Form*. This Bulletin reminds nominators to describe certain characteristics of the archaeological resource in its nomination, such as its environmental setting and the period of time when the resource is known or projected to have been used. But it is important to remember that listing on the National Register is not required for an archaeological resource to receive Section 106 protection. An archaeological resource that is eligible for listing will also be covered. Eligibility for listing is first assessed by the federal agency, and ultimately decided by the Keeper of the Register of Historic Places, in consultation with a state or tribal historic preservation officer, as applicable, using the designation criteria outlined above.

2.   DUTY TO IDENTIFY HIDDEN SIGNIFICANT PROPERTIES

Federal agencies often propose undertakings, which trigger Section 106 review, in areas where there are no properties listed on the National Register. In this case, the agency has a limited duty to identify significant archaeological resources within the area potentially affected by the undertaking. Specifically, the agency must make "a reasonable and good faith effort to carry out appropriate identification efforts, which may include background research, consultation, oral history interviews, sample field investigation, and field survey." 36 C.F.R. § 800.4(b)(1).

But what constitutes a "reasonable and good faith effort"? This standard can be particularly difficult to divine in the context of an agency trying to identify the archaeological resources related to Indian tribes, due to tribal concerns about revealing sites that are culturally significant and/or sacred. *See, e.g.*, Pueblo of Sandia v. United States, 50 F.3d 856 (10th Cir. 1995) (finding that an agency did not make a reasonable and good faith effort when it simply mailed letters to Indian tribes inviting them to meetings, did not include any tribal traditional cultural sites in the potential affected area despite having reliable information that such sites were in the area, and withheld information from the state historic preservation officer); Muckleshoot Indian Tribe v. U.S. Forest Serv., 177 F.3d 800 (9th Cir. 1999) (holding that an agency made a reasonable and good faith effort by cooperating fully with the state historic preservation officer, making continued efforts to obtain information from the Indian tribe about archaeological and culturally significant sites, and conducting its own research to try to identify tribal cultural properties).

Indeed, regulations caution agencies regarding sensitive, confidential information, stating that "an Indian tribe or Native Hawaiian organization may be reluctant to divulge specific information regarding the location, nature, and activities associated with such sites." 36 C.F.R. § 800.4(a)(4). Procedures for handling confidential information are outlined in the regulations, *id.* § 800.11, and in the National Park Service's Bulletin No. 38, *Guidelines for Evaluating and Documenting Traditional Cultural Properties.*

3. DUTY TO PROTECT ARCHAEOLOGICAL RESOURCES

Once an archaeological resource is listed on or deemed eligible for the National Register, Section 106 imposes a consultation duty on federal agencies. Consultation is the heart of the Section 106 process, as described in Chapter III. Agencies must consult with parties, including applicable Native American tribes and Native Hawaiian organizations, regarding the adverse effects that their undertakings would have on the archaeological resources within the project area. *See* 36 C.F.R. § 800.5(a)(1) (defining adverse effects). Some examples of adverse effects that agencies must assess include: physical destruction to any part of the property; introduction of visual, atmospheric, or audible elements that diminish the integrity of the property's historic features; or alteration of the property inconsistent with the Secretary's Standards for the Treatment of Historic Properties. *See id.* § 800.5(a)(2). Agencies must also work to mitigate adverse effects to archaeological resources through agreements with affected parties. *See id.* § 800.6.

Courts have interpreted whether agencies adequately consulted with affected parties and mitigated the effects of their undertakings on archaeological resources. *See, e.g.*, Quechan Tribe of Fort Yuma Reservation v. U.S. Dep't of the Interior, 755 F. Supp. 2d 1104 (S.D. Cal. 2010) (finding that the Department of the Interior failed to adequately consult with the tribe regarding the adverse effects that the siting of a solar energy project would have on hundreds of ancient cultural sites in the area); Muckleshoot Indian Tribe v. U.S. Forest Serv., 177 F.3d 800, 807–09 (9th Cir. 1999) (holding that the Forest Service failed to mitigate the adverse effects of transferring a portion of an important tribal ancestral transportation route to a private entity intent on logging the site).

It is important to note, however, that the protection of archaeological resources under Section 106 differs from the treatment of most other resources listed in or eligible for listing in the National Register. Unlike historic buildings, which have many uses, archaeological resources' primary value is informational, meaning that Section 106 protections may not cover these resources once the information has been collected. For instance, suppose that archaeological resources meeting the National Register criteria are found during the excavation of a foundation for an office building in an urban area. At this point, archaeologists may be called to the site to document, measure, categorize, photograph, and/or extract the resources to the extent they provide significant information. Once the archaeological dig is completed and the information has been collected, the construction work can resume.

4.   ARCHAEOLOGISTS AS CONSULTING PARTIES

Archaeologists may participate in the Section 106 consultation process in three ways. First, an archaeologist is required to participate in the consultation process in a formal capacity if she is an applicant for the federal funding assistance, permit, license, or other federal approval for the federal undertaking that activates Section 106 review. *See* 36 C.F.R. § 800.2(c)(4). Second, an archaeologist may become a formal consulting party if she is invited to participate by the federal agency. *See id.* § 800.2(c)(5). Finally, an archaeologist may participate in the Section 106 review process more informally as a member of the general public.

CHAPTER 12

NATIVE AMERICAN ISSUES

Long before Western Europeans "discovered" the American continents, hosts of indigenous peoples developed complex, thriving civilizations here. In the nascent United States, there was significant interest in examining and collecting the material remains of these Native American (including American Indian, Alaska Native, and Native Hawaiian) cultures. For most of the nineteenth and twentieth centuries, Native American sites and burial grounds received little protection, unless they were located on federal lands that were specifically protected by the statutes discussed in Chapter XI. Consequently, many Native American sites were looted, damaged, and destroyed, and scores of Native American human remains and cultural items found their way into private hands as well as collections of museums, federal agencies, and educational institutions.

This Chapter deals with federal rules pertaining to the protection of Native American sites and cultural items and to the repatriation of Native American human remains and cultural items from museums and federal agencies. It begins by discussing the Native American Graves Protection and Repatriation Act, the most important federal law related specifically to Native American artifacts. This Chapter then offers an overview of how Section 106 of the National Historic Preservation Act, discussed in Chapter III, protects

Native American sites and cultural items and provides tribes with an important consulting role.

A. NATIVE AMERICAN GRAVES PROTECTION AND REPATRIATION ACT

Since the early years of the United States, people have excavated and removed human remains and cultural items from Native American graves and burial sites. As a result, a large number Native American human remains and cultural items ended up in museums, educational institutions, and federal agency collections throughout the United States. After many years of various Native American groups striving to recover the remains and items associated with their ancestors, Congress passed the Native American Graves Protection and Repatriation Act in 1990. It is the only federal statute that exclusively deals with Native American artifacts. This Part begins with an overview of the Native American Graves Protection and Repatriation Act and includes an analysis of its key terms and application.

1.   OVERVIEW

As its name implies, NAGPRA has two purposes: protection and repatriation.

First, NAGPRA seeks to protect Native American human remains and cultural items on federal or tribal lands. Two of the relevant statutory provisions are as follows:

(c) Intentional excavation and removal of Native American human remains and objects

The intentional removal from or excavation of Native American cultural items from Federal or tribal lands for purposes of discovery, study, or removal of such items is permitted only if—

(1) such items are excavated or removed pursuant to a permit issued under section 4 of the Archaeological Resources Protection Act of 1979 (93 Stat. 721; 16 U.S.C. 470aa et seq.) which shall be consistent with this Act;

(2) such items are excavated or removed after consultation with or, in the case of tribal lands, consent of the appropriate (if any) Indian tribe or Native Hawaiian organization;

(3) the ownership and right of control of the disposition of such items shall be as provided in subsections (a) and (b); and

(4) proof of consultation or consent under paragraph (2) is shown.

(d) Inadvertent discovery of Native American remains and objects

Any person who knows, or has reason to know, that such person has discovered Native American cultural items on Federal or tribal lands * * * shall notify, in writing, the Secretary of the Department, or head of any other agency or instrumentality of the United States, having primary management authority with respect to Federal lands and the appropriate Indian tribe or Native Hawaiian organization with respect to tribal lands * * * If the discovery occurred in connection with an activity, including (but not limited to) construction, mining, logging, and agriculture, the person shall cease the activity in the area of the discovery, make a reasonable effort to protect the items discovered before resuming such activity, and provide notice under this subsection.

25 U.S.C. § 3002. NAGPRA thus protects tribal resources from unauthorized excavation and removal, and from inadvertent discovery. Anyone wishing to excavate or remove such items from federal or tribal lands must receive a permit under the Archaeological Resources Protection Act (discussed in Chapter XI). She must also comply with provisions governing the determination of ownership and control of items, consultation with the relevant tribes or Native Hawaiian organization, and appropriate disposition of items. Native American remains and cultural items that are discovered inadvertently are protected by similar measures. To enforce these provisions, NAGPRA prescribes civil and criminal penalties for the illegal trafficking of Native American human remains or cultural items. *See* 18 U.S.C. § 1170(b).

Second, NAGPRA provides a process for the repatriation of human remains and cultural items that are controlled by museums and federal agencies. The relevant provisions are as follows:

Each Federal agency and each museum which has possession or control over holdings or collections of Native American human remains and associated funerary objects shall compile an inventory of such items and, to the extent possible based on information possessed by such museum or Federal agency, identify the geographical and cultural affiliation of such item. * * *

Each Federal agency or museum which has possession or control over holdings or collections of Native American unassociated funerary objects, sacred objects, or objects of cultural patrimony shall provide a written summary of such objects based upon available information held by such agency or museum. The summary shall describe the scope of the collection, kinds of objects included, reference to geographical location, means and period of acquisition and cultural affiliation, where readily ascertainable.

25 U.S.C. §§ 3003(a) & 3004(a). According to these provisions, federal agencies and museums must create an inventory or summary of items in their control, identifying (if possible) the cultural affiliation of these items. They must also contact the appropriate Native American group to determine if they want the items back. NAGPRA authorizes federal grants to Native American groups to assist with documentation and repatriation of Native American cultural items, and the NAGPRA Review Committee has been established to monitor the

NAGPRA repatriation process and handle disputes and challenges arising from this process.

2.   KEY TERMS

NAGPRA has eight key terms that are critical in determining whether the statute applies, and, if it does, how it applies. Most legal disputes involving NAGPRA have turned on the scope of these terms. The first two terms, "Native American" and "Native Hawaiian," are foundational, because NAGPRA applies only to human remains and cultural items that are affiliated with these groups. Likewise, term number three, "museum," is important because only federal agencies and museums must comply with NAGPRA. The fourth key term, "Indian tribe," identifies groups that have standing to make claims for repatriation under NAGPRA. And terms five and six, "cultural items" and "cultural affiliation," are critical to understanding what objects are covered by NAGPRA and how affiliation to a Native American group (which leads to repatriation of the objects) may be shown. Finally, the last two terms— "federal land" and "tribal land"—are useful to know because NAGPRA's excavation and discovery provisions apply only to these lands.

a. Native American

NAGPRA only applies to human remains and cultural items that are determined to be "Native American" or "Native Hawaiian." NAGPRA defines "Native American" as follows: "of, or relating to, a tribe, people, or culture that is indigenous to the

United States." 25 U.S.C. § 3001(9). The statute implies that this term encompasses the definitions of both "Indian tribe" and "Native Hawaiian."

The use of the present tense verb "is" in this definition suggests that for NAGPRA to be applicable, the human remains or cultural items must relate to a presently existing tribe, people, or culture. The interpretation of "is" was at the heart of a famous dispute over the skeleton of a 9,000 year-old individual called "Kennewick Man" or "The Ancient One." Following an initial forensic anthropological study that dated the remains and concluded that they were unlike any known present day population, claims on the skeleton were placed by both Indian tribes and scientists. Tribes wanted the skeleton repatriated and reburied without undergoing more testing because they viewed the skeleton as an ancestor. Scientists, on the other hand, viewed the skeleton as a window into early New World populations that deserved careful scientific inquiry. Ultimately, the Ninth Circuit determined that the skeleton was not "Native American" and therefore not subject to NAGPRA because it bore no relationship to a presently existing tribe, people, or culture. Bonnichsen v. U.S., 367 F.3d 864 (9th Cir. 2004).

b. Native Hawaiian

Compared to the statutory definition of "Native American," NAGPRA's definition for "Native Hawaiian" is quite specific. It includes "any individual who is a descendant of the aboriginal people who, prior to 1778, occupied and exercised sovereignty in the area that now constitutes the State of Hawaii." 25 U.S.C. § 3001(10). This definition has never been tested in court, but its application would prove an interesting genealogical exercise.

The State of Hawaii has established an Office of Hawaiian Affairs and a nonprofit, Hui Malama I Na Kupuna O Hawai'i Nei, to assist Native Hawaiians in decisions dealing with cultural issues, particularly burials. Both of these entities are specifically recognized in NAGPRA as entities with authority to represent Native Hawaiian individuals. *See id.* §§ 3001(6) & (10). Contrast this approach with the representation of Native Americans by tribes—assemblies of people with more experiences in common than an individual Hawaiian might have with a state agency or nonprofit institution.

c. Museum

Museums and federal agencies must comply with NAGPRA's repatriation process. A "museum" for purposes of NAGPRA is much broader than one might think. It is: "any institution or State or local government agency (including any institution of higher learning) that receives federal funds and has possession of, or control over, Native American cultural items." 25 U.S.C. § 3001(8). The term "museum," however, does not include the Smithsonian Institution, which is subject to the repatriation provisions of the National Museum of the American Indian Act of 1989, 20 U.S.C. §§ 80q to 80q–15. *See id.*

A recent case shows how one court construed this term. Sons of the legendary Native American athlete, Jim Thorpe, brought suit under NAGPRA to repatriate their father's remains from the Borough of Jim Thorpe, Pennsylvania to Oklahoma. The Borough claimed that it was exempt from NAGPRA because it had not received any federal funds, and thus was not a "museum" under NAGPRA. The court disagreed, holding that the Borough was a "museum" for NAGPRA purposes because it had possession or control over Thorpe's remains and had received federal funds, albeit indirectly through the Commonwealth of Pennsylvania. *See* Thorpe v. Borough of Thorpe, No. 3:CV–10–1317 (M.D. Pa. Apr. 19, 2013).

d. Indian Tribe

Under NAGPRA, Indian tribes have standing to make claims for repatriation of human remains or cultural items. The statute defines "Indian tribe" as:

> any tribe, band, nation, or other organized group or community of Indians, including any Alaska Native village (as defined in, or pursuant to, the Alaska Native Claims Settlement Act) [43 U.S.C. §§ 1601 et. seq.], which is recognized as eligible for the special programs and services provided by the United States to Indians because of their status as Indians.

25 U.S.C. § 3001(7). This broad definition may conflict with definitions of "tribe" in other federal statutes, such as the Clean Water Act. *See* Abenaki Nation of Mississquoi v. Hughes, 805 F. Supp. 234 (D. Vt. 1992) (holding that even if the plaintiffs were not included in the Clean Water Act's definition of "tribe," they met NAGPRA's more expansive definition of "Indian tribe" and were thus entitled to its protection).

e. Cultural Items

NAGPRA does not apply to all objects, just those that are "cultural items." This term includes four categories of items: human remains, funerary objects, sacred objects, and objects of cultural patrimony.

Human remains are the "physical remains of the body of a person of Native American ancestry." 43 C.F.R. § 10.2(d)(1). This term excludes remains that "may reasonably be determined to have been freely given or naturally shed," such as "hair made into ropes or nets." *Id.* If human remains are incorporated into a funerary object, sacred object, or object of cultural patrimony, the remains are considered part of the item. *Id.* Although many Native American cultures believe the human remains of their ancestors are spiritual beings possessing all the traits of a living person, courts have held that the remains themselves do not have standing to bring suit. *See, e.g.,* Na Iwi O Na Kupunu O Mokapu v. Dalton, 894 F. Supp. 1397 (D. Haw. 1995).

Funerary objects are items that "as part of the death rite or ceremony of a culture, are reasonably believed to have been placed intentionally at the time of death or later with or near individual human remains." 43 C.F.R. § 10.2(d)(2). These objects "must be identified by a preponderance of the evidence as having been removed from a specific burial site of an individual affiliated with a particular Indian tribe or Native Hawaiian organization or as being related to specific individuals or families or to known human remains." *Id.* To help federal agencies and museums complete their inventories, the term "funerary objects" has been subdivided into two smaller categories: associated funerary objects and unassociated funerary objects. Associated funerary objects are funerary objects "that were made exclusively for burial purposes or to contain human remains" or "for which the human remains with which they were placed intentionally are also in the possession or control of a museum or federal agency." *Id.* § 10.2(d)(2)(i). Unassociated funerary objects are funerary objects whose linked human remains are not in the possession or control of a federal agency or museum. *See id.* § 10.2(d)(2)(ii).

Sacred objects are "specific ceremonial objects needed by traditional Native American religious leaders for the practice of traditional Native American religions by their present-day adherents." *Id.* § 10.2(d)(3). While "ancient pottery sherds" or "arrowheads" might be venerated by an individual, sacred objects under NAGPRA are "limited to objects that were used in traditional Native

American religious ceremonies or rituals and which have religious significance or function in the continued observance or renewal of such ceremony." *Id.*

Objects of cultural patrimony are "items having ongoing historical, traditional, or cultural importance central to the Indian tribe or Native Hawaiian organization itself, rather than property owned by an individual or organization member." *Id.* § 10.2(d)(4). Such objects are communally owned and may not be alienated by any individual tribal or organization member. Furthermore, objects of cultural patrimony "must have been considered inalienable by the culturally affiliated Indian tribe or Native Hawaiian organization at the time the object was separated from the group." *Id.* Examples of such items include the Zuni War Gods (wooden, cylindrical statues standing two to three feet tall) and the Iroquois Confederacy wampum belts.

The broad scope of the term "cultural patrimony" has been attacked for being unconstitutionally vague, but it has withstood these challenges. In one case, an experienced Native American art dealer selling Hopi masks claimed that the term "cultural patrimony" was unconstitutional because it did not adequately inform him that the Hopi masks he was selling might be covered under NAGPRA. The Ninth Circuit disagreed, holding that the term "cultural patrimony" provided adequate notice to the defendant that some of the items which he traded might be illegal to sell, particularly since he was a dealer in Native American art and had previously been convicted under NAGPRA. *See* United States v. Tidwell, 191 F.3d 976 (9th Cir. 1999). In another case, an "aficionado of Navajo culture and religion" who had participated in Navajo religious ceremonies, also claimed that "cultural patrimony" was unconstitutionally vague. He was charged under NAGPRA with illegally trafficking Navajo ceremonial masks that are thought to embody living gods. The Tenth Circuit rejected his vagueness claim, finding him sufficiently knowledgeable in Navajo Indian traditions to have fair notice that buying the masks and reselling them on the open market violated NAGPRA. *See* United States v. Corrow, 119 F.3d 769 (10th Cir. 1997).

f. Cultural Affiliation

For an item to be repatriated under NAGPRA, it must be culturally affiliated. That is, it must have "a relationship of shared group identity that can reasonably be traced historically or prehistorically between members of a present-day Indian tribe or Native Hawaiian organization and an identifiable earlier group." 43 C.F.R. § 10.2(e)(1). Cultural affiliation is proved when the preponderance of the following types of evidence—geographical, kinship, biological, archaeological, anthropological, linguistic, folklore, oral tradition, historical evidence, expert opinion, or other information—reasonably leads to such a conclusion. *Id.; see also id.* §§ 10.14(c)–(f).

g. Federal Land

NAGPRA's protections over Native American and Native Hawaiian human remains and cultural objects extend to all federal lands. Federal lands are all lands:

> other than tribal lands that are controlled or owned by the United States Government, including lands selected by but not yet conveyed to Alaska Native Corporations and groups organized pursuant to the Alaska Native Claims Settlement Act (43 U.S.C. 1601 *et seq.*). United States "control," as used in this definition, refers to those lands not owned by the United States but in which the United States has a legal interest sufficient to permit it to apply these regulations without abrogating the otherwise existing legal rights of a person.

43 C.F.R. § 10.2(f)(1). It is important to note that federal government supervision or permits for construction projects on state or local land does not transform state or local land into federal land subject to NAGPRA. *See, e.g.,* Castro Romero v. Becken, 256 F.3d 349 (5th Cir. 2001) (holding that where the federal agency acted in a supervisory role during the construction of a golf course on municipal lands on which Native American human remains were found, the municipal lands were not federal lands within the meaning of NAGPRA); W. Mohegan Tribe & Nation of N.Y., 100 F. Supp. 2d 122 (N.D.N.Y. 2000), *aff'd in part, vacated in part on other grounds*, 246 F.3d 230 (2d Cir. 2001) (finding that a construction permit from a federal agency for

the creation of state park did not transform state land into federal land subject to NAGPRA).

h. Tribal Land

The excavation and discovery provisions of NAGPRA also apply to tribal lands. Tribal lands are all lands which:

(i) Are within the exterior boundaries of any Indian reservation including, but not limited to, allotments held in trust or subject to a restriction on alienation by the United States; or

(ii) Comprise dependent Indian communities as recognized pursuant to 18 U.S.C. 1151; or

(iii) Are administered for the benefit of Native Hawaiians pursuant to the Hawaiian Homes Commission Act of 1920 and section 4 of the Hawaiian Statehood Admission Act

43 C.F.R. § 10.2(f)(2). Where the exact location of an Indian reservation is in question, courts require that the Indian tribe show title through a treaty or other means. *See*, *e.g.*, Robinson v. Salazar, 885 F. Supp. 2d 1002 (E.D. Cal. 2012) (holding that land on which the excavation, damage, and destruction of seven Indian cemeteries, sacred sites, and artifacts allegedly took place in connection with a development project did not constitute "tribal lands" under NAGPRA because the Indian tribe could not prove its title to the land under treaty).

3. APPLICATION

NAGPRA establishes two processes designed to ensure that Native American human remains and cultural items are returned to those to whom they belong. The first process is concerned with the intentional excavation or removal, or inadvertent discovery of, Native American human remains and cultural items on federal and tribal lands. The second process deals with cataloguing and repatriating Native American human remains and cultural items from federal agencies and museums. Below, we cover these two processes, and we explain what happens when human remains are not culturally identifiable. Comments about the role of the NAGPRA Review Committee and penalties associated with violations of NAGPRA are also included.

a. Intentional Excavations and Removals

Anyone wishing to excavate or remove Native American human remains or cultural items from federal or tribal lands must comply with several conditions. First, she must receive a permit for the excavation or removal under the Archaeological Resources Protection Act (ARPA). *See* 43 C.F.R. § 10.3(b)(1). In addition to following the ARPA permitting process described in Chapter XI, she must consult with the appropriate Indian tribe or Native Hawaiian organization before excavating and provide proof of that consultation to the federal agency responsible for issuing the ARPA permit. *See id.* §§ 10.3(b)(2) & (4); 10.5. And if any Native

American remains or cultural items covered by NAGPRA are discovered during the excavation, the excavator must dispose of these items in the following priority order: (1) to lineal descendants; (2) to the Indian tribe on whose land the excavation took place; (3) to the Indian tribe or Native Hawaiian organization with the closest cultural affiliation; (4) where cultural affiliation cannot be ascertained, to the Indian tribe aboriginally occupying the federal land that was excavated unless a different Indian tribe or Native Hawaiian organization can demonstrate a stronger relationship with the objects. *Id.* §§ 10.3(b)(3) & 10.6(a).

b. Inadvertent Discoveries

NAGPRA also deals with instances when Native American human remains or cultural items are inadvertently discovered on federal or tribal lands during activities such as logging or construction. Inadvertent discovery does not mean physically handling items and wondering what they are; observation is enough. *See* Yankton Sioux Tribe v. U.S. Army Corps of Engineers, 83 F. Supp. 2d 1047 (D. S.D. 2000) (holding that observation of exposed bones by the Corps at a cemetery site constituted "inadvertent discovery" of human remains when the Corps knew of the cemetery but assumed all remains had already been moved). Such observation, however, must be of items actually subject to NAGPRA. *See* San Carlos Apache Tribe v. United States, 272 F. Supp. 2d 860 (D. Ariz. 2003), *aff'd on other grounds*, 417 F.3d 1091 (9th Cir. 2005) (holding that a drawdown of a reservoir for irrigation purposes that exposed a cemetery capped with concrete grout did not constitute an "inadvertent discovery" because no human remains or protected objects were discovered and cemeteries are not per se protected by NAGPRA).

When anyone "knows are has reason to know" that she has inadvertently discovered Native American human remains or cultural items, she must immediately notify the requisite federal agency or tribal official, cease the activity, and "make a reasonable effort to protect" the objects. 43 C.F.R. §§ 10.4(b) & (c). The appropriate federal agency or tribal official must then certify receipt of the notification, determine how best to protect the objects, and, if necessary, excavate and dispose of them in the same priority order as that for intentional excavations and removals. *See id.* §§ 10.4(d)(2) & (e)(iv); 10.6(a). Activities that resulted in the inadvertent discovery of Native American human remains and cultural items may resume thirty days after the federal agency or tribe certifies that they have been notified, or before, if a binding recovery plan for the items is signed. *See id.* §§ 10.4(d)(2) & (e)(2).

Native American human remains and cultural objects that are intentionally excavated or removed, or inadvertently discovered, are particularly at risk of being trafficked illegally. Anyone illegally trafficking in these items is subject to criminal penalties under NAGPRA. Illegal trafficking and the attendant criminal penalties are discussed in more detail below.

c. Inventory

NAGPRA also established a process to repatriate Native American human remains and cultural items from historical collections in museums and federal agencies. The first step in this process is for each museum and federal agency to understand what NAGPRA items are in their collections and to determine their cultural affiliation, if possible. This step can occur through the inventory process described in this subsection, or the summary process described in the next subsection.

Museums and federal agencies holding Native American human remains and associated funerary objects must compile a detailed inventory of each item and attempt to identify its geographical and cultural affiliation. 43 C.F.R. § 10.9(a)(c). These inventories must be completed in consultation with the appropriate Indian tribe or Native Hawaiian officials. *Id.* § 10.9(b). A completed inventory consists of two documents: (1) a list of all Native American human remains and associated funerary objects that have been culturally affiliated with one or more present-day Indian tribes or Native Hawaiian organizations; (2) a list of all culturally unidentifiable human remains and associated funerary objects for which no affiliation can be determined. *Id.* § 10.9(d). If the inventory results in the identification or likely identification of Native American human remains and/or cultural items, the museum or federal agency must notify the affiliated Indian tribe or Native Hawaiian organization within six months of inventory completion. *Id.* § 10.9(e).

Courts are reluctant to grant injunctions against museums or federal agencies for failure to properly inventory Native American human remains or cultural items, particularly when the museum or agency is taking steps to improve its inventory processes. *See, e.g.,* Brown v. Hawaii, 424 Fed. Appx. 642 (9th Cir. 2011) (finding a permanent injunction was unwarranted in an action alleging that State of Hawaii was in violation of NAGPRA's inventorying procedures because the State was consulting with the National NAGPRA Program to improve compliance).

d. Summary

Museums or federal agencies controlling collections that may contain unassociated funerary objects, sacred objects, or objects of cultural patrimony must complete a summary rather than an inventory. 43 C.F.R. § 10.8(a). This summary serves in lieu of an object-by-object inventory described above, and is based upon available information held by the agency or museum in consultation with the appropriate Indian tribe or Native Hawaiian officials. *Id.* § 10.8(a)(d). A summary must contain the following four elements: (1) an estimate of the number of objects in the collection or portion of the collection; (2) a description of the kinds of objects included; (3)

reference to the means, date(s), and location(s) in which the collection or portion of the collection was acquired, where readily ascertainable; and (4) information relevant to identifying lineal descendant and cultural affiliation. *Id.* § 10.8(b).

e. **Repatriation**

Once Native American human remains and cultural items have been culturally affiliated, they must be repatriated if the culturally affiliated lineal descendant, Indian tribe, or Native Hawaiian organization requests that the museum or federal agency do so. 25 U.S.C. § 3005(a). Once a museum or federal agency receives a valid, written request for repatriation, the museum or agency has the opportunity to prove that it has the right of possession to the item by showing that it obtained the item with the voluntary consent of an individual or group able to alienate the item. 43 C.F.R. §§ 10.10(a) & (b). If the museum or federal agency cannot prove that it has the right of possession then it must publish a notice of intent to repatriate in the Federal Register and return the item within ninety days of the request, unless the item is "indispensable to the completion of a specific scientific study which would be a major benefit to the United States." *Id.* §§ 10.10(a) & (b), (c)(1). An item subject to the scientific study exception must be returned no later than ninety days after the date on which the scientific study is completed. *Id.* § 10.10(c)(1).

Repatriation of an item might also be delayed by multiple claims. If there are multiple requests for repatriation of Native American human remains or cultural items, and the museum or federal agency cannot determine by the preponderance of the evidence the most appropriate claimant, then the museum or agency retains the item in dispute until the matter is resolved. *Id.* § 10.10(e)(2).

Given that repatriation can be a sensitive issue, particularly when there are several possible claimants but the item can only be returned to one of them, NAGPRA immunizes museums from liability as long as they repatriate the item in good faith pursuant to the Act. 25 U.S.C. § 3005(f). Costs of repatriation may be defrayed through grants administered by the National NAGPRA Program.

f. Disposition of Culturally Unidentifiable Human Remains

What happens to Native American human remains and associated funerary objects that are culturally unidentifiable? Typically, these remains stay in the custody of the museum or agency, until it offers to transfer control of these items, or receives a request from an Indian tribe or Native Hawaiian organization which wants control of them. 43 C.F.R. §§ 10.11(a) & (b). Then a museum or agency must consult with religious leaders of all Indian tribes and Native Hawaiian organizations who have a present or aboriginal claim to the land from which the items were removed. *Id.* § 10.11(b). Following consultation, the museum or agency must offer to transfer control of the items in the following priority order: (1) to the Indian tribe or Native Hawaiian organization who had claim to the land at the time of removal; or (2) to the Indian tribe or tribes with aboriginal claim to the area from which the remains were removed. *Id.* § 10.11(c)(1).

If none of the aforementioned Indian tribes or Native Hawaiian organizations agrees to accept control, the museum or federal agency may transfer control of the items to other Indian tribes, Native Hawaiian organizations, or tribes that are not federally recognized. *Id.* § 10.11(c)(2). Alternatively, the museum or agency may also reinter the items according to state law. *Id.* Actual disposition of the culturally unidentifiable Native American human remains and associated funerary objects may occur thirty days after the public has been notified by a notice in the Federal Register. Disputes, if any, are facilitated by the NAGPRA Review Committee. *Id.* § 10.11(e).

g. **Review Committee**

NAGPRA established a Review Committee to advise Congress and the Secretary of the Interior on matters relating to the Act. *See* 25 U.S.C. § 3006. Among the Review Committee's duties are: (1) monitoring museums and federal agencies to ensure they comply with NAGPRA; (2) facilitating dispute resolution protocols and making recommendations on the resolution of disputes; (3) compiling a record of culturally unidentifiable human remains controlled by museums and federal agencies as well

as recommendation actions for their disposition. 43
C.F.R. § 10.16(a).

To provide transparency in Review Committee
actions, the National NAGPRA Program website
contains several databases tracking, among other
things: inventories of culturally affiliated items and
culturally unidentifiable items; summaries provided
by museums and federal agencies; notices of inventory
completion; and notices of intent to repatriate. *See*
National NAGPRA Online Databases, www.nps.gov/
nagpra/onlinedb/index.htm. The Review Committee
must also submit an annual report to Congress. 25
U.S.C. § 3006(h). All Review Committee
recommendations, reports, and actions are non-
binding and advisory only. 43 C.F.R. § 10.16(b).

However, Review Committee recommendations
appear to garner some deference from the courts.
For example, a federal district court in Nevada
found that the Bureau of Land Management's
determination that ancient human remains found
adjacent to tribal land were not culturally affiliated
with any modern-day tribe was arbitrary and
capricious because the agency failed to consider the
findings of the Review Committee linking the tribe
to the remains. Fallon Paiute-Shoshone Tribe v.
U.S. Bureau of Land Mgmt., 455 F. Supp. 2d 1207
(D. Nev. 2006). That court took the somewhat odd
position that federal agencies need not amend or
review their decisions solely on the basis of a
Review Committee decision, but that courts should
give Review Committee findings on cultural

affiliation "substantial weight should a dispute reach the courts." *Id.* at 1222.

h. Penalties

Criminal and civil penalties are available for violations of NAGPRA. Criminal penalties are available under NAGPRA for the illegal trafficking in Native American human remains or cultural items. Anyone caught illegally trafficking in Native American human remains or cultural items can be fined and/or imprisoned for up to one year for the first violation, with subsequent violations extending the jail sentence for up to five years. *See* 18 U.S.C. § 1170. What, then, constitutes illegal trafficking? Well, it depends on how much you know. Anyone who "knowingly sells, purchases, uses for profit, or transports for sale or profit" any Native American human remains to which they do not have lawful title or that were obtained in violation of NAGPRA may be prosecuted for illegal trafficking. 18 U.S.C. §§ 1170(a) & (b).

Courts interpreting this "knowledge" requirement have focused on how informed the defendant was regarding the character of the items she was selling. *See*, *e.g.*, United States v. Corrow, 119 F.3d 769 (10th Cir. 1997) (finding that an "aficionado of Navajo culture and religion" who had participated in Navajo religious ceremonies was sufficiently knowledgeable in Navajo Indian traditions to have fair notice that purchasing and reselling Navajo ceremonial masks thought to embody living gods on the open market violated NAGPRA); United States

v. Tidwell, 191 F.3d 976 (9th Cir. 1999) (holding that an experienced Native American art dealer with prior convictions under NAGPRA was adequately informed that the Hopi masks he was trying to sell were protected by NAGPRA).

In addition to the criminal penalties described above, museums that fail to comply with the NAGPRA repatriation process may be assessed a civil penalty, with each violation considered to be a separate offense. 43 C.F.R. §§ 10.12(a) & (b)(2). Violations include, among other things: (1) selling or transferring Native American human remains or cultural items to any individual or institution not subject to the purview of NAGPRA; (2) failure to complete inventories and summaries; (3) refusing to repatriate Native American human remains or cultural items to authorized parties; (4) failure to consult with Native American groups as required during the repatriation process; and (5) repatriating Native American human remains or cultural items before publishing the required notice in the Federal Register. *Id.* § 10.12(b). The amount of the penalty assessed takes into account a variety of factors, including: the archaeological, historical, or commercial value of the item; economic and non-economic damages suffered by the plaintiff; and the number of violations that have occurred. 25 U.S.C. § 3007(b). Any person may file an allegation of failure to comply with the NAGPRA Civil Penalties Coordinator using the National NAGPRA Contact Information website: www.nps.gov/nagpra/contacts/index.htm.

Civil penalties apply only to museums, not federal agencies. This difference may account for the findings of a July 2010 report by the U.S. Government Accountability Office—*The Native American Graves Protection and Repatriation Act: After Almost 20 Years, Key Federal Agencies Still Have Not Fully Complied with the Act*—that none of eight key federal agencies with significant historic collections had fully complied with NAGPRA. Only three of them had vigorously attempted to identify their NAGPRA items.

B. THE NATIONAL HISTORIC PRESERVATION ACT AND NATIVE AMERICAN ISSUES

Given the unique legal status of Native Americans (including American Indians, Alaska Natives, and Native Hawaiians) and the sacred links that Native Americans have to many of their historic resources, the National Historic Preservation Act (NHPA) makes special provisions relevant to Native American resources and Native Americans. This Chapter will focus on two aspects of the NHPA where Native American issues come into play. The first is in the evaluation of the historic significance of Native American properties and their eligibility for listing on the National Register of Historic Places. As discussed below, Native American properties are evaluated differently from non-Native American properties. The second is in NHPA Section 106, which requires federal agencies to consider the effect their undertakings will have on historic resources.

Section 106 requires federal agencies to consult with relevant stakeholders, which, in the case of an undertaking on tribal land, may proceed in a different fashion than a consultation for an undertaking on non-tribal land.

This Part begins with an overview of how the NHPA helps protect Native American resources and includes an analysis of its key terms. It then describes how the NHPA evaluates the historic significance of Native American properties and incorporates Native Americans in the Section 106 review process.

1.   OVERVIEW

The National Historic Preservation Act includes provisions specific to Native Americans to assist them in protecting their historic properties and preserving their traditional values. It summarizes the obligations of the Secretary of the Department of the Interior as follows:

> The Secretary shall establish a program and promulgate regulations to assist Indian tribes in preserving their particular historic properties. The Secretary shall foster communication and cooperation between Indian tribes and State Historic Preservation Officers in the administration of the national historic preservation program to ensure that all types of historic properties and all public interests in such properties are given due consideration, and to encourage coordination among Indian tribes, State Historic Preservation Officers, and

Federal agencies in historic preservation planning and in the identification, evaluation, protection, and interpretation of historic properties.

16 U.S.C. § 470a(d)(1)(A).

As this excerpt suggests, the NHPA has several mechanisms designed to preserve Native American historic properties. Most significantly, the NHPA sets forth a framework for cooperation between federal, state, and tribal authorities to plan, identify, and protect historic properties. In certain circumstances, the NHPA allows for Native American groups to identify their own representatives within this cooperative framework. The NHPA also establishes procedures for tribal resources to be listed on the National Register of Historic Places. Finally, it anticipates the provision of direct assistance—in the form of technical expertise and grants—to Indian tribes in preserving their own historic properties. The discussion below focuses on two mechanisms the NHPA establishes to protect Native American resources: (1) the framework within which the significance of Native American resources is evaluated for placement on the National Register, and (2) the role of Native Americans in the Section 106 review process.

2. KEY TERMS

Although many key terms in the National Historic Preservation Act (NHPA) were discussed in Chapters II and III, four additional terms have relevance here: Indian tribe, tribal historic preservation officer, Native Hawaiian, and Native Hawaiian organization. Given that the NHPA affords special protections to the properties of Indian tribes and Native Hawaiians, it is important to understand who these groups are and who represents their interests regarding the NHPA.

a. Indian Tribe

NHPA regulations define an "Indian tribe" broadly. The definition includes any:

Indian tribe, band, nation, or other organized group or community, including a native village, regional corporation, or village corporation, as those terms are defined in section 3 of the Alaska Native Claims Settlement Act, 43 U.S.C. § 1602, which is recognized as eligible for the special programs and services provided by the United States to Indians because of their status as Indians.

36 C.F.R. § 800.16(m). This definition overlaps substantially with the provisions of the Native American Graves Protection and Repatriation Act of 1990, described in Part A of this Chapter. *See* 25 U.S.C. § 3001(7).

b. Tribal Historic Preservation Officer

When a tribe appoints a "tribal historic preservation officer" (THPO) pursuant to NHPA regulations, the federal government views the THPO as the key representative of the tribe for all NHPA purposes. A THPO is defined as "the tribal official appointed by the tribe's chief governing authority or designated by a tribal ordinance or preservation program who has assumed the responsibilities of the SHPO [state historic preservation officer] for purposes of Section 106 compliance on tribal lands." 36 C.F.R. § 800.16(w). Some tribes do not have THPOs, in which case the SHPO is responsible for Section 106 compliance. Thus, in a federal undertaking on tribal lands where the tribe has a THPO, agencies must consult with the THPO, not the SHPO.

c. Native Hawaiian

A "Native Hawaiian" means "any individual who is a descendant of the aboriginal people who, prior to 1778, occupied and exercised sovereignty in the area that now constitutes the State of Hawaii." 36 C.F.R. § 800.16(s)(2). This definition is identical to the definition of "Native Hawaiian" in the Native American Graves Protection and Repatriation Act of 1990, discussed in Part A of this Chapter *See* 25 U.S.C. § 3001(10).

d. Native Hawaiian Organization

The Department of the Interior recognizes that, in the application of certain provisions of NHPA, "Native Hawaiian organizations" are authorized to represent the interests of Native Hawaiians. A Native Hawaiian organization is "any organization which serves and represents the interests of Native Hawaiians; has as a primary and stated purpose the provision of services to Native Hawaiians; and has demonstrated expertise in aspects of historic preservation that are significant to Native Hawaiians." 36 C.F.R. § 800.16(s)(1). The most significant of these organizations is Hui Malama I Na Kupuna O Hawai'I Nei, a nonprofit Native Hawaiian organization that works with the Office of Hawaiian Affairs in decisions dealing with cultural issues, particularly burials. *See* 25 U.S.C. §§ 3001(6) & (10).

Some may question the ability of a Native Hawaiian organization to represent Native Hawaiian people. Native Hawaiians are represented by a state agency or nonprofit institution, while Indians are typically represented by a tribal historic preservation officer (THPO)—a member of the tribe itself. Arguably, the THPO is likely to have more experiences in common with the Indians she represents than a state agency or nonprofit institution has with an individual Native Hawaiian.

3. EVALUATING THE HISTORIC SIGNIFICANCE OF NATIVE AMERICAN PROPERTIES

Protection under the National Historic Preservation Act (NHPA) of Native American historic properties is only available for properties that are listed on or eligible for listing on the National Register of Historic Places. As Chapter II describes, properties worthy of the National Register must follow a two-step process before they are officially listed (or deemed eligible). First, they must be nominated. Second, they must be evaluated. Here, we consider how the nomination and evaluation process differs for Native American properties, as opposed to non-Native American properties.

The nomination of a property for the National Register requires that key aspects of the property, such as its location or its historic or cultural significance, be thoroughly documented. This documentation requirement can be challenging for tribes, however, for two reasons. First, the significance of many tribal properties and sites may be preserved in oral tradition only—evidence that courts typically find unpersuasive. *See, e.g.*, Hoonah Indian Ass'n v. Morrison, 170 F.3d 1223 (9th Cir. 1999) (finding that conflicting oral traditions as to the location of a tribal retreat path was insufficient to document the site). Second, tribes may also be reluctant to document certain sacred properties and sites because they do not want to reveal them to outsiders. In such a case, NHPA provides that any information tribes offer about these significant sites can be kept strictly confidential. *See* 16 U.S.C. § 470w(3). To provide further guidance on how to sensitively use the confidentiality provisions of NHPA with respect to significant tribal resources, the National Park Service has released Bulletin No. 38, *Guidelines for Evaluating and Documenting Traditional Cultural Properties.*

The evaluation of a Native American property nominated for the National Register also presents an important area of difference. In general, Native American resources must meet all of the criteria for designation on the National Register, including the key criterion of "significance." But there is one extra avenue for tribal properties to be listed on the National Register. The NHPA and its regulations have expanded the meaning of significance when evaluating Native American properties by explicitly allowing religious significance as factor for Native American properties while rejecting religious significance as a factor when evaluating non-tribal properties. The specific NHPA provision states: "Properties of traditional religious and cultural importance to an Indian tribe or Native Hawaiian organization may be determined to be eligible for inclusion on the National Register." 16 U.S.C. § 470a(d)(6)(A). There is no simple explanation for this juxtaposition, but some of it may be due to the historical trust responsibility the United States owes to Native Americans through its treaties and agreements for ownership of Native American lands.

4. INCORPORATING NATIVE AMERICANS IN THE SECTION 106 PROCESS

Once a property is listed on or deemed eligible for the National Register, it is protected by the National Historic Preservation Act (NHPA) through a provision known as Section 106. As Chapter III describes in further detail, Section 106 requires federal agencies to "take into account the effect of the[ir] undertaking[s] on any district, site, building, structure, or object that is included in or eligible for inclusion in the National Register." 16 U.S.C. § 470f. The NHPA sets forth a process through which a representative of a state or Native American group may play a consulting role during the Section 106 review process. This section describes both the role of the Native American representative and the requirements for consultation during the Section 106 review process.

a. Role of the Native American Representative

For the Section 106 review process, Indian tribes may identify an individual, known as the tribal historic preservation officer (THPO), who can assume all or any part of the functions of a state historic preservation officer (SHPO) for tribal land. To ensure that the Department of the Interior recognizes this individual as the THPO, the following must occur: (1) the tribe's chief governing authority must request the designation of a THPO from the Secretary of the Interior; (2) the tribe must designate a tribal preservation official to administer the tribal historic preservation program; (3) the tribe must provide the Secretary with a plan describing how the functions the THPO proposes to assume will be carried out; (4) the Secretary of the Department of the Interior, after consultation with the tribe, decides whether the tribal preservation program is fully capable of carrying out the functions specified in the plan. *See* 16 U.S.C. § 470a(d)(2). Note that in this instance, the NHPA does not treat Indian tribes as sovereigns, but assumes that the federal government must play an initial supervisory role to ensure that tribal historic properties are adequately protected.

The THPO, where designated, takes the place of the SHPO for ensuring Section 106 compliance for federal undertakings on tribal lands. Like the SHPO, the THPO has several responsibilities under Section 106. She fulfills a consulting role where federal agencies are considering an undertaking on tribal land. She also reviews whether the federal agency has adequately identified, assessed, and addressed the impacts of its undertaking. Federal agencies must have the THPO's concurrence to proceed with the undertaking; otherwise, the agency must follow the termination procedures discussed in Chapter III.

Unlike Indian tribes, Native Hawaiians do not have a tribal historic preservation officer. Rather, the NHPA states that they engage in the Section 106 consultation process through the Hawaii state historic preservation officer. *Id.* § 470a(d)(6)(C). This arrangement effectively means the state, rather than a Native Hawaiian, is representing the needs of Native Hawaiians. The Hawaii state historic preservation officer consults under Section 106 with Native Hawaiian organizations, the most significant of which is Hui Malama I Na Kupuna O Hawai'i Nei. *See id.* § 470a(d)(6)(C); 36 C.F.R. § 800.16(s)(1). There may be other smaller Native Hawaiian organizations that may also need to be consulted, which could lead to competing consultation viewpoints about historic Native Hawaiian properties.

b. Adequacy of the Consultation Process

When agencies engage in an "undertaking" triggering Section 106 review, they must consult with certain groups, including Native American tribes and Native Hawaiian organizations. Consultation is the heart of the Section 106 process as described in Chapter III. One area where consultation is required is in the identification of historic properties that would be subject to the protections of Section 106. An agency must make a "reasonable and good faith effort" to identify historic properties. 36 C.F.R. § 800.4(b)(1). Another area requiring consultation is whether the agencies adequately assessed the effects that the undertaking would have on historic properties.

What constitutes a "reasonable and good faith effort"? This standard can be particularly difficult to divine in the context of an agency trying to identify the cultural resources of Indian tribes, due to tribal concerns about revealing sacred sites. Indeed, NHPA regulations caution agencies regarding this very problem, stating that "an Indian tribe or Native Hawaiian organization may be reluctant to divulge specific information regarding the location, nature, and activities associated with such sites." *Id.* § 800.4(a)(4). To overcome this problem, agencies must do their due diligence:

which may include background research, consultation, oral history interviews, sample field investigation, and field survey. The agency official shall take into account past planning, research and studies, the magnitude and nature of the undertaking and the degree of Federal involvement, the nature and extent of potential effects on historic properties, and the likely nature and location of historic properties within the area of potential effects. The Secretary's standards and guidelines for identification provide guidance on this subject. The agency official should also consider other applicable professional, State, tribal, and local laws, standards, and guidelines. The agency official shall take into account any confidentiality concerns raised by Indian tribes or Native Hawaiian organizations during the identification process.

Id. § 800.4(b)(1). Procedures for handling confidential information are also outlined in the regulations, *id.* § 800.11, and in the National Park Service's Bulletin No. 38, *Guidelines for Evaluating and Documenting Traditional Cultural Properties.*

Several federal circuit courts have assessed the adequacy of the Section 106 consultation process with respect to identifying tribal cultural properties. In *Pueblo of Sandia v. United States*, 50 F.3d 856 (10th Cir. 1995), the Tenth Circuit found that an agency did not make a reasonable and good faith effort when it simply mailed letters to identified Indian tribes inviting them to meetings, did not include any tribal traditional cultural sites in the affected areas despite having reliable information that culturally significant sites were in the area, and withheld information from the SHPO until after the SHPO issued its concurrence. In contrast, the

Ninth Circuit in *Muckleshoot Indian Tribe v. U.S. Forest Service*, 177 F.3d 800 (9th Cir. 1999) held that an agency had acted in compliance with the NHPA reasonable and good faith effort standard by cooperating fully with the SHPO, making continued efforts to obtain information from the Indian tribe, and conducting its own research to try to identify tribal cultural properties. And in *Te-Moak Tribe of Western Shoshone of Nevada v. U.S. Department of Interior*, 608 F.3d 592 (9th Cir. 2010), the court found that, although the agency failed to consult with the tribe about an amendment to a plan of operations for an existing mineral exploration project for over a year after its proposal, the agency provided the tribe sufficient opportunity to identify its concern about cultural properties, because the agency consulted with the tribe before the original mineral exploration project was approved and there was no new information that the tribe would have raised if it had been consulted earlier about the amendment to the plan of operations. *See also* Pit River Tribe v. Bureau of Land Mgmt., 306 F. Supp. 2d 929 (E.D. Cal. 2004) (upholding agency process of identifying tribal cultural properties where the agency requested information from tribes and conducted interviews and field studies).

Agencies must also consult with tribes regarding the adverse effects that their undertakings would have on tribal historic properties within the project area. An adverse effect is found when:

an undertaking may alter, directly or indirectly, any of the characteristics of a

> historic property that qualify the property for inclusion in the National Register in a manner that would diminish the integrity of the property's location, design, setting, materials, workmanship, feeling, or association. * * * Adverse effects may include reasonably foreseeable effects caused by the undertaking that may occur later in time, be farther removed in distance or be cumulative.

36 C.F.R. § 800.5(a)(1). Examples of adverse effects that must be assessed include, among other things: physical destruction to any part of the property; introduction of visual, atmospheric, or audible elements that diminish the integrity of the property's historic features; or alteration of the property inconsistent with the Secretary's standard for the treatment of historic properties. *See id.* § 800.5(a)(2). Agencies must work to mitigate adverse effects to tribal historic properties through agreements with the tribe and other affected parties using procedures outlined in 36 C.F.R. § 800.6.

Federal appellate and district courts have interpreted whether an agency adequately assessed the effects their undertaking would have on tribal historic properties. For example, the Ninth Circuit found that the Forest Service failed to mitigate the adverse effects of transferring a portion of an important tribal ancestral transportation route to a private entity intent on logging the site. *Muckleshoot Indian Tribe*, 177 F.3d at 807–09. And a district court held that the Department of the Interior failed to adequately consult with the tribe regarding the adverse effects that the siting of a solar energy project would have on hundreds of ancient cultural sites in the area. Quechan Tribe of Fort Yuma Reservation v. U.S. Dep't of the Interior, 755 F. Supp. 2d 1104 (S.D. Cal. 2010).

CHAPTER 13

CONSERVATION AND PRESERVATION RESTRICTIONS

This Chapter focuses on conservation and preservation restrictions: private, legal real property interests conveyed by a property owner to a qualified nonprofit organization (such as the Nature Conservancy) or government agency (such as the Department of the Interior) to limit development or activity on the property in order to protect vital resources. Such restrictions are becoming increasingly popular and already affect tens of millions of acres of land in the United States.

In general, "conservation restrictions" protect landscapes, land with historic or archaeological significance, wetlands, environmentally sensitive areas, and open space, while "preservation restrictions" protect historic structures. These restrictions burden one property while benefiting another property or persons, and they run with the land to successive owners, typically lasting forever. Conservation and preservation restrictions usually include provisions requiring the property owner to preserve and maintain the property, prohibiting changes that are inconsistent with the character of the property, and allowing third party access to some or all of the property. They may also prohibit demolition and detrimental uses. In exchange for relinquishing certain rights, a property owner may receive certain benefits, including federal and state tax deductions or credits.

Restrictions are sometimes known by the common law terms of "servitudes," "easements," or "covenants," which are often used interchangeably. We favor the term "restriction" because it clarifies that conservation and preservation restrictions are relatively recent legal tools that are created by state statute rather than common law.

This Chapter describes how conservation and preservation restrictions are created, altered, and terminated. Moreover, it highlights how their growth has been influenced by federal and state tax rules.

A. CREATION

Conservation and preservation restrictions are useful and flexible historic preservation tools created pursuant to state statutes. Under the terms of a typical conservation or preservation restriction, a property owner places restrictions on the development of, or changes to, the property and transfers these restrictions (usually through a deed) to a nonprofit organization or government agency whose mission includes environmental conservation, land conservation, or historic preservation.

This Part discusses how conservation and preservation restrictions are created voluntarily through adherence to different types of state statutes as well as how they are involuntarily created through exactions.

1. VOLUNTARY CREATION THROUGH STATE STATUTES

There are two primary types of conservation and preservation restrictions: those that are based on the Uniform Conservation Easement Act (UCEA), and those that are not. Twenty-one states and the District of Columbia have adopted the UCEA. The UCEA was drafted by the National Conference of Commissioners on Uniform State Laws, approved by the American Bar Association in 1981 and amended in 2007. The remaining states have unique state-specific statutes dealing with conservation and preservation restrictions. Each of these will be discussed in turn below.

a. States Adopting the Uniform Conservation Easement Act

Nearly half of the states have adopted the Uniform Conservation Easement Act (UCEA). According to its preface, the UCEA has three purposes: (1) to enable "durable restrictions and affirmative obligations to be attached to real property to protect natural and historic resources"; (2) to render these restrictions immune from "certain common law impediments which might otherwise be raised"; and (3) to maximize "the freedom of the creators of the transaction to impose restrictions on the use of land and improvements in order to protect them." UNIF. CONSERVATION EASEMENT ACT (1981).

The UCEA offers a comprehensive and coherent framework for identifying and protecting private land use restrictions designed to preserve important natural and historic resources. Specifically, it defines a "conservation easement" as:

> a nonpossessory interest of a holder in real property imposing limitations or affirmative obligations the purposes of which include retaining or protecting natural, scenic, or open-space values of real property, assuring its availability for agricultural, forest, recreational, or open-space use, protecting natural resources, maintaining or enhancing air or water quality, or preserving the historical, architectural, archaeological, or cultural aspects of real property.

Id. § 1(1). The UCEA further delineates how conservation and preservation restrictions may be created and recorded, their validity and application, and who may hold and enforce these restrictions. *Id.* §§ 1–5. Some states that have adopted the UCEA have made minor modifications.

b. States Not Adopting the Uniform Conservation Easement Act

A little more than half of the states have unique statutes governing conservation and preservation restrictions. Since these state statutes vary widely in content and scope, we cannot give them comprehensive treatment here. Instead we offer a brief discussion of how four key features—the definition of restriction, recording requirements, the identity of the enforcing party, and public review— of unique state-specific conservation and preservation restriction statutes may differ from the UCEA.

One of the most salient differences is the definition of what counts as a restriction. For instance, unlike the UCEA, Connecticut has separate definitions for "conservation restriction" and "preservation restriction" and the values that Connecticut's restrictions are designed to protect do not track the UCEA exactly. *See* CONN. GEN. STAT. ANN. § 47–42a(a–b).

Another difference is that many states, while requiring easements and covenants to be recorded on land records, make no provision in their statutes on how conservation or preservation restrictions must be recorded. California is one of handful of states that specifically address the recordation of conservation and preservation restrictions. CAL. CIV. CODE § 815.5 (requiring instruments creating or transferring conservation easements to "be recorded in the office of the county recorder of the county where the land is situated").

Furthermore, unlike the UCEA, some states, such as Connecticut, do not specify who, besides the attorney general, may enforce a conservation or preservation restriction. *See* CONN. GEN. STAT. §§ 47–42(b)–(c). The question of whether a Connecticut property owner who was aware of a conservation restriction on an abutting piece of property could sue his neighbor to prevent him from logging came before a Connecticut state court in 1995. With no statutory guidance on the issue, the court relied on common law principles related to the enforceability of easements to hold that only the easement holder (in this case, a nonprofit organization), not the neighbor, was entitled to relief. Burgess v. Breakell, 1995 WL 476782 (Conn. Super. 1995).

Some states have also differentiated themselves from the UCEA by adopting limited public review requirements relating to the enforceability of conservation and preservation restrictions. For instance, Nebraska requires local or county government approval for conservation easements not held by the state. *See* NEB. REV. STAT. §§ 76–2, 112(3). Virginia requires only that the conservation easement "conform in all respects to the comprehensive plan at the time the easement is granted for the area in which the real property is located." VA. CODE ANN., § 10.1–1010E.

2.   INVOLUNTARY CREATION
THROUGH EXACTIONS

Conservation and preservation restrictions are usually voluntary agreements entered into by a property owner. In some cases, however, restrictions are created when government agencies require developers to conserve land in exchange for a public approval of their projects (typically the issuance of a permit). In these cases, the developers who own the property promise to restrict the use of some of their land and devote it to conservation or preservation purposes.

These involuntary conservation and preservation restrictions create a host of issues, some of which have been confronted by courts. *See, e.g.*, Smith v. Town of Mendon, 822 N.E.2d 1214 (N.Y. 2004) (finding that a town's conservation restriction condition on a site plan approval for a single-family home was valid because it neither qualified as an exaction nor constituted a regulatory taking); Rossco Holdings, Inc. v. State of California, 260 Cal.Rptr. 736 (Ct. App. 1989) (holding that a landowner in a coastal zone who complied with a permit condition and started development could not later challenge the permit condition).

B.   ALTERATION AND TERMINATION

While state statutes specify how conservation and preservation restrictions may be created, they are often silent as to how or whether these restrictions may be altered or terminated. And the Uniform Conservation Easement Act, described further in Part A, defers to state law on these two matters. Given this lack of guidance, that conservation and preservation restrictions are relatively recent legal tools, and that these restrictions are usually meant to be perpetual, it is difficult to determine whether, or to what extent, alteration or termination should be allowed. Public authorities and courts may look to traditional servitudes law for guidance, or to other states' practices. This Part examines state supervised alterations to conservation and preservation restrictions as well as applicable doctrines that courts might use to analyze requests for alteration. Finally this Part concludes by examining termination procedures for conservation and preservation restrictions.

1. ALTERATION

Conservation and preservation restrictions are usually drafted to last in perpetuity. However, changed circumstances may require that a conservation or preservation restriction be altered. For example, the nonprofit holder of the restriction may have ceased to exist, the protected historic structure may require repairs prohibited by the restriction, or the amount of public access to the site may need to be modified. Currently, most states allow the relevant parties to a conservation or preservation restriction to amend the restriction without any government interference. Indeed, this flexibility is one of the most attractive features of such restrictions.

Sometimes, however, additional oversight of alterations may be required. In some states, for example, the state judicial or executive branch must consent to any proposed alterations. In other places, an alteration may be presented to a judicial decision-maker for review; here, we consider two judicial doctrines that may be utilized during this analysis.

a. State Supervised Alterations

While many states take a hands-off approach to conservation and preservation restriction amendments, a growing number of states—including Louisiana, Maine, Massachusetts, and New Jersey—require the review and consent of a court or other public official or entity before a restriction may be modified.

In Maine, for example, where conservation restrictions cover nearly 10 percent of the state, courts are empowered to decided whether or not a conservation or preservation restriction may be amended. Maine courts may allow amendments if two conditions are met: (1) the conservation or preservation restriction includes a statement of the holder's power to agree to amendments to the terms of the conservation or preservation restriction; and (2) the amendment may not "materially detract from the conservation values intended for protection" in the original conservation or preservation restriction. ME. REV. STAT. ANN. tit. 33, § 477–A2(A–B). In making its determination, a Maine court must consider, among other things, the purposes expressed by the parties in the original conservation or preservation restriction and the public interest. *See id.* § 477–A2(B). And should the amendment of a conservation or preservation restriction result in an increase in the landowner's estate, that increase must be paid over to the holder of the restriction or to a nonprofit or governmental entity chosen by the court and used to protect the values for which the original conservation or preservation restriction was made. *See id.* Maine's statutory amendment procedures, therefore, seek to strike a balance between denying restriction modifications altogether and allowing alterations at will.

b. Judicial Review of Alterations

In addition to the consent procedures described in the preceding section, a person wanting to alter a conservation or preservation restriction may turn to the courts. Courts may evaluate proposed alterations through a variety of traditional legal doctrines. Here, we mention only two: the changed condition doctrine and the charitable trust analogy.

The doctrine of changed conditions (sometimes called changed circumstances) applies to traditional common law servitudes. It states that when:

> a change has taken place since the creation of a servitude that makes it impossible as a practical matter to accomplish the purpose for which the servitude was created, a court may modify the servitude to permit the purpose to be accomplished. If modification is not practicable, or would not be effective, a court may terminate the servitude. Compensation for resulting harm to the beneficiaries may be awarded as a condition of modifying or terminating the servitude.

RESTATEMENT (THIRD) OF PROPERTY: SERVITUDES § 7.10(1) (2000). Thus, the changed condition doctrine calls on courts to decide whether changes that have taken place since the inception of the conservation or preservation restriction are so substantial that the restriction should be modified to better accomplish its original purpose.

In the alternative, courts might analyze proposed alterations to conservation and preservation restrictions using rules that apply to charitable trusts. A charitable trust is simply a trust created by agreement or operation of law for charitable purposes with a public benefit. Many conservation and preservation restrictions are created under charitable trust type arrangements: the organization or government agency holding the restriction is the trustee; the public is the beneficiary; and the property owner creating the restriction is the grantor. Similar to the changed conditions doctrine outlined above, charitable trust rules allow courts to modify charitable trust documents if the means of achieving the aims of the trust have become impossible or impracticable due to changed circumstances and the proposed alterations would conform with the original intent of the trust. To date, only the Supreme Court of Wyoming has found that charitable trust rules should apply to conservation restrictions. *See* Hicks v. Dowd, 157 P.3d 914, 919 (Wyo. 2007).

2.   TERMINATION

When conservation or preservation restrictions are created, they can be very difficult to extinguish. Many states mandate perpetual terms for conservation and preservation restrictions, and many nonprofit organizations and government agencies accepting conservation and preservation restrictions require that restrictions last forever.

Nevertheless, there are several ways to extinguish perpetual conservation or preservation restrictions. First, a court may extinguish a restriction in law or equity. For instance, courts are likely to extinguish a preservation restriction if the structure being protected by the restriction has been destroyed. A court may also extinguish a conservation or preservation restriction if the nonprofit organization holding the restriction dissolves.

Second, federal tax regulations allow conservation restrictions to be extinguished if it becomes impossible or impracticable to use the restricted property for conservation purposes, as long as any proceeds from the sale of the property (absent the restriction) are used for conservation purposes. *See* Treas. Reg. § 1.170A–14(c)(2) (2011).

Finally, conservation or preservation restrictions may be extinguished by government condemnation (also called eminent domain). Some states, like Virginia and Mississippi, mandate that compensation be given when government action condemns land burdened by a conservation restriction. *See* VA. CODE ANN. § 10.1–1010(F) (2011); MISS. CODE ANN. § 89–19–7 (2007). In states that do not explicitly require compensation, donors typically provide in their restriction documents that should the land be condemned, the restriction will revert and the full value will return to the property owner.

C.   VALUE OF CONSERVATION AND PRESERVATION RESTRICTIONS

The value of conservation and preservation restrictions is a topic of significant controversy and has given rise to several legal challenges. This Part first considers how the law calculates the worth of these restrictions and potential abuses of such calculations, and then describes how tax law and policy have affected the development of conservation and preservation restrictions.

1. VALUATION

Assessing the value of any interest in real property is an arduous task, as it typically requires a specially trained appraiser. Accurate valuations of conservation and preservation restrictions are even more difficult because compared to other real estate interests there are few market purchases and sales of such restrictions. Nevertheless, there are several reasons to get a valuation on a conservation or preservation restriction: the property's overall value may be reduced by the value of the restriction allowing the property owner to pay fewer taxes; the holder of a restriction may require a valuation for inventory purposes and to determine the extent of its administration and maintenance expenses for the restricted parcel; programs purchasing restrictions must assess their value prior to buying them; and, perhaps most significantly, the value of the restriction determines the tax advantages available to a property owner who is donating it for charitable purposes.

While in many cases, the value of a restriction acts to diminish the value of the overall property, this is not always the case. Sometimes restrictions have no effect on the overall value of property, or may even enhance its value, as the Treasury Department has recognized. *See* Treas. Reg. § 1.170A–14(h)(3)(ii) (2009). It is important,

therefore, to consult with a qualified appraiser
before creating a conservation and preservation
restriction to ensure that the desired financial
result will be reached.

a. Methods of Appraisal

Methods of appraisals vary, but there are three
primary methods of valuing donated property that
have been validated by the Internal Revenue
Service: comparable sales, replacement cost, and
income capitalization. *See* I.R.S., PUB. 561,
DETERMINING THE VALUE OF DONATED PROPERTY 6–
7 (2007).

The first method is the comparable sales
methodology. Here, an appraiser will review sales of
conservation and preservation restrictions in
roughly the same geographic area as the subject
property and adjust the average value either
upward or downward depending upon the unique
characteristics of the subject property. This method
is problematic for conservation or preservation
restrictions because there is typically a lack of
relevant market data.

The second method is the replacement cost
method. Under this method, an appraiser would
separate the value of the land from the value of any
improvements. This may allow for consideration of
the costs imposed on property owners by restrictions
that require the owner to replace or reproduce
protected features. Furthermore, the replacement
cost method may account for restrictions that
require direct expenditures on capital

improvements, or those that require the retention of obsolete or otherwise unfavorable improvements that may impose future rehabilitation costs.

The third method is income capitalization. This approach assesses a restriction's impact on a range of financial streams: tenant rents, operating expenses, insurance costs, repairs, additional reserves, and marketing costs. All of these approaches are covered in greater detail by Richard Roddewig, a preservation expert. *See* RICHARD J. RODDEWIG, APPRAISAL INST. & LAND TRUST ALLIANCE, APPRAISING CONSERVATION AND HISTORIC PRESERVATION EASEMENTS (2011).

In sum, all three methods discussed above utilize some well-accepted form of "before and after" analysis. That is, an appraiser determines the fair market value of the overall parcel without the restriction (the "before" value) and the fair market value taking into account the restriction (the "after" value). *See, e.g.*, Browning v. Comm'r, 109 T.C. 303 (1997) (using "before and after" analysis to determine the value of a conservation restriction). The difference between the "before" value and the "after" value is the value of the restriction. An appraiser must use a consistent approach in her "before and after" analysis, or courts will ignore the appraisal. *See, e.g.*, Dunlap v. Comm'r, T.C.M. (RIA) 2012–126 (finding a report of taxpayer's appraiser lacked any probative weight as to the fair market value of a donated historic preservation façade restriction because the appraiser switched from a comparable-sales approach to an income approach in her before-and-after valuation).

b. Difficulties in Making Valuations

Conservation or preservation restrictions are very difficult to value for several reasons. Restrictions are often unique and vary widely in scope and applicability. They may range from protections for a single architectural element of a historic interior to an exterior façade to a cluster of outbuildings, or even hundreds of acres of open space. The financial impact of a restriction must also be measured against the current level of protection offered by local ordinances, taking into account any special conditions attached to the restriction. Given the lack of relevant market data to guide restrictions assessments, as noted above, valuations have varied widely. This has raised concerns that some property owners have overestimated the value of restrictions they donated to charitable organizations, allowing them to unduly benefit from federal tax breaks.

Furthermore, given the variability and complexity of conservation and preservation restrictions, there has been a tendency to oversimplify the value of particular types of restrictions. For example, some thought that a series of court decisions had created an informal rule that historic façade restriction donations would automatically reduce the value of a historic property between 10 and 15 percent. *See, e.g.*, Hilborn v. Comm'r, 85 T.C. 677 (1985); Richmond v. United States, 699 F. Supp. 578 (E.D. La. 1988). However, the Tax Court has explicitly disavowed the notion that historic façade donations receive some set percentage reduction. *See* Nicoladis v. Comm'r, T.C.M. (P–H) 1988–163 (1988). And a federal court has recently enjoined an organization from advertising that historic façade donations would automatically result in reductions of certain amounts. *See* United States v. McClain, No. 1:11–cv–01087–GK (D.D.C. 2011). While conservation or preservation restrictions are flexible, individualized tools for protecting particular features of land and/or property, each restriction must be assessed by a qualified appraiser to gain an accurate understanding of its worth.

2. TAX TREATMENT

Perhaps the single greatest impact on the number and scope of conservation and preservation restrictions has been the tax benefits associated with them. The most significant rule affecting restrictions is section 170(h) of the Internal Revenue Code, which allows donors to receive a federal tax deduction for qualified conservation contributions. Many states also boast important tax benefits tied to conservation or preservation restrictions. This Part examines federal and state tax incentives associated with creating a conservation or preservation restriction.

a. Federal Tax Incentives

Federal tax incentives for conservation or preservation restrictions have increased the use of restrictions to protect important historic resources.

In 1976, Congress authorized temporary tax deductions for conservation and preservation restrictions that lasted at least thirty years. Given the success of the program, Congress made these tax deductions a permanent feature in 1980 and added requirements—including a provision that restrictions must be granted in perpetuity—which remain the core of the tax program today. Following stories of widespread abuse of conservation and preservation restriction tax deductions, Congress revised section 170 of the Internal Revenue Code in 2006. Among other things, these changes: clarified the type of property eligible for deductions, including property already in historic districts; required certified statements from donors and donees regarding the donee's capability to hold the conservation or preservation restriction; required more documentation regarding the value of the restriction; and imposed standardized qualifications for appraisers. *See* 26 U.S.C. § 170.

The most important part of the Internal Revenue Code for conservation and preservation restrictions is section 170(h), which outlines the provisions for qualified conservation contributions. To be eligible for federal tax deductions, a conservation or preservation restriction must meet three requirements. It must be a contribution:

(A) of a qualified real property interest,

(B) to a qualified organization,

(C) exclusively for conservation purposes.

Id. § 170(h)(1). The Code defines in detail what constitutes a qualified real property interest, a qualified organization, and conservation purposes. *See id.* § 170(h)(2–4). Importantly, conservation purposes include land areas for outdoor recreation; relatively natural habitat of fish, wildlife, or plants, or similar ecosystem; open space that will yield a significant public benefit; and a historically important land area or a certified historic structure. *See id.* § 170(h)(4)(A). The term "certified historic structure" is further defined to mean "any building, structure, or land area which is listed in the National Register, or any building which is located in a registered historic district* * * and is certified by the Secretary of the Interior as being of historic significance to the district." *Id.* § 170(h)(C). To guard against valuation abuse, the Code also outlines special rules with respect to restrictions covering the exterior of buildings in a registered historic district. *See id.* § 170(h)(4)(B).

There has been a significant amount of litigation regarding various aspects of conservation and preservation restrictions and federal tax deductions, not all of which can be summarized here. One recurring source of litigation is whether a donated conservation or preservation easement has been "granted in perpetuity" according to 26 U.S.C. § 170(h)(2)(C). Treasury regulations clarify that for a restriction to be enforceable in perpetuity, any mortgage encumbering it must be subordinate to the qualified organization that is tasked with preserving the restricted property in perpetuity. *See* Treas. Reg. § 1.170A–14(g)(2). Courts have consistently held that when a mortgagee (a lender) has superior claim to proceeds from the property over the qualified organization holding the donated restriction, the restriction was not granted in perpetuity. Thus, the donated restriction would not constitute a qualified conservation contribution under section 170(h) and no tax deduction can be given. *See, e.g.,* Wall v. Comm'r, T.C.M. (RIA) 2012–69; Kaufman v. Comm'r, 136 T.C. No. 13 (2011); 1982 East, LLC v. Comm'r, T.C.M. (RIA) 2011–84. Courts have also declined to extend tax deductions to donated conservation restrictions that could be extinguished by the parties' mutual consent because this would violate the perpetuity requirement. *See* Carpenter v. Comm'r, T.C.M. (RIA) 2012–001. However, façade preservation restrictions which allow the holding qualified organization to approve changes or abandon its rights to the restrictions meet the perpetuity requirement and thus qualify for the deduction. *See, e.g.,* Kaufman v. Shulman, 687 F.3d 21 (1st Cir. 2013); Comm'r v. Simmons, 646 F.3d 6 (D.C. Cir. 2011).

Another issue that has received attention is whether the conservation or preservation restriction was donated "exclusively for conservation purposes." 26 U.S.C. § 170(h)(1)(C). In *Glass v. Commissioner,* the Sixth Circuit held that the donation of two, small discontinuous conservation restrictions on a single lakefront parcel satisfied the "conservation purposes" requirement and qualified for the tax deduction. 471 F.3d 698 (6th Cir. 2006). Similarly, a conservation restriction that reserved rights to the owners to develop portions of the properties and alter the properties' current conditions met the "conservation purposes" requirement because the reserved rights were consistent with a conservation purpose, and the land trust retained the right to enforce the conservation restriction. *See* Butler v. Comm'r, T.C.M. (RIA) 2012–072. However, a preservation restriction that does not directly preserve a "historically important land area" or "certified historic structure" will fail the "conservation purposes" requirement and be ineligible for a tax deduction. *See, e.g.,* Herman v. Comm'r, T.C.M. (RIA) 2009–205 (finding that a preservation restriction on unused development rights within a historic district did not preserve a certified historic structure rendering it ineligible for a tax deduction); Turner v. Comm'r, 126 T.C. 299 (2006) (holding that a preservation restriction on a parcel adjacent to a historic grist mill did not preserve any historically important land area and did not qualify for a tax deduction).

b. State Tax Incentives

Many states offer income tax credits or deductions for conservation and preservation restrictions. Colorado is one of the most generous states, offering a tax credit of 50 percent of the fair market value of a qualifying charitable contribution up to $375,000, which can be transferred to other taxpayers. *See* COLO. REV. STAT. § 39–22–522. South Carolina allows a tax credit of 25 percent of the amount of a qualified charitable contribution up to $250 per acre, with a maximum annual limit of $52,500. *See* S.C. CODE ANN. § 12–6–3515. And

Virginia offers an income tax deduction of up to 40 percent of the value of a qualifying open-space easement up to $100,000 that may be transferred or carried forward for a decade. *See* VA. CODE ANN. § 58.1–512. These three states, like others, require that taxpayers submit relevant documentation certifying their donations and mandate that appraisals be performed by a qualified appraiser, as defined in 26 U.S.C. § 170(f)(11). But unlike most states, Colorado has established a regulatory agency, the Conservation Easement Oversight Commission, to supervise conservation and preservation restrictions within the state. *See* COLO. REV. STAT. § 39–22–522(2.5).

States vary as to size, transferability, carry-forward possibilities, and type of land qualifying for state tax incentives. But it is important to note that approximately one third of the states allow property owners who donate conservation or preservation restrictions to deduct the value of the restriction from the assessed value of their property, resulting in a reduction of property taxes. Thus, in addition to one-time credits or deductions on income tax, a property owner in many states who donates a conservation or preservation restriction may continue to receive tax benefits on an ongoing basis.

CHAPTER 14
TAX CREDITS

Tax credits are the single most effective public program supporting private development of historic buildings. They provide an incentive for property owners and developers to rehabilitate historic buildings in the form of a "refund" equal to a percentage of project costs. Tax credits are attractive because they reduce a taxpayer's tax liability on a dollar-for-dollar basis—unlike, say, tax deductions, whose value is reduced according to the marginal income rate paid by the taxpayer. Eligibility for tax credit programs varies but often requires that a property be listed on the National Register of Historic Places or a state equivalent.

The federal rehabilitation tax credit program is run by the National Park Service and, over the years, has varied in value and scope. Currently, the federal program offers a 20 percent credit for certain rehabilitations of historic buildings and a 10 percent credit for certain rehabilitations of non-historic buildings constructed before 1936. Since the program's inception in 1978, the credits have leveraged over $106 billion in private investment to preserve nearly 40,000 historic properties.

Thirty-one states also have historic tax credit programs. Many are based on the federal credit—and may even be coupled with the federal credit to make qualifying projects more attractive to historic preservation developers.

This Chapter offers a detailed analysis of the federal rehabilitation tax credit program and provides an overview of state tax credit programs.

A. FEDERAL REHABILITATION TAX CREDITS

The federal rehabilitation tax credit program has effectively catalyzed billions of dollars' worth of historic preservation development. An understanding of this program is critical for historic preservation developers (and their attorneys).

This Part provides an overview of the provisions of the Internal Revenue Code which establish the program, as well as an in-depth treatment of several key terms. It then describes the process that taxpayers must follow to use the program and issues that may arise after credits are awarded.

1. OVERVIEW

The federal rehabilitation tax credit program— the most significant direct federal financial aid to private historic preservation development projects— was created in 1978. At this time, cities around the country were experiencing high rates of vacant and neglected structures in urban neighborhoods with historic buildings. To spur economic development in these neighborhoods, Congress passed the Revenue Act of 1978. It authorized a 10 percent tax credit for rehabilitations of certain nonresidential properties. Three years later, Congress passed the Economic Recovery Tax Act, expanding the tax credit program to a three-tier system that authorized a 15 percent credit for rehabilitations of nonresidential buildings at least thirty years old, a 20 percent credit for nonresidential buildings at least forty years old, and a 25 percent credit for certified historic structures (residential and nonresidential alike).

In 1986, the Tax Reform Act replaced the three-tier system with a two-tier system, which is codified today in the following language:

(a) General rule. For purposes of section 46, the rehabilitation credit for any taxable year is the sum of—

(1) 10 percent of the qualified rehabilitation expenditures with respect to any qualified rehabilitated building other than a certified historic structure, and

(2) 20 percent of the qualified rehabilitation expenditures with respect to any certified historic structure.

(b) When expenditures taken into account.

(1) In general. Qualified rehabilitation expenditures with respect to any qualified rehabilitated building shall be taken into account for the taxable year in which such qualified rehabilitated building is placed in service. * * *

26 U.S.C. § 47. The language clarifies that the tax credit applies only to buildings (and related structural components), while other types of resources (structures unrelated to buildings, sites, objects, or districts) are ineligible. It establishes two

tiers of credits to be used for "qualified rehabilitation expenditures": a 20 percent credit for the rehabilitation of a "certified historic structure" and a 10 percent credit for a "qualified rehabilitated building other than a certified historic structure." These key terms are described in greater detail below, but for now it suffices to say that the 10 percent credit does not require properties to be designated historic, while the 20 percent tax credit does. Another difference is that the 20 percent credit has, in practice, proven to be more heavily utilized by taxpayers for obvious reasons (it is twice as generous!).

This excerpted language implies that the federal government will offer the tax credit to any qualifying project. Indeed, there is no cap on the amount of credits the federal government will disburse in any given year. The credits will be offered the year the building is "placed in service," a term described in the next section. With a few limited exceptions, the only party who may receive tax credit is the owner of the property for which the credits are being sought.

2.   KEY TERMS

As is the case with any portion of the Internal Revenue Code, the federal historic tax credit provision hinges on the details of the key statutory terms. The first three terms identify the types of buildings eligible for credits. A fourth term to know, "qualified rehabilitation expenditures," dictates the project costs that are eligible for a credit. The last term, "placed in service," is not defined in the statute but is important because it tells taxpayers when they will be able to start taking a credit.

a. Qualified Rehabilitated Building

Only projects related to "qualified rehabilitated buildings" are eligible for the federal rehabilitation tax credit. There are two types of qualified rehabilitated buildings: (1) certified historic structures and (2) buildings placed in service before 1936 that are not certified historic structures. Certified historic structures will receive a 20 percent tax credit, while other qualified rehabilitated buildings will receive a 10 percent tax credit.

The Internal Revenue Code expands on the meaning of qualified rehabilitated buildings as follows:

(A) In general. The term "qualified rehabilitated building" means any building (and its structural components) if—

(i) such building has been substantially rehabilitated,

(ii) such building was placed in service before the beginning of the rehabilitation,

(iii) in the case of any building other than a certified historic structure, in the rehabilitation process—

(I) 50 percent or more of the existing external walls of such building are retained in place as external walls,

(II) 75 percent or more of the existing external walls of such building are retained in place as internal or external walls, and

(III) 75 percent or more of the existing internal structural framework of such building is retained in place, and

(iv) depreciation (or amortization in lieu of depreciation) is allowable with respect to such building.

(B) Building must be first placed in service before 1936. In the case of a building other than a certified historic structure, a building shall not be a qualified rehabilitated building unless the building was first placed in service before 1936.

26 U.S.C. § 47(c)(1). The first limitation on the "qualified rehabilitated building" term is "any building." Federal regulations define the term building to mean "any structure or edifice enclosing a space within its walls, and usually covered by a roof, the purpose of which is, for example, to provide shelter or housing, or to provide working, office, parking, display, or sales space." Treas. Reg. § 1.48–1(e)(1). This term includes "apartment houses, factory and office buildings, warehouses, barns, garages, railway or bus stations, and stores," as well as stadiums. *Id.*; Rev. Rul. 69–170, 1969–1 C.B. 28.

A building must have been "placed in service" (occupied by humans) at some point prior to the rehabilitation, and must be placed in service again after the rehabilitation. *See* 26 U.S.C. § 47(c)(1)(A)(ii); Treas. Reg. § 1.46–3(d)(1). Thus bridges, statues, landscapes, and ancient archaeological artifacts will not be considered buildings, even if such resources may be listed on registers of historic places.

Moreover, a building must have been "substantially rehabilitated," a term discussed next. It must also be depreciable, using the straight line depreciation method. *Id.* § 47(c)(2)(B)(i). Taxpayers who fail to use a straight line method of depreciation will be prevented from taking a tax credit. *See*, *e.g.*, DeMarco v. Comm'r, 87 T.C. 518 (T.C. 1986), *aff'd* 831 F.2d 281 (1st Cir. 1987).

Pre-1936 buildings that are not certified historic structures deserve additional commentary. The rehabilitation of these buildings must retain a percentage of existing external and internal walls or framework and must have been placed in service prior to 1936. *See* Depot Investors Ltd., 63 T.C.M. (CCH) 2344 (T.C. 1992) (disallowing a rehabilitation credit for a project that did not retain the required percentage of walls). In addition, they must be used for non-residential rental purposes, 26 U.S.C. § 50(b)(2), and must have remained in the same location since 1936, Treas. Reg. § 1.48–12(b)(5). A taxpayer cannot claim a 10 percent rehabilitation credit on a building listed individually on the National Register or one that is contributing to the significance of a registered historic district. She may only claim the 10 percent rehabilitation credit on an unlisted property or on a property within a registered historic district that is "decertified"—a process through which the NPS acknowledges that the building does not contribute to the significance of the district. Decertification may be completed during Part 1 of the federal rehabilitation tax credit application process.

b. Substantial Rehabilitation

A building will not be considered to be a "qualified rehabilitated building" unless it has been "substantially rehabilitated" prior to being placed in service. Rehabilitation is substantial if the qualified rehabilitation expenditures incurred over a twenty-four month period exceed the greater of the adjusted basis of the building or $5,000. 26 U.S.C. § 47(c)(1)(C)(i). Basis is a term that refers to a property owner's capital investment in a property for tax purposes, and is reduced by annual depreciation. On occasion, if a building is held for many years, the property owner's basis in the building will depreciate to zero. In such situations, the $5,000 figure provides a minimum investment for qualification for the tax credit. Note that for a project that was expected to be phased prior to the start of the rehabilitation work, the expenditures may occur over a sixty-month period. *Id.* § 47(c)(1)(C)(ii).

The $5,000 minimum and the tying of qualified rehabilitation expenditures to basis ensures that substantial rehabilitations may be measured objectively. The Internal Revenue Service requires that qualified rehabilitation expenditures must exceed the basis in the building as a whole, not just in the portion being renovated. *See* Alexander v. Comm'r, 97 T.C. 244, 247–49 (1991) (upholding this approach). Numerous example scenarios showing how basis, measuring period, and rehabilitation expenditures work in practice are provided in Treasury Regulation section 1.48–12.

There are no objective thresholds for the substantial rehabilitation. For example, there is no percentage of a building that must be touched by the rehabilitation project before a tax credit is awarded. However, work on certified historic structures must be completed in accordance with the subjective requirements of the Secretary of the Interior's Standards for Rehabilitation. *See* 36 C.F.R. § 67.6(b)(1).

c. Certified Historic Structure

"Certified historic structures" are given a higher tax credit (20 percent) than qualified rehabilitated buildings that are not certified historic structures (10 percent). The term's definition is self-explanatory:

(A) In general. The term "certified historic structure" means any building (and its structural components) which—

(i) is listed in the National Register, or

(ii) is located in a registered historic district and is certified by the Secretary of the Interior to the Secretary as being of historic significance to the district.

(B) Registered historic district. The term "registered historic district" means—

(i) any district listed in the National Register, and

(ii) any district—

(I) which is designated under a statute of the appropriate State or local government, if such statute is certified by the Secretary of the Interior to the Secretary as containing criteria which will substantially achieve the purpose of preserving and rehabilitating buildings of historic significance to the district, and

(II) which is certified by the Secretary of the Interior to the Secretary as meeting substantially all of the requirements for the listing of districts in the National Register.

26 U.S.C. § 47(c)(3). Only properties actually listed on the National Register or contributing to a registered historic district are eligible for the tax credit; properties that are merely eligible for listing are excluded.

The one exception to this general rule is contained in subsection (B)(II), which allows the

Secretary of the Interior to certify a state or local historic district "as meeting substantially all of the requirements for the listing of districts in the National Register." This language ensures that incentives may be provided to taxpayers to rehabilitate historic properties where there is some technical or political reason why a district is not listed on the National Register. The Secretary of the Interior may not, however, unilaterally declare individual buildings not located within state or local historic districts to be eligible for the tax credit program.

It may be tempting for taxpayers to try to manipulate whether a building is considered to be a certified historic structure. For example, a taxpayer may wish to petition for the de-listing of a property on the National Register to render that building a qualified rehabilitated building other than a certified historic structure, thus making it eligible for the lower 10 percent credit and avoiding the more rigorous scrutiny of the 20 percent credit. Courts may be reluctant, however, to grant taxpayers this ability to game the system. *See, e.g.,* Amoco Prod. Co. v. U.S. Dep't of the Interior, 763 F. Supp. 514, 523 (N.D. Okla. 1990).

d. Qualified Rehabilitation Expenditures

Rehabilitation projects have many different costs, but only certain costs will be covered by the federal rehabilitation tax credit. A taxpayer may only recover costs that can be characterized as "qualified rehabilitation expenditures." This term is defined as follows:

any amount properly chargeable to capital account—

(i) for property for which depreciation is allowable under [26 U.S.C.] section 168 and which is—

(I) nonresidential real property,

(II) residential rental property,

(III) real property which has a class life of more than 12.5 years, or

(IV) an addition or improvement to property described in subclause (I), (II), or (III), and

(ii) in connection with the rehabilitation of a qualified rehabilitated building.

26 U.S.C. § 47(c)(2)(A). Clause (i) identifies what kinds of properties may qualify for the tax credit. Clause (ii) specifies that the rehabilitation must be of a qualified rehabilitated building.

Federal regulations provide additional guidance. Expenditures (including materials and trade and subcontractor costs) related to:

walls, partitions, floors, and ceilings, as well as any permanent coverings therefor such as paneling or tiling; windows and doors; . . . central air conditioning or heating system . . .; plumbing and plumbing fixtures, such as sinks

and bathtubs; electric wiring and lighting
fixtures; chimneys; stairs, escalators, and
elevators, including all components thereof;
sprinkler systems; [and] fire escapes

are all eligible for the tax credit. Treas. Reg. § 1.48–
1(e)(2). All of these items are permanently attached
to the building and would normally be considered to
contribute to a building's tax basis. In addition,
developers' fees, "soft costs" for architects and
engineers, construction loan interest, site surveys,
insurance premiums, legal fees, and other fees
normally chargeable to a capital account may all be
eligible for the tax credit. *Id.* § 1.48–12(c)(2). Note
that the Internal Revenue Service may challenge
certain expenditures that have not been adequately
substantiated. *See, e.g.*, Carp v. Comm'r, 62 T.C.M.
(CCH) 658 (T.C. 1991) (agreeing with the IRS that
taxpayers had failed to show that they performed
services to earn a developers' fee equal to 20 percent
of total expenditures).

The Internal Revenue Code also identifies certain
costs that are not qualified rehabilitation
expenditures. Excluded costs include costs related
to: site acquisition (including costs related to moving
buildings); enlargements of existing buildings;
certain rehabilitations that are not certified
rehabilitations; portions of properties that are more
than 50 percent leased to tax-exempt organizations;
and expenditures of lessees if their lease is shorter
than the recovery period for property depreciation.
See 26 U.S.C. § 47(c)(2)(B). (Note that enlargements
of existing buildings only occur "to the extent that

the total volume of the building is increased." Treas. Reg. § 1.48–12(c)(10).)

In addition, landscaping and other site work, such as decking, fencing, new porches or porticos, outdoor lighting, paving, retaining walls, sidewalks, and storm sewer costs, may not be included in qualified rehabilitation expenditures. *Id.* § 1.48–12(c)(5). Finally, items that are easily removed from the building—appliances, cabinetry, carpets tacked in place (not glued), furniture, signage, and window treatments—are not eligible for the tax credit.

e. Placed in Service

Federal regulations describe what the term "placed in service" means, as follows:

[P]roperty shall be considered placed in service in the earlier of the following taxable years:

(i) The taxable year in which, under the taxpayer's depreciation practice, the period for depreciation with respect to such property begins; or

(ii) The taxable year in which the property is placed in a condition or state of readiness and availability for a specifically assigned function, whether in a trade or business, in the production of income, in a tax-exempt activity, or in a personal activity.

Treas. Reg. § 1.46–3(d)(1). Buildings subject to the federal rehabilitation tax credit will be considered to be placed in service the year they are first used for the purpose for which they were substantially rehabilitated. Often, this is the same year that they receive a certificate of occupancy. The substantial rehabilitation test must have been met by the time a building is actually placed in service, or it will not qualify as a qualified rehabilitated building. If a building is continually used throughout the rehabilitation, then the date it was placed in service is the project completion date.

Taxpayers may care a lot about the year their building is determined to be placed in service, because their tax liabilities may change from year to year. On the other hand, the ability to carry forward or carry back the tax credit may help them choose the year that is most advantageous.

3. APPLICATION

Taxpayers wishing to take advantage of the 20 percent federal rehabilitation tax credit must deal with two federal agencies: the National Park Service (NPS) of the Department of the Interior and the Internal Revenue Service (IRS) of the Department of the Treasury. First, the taxpayer must submit to the state historic preservation officer (SHPO) a three-part application that includes project plans and proof that the project was completed in accordance with those plans. The three parts of the application are submitted independently and in sequential order. The SHPO reviews each part of application, sends each part on to the NPS, and serves as a liaison between the NPS and the taxpayer. That the NPS reviews all parts of the applications for substantive compliance before tax credits are issued seems to have greatly limited the number of cases regarding the federal rehabilitation tax credit. Once the NPS certifies the work, the taxpayer must submit relevant documentation to the IRS to actually apply the credit to her tax liability.

Below we will discuss each part of the three-part application to the NPS, the appeals process, and issues that may arise after tax credits have been awarded.

a. Part 1

Part 1 is an "evaluation of significance," in which the NPS determines whether the building is a "certified historic structure" contained in 26 U.S.C. § 47(c)(3) or may otherwise be eligible for the tax credit program. The Part 1 application may be submitted after a building is rehabilitated and placed in service only if the building is individually listed on the National Register. If the building is located within a registered historic district, then the taxpayer must submit Part 1 of the application before the building is placed in service.

In the Part 1 application, the taxpayer submits documentation, including a statement of significance, photographs, and maps. If the property is already individually listed on the National Register or contributes to the significance of a registered historic district, then Part 1 is easy.

If the building is not yet listed, then the NPS will evaluate whether the building should be listed on the National Register. In this case, the applicant will request in the Part 1 application that the NPS make a preliminary determination about the eligibility of the building. The Keeper of the National Register of Historic Places makes the final determination, but in any event the taxpayer will not receive any tax credits unless and until the building is listed.

b. Part 2

Part 2, the "description of rehabilitation," is the most intensively reviewed part of the application. The NPS encourages taxpayers to submit the Part 2 application prior to commencing the work, but this is not required. *See* 36 C.F.R. § 67.6(a)(1). Submitting early is wise, however, because a taxpayer may incur significant costs and make decisions that render a building ineligible for tax credits. *See, e.g.*, Amoco Prod. Co. v. U.S. Dep't of the Interior, 763 F. Supp. 514, 523 (N.D. Okla. 1990).

In Part 2, the taxpayer provides information about the floor area, use, and estimated cost, as well as a detailed description (in writing, photographs, and architectural plans) of each aspect of the rehabilitation work. The ultimate use of the building is important: only properties rehabilitated for commercial, industrial, agricultural, or income-producing residential uses are eligible for the credit. It may not be used for an owner-occupied residence.

See Dennis v. Comm'r, 66 T.C.M. (CCH) 319 (T.C. 1993). The taxpayer must also provide information about all aspects of the rehabilitation, even those aspects (such as landscaping or enlargements) that are not eligible for the tax credit. Claims that NPS review of non-eligible expenses extends beyond NPS's authority have failed in court. *See, e.g.,* Schneider P'ship v. U.S. Dep't of the Interior, 693 F. Supp. 223 (D. N.J. 1988).

The SHPO and then the NPS will review whether the plans conform with the Secretary's Standards for Rehabilitation. *See* 36 C.F.R. § 67.7. These Standards provide general guidelines, but not specific mandates, for the rehabilitation of historic buildings to ensure that historic character is maintained. For example, the Standards say: "Distinctive features, finishes, and construction techniques or examples of craftsmanship that characterize a historic property shall be preserved." *Id.* § 67.7(b)(5). The Standards do not, however, dictate what specific kinds of features, finishes, or techniques are appropriate, because appropriateness will depend on the historical context of the building. If the taxpayer's plans do not conform with the Secretary's Standards, the taxpayer may be given an opportunity to revise her plans. Only conforming projects will be allowed to proceed to Part 3.

To avoid any surprises in the Part 3 certification, applicants should keep the SHPO and NPS aware of any changes that may be made to plans for the building. Failure to do so may result in a denial of tax credits. *See* St. Charles Assocs., Ltd. v. United States, 671 F. Supp. 1074 (D. Md. 1987) (denying tax credits to a taxpayer that commenced new, unapproved construction adjacent to historic properties that had been the subject of Part 2 approval).

c. Part 3

Part 3 of the application is a "request for certification of completed work" and is submitted after the work has been completed.

In Part 3, the taxpayer must submit a description and photographs of the completed rehabilitation project. The SHPO and NPS will again review whether the completed project conforms with the Secretary's Standards for Rehabilitation. The SHPO or NPS may inspect the completed work to ensure that it meets the Secretary's Standards at this time, and for a period of five years after completion of the rehabilitation. If the NPS finds the project conforms, then the project will be a "certified rehabilitation," meaning it is a "rehabilitation of a certified historic structure which the Secretary of the Interior has certified to the Secretary [of the Treasury] as being consistent with the historic character of such property or the district in which such property is located." 26 U.S.C. § 47(c)(2)(C).

Once Part 3 approval is obtained, tax credits will be awarded to the taxpayer, who must own title to the property. The taxpayer may transfer the credits in some limited circumstances, as described below. To claim the credit to her income, the taxpayer must file Form 3468 with the IRS, attaching a copy of the Part 3 approval. The taxpayer may carry back the credit for one year and may carry it forward for twenty years. *Id.* § 39(a).

d. Appeals

Taxpayers who are denied NPS approval at any stage may appeal the decision to a hearing officer. The officer usually hears just a few dozen appeals each year. The key factor in the relatively small number of appeals seems to be that the SHPO—who has significant expertise in working with NPS staff and in evaluating the appropriateness of architectural plans—often helps applicants to craft applications that the NPS will deem eligible for the tax credit.

4. POST-AWARD ISSUES

Three additional considerations are relevant after a tax credit award has been made: transfers, recaptures, and combinations of the federal tax credit with other programs.

a. Transfers

If a taxpayer is awarded tax credits, she may not be able to fully utilize the credits. For example, she may not have enough tax liability to take advantage of the credit offsets, or she may be subject to the alternative minimum tax. She may therefore wish to transfer some or all of the credits to another party.

Under federal tax law, she has the option of transferring the benefits of the credits, but only under very limited circumstances. She cannot transfer them through a direct sale, and the parties to which she may make a transfer are limited to: (1) new owners of the property, as long as the prior owner did not place the property in service, see Treas. Reg. § 1.48–12(b)(2)(B)(vii); and (2) those with a sufficient level of participation in the investment, pursuant to the economic substance doctrine, see 26 U.S.C. § 7701(o)(5)(A) (disallowing tax benefits for a transaction that "does not have economic substance or lacks a business purpose").

With regard to the latter group—participating investors—developers have implemented various syndication and structuring schemes that have allowed them to leverage resources from parties other than the property owner/taxpayer. A 2012 Third Circuit decision, *Historic Boardwalk Hall, LLC v. Commissioner*, threw some past practices into question. 694 F.3d 425 (3rd Cir. 2012), *cert. denied* 133 S.Ct. 2734 (2013). In that case, a private firm invested capital contributions in a limited liability company set up by the developer to facilitate the transfer of tax credits to the firm. In exchange for this investment, the firm was entitled to a 3 percent priority return with put and call arrangements and had a 99.9 percent interest in the federal tax credits. *See id.* at 435–42. The court found that the limited liability company was an impermissible mechanism to transfer the tax credits because the tax credit investor lacked meaningful downside risk or meaningful upside potential. *Id.* at 454–55.

Prior to *Historic Boardwalk Hall*, mere investment in a limited liability company or partnership was considered to be an acceptable level of participation. The decision did not clarify what types of participation would be acceptable, and as a result, there was a noticeable chilling effect on private investment in historic tax credit projects. In early 2014, the Internal Revenue Service issued guidance that clarified what kind of investment was sufficient. *See* Rev. Proc. 2014–12. This guidance allowed many projects that were stalled to proceed within a "safe harbor" framework.

b. Recapture

Tax credits awarded through the process may be recaptured if the taxpayer falls out of compliance with the tax credit program. One way that taxpayers fall out of compliance is by failing to retain ownership of the building for five years after completion of the work, as is required by law. Another way is if the property owner ceases to use the property in a way that would qualify for the tax credits—for example, if the property owner converted the building to become her own residence, a use not supported by the tax credit program.

c. Combination with Other Credits

Historic preservation developers often find it beneficial to combine the federal rehabilitation tax credit with other incentives, including other federal credits and state tax credits. The most common federal tax credit combination is with the federal low income housing tax credit, which provides either a 4 percent or 9 percent credit on a certain percentage of a building's qualified basis. However, some federal programs may not be combined with the federal rehabilitation tax credits, such as federal credits given to certain businesses that make their properties more accessible to the disabled. *See* 26 U.S.C. § 44(d)(7).

Developers utilizing federal rehabilitation tax credits may also combine them with state credits, as long as the building and the rehabilitation are eligible for both programs.

B. STATE REHABILITATION TAX CREDITS

Thirty-one state legislatures—many inspired by the success of the federal rehabilitation tax credit—have passed laws authorizing state rehabilitation tax credits. Some of these credits may be combined with the federal credits. Other credits are offered for owner-occupied residences or other projects that are ineligible for the federal credit. In this Part, we provide an overview of some of the common types of state rehabilitation tax credit programs and describe two issues that may arise after a credit is awarded.

1. OVERVIEW

State rehabilitation tax credits come in many different forms. Many programs mirror the federal rehabilitation tax credit; some even require applicants to submit copies of the federal application instead of offering a separate state-level application. Other programs target different kinds of properties.

Whether they track the federal credit or not, state rehabilitation tax credits share many of same characteristics. Almost all programs specify building uses targeted by the credits, and many programs require that projects adhere to the Secretary of the Interior's Standards for Rehabilitation, codified at 36 C.F.R. § 67.7, which provide guidance to property owners as to how to complete rehabilitation projects that are compatible with historic properties. The mechanism for calculating the amount of the tax credit award varies, but many follow the federal credit's formula of providing an award equal to a percentage of specified project expenditures, and requiring a minimum investment (either a fixed dollar amount or a percentage of the property owner's adjusted basis in the property). Sometimes, there is a per-project cap, which limits any potential credits that a single property owner may earn. In addition, there may be a program cap, which limits the total amount of tax credits allocated by a state in any given year. (The federal program does not have a per-project or program cap.)

The National Trust for Historic Preservation, a nonprofit advocacy group, has identified a few areas that make some state tax credit programs more successful in attracting investment than others. These include:

• Having a broad definition of eligible properties that includes properties designated at the local level and National Register

• Adopting the Secretary of the Interior's Standards for Rehabilitation

• Making the credit available for homeowners, who are ineligible for the federal credit

• Fixing a percentage rate for qualified rehabilitation expenditures between 20 and 30 percent, to provide meaningful assistance

• Making the credit transferable or refundable

• Eliminating any caps on programs

• Allowing the credit to apply to a range of taxable incomes

• Being cautious in implementing credits that target specific geographic areas.

See HARRY K. SCHWARTZ, NAT'L TRUST FOR HISTORIC PRES., STATE TAX CREDITS FOR HISTORIC PRESERVATION: A PUBLIC POLICY REPORT 2–4 (2011). We think these eight suggestions are wise, but few states have adopted them in their entirety. The National Trust for Historic Preservation maintains a website that lists key characteristics of the current state programs, available here: www. preservationnation.org/take-action/advocacy-center/ additional-resources/historic-tax-credit-maps/state-rehabilitation-tax.html

Although federal credits are always subject to political pressure, state credits seem to be more volatile. Key provisions, including program caps and eligibility requirements, are changed with frequency. Some programs have been shut down completely, only to be partly restored. For example, a Rhode Island program that increased investment activity by 700 percent during its six-year run was shut down in 2008, only to be reopened in 2013 in a limited form (which was immediately over-subscribed). Other programs have never made it off the ground due to political concerns. In New Jersey, for example, governor after governor has cited economic concerns when vetoing state tax credit legislation. The volatility of state rehabilitation tax credit programs can make investors wary of planning projects too far in advance, or investing in all but the most stable states.

2. POST-AWARD ISSUES

As is the case with the federal rehabilitation tax credit, there are several issues that a taxpayer may deal with even after her application for state rehabilitation credits is approved. These post-award issues are identical to the issues described above for federal rehabilitation tax credit.

We add that with regard to transferability of credits and investor participation in state rehabilitation tax credit schemes, a recent court decision regarding third party investments has limited the effectiveness of the Virginia state tax credit (and possibly other states' programs). In 2011, the Fourth Circuit disallowed an investor to benefit from state rehabilitation tax credits, in part due to the fact that the developers did not face sufficient entrepreneurial risk. Va. Historic Tax Credit Fund v. Comm'r, 639 F.3d 129 (4th Cir. 2011). In that case, the court found that the property was acquired through a disguised sale and that the gain must be taxed at the higher marginal tax rate required for ordinary income. *Id.* at 145. This case does not appear to have had as dramatic a chilling effect as *Historic Boardwalk Hall, LLC v. Commissioner*, described above, had on federal rehabilitation tax credit investment. *See* 694 F.3d 425 (3rd Cir. 2012), *cert. denied* 133 S.Ct. 2734 (2013). Still, its effect on third party investments in state tax credit projects should be watched closely.

CHAPTER 15

ISSUES IN BUILDING REHABILITATION

This Chapter focuses on one type of historic resource—buildings—and two areas of law related to the rehabilitation of historic buildings. The first area is building codes, which dictate construction techniques, materials, and configurations. The second area is the federal Americans with Disabilities Act, which mandates physical accessibility of certain public buildings and programs.

A. BUILDING CODES

Ten thousand jurisdictions in the United States have adopted building codes: legal documents, drafted for architects and engineers, which explain the kinds of construction techniques, materials, and configurations that are acceptable for certain building types. This Part illuminates the relationship between coding and rehabilitation; it does not delve into technical details of specific code provisions. An overview of modern building codes, including their impact on historic properties, is followed by a brief summary of rehabilitation building codes—a special kind of building code that specifically addresses historic and older buildings.

1. OVERVIEW

Building codes dictate how almost every building in this country is built. Among other areas, they regulate: structural element strength, fireproofing and insulation materials, electrical and plumbing connections, wall and floor framing dimensions, windows and doorways, hallway widths, ceiling heights, stairway geometry, and accessibility clearances. Code provisions are carefully drafted to protect building occupants and neighbors from the direct and indirect consequences of poorly constructed buildings.

How do building codes work? They are adopted at either the state or local level and implemented and enforced by local building code officials. Property owners must submit plans to these officials, who review the plans for conformity with code requirements and inspect the construction activity at various stages to ensure compliance. For the most part, property owners need only comply with the code in existence when a particular construction activity occurred and need not continuously update their buildings to comply with new or modified code provisions. However, some states authorize localities to allow building inspectors to assess ongoing compliance with building codes. *See, e.g.,* VA. CODE ANN. § 36–105C.

This overview of building codes provides a brief history of coding, an explanation of code adoption, and an assessment of the impact of modern codes on historic and older buildings.

a. History

Building codes have existed for thousands of years, from Hammurabi's "eye for an eye" code (requiring architects whose buildings collapsed on others to lose their own lives!) to modern-day versions. In what would become the United States, the first codes originated in the colonial era. New Amsterdam, for example, "introduced ordinances prohibiting wooden or plaster chimneys, straw or reed roofs, hayricks or haystacks; requiring each household to have a ladder; appointing fire wardens and inspectors with powers to levy harsh fines (up to 100 guilders); and compelling householders to keep chimneys clean." WILLIAM J. NOVAK, THE PEOPLE'S WELFARE: LAW AND REGULATION IN NINETEENTH-CENTURY AMERICA 56–57 (1996). But it was not until 1850 that a comprehensive, modern building code was enacted, in New York City. Other cities, notably Philadelphia in 1855 and New Orleans in 1865, followed New York's lead and passed laws allowing for building inspection and design review. The real wave of code adoption began in the 1870s, after the devastation caused by the 1871 Chicago fire drew nationwide attention to the importance of building safety and proper construction.

Codes again returned as a policy issue in the two decades following World War II, when major federal housing acts created a boom in construction. A quarter of extant building codes were enacted or comprehensively revised between 1962 and 1965; this proportion rose to over a third during 1966 and 1967. *See* ALLEN D. MANVEL, NAT'L COMM'N ON URB. PROBLEMS RES. REP. NO. 6, LOCAL LAND AND BUILDING REGULATION 11 (1968). By the 1970s, about 8,000, or nearly half, of the 18,000 local governments in America had a building code, including eighty percent of local governments serving populations over 5,000 people. By the 1990s, approximately ten thousand jurisdictions were equipped with building codes.

b. Code Adoption

Except for a few areas, such as accommodations for the disabled and manufactured housing, the federal government delegates the right to initiate building legislation to the fifty states. *See* Americans with Disabilities Act, 42 U.S.C. §§ 12101–12213; National Manufactured Home Construction and Safety Act of 1974, 42 U.S.C. §§ 5401–5426. Many states have established statewide building codes, or at least some statewide building regulations, but some assign building code adoption and enforcement to counties and municipalities. As a result, codes vary tremendously in scope and content.

The numerous possible variations in coding prompted several groups to work toward consistency through the promulgation of model codes. In 1905, the National Board of Fire Underwriters drafted a model building code for local governments. The provisions of that code primarily aimed to protect against fire loss and to shield the fire insurance companies from bankruptcy resulting from massive payouts. Building codes assuaged fire safety concerns through area and height limits, special occupancy requirements, fire resistant materials and configurations, and exit requirements facilitating fast escape.

Over time, three regional organizations emerged that developed building codes that went beyond fire safety issues. These three groups merged in 1994, creating the International Code Council (ICC), which develops a single set of comprehensive, coordinated national model construction codes. The ICC adopts new codes every three years after consultation with members. The process for considering a code change involves a hearing and debate before an ICC committee composed of both code officials and construction industry representatives. The committee makes a recommendation, and eligible members of the ICC vote on it. Though this system seems onerous, the ICC has managed to adopt a uniform building code as well as plumbing, electrical, mechanical, maintenance, energy conservation, and other codes in less than twenty years.

The ICC has tremendous influence on the content of codes in the United States. Today, all fifty states and Washington, D.C. have adopted (or have localities that have adopted) some version of the International Building Code (IBC). These figures imply that a high level of uniformity has been achieved. However, this is not the case. Only thirty-two states have adopted the IBC for statewide application without limitation, and among those thirty-two states, four different versions of the IBC have been adopted. In addition, thirteen states have adopted the IBC statewide with limitations, which usually means that local governments may adopt the IBC but make their own revisions. *See* INTERNAT'L CODE COUNCIL, INTERNATIONAL CODES— ADOPTION BY STATES (2013). Local governments often fail to update codes as updates become distributed by the ICC; many have adopted versions of the model codes dating back ten years or more.

c. Impact on Rehabilitation

Modern codes have had a negative effect on the number of rehabilitations of historic and older buildings. They often require rehabilitations to comply with the same standards as new construction, but strict compliance with modern standards can make rehabilitation too expensive, deterring investment in older and historic properties. Take, for example, a historic building with a 32″ wide interior stair. Modern building codes require that the stair be 36″ wide. Replacing the existing stair with a wider one would impose excessive demolition and reconstruction costs, and would change the dimensions of interior hallways and rooms in the process. A property owner's willingness to proceed with a rehabilitation may thus depend on the way the modern building code would be enforced upon her project—in the example, whether she would be allowed to keep the 32″ stair or would be forced to replace it with a 36″ stair. Property owners may not be able to determine, however, how an individual inspector—who typically has wide discretion over how codes are enforced—might respond to site conditions. As a result, they may not be able to adequately assess their budget and may not proceed with the project at all. In this way, enforcement unpredictability deters investment in rehabilitation.

There have been attempts to address the dual problems of expense and unpredictability by revising building codes to facilitate rehabilitation. For example, each of the three original model code organizations at some point during their existence adopted a "25-or-50 percent rule." This rule set out three thresholds for rehabilitation projects based on the proportion of rehabilitation project costs to the replacement cost of the project. If the cost of the rehabilitation exceeded 50 percent of the replacement cost of the building, full compliance with the modern code was required. If the rehabilitation cost fell between 25 and 50 percent of the replacement cost, then only partial compliance was required. If the rehabilitation cost fell below 25 percent, a correspondingly diminished amount of partial compliance was required. All three organizations abandoned this rule after fair and consistent administration proved difficult, though some jurisdictions still use it as an informal rule of thumb.

Another attempt at addressing rehabilitation still operating in some jurisdictions is an exception made to what is known as the "change-of-occupancy rule." The change-of-occupancy rule holds that when construction creates a change in use or occupancy, the building must comply with modern construction standards. An exception for rehabilitation projects would occur if a building inspector certifies that either: (1) the construction activities satisfied the intent of the modern building code; or (2) the new use or occupancy was less hazardous than the existing use. Although this exception offers some property owners a reprieve from strict compliance with modern standards, it is difficult to predict when the exception will be allowed.

Difficulties in applying the 25-or-50 percent rule and change-of-occupancy rule inspired states and localities to experiment with other ways to facilitate rehabilitation. For example, some states have expressly exempted historic buildings from special codes, such as energy conservation codes, altogether. *See, e.g.*, N.Y. ENERGY LAW § 11–104.5 (exempting historic structures from the state's energy conservation code); N.C. GEN. STAT. § 143–135.36 (excluding historic buildings from the list of facilities required to comply with the state's energy efficiency performance standards). But only a minority of states, and some localities, have comprehensively addressed differences between new construction and rehabilitation through rehabilitation building codes—a topic we turn to next.

2.   REHABILITATION BUILDING CODES

Few modern building codes specifically address older and historic buildings. In some jurisdictions, however, supplemental building codes known as rehabilitation building codes have been implemented to better address the rehabilitation of existing buildings. These codes attempt to reduce expenditures and apply code requirements in proportion to risk.

The first rehabilitation code was the New Jersey Rehabilitation Subcode, developed in the late 1990s. *See* N.J. ADMIN CODE § 5:23–6.2(b)(2). The Subcode recognizes six different types of projects, listed in order of increasing impact on the building: repair, renovation, alteration, reconstruction, change of use, and addition. The rules applicable to each type of project vary according to the scope of work: while a repair triggers very few constraints, an addition requires full compliance with modern codes. Specific provisions improve predictability and ensure consistent enforcement. For renovation and reconstruction projects, for instance, the Subcode allows for certain window replacements to be the same size as existing windows (which can be small and irregular) and does not require them to be the larger, more regular sizes required by modern code. *Id.* §§ 5:23–6.5(h), 5:25–6.7(g). The Subcode is clear as to when existing materials may be replaced in kind and when life safety requires upgrades. For alterations, the Subcode allows for existing electrical wiring and equipment to be replaced with like material, except for electrical receptacles (plugs). *Id.* § 5:23–6.6. An owner of a historic building may ask for additional variances if, among other things, they can show that "strict compliance . . . would result in practical difficulties or would detract from the historic character of the building." *Id.* § 5:23–6.33(a)(2).

The New Jersey Subcode establishes clear and reasonable guidelines for rehabilitation projects, making enforcement more predictable and lowering costs for property owners. It was drafted to meet the needs of one state and was not meant to be a model code. It has, however, been used as a basis for two different model rehabilitation codes, meant to be adopted more broadly: the U.S. Department of Housing and Urban Development's Nationally Applicable Recommended Rehabilitation Provisions and the International Code Council's International Existing Building Code (IEBC). Of these two model rehabilitation codes, the IEBC has had more impact. Seventeen states have adopted the IEBC on a statewide basis, seven states have adopted it with some limitations, and in eleven states, a variety of localities (but not the state itself) have adopted the IEBC. *See* INTERNAT'L CODE COUNCIL, INTERNATIONAL CODES—ADOPTION BY STATES (2013). The number of states adopting rehabilitation building codes is growing, and attorneys assisting clients with rehabilitation projects should be aware of their existence and basic content.

B.   AMERICANS WITH DISABILITIES ACT

With the Americans with Disabilities Act of 1990 (ADA), Congress enacted sweeping prohibitions on discrimination against disabled persons in areas ranging from employment to telecommunications. The ADA affects rehabilitations of historic buildings in two ways. First, Title II of the ADA requires public entities to provide access to services, programs, and activities regardless of disability status; public buildings that are designated historic may have to be rehabilitated to comply. Second, Title III of the ADA requires private owners of historic buildings that are considered to be "public accommodations" to ensure a certain level of physical accessibility—again, possibly requiring rehabilitation. For some rehabilitations required by the ADA, the need to provide access for the disabled may necessitate changes that compromise significant characteristics of historic buildings. For example, installing an exterior ramp to provide for access by the mobility impaired may interfere with the visual coherence of a historic façade. In such cases, the ADA works to resolve potential conflicts. Most importantly, it generally excuses owners or operators of historic properties from making any changes that would threaten or destroy historically significant features.

This Part provides an overview of Titles II and III, addresses key terms, and discusses how each Title applies to the rehabilitation of historic buildings.

1.   OVERVIEW

Titles II and III of the ADA impact rehabilitations of historic buildings. The basic difference between the two is that Title II addresses the facilities of public entities, while Title III targets private facilities that are either public accommodations or commercial facilities. Both Titles have provisions that soften compliance requirements for owners and operators of historic buildings where strict compliance would threaten or destroy the buildings' historic significance. This section identifies and explains the relevant statutory provisions.

a. Title II: Regarding Access to Public Programs

Title II of the ADA provides that "no qualified individual with a disability shall, by reason of such disability, be excluded from participation in or be denied the benefits of the services, programs, or activities of a public entity, or be subjected to discrimination by any such entity." 42 U.S.C. § 12132. This language requires public entities to refrain from discrimination in essentially everything they do.

For our purposes, an important implication of Title II is that public buildings—including those that have been designated historic—must be made accessible to persons with disabilities, with limited exceptions. Existing facilities must, "to the maximum extent feasible, be altered in such manner that the altered portion of the facility is readily accessible to and usable by individuals with disabilities." 28 C.F.R. § 35.151(b)(1). The regulations proceed to carve out an exception for historic properties, saying that: "If it is not feasible to provide physical access to an historic property in a manner that will not threaten or destroy the historic significance of the building or facility, alternative methods of access shall be provided pursuant to the requirements of § 35.150." *Id.*

§ 35.151(b)(3). There is another provision regarding "historic preservation programs," a term defined below. It says that although physical access to such programs is preferred, alternative methods of achieving accessibility include audio-visual materials, personal guides, or "other innovative methods." *Id.* § 35.150(b)(3). Because the primary benefit of such programs is the preservation of historic resources, the public entity must prioritize alternative methods that best approximate the experience of having physical access to the historic property.

Another part of Title II applies specifically to public transportation. It says that with respect to alterations of an existing public transportation facility:

> it shall be considered discrimination * * * for a public entity to fail to make such alterations (or to ensure that the alterations are made) in such a manner that, to the maximum extent feasible, the altered portions of the facility are readily accessible to and usable by individuals with disabilities, including individuals who use wheelchairs, upon the completion of such alterations.

42 U.S.C. § 12147(a). Included in the types of facilities subject to this provision are transportation stations that have been identified as "key stations." *Id.* § 12147(b)(1). Federal regulations clarify that "the phrase to the maximum extent feasible applies to the occasional case where the nature of an existing facility makes it impossible to comply fully

with applicable accessibility standards through a planned alteration." 49 U.S.C. § 37.43. In such cases, the public entity must do everything that it can to make the public transportation facility accessible.

b. Title III: Regarding Public Accommodations and Commercial Facilities

Title III of the Americans with Disabilities Act imposes two distinct obligations on private owners of public accommodations: (1) removal of architectural barriers (or provision of alternative methods if removal is not readily achievable), and (2) ensuring that any alterations done on the properties are accessible to those with disabilities, to the maximum extent feasible. An exception will be made for historic properties if engaging in either of these two activities will threaten or destroy the historic significance of the property. The second obligation also applies to private owners and operators of commercial facilities. Owners and operators of commercial facilities need not remove architectural barriers, as owners and operators of public accommodations must do.

With respect to the first obligation (removing architectural barriers), the ADA provides, in relevant part:

(a) General rule

No individual shall be discriminated against on the basis of disability in the full and equal enjoyment of the goods, services, facilities, privileges, advantages, or accommodations of any place of public accommodation by any person who owns, leases (or leases to), or operates a place of public accommodation.

(b) Construction * * *

(2) Specific prohibitions

(A) Discrimination

For purposes of subsection (a) of this section, discrimination includes—* * *

(iv) a failure to remove architectural barriers * * * in existing facilities, * * * where such removal is readily achievable; and

(v) where an entity can demonstrate that the removal of a barrier under clause (iv) is not readily achievable, a failure to make such goods, services, facilities, privileges, advantages, or accommodations available through alternative methods if such methods are readily achievable.

42 U.S.C. § 12182. According to the statute, discrimination may occur when architectural barriers in existing facilities are not removed. Removing architectural barriers—physical elements impeding access by the disabled—might include widening doorways, installing ramps, repositioning accessories such as paper towel dispensers, removing high pile carpeting, making sidewalks and curbs more accessible, and installing raised toilet seats and grab bars. *See* 28 C.F.R. § 36.304(b). The statutory language excerpted above says that an

entity may be exempted from having to remove architectural barriers if removal is not readily achievable, in which case the entity must modify the facility to make alternative methods of access available, if such methods are readily achievable. According to the regulations, one example of an alternative to barrier removal might include relocating activities to accessible locations. *Id.* § 36.305. Importantly for historic properties, barrier removal will not be considered to be readily achievable if removal would "threaten or destroy the historic significance" of the historic property. *See id.* § 36.304(d)(1) (incorporating by reference 28 C.F.R. § 36.405, which contains the "threaten or destroy" exception).

With respect to the second obligation (making alterations accessible), Title III also includes in its concept of discrimination "a failure to make alterations [to public accommodations or commercial facilities] in such a manner that, to the maximum extent feasible, the altered portions of the facility are readily accessible to and usable by individuals with disabilities, including individuals who use wheelchairs." 42 U.S.C. § 12183(a)(2). The regulations carve out an exception for historic properties nearly identical to that contained in Title II. They say that alterations to historic properties covered by Title III "shall comply to the maximum extent feasible," and if "it is not feasible to provide physical access to an historic property that is a place of public accommodation in a manner that will not threaten or destroy the historic significance of the building or the facility, alternative methods of access shall be provided." 28 C.F.R. § 36.405.

2.   KEY TERMS

The scope of the Americans with Disabilities Act is dictated by numerous important terms. The first three terms included here are specific to Title II. Title II only applies to a "public entity" and has special rules applicable to "historic preservation programs" and "historic properties." The fourth term, "disability" may be found in both Titles II and III and identifies which individuals are protected by the ADA.

The last four terms are specific to Title III. Title III only applies to "public accommodations" and "commercial facilities." It uses the term "readily achievable" in relation to the first obligation it may place on owners and operators of places of public accommodation to remove architectural barriers. The final term, "alteration," relates to the second obligation Title III places on owners and operators of places of public accommodation and commercial facilities to make alterations accessible.

a. Public Entity

Title II of the Americans with Disabilities Act applies to every "public entity," which the statute defines very broadly to mean:

(A) any State or local government;

(B) any department, agency, special purpose district, or other instrumentality of a State or States or local government; and

(C) the National Railroad Passenger Corporation, and any commuter authority (as defined in section 24102(4) of Title 49).

42 U.S.C. § 12131(1). There is no requirement that the public entity be a recipient of federal financial assistance for it to be covered by Title II.

b. Historic Preservation Programs

Title II has a provision specific to the alterations for accessibility of the historic preservation programs of public entities. The regulations define "historic preservation programs" as "programs conducted by a public entity that have preservation of historic properties as a primary purpose." 28 C.F.R. § 35.104. Such programs include the ownership and operation of historic house museums or other historic properties that members of the public might visit specifically to enjoy their historic characteristics. The definition also includes those programs—such as the Advisory Council on Historic Preservation and the fifty state historic preservation offices—that have as their primary purpose the preservation of historic properties. The Title II provision on alteration may have less relevance to these programs unless their offices are housed in historic buildings that are also meant to be enjoyed by the public.

Many public programs that do not specifically address historic preservation are located in historic properties. For example, a state public health office may be housed in a National Register designated historic building, or a county courthouse may be located in a building in a state register historic district. These types of programs are not included in the definition of "historic preservation programs" because they do not have the preservation of historic properties as their primary goal.

c. Historic Properties

As the preceding section shows, the definition of "historic preservation programs" in Title II of the Americans with Disabilities Act is linked to the definition of "historic properties." The regulations define historic properties as "those properties that are listed or eligible for listing in the National Register of Historic Places or properties designated as historic under State or local law." 28 C.F.R. § 35.104. Thus properties that are otherwise unlisted but could be eligible for the National Register will be covered by the ADA.

Note that the Title III regulations contain a similar concept for historic properties, without using the term "historic properties." *See* 28 C.F.R. § 36.405 (applying a different rule for Title III alterations only to those buildings or facilities "that are eligible for listing in the National Register of Historic Places ... or are designated as historic under State or local law").

d. Disability

The Americans with Disabilities Act protects those individuals with disabilities. More specifically, Title II of the Americans with Disabilities Act protects each "qualified individual with a disability," while Title III prohibits discrimination "on the basis of disability." Both Titles define the word "disability" in the same way:

> Disability means, with respect to an individual, a physical or mental impairment that substantially limits one or more of the major life activities of such individual; a record of such an impairment; or being regarded as having such an impairment.

28 C.F.R. §§ 35.104 & 36.104. The phrase "major life activities" means "functions such as caring for one's self, performing manual tasks, walking, seeing, hearing, speaking, breathing, learning, and working." *Id.*

Title II adds the term "qualified individual with a disability," which means:

> an individual with a disability who, with or without reasonable modifications to rules, policies, or practices, the removal of architectural, communication, or transportation barriers, or the provision of auxiliary aids and services, meets the essential eligibility requirements for the receipt of services or the participation in programs or activities provided by a public entity.

42 U.S.C. § 12131(2).

e. Public Accommodation

A concept central to Title III of the Americans with Disabilities Act is "public accommodation," defined as "a private entity that owns, leases (or leases to), or operates a place of public accommodation." 28 C.F.R. § 36.104. The term "place of public accommodation" provides further detail. It includes all facilities that "affect commerce" and fall into one of the following twelve categories:

(A) an inn, hotel, motel, or other place of lodging, except for an establishment located within a building that contains not more than five rooms for rent or hire and that is actually occupied by the proprietor of such establishment as the residence of such proprietor;

(B) a restaurant, bar, or other establishment serving food or drink;

(C) a motion picture house, theater, concert hall, stadium, or other place of exhibition or entertainment;

(D) an auditorium, convention center, lecture hall, or other place of public gathering;

(E) a bakery, grocery store, clothing store, hardware store, shopping center, or other sales or rental establishment;

(F) a laundromat, dry-cleaner, bank, barber shop, beauty shop, travel service, shoe repair service, funeral parlor, gas station, office of an accountant or lawyer, pharmacy, insurance office, professional office of a health care provider, hospital, or other service establishment;

(G) a terminal, depot, or other station used for specified public transportation;

(H) a museum, library, gallery, or other place of public display or collection;

(I) a park, zoo, amusement park, or other place of recreation;

(J) a nursery, elementary, secondary, undergraduate, or postgraduate private school, or other place of education;

(K) a day care center, senior citizen center, homeless shelter, food bank, adoption agency, or other social service center establishment; and

(L) a gymnasium, health spa, bowling alley, golf course, or other place of exercise or recreation.

42 U.S.C. § 12181(7). These twelve categories provide an exhaustive list of all entities subject to Title III. Of course, many types of entities are covered in the various phrases containing the word "other," even if they are not specifically listed. For example, "other establishment serving food or drink," id. § 12181(7)(B), includes coffeeshops, even though coffeeshops are not specifically listed in the

statute. Apartment buildings are not places of public accommodation, although common facilities (such as laundromats or pools) in apartment buildings that are open to the general public may be considered to be places of public accommodation. Similarly, homes are not places of public accommodation, but if some parts of the home are open to the public at certain times—for example, a home day care center—then those areas must be compliant with Title III. 28 C.F.R. § 36.207.

A place must "affect commerce" for it to be regulated by Title III, meaning that it must affect interstate or foreign "travel, trade, traffic, commerce, transportation or communication." 42 U.S.C. § 12181(1). Note that Title III does not apply to many private clubs or to religious organizations (including places of worship). *See id.* § 12187. The religious organization exemption also extends to entities affiliated with religious institutions, such as private schools, and secular activities (such as day care centers) of religious institutions.

f. Commercial Facilities

Title III of the Americans with Disabilities Act also applies to "commercial facilities" which are facilities: "(A) that are intended for nonresidential use; and (B) whose operations will affect commerce." 42 U.S.C. § 12181(2). To "affect commerce," a commercial facility must affect interstate or foreign "travel, trade, traffic, commerce, transportation or communication." *Id.* § 12181(1). This definition thus includes many private businesses, including industrial factories, warehouses, and office buildings, which are not accessible to the general public. It excludes residential buildings.

g. Readily Achievable

Title III of the American with Disabilities Act requires the removal of architectural barriers where such removal is "readily achievable." It explains:

> The term "readily achievable" means easily accomplishable and able to be carried out without much difficulty or expense. In determining whether an action is readily achievable, factors to be considered include—

> (A) the nature and cost of the action needed under this chapter;

> (B) the overall financial resources of the facility or facilities involved in the action; the number of persons employed at such facility; the effect on expenses and resources, or the impact otherwise of such action upon the operation of the facility;

> (C) the overall financial resources of the covered entity; the overall size of the business of a covered entity with respect to the number of its employees; the number, type, and location of its facilities; and

> (D) the type of operation or operations of the covered entity, including the composition, structure, and functions of the workforce of such entity; the geographic separateness,

administrative or fiscal relationship of the facility or facilities in question to the covered entity.

42 U.S.C. § 12181(9). The regulations add a fifth factor, which is "[t]he geographic separateness, and the administrative or fiscal relationship of the site or sites in question to any parent corporation or entity." 28 C.F.R. § 36.104. Determining whether an activity is readily achievable, therefore, requires a balancing of various factors on a case-by-case basis. What is readily achievable for a large corporation may not be readily achievable for a small business. In the case of historic buildings, barrier removal is not readily achievable if such removal would threaten or destroy the historic significance of the building.

h. Alterations

Title III of the Americans with Disabilities Act, which imposes certain obligations on private entities when they alter places of public accommodation or commercial facilities, includes in its conception of the term "alteration" activities that affect the usability of the facility. The regulations clarify:

> [A]n alteration is a change to a place of public accommodation or a commercial facility that affects or could affect the usability of the building or facility or any part thereof.

> (1) Alterations include, but are not limited to, remodeling, renovation, rehabilitation,

reconstruction, historic restoration, changes or rearrangement in structural parts or elements, and changes or rearrangement in the plan configuration of walls and full-height partitions. Normal maintenance, reroofing, painting or wallpapering, asbestos removal, or changes to mechanical and electrical systems are not alterations unless they affect the usability of the building or facility.

(2) If existing elements, spaces, or common areas are altered, then each such altered element, space, or area shall comply with the applicable provisions * * *

28 C.F.R. § 36.402(b). According to this language, major renovations will be considered to be alterations that must comply with ADA rules, while minor activities not affecting usability—such as rewiring and painting—will not.

3.   APPLICATION

The Americans with Disabilities Act ensures the accessibility of public facilities and many private facilities, within certain limitations. In our overview, we covered the legal standards required by the ADA. Below we supplement that discussion with notes on how Titles II and III have been applied to the rehabilitation of historic properties by the handful of courts that have dealt with the question.

a. Title II: Regarding Access to Public Programs

As explained above, Title II of the ADA prohibits public entities from discriminating against qualified individuals with disabilities. *See* 42 U.S.C. § 12132. To comply with this provision, most public buildings, including public transportation facilities, see id. § 12147, must be made fully accessible to the disabled. For historic buildings, alterations need not be made if they will "threaten or destroy the historic significance of the building"; in such cases, alternative means of access must be provided. 28 C.F.R. § 35.151(b)(3).

A plaintiff making a claim under Title II must present evidence showing three things to prove a violation: (1) she is a qualified individual with a disability; (2) she was excluded from participation or denied benefits of a public entity's services, programs, or activities or was otherwise discriminated against; and (3) such exclusion, denial of benefits, or discrimination was by reason of the disability. *See* Layton v. Elder, 143 F.3d 469, 472 (8th Cir. 1998). Once the plaintiff successfully makes these showings, the public entity defendant may present affirmative defenses.

The only federal case involving Title II's applicability to historic properties, *Neighborhood Association of the Back Bay, Inc. v. Federal Transit Administration*, does not actually involve an allegation of an ADA violation. *See* 463 F.3d 50 (1st Cir. 2006). In that case, a local public transit authority attempted to make one of its key stations compliant with Title II by, among other things, constructing two elevators directly adjacent to a library and a church, both of which were designated National Landmarks. The plaintiff organizations alleged that the transit authority had not adequately considered the effect of the proposed elevators on the two National Landmarks as it was required to do by the National Historic Preservation Act (NHPA) (discussed in Chapter III) and Section 4(f) of the Department of Transportation Act (discussed in Chapter V). In considering the NHPA claim, the court said that projects with no "adverse effect" under the National Historic Preservation Act cannot "threaten or destroy" historic fabric in violation of the ADA, calling it "inconceivable, that the ADA was designed to be more protective of historical properties than the primary historical preservationist statutes themselves." *Neighborhood Association*, 463 F.3d at 66. For the Section 4(f) claim, the court reviewed whether one possible alternative to the proposed design—placing one elevator 150 feet from the main entrance—was prudent and feasible, in which case the transit authority would have to choose that alternative. *Id.* at 65. The trial court found that the transit authority's conclusion that this alternative was imprudent was not arbitrary or capricious, in part, because the transportation needs of the project included ADA compliance. *Id.* Such compliance was achieved by placing the elevator closer to the main entrance, in accordance with ADA regulations stating that the circulation path for the disabled should, "to the maximum extent practicable, coincide with the circulation path for the general public." *See* 49 C.F.R. Part 37, app. A 10.3.1(1) & 10.3.2(2). Even without an alleged ADA violation, this case highlights the interplay between the ADA, the NHPA, and Section 4(f).

Judicial enforcement of Title II of the ADA is based on the procedures of Title VI of the Civil Rights Act of 1964, 42 U.S.C. §§ 2000d–2000d–4a. *See* 42 U.S.C. § 12133. The Attorney General may file a lawsuit in federal district court, or private persons with disabilities have a private right of action. Administrative complaints may be filed by individuals who believe that she or a class of individuals has been subject to discrimination on the basis of a disability in violation of Title II of the ADA. *See* 28 C.F.R. § 35.170. The agency may investigate complaints and must refer the matter to the Attorney General if it cannot come to a resolution. *Id.* §§ 35.172 & 35.174. Finally, it is important to note that states are not immune to ADA claims. *Id.* § 35.178.

b. Title III: Regarding Public Accommodations and Commercial Facilities

Within certain limitations, Title III of the Americans with Disabilities Act requires private owners, tenants, and operators of places of public accommodation to: (1) remove architectural barriers and (2) ensure that alterations provide access to the disabled. The second obligation also applies to commercial facilities. Here, we discuss how these barrier removal and alteration obligations play out in the rehabilitation of historic properties.

The first obligation imposed on private entities is the removal of architectural barriers in places of public accommodation where such removal is "readily achievable." If the removal is not readily achievable, then alternative methods of access must be provided. *See* 42 U.S.C. § 12182. Barrier removal for historic properties is not considered to be readily achievable "if it would threaten or destroy the historic significance" of the historic property. DEP'T OF JUSTICE, AMERICANS WITH DISABILITIES ACT TITLE III TECHNICAL ASSISTANCE MANUAL § 4.42. Of all the provisions of the ADA, the barrier removal provision has generated the most litigation involving historic properties (three federal court cases to date, all discussed below).

Courts have differed over which party has the burden of proof as to whether an architectural barrier exists and whether barrier removal is readily achievable. Several courts have followed a Tenth Circuit case, *Colorado Cross Disability Coalition v. Hermanson Family Limited Partnership*, which found that the plaintiff bears the initial burden of production of evidence on these points. 264 F.3d 999, 1005–06 (10th Cir. 2001). The plaintiff has to provide enough information to the defendant so that the defendant can evaluate the plaintiff's suggestion. When the plaintiff meets this burden, the defendant may rebut the evidence, as part of its affirmative defense, that the plaintiff's suggested method of barrier removal is not readily achievable. *Id.* The Ninth Circuit has declined to adopt the *Colorado Cross* approach, finding that it places an excessive burden on plaintiffs, especially when the defendant is in a better position to evaluate physical changes to its property. *See* Molski v. Foley Estates Vineyard and Winery, LLC, 531 F.3d 1043, 1048–49 (9th Cir. 2008).

A Maryland federal court considered the obligation to remove architectural barriers when a plaintiff charged that a bank failed to adequately remove barriers whose removal was readily achievable. Speciner v. NationsBank, N.A., 215 F. Supp. 2d 622 (D. Md. 2002). The bank occupied a historic building in downtown Baltimore. The plaintiff claimed that the bank was bound by the ADA (1) to remove barriers at one of its entrances by building a ramp and (2) to provide a more direct route to the main Banking Hall, which wheelchair-bound persons could only reach by following a complicated route through offices and multiple corridors. Adopting the burden of proof allocation of *Colorado Cross*, the Maryland court found that the plaintiffs had not shown that the construction of a ramp at another entrance was readily achievable. *Id.* at 632–33. Moreover, it found that interior alterations to make the Banking Hall more easily accessible were not readily achievable, because "[t]he tortuous assisted path to the Banking Hall is, unfortunately, of little real utility but is the only path possible due to the 1929 Building design." *Id.* at 631. The court was satisfied with the alternative means of access provided by the "curbside (in car) service, service in the lobby, the use of sidewalk ATM machines, . . . an unfortunately inconvenient route to the Banking Hall (described above)" and the existence of "a large, modern, completely accessible, full service branch within three city blocks." *Id.* at 630–31.

The Eleventh Circuit also considered the claim of two plaintiffs that an Atlanta theater individually listed on the National Register failed to remove barriers affecting access by wheelchair-bound persons. Gathright-Dietrich v. Atlanta Landmarks, Inc., 452 F.3d 1269 (11th Cir. 2006). The court adopted the *Colorado Cross* allocation of the burden of proof and found that while the plaintiffs submitted several options relating to wheelchair seating, they did not "produce any reliable evidence that those proposals were readily achievable." *Id.* at 1274. Additionally, the court found that even if the plaintiffs had met their burden of proof, the theater rebutted any showing that barrier removal could occur "without much difficulty or expense," pursuant to 42 U.S.C. § 12181(9). The theater did this by showing that the plaintiff's proposals would directly impact character-defining features and historically significant interior areas, and that implementation of the proposals would involve: "closing the theater for a period of time; . . . the elimination of seats belonging to season ticket holders; and a decrease in the number of regular theater seats." *Gathright-Dietrich*, 452 F.3d at 1275.

The most recent case involving the obligation to remove architectural barriers in a historic place of public accommodation is *Molski v. Foley Estates Vineyard and Winery, LLC*, 531 F.3d 1043 (9th Cir. 2008). In that case, the wheelchair-bound plaintiff visited a winery listed on the local register of historic places. The winery presented several barriers to accessibility, including (1) an exterior ramp with a variable slope, and (2) interior barriers such as narrow doorways and a high wine-tasting counter. *Id.* at 1045. The court considered the exterior and interior barriers separately. It remanded the question as to whether an exterior ramp would be readily achievable to the district court, which had failed to appropriately analyzed the issue. *Id.* at 1048. In considering the interior barrier removal, the court found that even if the exterior ramp was not altered, leaving patrons in wheelchairs without access to the interior, the winery still had the duty to remove interior barriers, where such removal was readily achievable. The court reasoned that disabled individuals who could navigate the ramp to access the interior of the building were entitled to barrier removal once they got inside. *Id.* at 1049–50. Note that in this case, the court rejected the approach of *Colorado Cross*, placing the burden of proof on the defendant winery—perhaps one of the reasons why this case (in contrast to *Speciner* or *Gathright-Dietrich*), found in favor of the plaintiff.

The second obligation imposed on private entities by Title III is the requirement that alterations to regulated facilities occur, to the maximum extent feasible, in a way that provides physical access to the disabled. 42 U.S.C. § 12183(a)(2). Alterations to historic properties must provide physical access only "to the maximum extent feasible." If access is not feasible without "threaten[ing] or destroy[ing] the historic significance of the building or the facility,

alternative methods of access shall be provided." 28
C.F.R. § 36.405. Further guidance on the
appropriateness of alterations to historic sites may
be found in the *ADA Accessibility Guidelines. See*
U.S. Architectural & Transportation Barriers
Compliance Board, ADA Accessibility Guidelines for
Buildings and Facilities 4.1.7 (2002). Among other
procedures, the guidelines suggest that the state
historic preservation officer make the final
determination as to whether alterations will
threaten or destroy the historic significance of the
historic property. If the alteration is subject to
increased federal review under Section 106 of the
National Historic Preservation Act, then the state
historic preservation officer and the Advisory
Council on Historic Preservation may work together
to make this determination.

Only one federal court has delved into the
question of ADA compliance of alterations involving
a historic property. This court, however, determined
that the alterations claim of the plaintiff was time-
barred and never reached the merits of the case.
Speciner v. NationsBank, N.A., 215 F. Supp. 2d 622,
634 (D. Md. 2002).

Private parties or the U.S. Attorney General may
enforce the provisions of the Title III of the ADA.
The Attorney General may investigate violations
and may commence civil actions in federal court if
she has reasonable cause to believe that
discrimination prohibited by the ADA occurred and
the issue raised is "of general public importance." 42
U.S.C. § 12188(b). Available remedies include

permanent and temporary injunctions, restraining orders, other orders, and reasonable attorneys' fees to the prevailing party. *Id.* § 2000a–3. In a lawsuit commenced by the Attorney General, monetary damages as well as civil penalties to vindicate the public interest may be awarded—up to $50,000 for a first violation and up to $100,000 for a subsequent violation. Injunctive relief may include an order to alter facilities to make them readily accessible to and usable by disabled individuals. *Id.* § 12188(a)(2).

CHAPTER 16

INTERNATIONAL PRESERVATION LAW

International laws protecting and preserving tangible cultural property (including historic buildings, sites, artifacts, and landscapes) were born of conflict. The first codified provisions for protecting tangible cultural property—the Lieber Code of 1863—stem from the United States Civil War. The Code sought to curb traditional military practices of looting, plundering, and destroying important buildings and sites belonging to the opposition. The systemic looting and mass destruction of World War II prompted more comprehensive international agreements designed to protect and preserve cultural property in times of both war and peace.

This Chapter discusses three important international conventions that deal with tangible cultural property and have been ratified, in whole or in part, by the United States. All three are administered by the United Nations Educational, Scientific, and Cultural Organization (UNESCO). This Chapter begins with a discussion of the 1954 Hague Convention for the Protection of Cultural Property in the Event of Armed Conflict—the first comprehensive treaty outlining warring parties' obligations to cultural heritage. Then follows an examination of the 1970 UNESCO Convention on the Means of Prohibiting and Preventing the Illicit Import, Export, and Transfer of Ownership of

Cultural Property, which requires States Parties (countries that have ratified the Convention) to regulate and document trafficking in cultural property in a manner consistent with their domestic laws. The third international convention—1972 UNESCO Convention Concerning the Protection of the World Cultural and Natural Heritage—is perhaps the most well-known international legal instrument protecting cultural property as it established the concept of World Heritage Sites.

A. 1954 HAGUE CONVENTION FOR THE PROTECTION OF CULTURAL PROPERTY IN THE EVENT OF ARMED CONFLICT

Following the unprecedented destruction and targeted looting of World War II, the international community decided to try and prevent the future destruction of irreplaceable historical and artistic treasures by creating an international agreement aimed at protecting and preserving cultural property caught in conflict. The 1954 Hague Convention for the Protection of Cultural Property in the Event of an Armed Conflict is the first international multilateral treaty exclusively focused on protecting cultural heritage in the event of an armed conflict. This Part begins with an overview of the 1954 Hague Convention and its accompanying Protocols, then analyzes an important key term and how the Convention has worked in practice in the United States.

1. OVERVIEW

The 1954 Hague Convention was the international response to the destruction and wholesale pillaging of cultural heritage during World War II. UNESCO, at the initiative of the Netherlands, called an international conference that was attended by eighty-six nations. This conference, held at the Hague, led to the adoption of the Convention and a First Protocol—a document supplementing the Convention that established a more robust legal framework for issues specifically relating to moveable cultural property. A Second Protocol, aimed at updating certain aspects of the Convention to respond to modern types of warfare and military techniques, was adopted in 1999. While the United States has ratified the Convention (thus becoming a "State Party" to it), it has not yet ratified either of the Protocols supplementing the Convention. Discussion of each of these three documents follows.

a. Convention (1954)

The international community knew that World War II would not end all wars or occupations. Foreseeing that military tactics endangering vast amounts of cultural property—such as widespread, regular interval aerial bombing—would become more sophisticated and destructive, the international community sought to ensure that cultural property would remain preserved for future generations. The 1954 Hague Convention specifically recognized:

that cultural property has suffered grave damage during recent armed conflicts and that, by reason of the developments in the technique of warfare, it is in increasing danger of destruction; being convinced that damage to cultural property belonging to any people whatsoever means damage to the cultural heritage of all mankind, since each people makes its contribution to the culture of the world; considering that the preservation of the cultural heritage is of great importance for all peoples of the world and that it is important that this heritage should receive international protection * * *

1954 Hague Convention for the Protection of Cultural Property in the Event of Armed Conflict, May 14, 1954, 249 U.N.T.S. 240 (hereinafter "Hague Convention"), at Preamble. Unfortunately, the grim legacy of the damage wreaked on cultural property during World War II endures to this day in gutted churches, historic urban cores almost entirely devoid of old buildings, the discovery of unexploded ordnance, and continuing disputes concerning cultural objects and artworks that were displaced or looted.

The United States participated extensively in the negotiations of the 1954 Hague Convention. But it was only in 2009, following the looting of the Iraq Museum in Baghdad and of several archaeological sites in Iraq, that the United States finally ratified the 1954 Hague Convention.

b. First Protocol (1954)

A Protocol specific to movable cultural property and the thorny issues surrounding restitution (the return of stolen or lost property to its rightful owner) was adopted at the same time as the 1954 Hague Convention. Countries that have ratified the First Protocol of the 1954 Hague Convention agree to: (1) prevent the exportation of movable cultural property from a territory occupied by it during an armed conflict; (2) ban the importation of movable cultural property from any occupied territory; (3) return movable cultural property exported in contravention to the occupant's obligations; (4) prohibit the retention of movable cultural property as war reparations; (5) pay an indemnity to good faith purchasers of movable cultural property that was exported from a territory occupied by it which has to be returned; and (6) return any movable cultural property in its custody for safekeeping to the competent authorities at the end of hostilities. *See* Hague Convention, arts. 1–5.

The United States has not yet ratified the First Protocol.

c. Second Protocol (1999)

Advances in weapons and the increased recognition of internal and/or ethnic conflicts since the middle of the twentieth century have posed great threats to cultural property. These threats have in turn fostered concern about the adequacy of the protections afforded to cultural property under the 1954 Hague Convention and its First Protocol.

This concern is perhaps best exemplified by the war in the former Yugoslavia in which opposing ethnic groups who were deeply aware of each other's culture deliberately destroyed cultural properties that were not military targets.

Internal and/or ethnic conflicts and their repercussions were not the focus of the 1954 discussions. So, the 1954 Hague Convention and its First Protocol were reviewed and a Second Protocol to the Convention was adopted in March 1999. The Second Protocol strengthened cultural property protections in the Convention by shrinking the scope of "military necessity" and creating a new category—enhanced protection—for cultural property of the greatest importance to humanity. *See* Second Protocol to the Hague Convention of 1954 for the Protection of Cultural Property in the Event of Armed Conflict, March 26, 1999, 2253 U.N.T.S. 212, at chs. 2–3. Cultural property qualifying for "enhanced protection" must be protected by national legislation, such as national registers of historic or cultural properties, and may not be used for military purposes. *See id.* at art. 10. The Second Protocol also increased effective enforcement mechanisms by: (1) creating individual, as opposed to governmental, responsibility for intentional, serious violations against cultural property; (2) clearly defining heavier sanctions for other offenses against cultural property; and (3) delineating conditions under which criminal responsibility applies. *See id.* at ch. 4. To oversee the implementation of its provisions, the Second Protocol formed the Committee for the Protection of

Cultural Property in the Event of Armed Conflict—a permanent, funded intergovernmental committee consisting of twelve States Parties. *See id.* at ch. 6.

The United States has not yet ratified the Second Protocol.

2.   KEY TERM: CULTURAL PROPERTY

There is only one key term in the 1954 Hague Convention and its two Protocols: cultural property. The Convention defines the term "cultural property" with breathtaking scope, sweeping into its protections a staggering range of both movable and immovable property. The term "cultural property" covers, irrespective of origin or ownership:

(a) movable or immovable property of great importance to the cultural heritage of every people, such as monuments of architecture, art or history, whether religious or secular; archaeological sites; groups of buildings, which, as a whole, are of historical or artistic interest; works of art; manuscripts, books and other objects of artistic, historical or archaeological interest; as well as scientific collections and important collections of books or archives or of reproductions of the property defined above;

(b) buildings whose main and effective purpose is to preserve or exhibit the movable cultural property defined in sub-paragraph (a) such as museums, large libraries and depositories of archives, and refuges intended to shelter, in the event of armed conflict, the movable cultural property defined in sub-paragraph (a);

(c) centers containing a large amount of cultural property as defined in sub-paragraph (a) and (b), to be known as "centers containing monuments."

Hague Convention, at art. 1. Deliberately broad, the term includes the smallest objects to the largest monuments; it includes literary, scientific, artistic, archaeological, and architectural works. It includes not just buildings that are culturally significant but also buildings that serve to warehouse other cultural property. Finally, the term includes items of religious significance, which may raise issues about who decides what is religiously significant.

All of the resources included in the meaning of cultural property—many of which were considered traditional "spoils of war"—are protected by the Convention from damage, destruction, and improper relocation. Note that the definition includes presumptions of egalitarianism and collectivism: every group of people has a cultural legacy that is worth preserving, and we all share in that heritage.

The term "cultural property" is also important in a different international agreement, the 1970 Convention on the Means of Prohibiting and Preventing the Illicit Import, Export and Transfer of Ownership of Cultural Property. Differences in the way the two documents define this term are described in the next Part.

3.   APPLICATION

The impact of the 1954 Hague Convention on the United States is still in flux, given that the United States only ratified the Convention in 2009. Here, we discuss the basic Convention requirement that States Parties adopt measures to protect and respect cultural property during peacetime and during armed conflict. Additional requirements for States Parties found in the First and Second Protocols will not be discussed, as the United States has not yet ratified either of these Protocols.

a. During Peacetime

During peacetime, the 1954 Hague Convention requires States Parties to adopt a series of measures designed to protect cultural property. First, States Parties should prepare "for the safeguarding of cultural property situated within their own territory against the foreseeable effects of armed conflict, by taking measures as they consider appropriate." Hague Convention, at art. 3. States Parties should also consider marking its cultural property with a distinctive emblem (the Blue Shield) to facilitate identification. *See id.* at arts. 6, 16–17. A limited number of refuges, monumental centers, and other immovable cultural property may be selected for "special" protection by entering these selected sites into the International Register of Cultural Property under Special Protection. In the event that armed conflict occurs, these sites receiving "special" protection will be marked with the Blue Shield and receive immunity from hostilities, provided they are not used for military objectives. *See id.* at arts. 8–10.

States Parties should also widely disseminate the text of the Convention (Article 25), and establish services and specialist personnel within their armed forces "whose purpose will be to secure respect for cultural property and to co-operate with the civilian authorities responsible for safeguarding it." *Id.* at art. 7, para. 2. And States Parties should take "within the framework of their ordinary criminal jurisdiction, all necessary steps to prosecute and impose penal or disciplinary sanctions upon those persons, of whatever nationality, who commit or order to be committed a breach of the present Convention." *Id.* at art. 28.

The United States has not yet engaged in any national efforts to protect significant resources from the foreseeable effects of armed conflicts. There are no American properties listed on the International Register of Cultural Property, which is a very short list (unlike the World Heritage List discussed in Part C). And there are no federal statutes imposing criminal or civil liability that specifically implement the Convention. Even extant statutes protecting cultural property, such as the National Historic Preservation Act of 1966 (NHPA), discussed in Chapter III, would not meet the standards of the Convention. While the NHPA provides a mechanism for identifying historically significant properties, the NHPA does not encompass all of the resources included in the Convention's definition of cultural property; it excludes properties with merely religious significance, for example, and would also exclude repositories of other cultural property unless the repositories were themselves historically significant.

b. During Armed Conflict

During armed conflict, the 1954 Hague Convention imposes several obligations on States Parties to protect cultural property. Perhaps most importantly, States Parties should respect cultural property by refraining from targeting it during hostilities, targeting it as an act of reprisal, or requisitioning movable cultural property. *See id.* at arts. 4, 19. States Parties should also "prohibit, prevent, and, if necessary, put a stop to any form of theft, pillage, or misappropriation of, and any acts of vandalism directed against, cultural property." *Id.* at art. 4, para. 3.

When a State Party occupies another territory, it should protect the cultural property in the occupied territory and take necessary measures for its preservation, including, if consistent with the interests of security, allowing personnel from the opposing side who are engaged in the protection of cultural property to continue to carry out their duties. *See id.* at arts. 5, 15. And States Parties should prosecute and impose penal or disciplinary sanctions upon anyone who breaches the Convention, within the framework of their ordinary criminal jurisdiction. *See id.* at art. 28.

Prior to ratification of the Hague Convention, the protection of cultural heritage during armed conflict

was already contemplated and practiced by the
United States Armed Forces. Article 103 of the
Uniform Code of Military Justice, for example,
outlines sanctions for soldiers who loot or pillage.
See 10 U.S.C. § 903. Further, the United States
Army manual on the law of land warfare contains
basic provisions for recognition and protection of
cultural sites. *See* U.S. DEP'T OF ARMY, FIELD
MANUAL 27–10, THE LAW OF LAND WARFARE (July
1956). Whether these practices are enough to satisfy
the dictates of the Convention remains unclear—but
they are a start. Not a single federal court has had
the opportunity to provide additional guidance.

B.   1970 UNESCO CONVENTION ON THE MEANS OF PROHIBITING AND PREVENTING THE ILLICIT IMPORT, EXPORT AND TRANSFER OF OWNERSHIP OF CULTURAL PROPERTY

Beyond the 1954 Hague Convention, the
international community has recognized that
danger to cultural heritage is not limited to times of
armed conflict. Archaeological sites and museums,
particularly in developing nations, suffered from a
spate of thefts in the late 1960s. Looted artifacts
began turning up with increasing frequency in
wealthier countries with thriving art and
antiquities markets, such as the United States. In
this context, the international community adopted
the UNESCO Convention on the Means of
Prohibiting and Preventing the Illicit Import,
Export and Transfer of Ownership of Cultural
Property in 1970—the first international legal

framework aimed at combating the illicit trafficking of cultural property in times of peace.

This Part begins with an overview of the 1970 Convention and a later refinement of it (the 1995 UNIDROIT Convention on Stolen or Illegally Exported Cultural Objects). It then turns to key terms in the 1970 Convention and discusses how the 1970 Convention has been applied in the United States.

1.   OVERVIEW

The 1970 Convention on the Means of Prohibiting and Preventing the Illicit Import, Export and Transfer of Ownership of Cultural Property was the international response to illicit trafficking in cultural property during peacetime. In 1995, the UNIDROIT Convention on Stolen or Illegally Exported Cultural Objects was developed as a refinement of the 1970 Convention. While the United States has ratified the 1970 Convention, it has not yet ratified the 1995 UNIDROIT Convention. Discussion of each of these two documents follows.

a. Convention (1970)

The 1970 Convention recognized that the cultural property of every country is a valuable and fundamental part of national culture and should be protected from illicit trafficking. The Convention recognized the following considerations leading to its adoption:

Considering that the interchange of cultural property among nations for scientific, cultural and educational purposes increases the knowledge of the civilization of Man, enriches the cultural life of all peoples and inspires mutual respect and appreciation among nations,

Considering that cultural property constitutes one of the basic elements of civilization and national culture, and that its true value can be appreciated only in relation to the fullest possible information regarding its origin, history and traditional setting,

Considering that it is incumbent upon every State to protect the cultural property existing within its territory against the dangers of theft, clandestine excavation, and illicit export, * * *

Considering that the protection of cultural heritage can be effective only if organized both nationally and internationally among States working in close cooperation

1970 Convention on the Means of Prohibiting and Preventing the Illicit Import, Export and Transfer of Ownership of Cultural Property, Nov. 14, 1970, 823 U.N.T.S. 231 (hereinafter "1970 Convention"), at Preamble. Accordingly, the 1970 Convention calls on States Parties to take a variety of measures, consistent with their national laws, to better regulate and document traffic in cultural property. These measures include protecting cultural property in their territories, regulating the movement of cultural property, and returning stolen cultural property to the source nation. *See id.* at arts. 5–9.

Currently, 123 countries have ratified the 1970 Convention. The United States ratified this Convention on September 2, 1983.

b. UNIDROIT Convention on Stolen or Illegally Exported Cultural Objects (1995)

Two decades after the 1970 Convention, the international community recognized that the 1970 Convention inadequately addressed certain private law aspects of illicit trafficking in cultural property. UNESCO asked UNIDROIT, an independent intergovernmental organization, to develop the 1995 Convention on Stolen or Illegally Exported Cultural Objects. The 1995 UNIDROIT Convention is a complement to the 1970 Convention, refining the legal standards for trade and protection of cultural property by formulating minimal legal rules for the restitution and return of illicitly trafficked cultural property. It grants a general right of restitution to persons or States from whom cultural property was stolen or illegally exported. States Parties commit to a uniform treatment for restitution of stolen or illegally exported cultural objects and allow restitution claims to be processed directly through national courts.

To date, thirty-three countries have ratified the 1995 UNIDROIT Convention. The United States, and most primary art and antiquities market countries of Asia and Europe, have not ratified this Convention.

2.   KEY TERM: CULTURAL PROPERTY

One term in the 1970 Convention is of highest significance: cultural property. (The 1995 UNIDROIT Convention incorporated the definition of cultural property from the 1970 Convention.) States Parties must designate specific cultural properties within the confines of this term, which means:

property which, on religious or secular grounds, is specifically designated by each State as being of importance for archaeology, prehistory, history, literature, art or science and which belongs to the following categories:

(a) Rare collections and specimens of fauna, flora, minerals and anatomy, and objects of palaeontological interest;

(b) property relating to history, including the history of science and technology and military and social history, to the life of national leaders, thinkers, scientists and artist and to events of national importance;

(c) products of archaeological excavations (including regular and clandestine) or of archaeological discoveries;

(d) elements of artistic or historical monuments or archaeological sites which have been dismembered;

(e) antiquities more than one hundred years old, such as inscriptions, coins and engraved seals;

(f) objects of ethnological interest;

(g) property of artistic interest, such as:

(i) pictures, paintings and drawings produced entirely by hand on any support and in any material (excluding industrial designs and manufactured articles decorated by hand);

(ii) original works of statuary art and sculpture in any material;

(iii) original engravings, prints and lithographs;

(iv) original artistic assemblages and montages in any material;

(h) rare manuscripts and incunabula, old books, documents and publications of special interest (historical, artistic, scientific, literary, etc.) singly or in collections;

(i) postage, revenue and similar stamps, singly or in collections;

(j) archives, including sound, photographic and cinematographic archives;

(k) articles of furniture more than one hundred years old and old musical instruments.

1970 Convention, art. 1. The term thus focuses on objects that may be moved—that is, objects that are most likely to be subject to theft, illegal export, or other trafficking. While undoubtedly expansive, one limiting feature of this definition is that the resource must relate to human activity in the realms of "archaeology, prehistory, history, literature, art or science." Thus the items listed in subsection (a) may not be designated cultural property unless they have some relationship with the human experience.

Like the definition of cultural property in the 1954 Hague Convention for the Protection of Cultural Property in the Event of an Armed Conflict, this term is defined very broadly. The 1970 Convention definition, however, differs in several key ways. Most significantly, the 1970 Convention excludes from the definition of cultural property all immovable properties, including buildings, large monuments, museums, libraries, and cultural centers. This is because the focus of the 1970 Convention is to stem illicit trafficking, not to achieve the broader mission of the 1954 Hague Convention of preventing destruction to large-scale resources.

3. APPLICATION

The 1970 Convention requires that States Parties establish measures to protect cultural property, cooperate with other States Parties to protect cultural property, and restore stolen or looted items to their source countries. The United States has implemented three key provisions of the 1970 Convention: (1) Article 7(b)(i), prohibiting the import of cultural property stolen from certain institutions in other state parties; (2) Article 9, assisting other countries in cases of potential pillage of archaeological and ethnological materials; and (3)

Article 7(b)(ii), dealing with the return of any illegally imported cultural property. All three provisions were implemented with Congress's passage of the Cultural Property Implementation Act (CPIA) in 1983. *See* 19 U.S.C. §§ 2601–2613. The 1970 Convention and the CPIA are not retroactive; they only cover offenses occurring after their enactment.

This section first discusses the manner in which the CPIA has implemented Articles 7(b)(i) and 9, and then discusses the way CPIA enforces these provisions. It concludes with an analysis of CPIA's implementation of Article 7(b)(ii)—including the return of property discovered through the enforcement process. Additional requirements for States Parties found in the 1995 UNIDROIT Convention will not be discussed in this section, as the United States has not ratified this Convention.

a. CPIA Implementation of Article 7(b)(i): Prohibiting Import

The Cultural Property Implementation Act (CPIA) codified Article 7(b)(i) of the 1970 Convention, which requires States Parties:

> to prohibit the import of cultural property stolen from a museum or a religious or secular public monument or similar institution in another State Party to this Convention after the entry into force of this Convention for the States concerned, provided that such property is documented as appertaining to the inventory of that institution

Section 308 of the CPIA states that "[n]o article of cultural property documented as appertaining to the inventory of a museum or religious or secular public monument or similar institution in any State Party which is stolen from such institution" may be imported into the United States. 19 U.S.C. § 2607. For example, looted items listed on the register of a museum in Peru (a State Party to the 1970 Convention) cannot enter the United States. These items will be seized, forfeited to the United States, and restored to the source country, as described below.

b. CPIA Implementation of Article 9: International Assistance

Article 9 of the 1970 Convention calls on States Parties to assist each other in cases of potential pillage of archaeological and ethnological materials:

Any State Party to this Convention whose cultural patrimony is in jeopardy from pillage of archaeological or ethnological materials may call upon other States Parties who are affected. The States Parties to this Convention undertake, in these circumstances, to participate in a concerted international effort to determine and to carry out the necessary concrete measures, including the control of exports and imports and international commerce in the specific materials concerned. Pending agreement each State concerned shall take provisional measures to the extent feasible to prevent irremediable injury to the cultural heritage of the requesting State.

To implement Article 9, the Cultural Property Implementation Act (CPIA) authorizes the United States to impose import restrictions for cultural patrimony that is in jeopardy of pillage. Upon the request of another State Party, the President of the United States, typically through the State Department's Bureau of Educational and Cultural Affairs and the Department of Homeland Security, may impose import restrictions through bilateral agreements on designated categories of archaeological and ethnological materials. *See* 19 U.S.C. § 2602(a).

To assist the President, or her delegate, in the decision of whether or not to impose import restrictions, CPIA established a panel of eleven experts appointed by the President: the Cultural Property Advisory Committee (CPAC). CPAC examines States Parties' requests for import restrictions, and after public involvement, makes recommendations to the President, or her delegate. *See id.* § 2605. CPAC's closed proceedings are typically not subject to disclosure pursuant to the Freedom of Information Act. *See* Ancient Coin Collector's Guild v. U.S. Dep't of State, 673 F. Supp 2d 1 (D.D.C. 2009) (holding that CPIA barred the disclosure of information submitted in confidence either to or from CPAC). Import restrictions become effective after a notice designating the restricted items is published in the Federal Register. *See* 19 U.S.C. § 2602(f). In the case of an emergency, CPIA allows the United States to unilaterally impose import restrictions, but only if the State Party has already submitted a request for a bilateral agreement. *See id.* § 2603.

CPIA's requirements for import restriction requests are stringent. The requesting State Party must state that its cultural patrimony is in jeopardy, that import restrictions would be of substantial benefit in deterring the situation, and that less drastic remedies are unavailable. *See id.* § 2602(a)(1). Even after a bilateral agreement has been finalized, the United States might suspend the import restrictions if they prove ineffective or if other importing countries do not implement similar restrictions. *See id.* § 2602(d). And CPIA restrictions do not apply to cultural property that has been in the United States for a specified period of time: as brief as three years in the case of well-publicized museum purchases, or as long as twenty years in the case of any bona fide purchaser. *See id.* § 2611(2).

There has been one federal case involving a direct challenge to import restrictions imposed by CPIA. In *Ancient Coin Collector's Guild v. U.S. Customs and Border Protection*, the 4th Circuit found that the State Department complied with CPIA procedures in conducting diplomatic negotiations with foreign states and in obtaining recommendations from CPAC experts prior to levying import restrictions on ancient Cypriot and Chinese coins. 698 F.3d 171, 182–83 (4th Cir. 2012). It also held that even though China's request under CPIA did not mention coins, imposing import restrictions on ancient Chinese coins did not violate CPIA because the statute does not require a comprehensive list of all items that might be found appropriate for inclusion in import restrictions after negotiations between the U.S. State Department and China. *Id.* at 181.

Since CPIA's enactment, the United States has entered into bilateral agreements with only fourteen nations, half of which are located in Central and South America.

c. CPIA Enforcement

Congress established clear authority to enforce articles 7(b)(i) and 9 of the 1970 Convention. CPIA provides that any item of cultural property illegally imported into the United States—whether stolen or otherwise—may be subject to the civil penalty of seizure and forfeiture. *See* 19 U.S.C. § 2609. When the United States initiates forfeiture proceedings, it bears the initial burden of proving by probable cause that the items were stolen or illegally imported. *See id.* § 2610.

There are two federal cases dealing directly with the issue of whether an item was properly subject to forfeiture under CPIA. In *United States v. Eighteenth Century Peruvian Oil on Canvas Painting of Doble Trinidad*, the court held that two paintings that the defendant imported into the United States were subject to CPIA where the defendant's admissions and reports of art experts concluded that the paintings were designated cultural property originating from Peru. 597 F.

Supp. 2d 618 (E.D. Va. 2009). And in *United States v. An Original Manuscript Dated November 19, 1778,* the court held that an eighteenth century Mexican manuscript was subject to CPIA when there was probable cause to believe that the manuscript was the same one that had been reported stolen from the Mexican national archives. No. 96 Civ. 6221(LAP), 1999 WL 97894 (S.D.N.Y Feb. 22, 1999).

Once the United States meets its burden of proving by probable cause that cultural property was stolen or illegally imported, the burden of proof switches to the defendant, who must establish by a preponderance of the evidence that the property was not subject to forfeiture or establish an applicable affirmative defense (*i.e.,* innocent ownership). *See United States v. An Original Manuscript,* 1999 WL 97894, at *6–*7 (holding that the defendant had not established an innocent owner affirmative defense); *United States v. Eighteenth Century Peruvian Oil on Canvas,* 597 F. Supp. 2d at 624–26 (holding that the defendant did not prove by a preponderance of the evidence that paintings were not subject to forfeiture).

CPIA has been criticized for its lack of criminal penalties. However, an important federal case from California suggests that CPIA's import restrictions may be enforced by criminal penalties under other statutes. In *United States v. Perez,* Robert Perez illegally imported a melon-shaped, pre-Hispanic ceramic bowl into the United States from El Salvador and sold it. CR 07–00499 (C.D. Ca. 2007).

The United States had, and continues to have, a bilateral agreement with El Salvador imposing import restrictions on cultural property from that country under CPIA. Referencing the import restrictions in CPIA (19 U.S.C. § 2606(a)), a grand jury indicted Perez on one count of smuggling under the 1948 federal anti-smuggling statute, 18 U.S.C. § 545. *See id.* at Indictment, June 6, 2007. Perez eventually reached a plea agreement in which he forfeited the bowl, was sentenced to three years probation (with a term of six months home confinement), and fined $10,100. *See id.* at Plea Agreement for Defendant Robert Perez.

d. CPIA Implementation of Article 7(b)(ii): Restitution

Article 7(b)(ii) of the 1970 Convention requires States Parties:

> at the request of the State Party of origin, to take appropriate steps to recover and return any such cultural property imported after the entry into force of this Convention in both States concerned, provided, however, that the requesting State shall pay just compensation to an innocent purchaser or to a person who has valid title to that property. Requests for recovery and return shall be made through diplomatic offices. The requesting Party shall furnish, at its expense, the documentation and other evidence necessary to establish its claim for recovery and return. The Parties shall impose no customs duties or other charges upon cultural property returned pursuant to this

Article. All expenses incident to the return and delivery of the cultural property shall be borne by the requesting Party.

1970 Convention, art. 7(b)(ii). The Cultural Property Implementation Act (CPIA) contains restitution provisions implementing this Article. Any cultural property that has been seized and forfeited to the United States must first be offered for return to the State Party. *See* 19 U.S.C. § 2609. However, in the case of stolen property, a United States bona fide purchaser who had no reason to believe the property was stolen is entitled to recover the purchase price, unless the laws of the source country would "recover and return an article stolen from an institution in the United States without requiring the payment of compensation." *Id.* § 2609(c); *see also United States v. An Original Manuscript*, at 1999 WL 97894, at *7–*8 (holding that the defendant was not entitled to compensation because he was not an innocent purchaser and because there was sufficient evidence to prove that Mexico would recover and return and article to the United States without requiring compensation). The State Party must also pay any expenses incident to the return and delivery of the cultural property. *See id.* § 2609.

Restitution has become an increasingly important component of American relations with other countries. Immigration and Customs Enforcement (ICE), the investigative arm of the Department of Homeland Security, is tasked with investigating cases of illegal importation of cultural property. ICE has reported numerous restitutions of illegally imported cultural property, among them the return to China of one hundred ancient fossils belonging to a 525 million-year-old animal.

C. 1972 UNESCO CONVENTION CONCERNING THE PROTECTION OF THE WORLD CULTURAL AND NATURAL HERITAGE

The 1972 Convention Concerning the Protection of the World Cultural and Natural Heritage (commonly called the 1972 World Heritage Convention) addresses the aims of two international movements: one interested in preserving outstanding cultural sites and the other interested in conserving nature. The decision to build the Aswan Dam in the 1950s was the catalyst for galvanizing international concern for cultural sites, as erection of the dam meant flooding the valley containing the temples of Abu Simbel, priceless structures and monuments of ancient Egyptian civilization. UNESCO launched an international safeguarding campaign that raised eighty million dollars, half of which was donated by fifty different countries. These efforts demonstrated international solidarity and shared responsibility in conserving outstanding cultural sites.

The idea for combining conservation of cultural sites with those of nature came from the United States. In 1965, a White House Conference called for a "World Heritage Trust" to protect the world's superb natural and scenic areas and historic sites for present and future generations. At the 1972

United Nations Conference, a single text—melding the concepts of nature conservation and the preservation of cultural properties—was agreed upon by key parties and adopted by UNESCO.

This Part begins with an overview of the 1972 World Heritage Convention and includes an analysis of its key terms and application.

1.   OVERVIEW

By linking the concepts of nature conservation and the preservation of cultural properties, the 1972 World Heritage Convention recognizes that it is critical to preserve the balance between humans and nature. Among other things, the Convention recognized that "the cultural heritage and the natural heritage are increasingly threatened with destruction not only by the traditional causes of decay, but also by changing social and economic conditions" and that simultaneously the "protection of this heritage at the national level often remains incomplete" because of resource scarcity. 1972 Convention Concerning the Protection of the World Cultural and Natural Heritage, Nov. 16, 1972, 1037 U.N.T.S. 151 (hereinafter "1972 World Heritage Convention"), at Preamble.

To stem the disappearance and degradation of outstanding natural sites and cultural properties, the Convention established a framework for identifying, protecting, and preserving outstanding sites in perpetuity. States Parties identify potential sites within their respective territories and submit these sites to the World Heritage Committee (an entity further described below) for review and inscription on the World Heritage List. States Parties must protect and preserve these sites through national laws and report regularly to the World Heritage Committee on the state of conservation. International financial assistance may also be available to help protect sites in peril.

Currently, 190 nations adhere to the 1972 World Heritage Convention. The United States ratified this Convention on December 7, 1973.

2.   KEY TERMS

There are three key terms in the 1972 World Heritage Convention. The first two—"cultural heritage" and "natural heritage"—define the scope of resources that are protected under the Convention. The third term, "outstanding universal value," delineates criteria used by the World Heritage Committee to decide if a resource merits inscription on the World Heritage List.

a. Cultural Heritage

The term "cultural heritage" covers three broad categories in the 1972 World Heritage Convention. These are:

monuments: architectural works, works of monumental sculpture and painting, elements or structures of an archaeological nature, inscriptions, cave dwellings and combinations of features, which are of outstanding universal value from the point of view of history, art or science;

groups of buildings: groups of separate or connected buildings which, because of their architecture, their homogeneity or their place in the landscape, are of outstanding universal value from the point of view of history, art or science;

sites: works of man or the combined works of nature and man, and areas including archaeological sites which are of outstanding universal value from the historical, aesthetic, ethnological or anthropological points of view.

1972 World Heritage Convention, at art. 1. These three categories are very broad and allow for a certain degree of subjectivity. The United States currently has eight cultural heritage properties inscribed on the World Heritage List, including the Statue of Liberty, Independence Hall, and Mesa Verde.

b. Natural Heritage

The term "natural heritage" also ranges over three broad categories in the 1972 World Heritage Convention. They are:

natural features consisting of physical and biological formations or groups of such formations, which are of outstanding universal value from the aesthetic or scientific point of view;

geological and physiographical formations and precisely delineated areas which constitute the habitat of threatened species of animals and plants of outstanding universal value from the point of view of science or conservation;

natural sites or precisely delineated natural areas of outstanding universal value from the point of view of science, conservation or natural beauty.

Id. at art. 2. Like the categories of cultural heritage, those of natural heritage are wide-ranging and context dependent. Currently, the United States has twelve natural heritage properties on the World Heritage List, including Yellowstone National Park and the Grand Canyon. In addition, the United States also has one mixed cultural and natural heritage property on the World Heritage List— Papahanaumokuakea—a cluster of small, low lying islands and atolls which is sacred in Hawaiian culture, located about 250 kilometers northwest of the main Hawaiian archipelago.

c. Outstanding Universal Value

For a cultural heritage or natural heritage site to warrant inclusion on the World Heritage List, the nation in which it resides and the World Heritage Committee must decide that it has "outstanding universal value," which means:

Cultural and/or natural significance which is so exceptional as to transcend national boundaries and to be of common importance for present and future generations of all humanity. As such the permanent protection of this heritage is of the highest importance to the international community as a whole.

UNESCO Intergovernmental Comm. for the Prot. of the World Cultural and Natural Heritage, *Operational Guidelines for the Implementation of the World Heritage Convention*, art. 49 (July 2012). The World Heritage Committee considers a site as having outstanding universal value if it meets the conditions of integrity and/or authenticity outlined in Articles 79–95 of the Operational Guidelines along with one or more of the following criteria:

(i) represent a masterpiece of human creative genius;

(ii) exhibit an important interchange of human values, over a span of time or within a cultural area of the world, on developments in architecture or technology, monumental arts, town-planning or landscape design;

(iii) bear a unique or at least exceptional testimony to a cultural tradition or to a civilization which is living or which has disappeared;

(iv) be an outstanding example of a type of building, architectural or technological ensemble or landscape which illustrates (a) significant stage(s) in human history;

(v) be an outstanding example of a traditional human settlement, land-use, or sea-use which is representative of a culture (or cultures), or human interaction with the environment especially when it has become vulnerable under the impact of irreversible change;

(vi) be directly or tangibly associated with events or living traditions, with ideas, or with beliefs, with artistic and literary works of outstanding universal significance. (The Committee considers that this criterion should preferably be used in conjunction with other criteria);

(vii) contain superlative natural phenomena or areas of exceptional natural beauty and aesthetic importance;

(viii) be outstanding examples representing major stages of earth's history, including the record of life, significant on-going geological processes in the development of landforms, or significant geomorphic or physiographic features;

(ix) be outstanding examples representing significant ongoing ecological and biological processes in the evolution and development of terrestrial, fresh water, coastal and marine ecosystems and communities of plants and animals;

(x) contain the most important and significant natural habitats for in-situ conservation of biological diversity, including those containing threatened species of Outstanding Universal

Value from the point of view of science or
conservation.

Id. at arts. 77–78. The concept of integrity in the
1972 World Heritage Convention is similar to that
used in the National Register of Historic Places—
the United States' list of properties and sites that
have been designated historic (further described in
Chapter II). Essentially, the resource or landscape
must be in such physical condition that it can
convey its significance.

3.   APPLICATION

The United States has fully embraced the
requirements the 1972 World Heritage Convention
imposes on States Parties. States Parties to the
1972 World Heritage Convention voluntarily
nominate their own sites containing superlative
natural or cultural attributes. States Parties pledge
to identify and protect their key natural and
cultural sites through national legislation, as
inscription in the World Heritage List does not
confer any additional direct legal protections for the
sites beyond national law. States Parties also agree
to assist and cooperate with other signatories in
their preservation efforts. Among other
requirements, World Heritage sites must be
authentic and meet at least one of the several highly
stringent criteria for outstanding universal value
discussed above. States Parties retain sovereignty
over their World Heritage sites and are encouraged
to publicize the status of these sites and use them in
educational activities.

The Secretary of the U.S. Department of the Interior, through the Assistant Secretary for Fish and Wildlife and Parks and the National Park Service, has the responsibility for administering the 1972 World Heritage Convention in the United States. Under the authority of Title IV of the National Historic Preservation Act (discussed in Chapter III of this book), the National Park Service has promulgated regulations for identifying, selecting, and nominating U.S. sites to the World Heritage List. *See* 16 U.S.C. §§ 470a–1 & 36 C.F.R. 73.1–17. Proposed sites are then sent to the World Heritage Committee for review and a decision of whether the sites qualify for World Heritage status. Designated World Heritage Sites are eligible for financial assistance to aid in protection and conservation through the World Heritage Fund. This section discusses the nomination process, the evaluation of nominations, and benefits for listed sites from the World Heritage Fund.

a. Nomination Process in the United States

The National Park Service initiates the nomination process for American sites by publishing a notice in the Federal Register that describes the procedures and the schedule for consideration of proposed new nominations. *See* 36 C.F.R. § 73.7(a)(2). For an American site to be considered by the Assistant Secretary for Fish and Wildlife and Parks for nomination to the World Heritage List, it must meet at least one of the criteria for outstanding universal value listed above and must satisfy all of the following requirements:

• The property must be nationally significant (listed as a National Historic Landmark of National Natural Landmark, proclaimed a National Monument, or designated as nationally significant by Congress). *See* 36 C.F.R. § 73.7(1).

• The property's owner or owners must concur in writing to the nomination consideration. *See id.* § 73.7(2).

• The property must currently be legally protected to ensure its preservation in the United States. Private owners of sites to be nominated must commit in writing to preserve their property in perpetuity. *See id.* § 73.13.

Once the comments and suggestions are compiled, the Assistant Secretary for Fish and Wildlife and Parks and the Federal Interagency Panel for World Heritage—a group of representatives from seven different federal agencies established to advise the Department of Interior on implementation of the 1972 World Heritage Convention—decides whether to select any properties as proposed nominations. *Id.* §§ 73.7(c)–(e) & 73.11.

If any properties are selected as proposed United States nominations, there is a second notice in the Federal Register, and the property owner and others are notified in writing. *Id.* sec 73.7(f). Property owners and proponents of inscribing the property on the World Heritage List then prepare a nomination draft with the National Park Service, which is evaluated by the Federal Interagency Panel. *Id.*

§§ 73.7(g)–(h). If the draft nomination is approved, the U.S. State Department transmits it to the World Heritage Committee for consideration, and a third Federal Register notice announcing the World Heritage nomination is published. *Id.* §§ 73.7(i)–(j).

b. Evaluation of Nominations by the World Heritage Committee

Any nomination submitted by the United States to the World Heritage Committee is carefully evaluated to determine if it complies with the 1972 World Heritage Convention criteria. The World Heritage Committee is composed of representatives from twenty-one States Parties—each serving staggered six-year terms—and is responsible for the implementation of the 1972 World Heritage Convention. *See* 1972 World Heritage Convention, at arts. 8–9. When the U.S. State Department transmits a draft nomination to the World Heritage Committee, the Committee evaluates whether it deserves inscription on the World Heritage List by deciding if it meets one or more of the outstanding universal value criteria noted above along with the conditions of integrity and/or authenticity outlined in Articles 79–95 of the Operational Guidelines. The Committee may accept the proposed nomination, defer its decision and request further information on sites from the States Parties, or reject the proposed nomination.

Note that three international non-governmental or intergovernmental organizations play prominent advisory roles for the World Heritage Committee in its deliberations: (1) the International Union for the Conservation of Nature provides the Committee with technical evaluations of proposed natural heritage properties; (2) the International Council on Monuments and Sites provides the Committee with evaluations of proposed cultural and mixed properties; and (3) the International Centre for the Study of Preservation and Restoration of Cultural Property provides the Committee with expert advice on how to conserve listed properties as well as training and restoration techniques. *See id.* at art. 8, para. 3.

c. Implications of Inscription on the World Heritage List

Once a property is inscribed on the World Heritage List, the World Heritage Committee examines periodic reports on the state of conservation of the inscribed property, and may ask States Parties to take action when properties are not being properly managed. The Committee may also add World Heritage Sites needing major conservation, or those that are threatened by "serious and specific dangers," such as armed conflict, earthquakes, volcanic eruptions, large-scale public or private projects, to the World Heritage in Danger list. *Id.* at art. 11, para. 4.

Properties inscribed on the World Heritage List are also eligible for financial and technical assistance through the World Heritage Fund. The World Heritage Fund is administered by the World Heritage Committee and is designed to assist States

Parties in preserving and promoting World Heritage Sites. Contributions to the World Heritage Fund are made by States Parties on a compulsory or voluntary basis. *See* 1972 World Heritage Convention, at art. 15, para. 3(a). Compulsory contributions by a State Party consist of one percent of that State Party's annual UNESCO dues. *See id.* at art. 16, para. 1. From the years 2000 to 2010, the United States' compulsory contributions to the World Heritage fund ranged from a low of $428,604 (FY2000) to a high of $700,000 (FY2008–2010). United States federal agencies, such as the National Park Service and the U.S. Agency for International Development, also provide technical assistance to other States Parties. Other sources contributing to the World Heritage Fund include: private funds, funds-in-trust donated by countries for specific purposes, partnerships, and income from sales of World Heritage materials. *See id.* at art. 15, para. 3(b)–(e). The World Heritage Fund receives an annual total amount of just under four million dollars.

The World Heritage Committee allocates funding from the World Heritage Fund on a priority basis, with a particular focus on the most threatened sites. These sites are typically those listed on the World Heritage in Danger list, and properties located in developing countries. Assistance from the World Heritage Fund includes, among other things, low-interest or interest-free loans, non-repayable subsidies, supply of equipment, training expenses, and costs to perform particular studies. *See id.* at art. 22.

INDEX

References are to Pages

NATIONAL ENVIRONMENTAL POLICY ACT
Adequacy of Environmental Review, 134–137
Administrative Procedure Act, Interaction With, 33–34
Agency Requirements Under, 112–114, 143
Alternatives, 113, 117, 130, 131, 132, 135, 136, 143
Categorical Exclusion, 127–129
Environmental Assessment, 127, 129–130, 134
Environmental Impact Statement, 127, 130–133, 134
Generally, 5, 7, 33–36 111–114, 225–226
Key Terms, 114–126
National Historic Preservation Act, Interaction With, 137–143
Record of Decision, 132
Section 4(f), Interaction With, 176–177, 184
State Preservation Acts, Comparison With, 143–150
Supplemental Environmental Impact Statement, 133–134
Tiering Environmental Reviews, 134

NATIONAL HISTORIC LANDMARKS
Under Historic Sites Act, 11, 337
Under National Historic Preservation Act, 38, 39, 42, 46–47, 161
Under Section 4(f), 166

NATIONAL HISTORIC PRESERVATION ACT
Advisory Council on Historic Preservation (see "Advisory Council on Historic Preservation")
Agency Nomination of Properties Under, 50, 51, 52–53
Americans with Disabilities Act, Interaction With (see "Section 106")
Archaeological Resources, Interaction With (see "Section 106")
Confidentiality Provisions, 95, 97
Findings and Declarations, 16–17
Generally, 5, 11, 12, 16–17, 22, 27, 37–38, 47, 49, 65, 69–72, 112, 114, 126, 225, 337, 488, 494, 506, 531
Key Terms, 72–88
Motivations for Passage, 4–5
National Environmental Policy Act, Interaction With (see "Section 106")
National Register Criteria (see "National Register of Historic Places")
Purposes, 11–12, 16–17
Section 4(f), Interaction With (see "Section 106")

POLITICAL CONCERNS
Antiquities Act, 328
Conservation Districts, 211
Eminent Domain, 242
Federal Religious Liberty Rules, 295, 296
Free Speech, 309
National Register Designation, 443
Tax Credits, 457–458

PORT AUTHORITY OF NEW YORK AND NEW JERSEY, 116

PORTLAND, 210–211

PRESERVATION MOVEMENT, 1–12

PRESERVATION EASEMENTS (SEE "RESTRICTIONS")

PRESERVATION RESTRICTIONS (SEE "RESTRICTIONS")

PRIVATE PROPERTY RIGHTS (SEE "PROPERTY OWNER ISSUES" AND "TAKINGS")

PROGRAMMATIC AGREEMENTS (SEE "SECTION 106")

PROGRAMMATIC EVALUATIONS (SEE "SECTION 4(f)")

PROPERTY OWNER ISSUES
Due Process Rights (see "Due Process")
Generally, 26
Local Preservation Rules (see "Local Preservation Ordinances")
Private Owners' Rights During Designation Process, 19, 51, 54–56, 67
Private Restrictions on Land (see "Restrictions")
Takings Rights (see "Takings")
Tribal Ownership of Land, 93

PUBLIC INTEREST EXCEPTION (SEE "LOCAL PRESERVATION ORDINANCES")

RECORDATION OF RESTRICTIONS (SEE "RESTRICTIONS")

REGULATORY TAKINGS (SEE "TAKINGS")